Creativity in Performance

Publications in Creativity Research
Robert S. Albert, Series Editor

(formerly Creativity Research Monographs as edited by Mark A. Runco)

Achieving Extraordinary Ends: An Essay on Creativity, by Sharon Bailin, 1994
Beyond Terman: Longitudinal Studies in Contemporary Gifted Education, edited by Rena Subotnik and Karen Arnold, 1994
Counseling Gifted and Talented Children, edited by Roberta M. Milgram, 1991
Creative Thinking: Problem-Solving Skills and the Arts Orientation, by John Wakefield, 1992
Creativity and Affect, edited by Melvin P. Shaw and Mark A. Runco, 1994
Creativity in Government, by Thomas Heinzen, 1994
Creativity in Performance, by R. Keith Sawyer, 1997
Divergent Thinking, by Mark A. Runco, 1991
E. Paul Torrance: The Creativity Man (An Authorized Biography), by Garnet W. Millar, 1995
Eminent Creativity, Everyday Creativity, and Health: New Work on the Creativity/Health Interface, edited by Mark A. Runco and Ruth Richards
Fostering the Growth of High Ability: European Perspectives, edited by Arthur J.Cropley and Detlev Dehn, 1996
Genius and Creativity: Selected Papers by Dean Keith Simonton
Genius Revisited: High IQ Children Grown Up, by Rena Subotnik, Lee Kassan, Ellen Summers, and Alan Wasser, 1993
More Ways Than One: Fostering Creativity, by Arthur J. Cropley, 1992
Nurturing and Developing Creativity: The Emergence of a Discipline, edited by Scott G. Isaksen, Mary C. Murdock, Roger L. Firestien, and Donald J. Treffinger, 1993
The Person Behind the Mask: A Guide to Performing Arts Psychology, by Linda H. Hamilton, 1997
Perspectives on Creativity: The Biographical Method, by John E. Gedo and Mary M.Gedo, 1992
Problem Finding, Problem Solving, and Creativity, edited by Mark A. Runco, 1994
Top of the Class: Guiding Children Along the Smart Path to Happiness, by Arline L. Bronzaft, 1996
Understanding and Recognizing Creativity: The Emergence of a Discipline, edited by Scott G. Isaksen, Mary C. Murdock, Roger L. Firestien, and Donald J. Treffinger, 1993
Why Fly? A Philosophy of Creativity, by E. Paul Torrance, 1995

Creativity in Performance

edited by
R. Keith Sawyer
Washington University

Ablex Publishing Corporation
Greenwich, Connecticut
London, England

Figure 6.1 Reprinted with permission from Driver, Brousseau, & Hanscker. *The dynamic decision maker.* Copyright © Jossey-Bass Inc., Publishers. All rights reserved.

Copyright © 1997 by Ablex Publishing Corporation

Printed in the United States of America

Library of Congress Cataloging-in-Publication Data

Creativity in performance / R. Keith Sawyer [editor].
         p.   cm.—(Publications in creativity research)
    Includes bibliographical references and index.
    ISBN 1-56750-335-7 (cloth).—ISBN 1-56750-336-5 (pbk.)
    1. Performing arts. 2. Music. 3. Improvisation (Acting)
4. Inprovisation (Music) I. Sawyer, R. Keith (Robert Keith)
II. Series.
PN1584.C74   1997
791—dc21   97-25985
                                                      CIP

Ablex Publishing Corporation
55 Old Post Road #2
P.O. Box 5297
Greenwich, CT 06830

Published in the U.K. and Europe by:
JAI Press Ltd.
38 Tavistock Street
Covent Garden
London WC2E 7PB
England

Contents

chapter I

Introduction

R. Keith Sawyer
Washington University

This is a book for readers interested in the latest research on creativity in performance. It is relevant and accessible to students and researchers in many fields, including psychology, anthropology, musicology, and performance studies. I've designed the book to be accessible to this broad readership in two ways: By selecting chapter authors who represent a wide range of perspectives on the study of performance creativity, and by asking that the chapters be written using as little jargon and as few specialized concepts as possible. Each chapter is preceded with a short summary, stating how the chapter is related to the themes of the volume, and pointing out connections and parallels among the chapters. My goals for the volume are to help define creativity in performance as a productive new area of research, and to initiate a cross-disciplinary dialogue that I hope will continue.

The creative process that led to this volume began when Robert Albert, editor of the *Publications in Creativity Research* series, asked me to consider editing a reader of psychological research on performance. I have long felt that psychologists who study creativity have neglected performance, and Albert confirmed this by pointing out that there were no books available on the topic. As I began to consider the idea of a reader, I realized that there weren't enough chapters available to form a complete volume. To address this need, I decided to solicit original material from a wide range of colleagues working in this area: ethnomusicologists, anthropologists, folklorists, and philosophers, in addition to psychologists. I was pleasantly surprised, and I remain grateful, that so many preeminent researchers agreed to contribute material for this volume. From the beginning, I have been excited about the synergy and the timeliness of this topic, and the contributors exceeded my highest expectations. All of the chapters are well-written, speak to common themes yet from diverse disciplinary perspectives, and represent truly important and innovative research.

FROM PRODUCT TO PERFORMANCE

Creativity research has focused on activities that result in objective, ostensible products, which remain after the creative act is complete. In scientific disciplines, these creative products include theories, experimental results, and journal articles; in the arts, products include paintings, sculptures, and musical scores. While focusing on creative products and the psychological processes that generate them, creativity researchers have tended to neglect the creativity of performance (Sawyer, 1995). In Western cultures, creative individuals often choose to enter the sciences or the arts, where they will generate creative products such as journal articles, books, paintings, and orchestral scores. The focus in creativity research on *product* creativity is not surprising, because our goals are often to understand the histories of our own creative genres, and to identify and encourage creativity (particularly scientific creativity) in our own societies. However, theories that claim to be directed at underlying universals in the psychological and social processes of creativity must be cognizant of all manifestations of creativity, including both product creativity and performance. Cross-cultural study indicates that performance genres may be a much more common form of creativity worldwide. Unlike product creativity, which involves a long period of creative work leading up to the creative product, in performance creativity, the creative process and the resulting product are co-occurring. This is particularly true of improvisational performance. Although most Western performance genres are scripted or composed, most non-Western performances incorporate improvisational elements.

Because performance, particularly in the more improvisational genres, is ephemeral and does not generate any lasting ostensible product, it has been easy to neglect. Even though performance has rarely been a subject for creativity research, it may actually represent a more common, more accessible form of creativity than privileged domains such as the arts and sciences. If one recognizes that all social interactions display improvisational elements, then everyday activities such as conversation also become relevant to creativity theory. Creativity in interactional domains, including teaching, parenting, leadership, and mentoring, is recognized to be important to our lives and our culture. (Baker-Sennett & Matusov's chapter focuses on the improvisationality of teaching.)

In practice, creativity research has been a subdiscipline of psychology. However, several other disciplines represented in this volume have addressed performance and improvisation, including anthropology (the chapters by Bauman & Briggs, Hanna, and Silverstein), philosophy (Crease), and ethnomusicology (Berliner, Henderson, & Monson). Most empirical studies of performance have been ethnographic descriptions of musical and verbal performance genres. A recent ethnomusicological focus on jazz has emphasized the unique role that improvisation plays in performance (Berliner, Monson), and linguistic anthropologists and sociolinguists have studied the creativity of ritual verbal performance and of everyday speech genres (Bauman & Briggs, and Silverstein). These researchers focus on public verbal performance in a variety of cultures. In many non-Western and pre-literate cultures, performance is a daily, central aspect of the construction of meaning and identity. These genres incorporate more improvisational elements than Western performances. Despite the prevalence of improvisation in performance, many treatments have retained a "compositional" approach to the analysis of performance, often using techniques developed for the analysis of creative products. For example, musicologists who analyze performances tend to analyze transcripts of the performance, implicitly treating the performance as if it had been a composed creative product, and theater researchers have frequently analyzed scripts using the techniques of literary analysis. Unfortunately, these methods are often based on the implicit assumption that all performances are variations on a compositional model, when in fact, the socially embedded, interactional nature of improvised performance may require different theoretical and methodological approaches.

With the above observations in mind, I've grouped the chapters into three parts:

- *Musical performance*. Ethnomusicological and psychological studies of musical performances, including jazz (Berliner, Monson, Csikszentmihalyi & Rich) and Nepalese drumming (Henderson).
- *Creativity on stage*. Anthropological and psychological study of staged and situated performances, including dance (Hanna), improvisational theater (Sawyer), and TV sitcoms (Pritzker & Runco).
- *Performance in everyday life*. Psychological, philosophical, and anthropological approaches to the study of the performances of everyday life, including teaching and learning (Baker-Sennett & Matusov), scientific experiments and collaboration (Crease), formalized or "poetic" genres of discourse (Bauman & Briggs), and everyday conversation (Silverstein).

COMMON THEMES

I asked each author to address the following themes in their chapters: How do psychological and sociocultural factors combine in performance? Is creativity specific to a given performance genre, or are there universally creative personalities? What is the relationship between performance creativity and compositional creativity (for example, a first violinist contrasted with a composer)? How can we even define performance creativity? Is it a personality trait, or does it emerge from a specific sociocultural context? What are the relationships between creativity in performance and an individual's culture? Are there culture-specific or genre-specific "styles" of creativity? How are performance skills acquired, including both formal and informal learning contexts?

The following themes stand out as being particularly salient and pervasive throughout this volume.

1. Listening—Performers must always listen to the co-performers, responding to what they are doing, and remember many sub-events for potential connections later on.
2. Collectivity—Performances are collaborative and participatory; thus group processes are central.
3. Contingency—Performance is indeterminate and the performer must create on the spot, in response to the other performers. Performances are contingent, in part, because they are collective: No one person is in control.
4. Emergence—Performance emerges from the actions of all of the participants. The structure of the performance—especially if it is improvised—does not exist prior to the performance and cannot be predicted from any pre-existing mental state of any of the participants. This quality of emergence emphasizes a *level of analysis* issue: The central level of analysis for performance study is not the individual performer, but rather the event, the collective activity, and the the group.
5. Socialization and participatory learning—Knowing how to participate in a performance genre is a highly implicit, practice-based knowledge. Most performance genres socialize new members through a highly participatory form of apprenticeship, *not* by identifying a body of explicit knowledge and attempting to "transfer" it to the student. Most studies show that it takes at least a few years to become expert. In education research, Barbara Rogoff and her colleagues have determined that it takes at least two years before parents are socialized into the Open Classroom "community of learners." In jazz, it typically takes five to ten years, and continues

through a lifetime (Berliner, 1994). In improv theater, it takes at least a year and some actors who are accomplished at conventional theater never learn to do it well.

6. The importance of discourse—Perhaps the most sophisticated treatments of performance issues are found in linguistic anthropology, as exemplified in the chapter by Bauman and Briggs. But most studies of performance choose methodologies that focus closely on talk. Even the chapters on dance and music present analytic frameworks that share many characteristics with conversation. For example, jazz musicians compare their interactions on stage to a conversation.

These themes are central to a broad range of research in several social science disciplines, but especially psychology, sociology, and education. For psychologists and educators, most of the chapters will be of interest to those studying collaboration, group problem-solving, and participatory learning contexts because many performance genres evince the same group processes that are found in effective collaborations. For those studying everyday conversation and ritual verbal performance, many of the chapters will be helpful in thinking about the balance between individual creativity and collective group processes that is a central analytic issue in these studies. For those studying musical performance, many of the chapters emphasize the collective, contingent, and indeterminate aspects of performance, and demonstrate how researchers in different disciplines have conceptualized the tension between individual creativity on stage, and the influences and constraints of the performance context, the cultural situation and the collective influence of the other performers.

CENTRAL ISSUES

Both because creativity in performance is a relatively new area of inquiry and because the issues fall on fault lines between the social sciences, many important questions remain poorly understood. Below, I've listed some of the significant issues that are touched on throughout these chapters. The scope of these issues demonstrates that the study of performance has much to offer the social sciences more generally.

1. What is an appropriate methodology for studying these collective group creative processes? Post-performance interviews, historical and biographical studies, or observational studies of performances using ethnomusicological or conversation-analytic methodologies?

2. Is performance creativity different from other forms of creativity, such as scientific innovation and product-oriented creativity (e.g., painting and photography)?

3. Is there an intellectual history that can explain why psychologists have neglected performance creativity? Is it because we think it's "the same" as scientific and product creativity? Is it because performance is culturally devalued in the West? What does this neglect teach us about our own ethnotheories of creativity and agency?

4. To what extent is the metaphor of "everyday life as performance" accurate? Can we think of scientific collaborations, or of classroom interactions, as collective performances? Or is this metaphor misleading? What are the implications of this metaphor, if any, for social theoretic issues such as reproduction of the social order, micro/macro-level issues, the concept of emergence (of social structure from discursive interactions), the appropriation and resistance of discourse for transformative goals (cf. deCerteau, Bourdieu)?

5. What is it about performance that gives it its "aura," its sense of specialness, its immediacy? What qualities make watching a performance different from viewing an artwork? Are these distinctions significant, or trivial (as Dewey's aesthetic theory claims)?

6. What is the relationship between text and performance, between creative product and creative process (cf. Sawyer, 1997)? This is the crux of the structuralist/post-structuralist debate. To what extent is it meaningful for the analyst to look for structures (or texts) that guide social action (or performance)? What is the nature of such structures? Once identified, what is the relationship between structure and practice, between text and performance?

Obviously, these are issues for an interdisciplinary study of human action, not for any single discipline (cf. Wertsch, in press). I believe this volume helps to demonstrate just how central these issues are to the study of creativity in performance, and how much room there is for creative new theories, methodologies, and explanations.

REFERENCES

Berliner, P. (1994). *Thinking in jazz: The infinite art of improvisation*. Chicago: University of Chicago Press.

Sawyer, R.K. (1995). Creativity as mediated action: A comparison of improvisational performance and product creativity. *Mind, Culture, and Activity, 2*, 172–191.

Sawyer, R.K. (1997). *Pretend play as improvisation: Conversation in the preschool classroom*. Norwood, NJ: Lawrence Erlbaum Associates.

Wertsch, J. V. (in press). *Mind as mediated action*. London: Oxford.

part I

Musical Performance

chapter 2

Give and Take: The Collective Conversation of Jazz Performance*

Paul Berliner
Northwestern University

Dr. Berliner has written on a range of musical performance genres. His books include The Soul of the Mbira, *an ethnography of* mbira *performance in Zimbabwe, and* Thinking in Jazz: The Infinite Art of Improvisation. *In this chapter, Berliner draws from his 15-year study of the jazz community to describe how musicians perceive musical interaction during a live jazz performance. In one of the interviews quoted in this chapter, the bassist Chuck Israels says "Playing with musicians is like a conversation. If when I speak, you interject some comment of your own, that keeps me going." This chapter is an attempt to expand on this metaphor, frequently repeated by jazz musicians. The chapter raises such questions as: What does it mean to call musical interaction a "conversation"? How is it like a conversation? What are the moment-to-moment processes that musicians use to communication with each other, to intersubjectively create an improvised performance? The unique defining feature of Berliner's research is that he combines these in-depth interviews with rigorous analyses of performance transcripts, using musicological techniques to demonstrate specific cases of the interaction patterns that the musicians refer to in their interviews. Berliner gives specific examples of how musicians influence each other's creativity on stage, including a musical example that has been annotated so that non-musicians can follow the essential characteristics of the interaction, demonstrating how a performance can be a collective product, emergent from the actions of many individuals. This chapter demonstrates that the study of one musician's creative*

---

*This chapter is an edited and reduced version of material that originally appeared as chapter 13 of the book *Thinking in Jazz: The Infinite Art of Improvisation* (1994), Chicago: University of Chicago Press.

process cannot capture the essence of jazz, because more than any other perfor-mance genre, a jazz performance is a collective, emergent phenomenon.

Musicologists and anthropologists will find this chapter to be a concise intro-duction to Berliner's approach, and to contemporary issues in ethnomusicology. In addition, this chapter will be of interest to psychologists studying collaboration and participatory learning. For example, Berliner's focus on improvisational group processes touches on the themes of Baker-Sennett and Matusov's chapter on improvisation in participatory learning environments. Berliner's study is rele-vant to broad issues in social science: the relation between culture and perfor-mance, and processes of socialization into communities of practice.

Over the past 15 years, I have immersed myself in research in the jazz community, striving to understand a number of interrelated processes that are central to the production of the community's artworks. My focus has been on those creative processes that constitute improvisation and those through which artists absorb the knowledge sys-tem on which competence at improvisation depends. To generate data for the study, I adopted several complementary methods: extensive interviews with upwards of 50 professional musicians, observations of different bands in rehearsals and performances, private studies as a trumpeter with individual artists, direct participation in jazz workshops and bands, and finally, music transcriptions and analyses of improvised performances on jazz recordings. *Thinking in Jazz: The Infinite Art of Improvisation* speaks to many of the themes of *Creativity in Performance*: the production and transmission of performance culture; the individ-ual's development of knowledge and skill throughout the life cycle; and the distinctive features of collective improvisation.

In addressing the latter theme, this chapter takes up the larger story of the musical development of artists at the point at which they have already acquired a fundamental base of jazz knowledge (Berliner, 1994). Among other things, they have built up a repertoire of compositions that serve as vehicles for improvisation, mastering not only the pieces' melodies and harmonic forms, but various techniques for their transfor-mation. They have also acquired a repertoire of vocabulary patterns associated with their instruments' conventional roles within the ensem-ble. Applying and transforming these patterns in performance facilitates the invention of individual parts that complement those of other group members. Guiding the players further is their familiarity with the stylis-tic features and aesthetic values of jazz, including the changes and conti-nuities that have marked them over time. In part, it is through their study of the aural literature of jazz recordings that they have gained a broad perspective on their music's intellectual history. Within the context of their living tradition, the artists appreciate one another's ideas in relation to those of contemporaries and predecessors alike.

Despite the importance of collective improvisation for understanding jazz, the scholarly literature devoted to this subject was scant when I began my research in the late 1970s. Notable exceptions included works by Keil (1966) and Owens (1974). Subsequently, relevant articles appeared by Rinzler (1988) and Stewart (1986). The most valuable research was presented in Monson's dissertation (1991), an ethnomusicological study based in part on interviews with 14 professional jazz musicians. Monson's findings complement those of my own, providing rich data that amplifies the musical roles of the rhythm section instruments and the nature of collective improvisation. She situates her analysis within the framework of relevant issues in anthropology and interactional sociolinguistics (also see Monson, this volume).

Overall, this chapter is concerned with the complex and dynamic experiences that characterize improvised performance. It probes the mystery of how jazz players, who may meet for the first time at a music event and perform without a conductor to coordinate their operations, can create collective artworks of great rigor, elegance, and emotional power. Its emphasis is on a number of operations and challenges with which artists routinely contend. These include the development of precise timing and the process of striking a groove, the guiding roles of different instruments in the ensemble, the constant negotiation of musical relationships among performers, the integration of musical ideas across the parts, and the creative interplay between precomposed and spontaneous musical ideas during performances.

As such issues arose in my interviews with musicians, individuals confirmed the central importance of collective improvisation in the jazz tradition. At the same time, they sometimes cautioned me about the difficulty of explicating these features of the music. When discussing the background and knowledge they brought to performances, for example, musicians commented on how much more complex jazz was than was possible to express in an interview. Clearly, talking about the preparation for collective improvisation was one thing, the actual experience of improvising was quite another. "No matter what you're doing or thinking about beforehand," Chuck Israels explains, "from the very moment the performance begins, you plunge into that world of sounds. It becomes your world instantly and your whole consciousness changes." (Here, as below, quotations are taken from my own interviews unless otherwise indicated.)

Despite the difficulties of verbalizing about essentially nonverbal aspects of improvisation, artists favor two metaphors in their own discussion about the subject that provide insight into unique features of their experience. One metaphor likens group improvisation to a conversation that players carry on among themselves in the language of jazz. The second metaphor likens the experience to being on a demanding musical journey. From the performance's first beat, improvisers enter a rich, constantly changing musical stream of their own creation, a vibrant mix of shimmering cymbal patterns, fragmentary bass lines, luxuriant chords, and surging melodies, all winding in time through the channels of a composition's general form. Over its course, players are perpetually occupied: They must take in the immediate inventions around them while leading their own performances toward emerging musical images, retaining, for the sake of continuity, the features of a quickly receding trail of sound. They constantly interpret one another's ideas, anticipating them on the basis of the music's predetermined harmonic events.

Without warning, however, anyone in the group can suddenly take the music in a direction that defies expectation, requiring the others to make instant decisions as to the development of their own parts. When pausing to consider an option or take a rest, the musician's impression is of a "great rush of sounds" passing by, and the player must have the presence of mind to track its precise course before adding his or her powers of musical invention to the group's performance. Every maneuver or response by an improviser leaves its momentary trace in the music (cf. Sawyer, this volume, on improvisational theater). By journey's end, the group has fashioned a composition anew, an original product of their interaction.

STRIKING A GROOVE

Among all the challenges a group faces, one that is extremely subtle yet fundamental to its travels is a feature of group improvisation that requires the negotiation of a shared sense of the beat, known as striking a groove (Keil, 1966; Monson, 1991) or playing in the pocket (Don Friedman). Incorporating the connotations of stability, intensity, and swing, the groove provides the basis for "everything to come together in complete accord" (Harold Ousley). "When you get into that groove," Charlie Persip explains, "you ride right on down that groove with no strain and no pain—you can't lay back or go forward. That's why they call it a groove. It's where the beat is, and we're always trying to find that." The notion is shared. Lou Donaldson asserts

> I don't care what kind of style a group plays as long as they settle into a groove where the rhythm keeps building instead of changing around. It's like the way an African hits a drum. He hits it a certain way, and after a

period of time, you feel it more than you did when he first started. He's playing the same thing, but the quality is different—it's settled into a groove. It's like seating tobacco in a pipe. You put some heat on it and make it expand. After a while, it's there. It's tight.

Although potentially involving all band members, the groove depends especially on the rhythm section's precise coordination, the relationship between drummer and the bass player usually being the most critical. "For things to happen beautifully in the ensemble," Charli Persip metaphorizes, "the drummer and the bass player must be married. When I listen to the drummer and the bass player together, I like to hear wedding bells." One basic obligation of this union involves the synchronization between the walking bass line and the cymbal's time-keeping pattern. "You play every beat in complete rhythmic unison with the drummer," Chuck Israels explains, "thousands upon thousands of notes together, night after night after night. If it's working, it brings you very close. It's a kind of emotional empathy that you develop very quickly. The relationship is very intimate."

As players enter into successive musical relationships, they discover a world of subtle nuances involving the collective maintenance of the beat. At issue are concepts of rhythmic phrasing and differing timbral and acoustical qualities. As Akira Tana knows,

> Finding the time is very important. So is how the time feels. A drummer can be very stiff or loose when he plays in terms of the elasticity of the beat. He can play the beat very stiff and staccato, like a European march with a straight eighth-note feel, or he can play more with a swinging trip-let feel. I was recently talking to Percy Heath about this. Part of the elasticity of the beat also comes from the way the bass player articulates his notes together with the cymbal beat. It can be made to seem long or short, according to whether the bass player plays staccato or whether he sustains his notes between the cymbal beats.

Sensitive to specific timbral characteristics of different instruments and their particular attack envelope, Chuck Israels also listens for "a certain sound" that he and the drummer make together when they play.

Eventually, musicians learn to make distinctions in the interpretation of time that will enable them to articulate a regular four-beat pattern in slightly different positions—before, on top of, and after the beat—without changing the actual tempo. These precise positions are often imperceptible to the untrained ear. Yet for experienced improvisers, they assume such tangible qualities that the beat seems a physical object, a palpable force. "There's an edge I feel when I'm playing walking bass lines on top of the beat. It's like if you are walking into the wind," Rufus

Reid observes poetically, "you feel a certain resistance when your body is straight, but you feel a greater resistance if you lean into the wind."

Personal preferences sometimes require minor accommodations among group members. Leroy Williams discovered that saxophonist Johnny Griffin is "the type of player who likes a drummer to play way up on the beat." Although Williams "wasn't what you'd call an on-top-of-the-beat player at the time"—it wasn't "my natural flow," he says—he tried "to play more that way for Griffin." In another instance, a bass player known for playing "way behind on the beat" joined a drummer known for playing "way up on the beat." Despite their opposing tendencies, they adjusted their differences to maintain a "steady, swinging groove" throughout the performance (Howard Levy). Tied to individual preferences is the role that the drummer plays in discourse with the soloists. "If you play really ahead of the beat, where you're pushing everybody and telling them where to go," Paul Wertico says, "you're carrying a big responsibility [as to] the direction of a solo . . . [Whereas] if you just sit on the beat or on the back of the beat a little bit, you can just kind of cruise and add periods and commas to their statements."

Musicians strive to avoid major changes in tempo, although subtle fluctuations within the groove are tolerable. If one musician shifts positions from behind the beat to just before the beat and others follow suit, the group's overall tempo might edge ahead slightly, then steady itself, within a margin of acceptable variation. Rufus Reid refers to this practice when he explains that "some guys can play in tempo together as it swells in and out. As long as everybody is doing it together, they sound like they are perfectly in time." Indeed, when groups desire greater expressive freedom, such controlled flexibility enhances their music. "When you're in the rhythm section and everyone can play in all those places [i.e., on the beat, behind the beat, and on top of the beat]," Don Pate observes, "then you're not limited. . . . There can be a shift in where the beat is. Everyone responds to it . . . as opposed to the predictability of having to stay in one place."

At the same time that musicians introduce subtle variations in the tempo's ebb and flow as a matter of personal taste, the piece's structural features are also influencing them. "When I'm playing walking bass lines, I try to have the line moving somewhere," Reid says. "This has a lot to do with harmonic phrasing. If I'm playing a ii-V-I progression, I'm not just playing the notes of the chord. I'm moving toward V when I'm playing ii. I'm constantly flowing, pushing toward I. If you think consciously of moving somewhere harmonically when you play, it assimilates this swinging sound because harmonic sound is motion."

Improvisers sometimes increase the tempo slightly as a piece's harmonic rhythm increases and then relax it during static parts of the progression. They may increase the tempo slightly over the harmonic cadence at the close of a chorus, only to relax it with the beginning of the new cycle. Through the entire performance, group members alternate between asserting their own interpretations of time and adjusting them to those of other players.

THE RHYTHM SECTION'S IMPROVISATION WITHIN THE GROOVE

Defining the beat is an ongoing responsibility, but the rhythm section must also attend to other demands in order to assure a truly complementary performance. Toward such ends, the players in the rhythm section delineate the piece's harmonic-rhythmic form, support one another's evolving lines of thought, and fashion individual parts with "inherent interest and change." Musicians often rotate the responsibility for time-keeping. "You can play in a way that either states the time or implies it," Walter Bishop, Jr. explains. "My preference is to have someone state the time when the others aren't, so that what the others are doing works against the time. Then you have polytime and it becomes much more exciting, much more creative."

Typically, either the bass player or the drummer provides an anchor or rhythmic ground for the more adventurous performances of the rest of the band. According to Wynton Marsalis, "The bass player is the key. He needs to keep a steady pulse, to provide the bottom and to hold the music together. This frees the drummer up to play." Within this arrangement, it is a challenge for bass players to maintain a steady time-keeping pattern in relation to the tug and pull of the drummer's complex off-beat figures, even if the drummer includes a regular reference point within his or her part by playing the hi-hat cymbal on beats two and four. "Donald Bailey is an incredible drummer this way," Chuck Israels remembers. "I made a record with him and Hampton Hawes, and his playing was constantly churning and changing rhythmically. It was inventive and interesting all the time so that you never had a moment in which you were not being kept alert."

On the other hand, the bass can also "be free at times," Marsalis observes, "but when the bass player gets free, the drummer has to be restricted somewhat. It's just a tradeoff." Calvin Hill shares this view. "Last year when I heard Richard Davis, I was knocked out by the creative energy and natural flow to his bass playing," Hill recalls. "Something was always happening. Rhythmically, he'd walk for a while. Then, he'd stop and start playing a broken tempo for a while. Then, maybe, he'd switch to a little bit of arco [bowed bass]. It was very refreshing and very stimulating."

The accompaniment that Roy Haynes and Buster Williams provided Kenny Barron's solo at one New York concert demonstrated a particularly successful and sensitive interchange between bass player and drummer. When Haynes generated complicated rhythmic figures that obscured the beat, Williams stabilized the music with a steady walking bass line, but when Haynes reduced his part to a regular swing pattern, Williams varied his own part's rhythmic tension by repeatedly venturing outside the time, then returning to it. Typically, he entered the performance behind the beat and improvised intricate, gradually accelerating melodic phrases that aligned with the patterns of the other players at major structural points, resolving like successive waves that overtake one another, then break together.

Such examples suggest that improvisers are not only concerned with sharing their time-keeping role, but with occupying complementary space within the music's texture and achieving a collective transparency of sound in which each part is discernible. Through such temporal patterns, or "horizontal space," musicians seek to create a complementary level of rhythmic activity by improvising patterns whose rhythmic density is appropriate for the room that others leave for them. Through simultaneous harmonies, or "vertical space," they try to improvise in a melodic range that does not obscure the performances of others.

In this "vertical," harmonic space, the pianist figures prominently. In McCoy Tyner's group, Tyner "played a lot of notes on piano" and the drummer "played a lot of rhythmic things." Because their contributions "seemed to fill up every space" in the music, Calvin Hill confined his bass performance to "Eastern things like drones," playing them in a manner that was "not too rhythmic." Hill improvised parts with greater variety in Pharoah Sanders's band, however, because of the constraints on the pianist. "Pharoah liked to have the piano set up a bass-like vamp or ostinato, holding its fixed rhythm in" over the course of a performance. Other approaches that call attention to the piano part, even when it features spare comping rhythms are "relatively high registral placement" and dissonant voicings (Monson, 1991, p. 237). The range and configuration of chord voicings affects, as well, the bassist's inventive course. Larry Gray states that he can pursue greater options in formulating a bass line, without clashing with the pianist, when the pianist omits the chord's root and voices chords above the bass's range.

In other instances, the rhythmic density of the performances of all three accompanists remains fluid, and changes in any one can potentially influence the others. Ronald Shannon Jackson explains that if pianists switch from sustained chords to "playing driving eighth-notes," then he might switch from a regular quarter-note drum pattern to "sixteenth-notes, filling in between the spaces of what the piano player plays and increasing its intensity." John Hicks gives another example:

> In Arthur Blythe's group, we have this little break tune which sometimes takes the form of a very slow, almost dirge-like tempo. But then, sometimes, Fred will double it up on the bass and Steve will do the same thing on drums. So what I might do is double it up and stay with the double time for a while, then break it back down. Or I might just let them play the double time, and I would play something against that like the slower half time.

Besides shifting complementary positions among streams of patterns representing even-numbered subdivisions or multiples of the beat, performers also respond to one another by inventing asymmetrical counterposing patterns and interjecting fills between the discrete phrases of other artists. "Playing with musicians is like a conversation," Chuck Israels observes. "If when I speak, you say, 'Yes,' or you look at me and blink your eyes or interject some comment of your own, that keeps me going. Just listen to Roy Haynes! To say that he's a great rhythmic contrapuntal conversationalist doesn't do justice to what he does. What he does is just magic."

Elaborating upon the drummer's role as musical commentator, Ronald Shannon Jackson's early snare drum comping instruction was aimed at creating varied "polyrhythms" whose accents occur "either before or with or after the figures of the piano player." Today, if a pianist "plays something that is really driving," Jackson will hold the basic beat on the cymbals or the hi-hat "to provide a foundation," at the same time, "comping on the snare drum or the bass drum . . . to inspire the pianist's drive," he says. The two musicians "will work in and out of what each other is doing . . . calling and answering." Similarly, to prevent the music from becoming "stale," Michael Carvin features "short, staccato spurts . . . like a boxer, jabbin', jabbin', always keeping something happening" (Monson, 1991, p. 151). McCoy Tyner's drummer also conversed with other musicians by performing "lots of polyrhythms," Calvin Hill reports, adding that during breaks, the drummer usually superimposed "odd rhythms" like 7/4 over the simpler underlying meter of 4/4.

Within the music's ever-changing texture, new phrases that insinuate themselves above, beside, or below other phrases ultimately provide rich ideas that any of the players can seize and combine within their own. Musicians periodically depart from an independent course to echo fragmentary patterns just heard from another. Alternatively, they can reinforce a recurring phrase or any constant element within another member's performance by repeating it together with the inventor, perhaps with rhythmic embellishments. Common operations include accenting the second half of the fourth beat or briefly developing the effect of playing on different parts of the same beat. At times, increasing its coordinated punches leads the rhythm section to create intense developmental episodes; other times, sparser routines such as ostinato shout patterns result.

In college, Ronald Shannon Jackson, Julius Hemphill, and other class-mates provided John Hicks with invaluable coaching, deepening his understanding of such interplay. In addition to teaching him "how to loosen up rhythmically on piano, listening to the drummer, and locking into a groove," they demonstrated "different rhythmic things done by the drummer on the ride cymbal." This clarified specific figures and "lit-tle nuances" that had never been as clear to him from recordings, such as "the drummer's hi-hat cymbal pattern on beats two and four."

Pianist Kenny Barron recalls the relevance of comparable discoveries to his own comping skills. "The drummer has become a very, very important partner for me as my playing has evolved. At one point, I started really listening to the things the drummer would play, and I'd play the same things rhythmically." Barron initially adapted his perfor-mances to those of "older drummers" who maintained a regular "almost staccato" four-beat pattern on the bass drum. He subsequently collabo-rated with younger drummers who performed with a different "time-feel" and with surprising off-beat accents that, he admits, "forced me to play another way. At the time, I loved that."

As Barron's own musical vocabulary grew, he found that "some of the patterns drummers played were standard," and he could periodically anticipate their performance, even within the improvisations of musi-cians he played with for the first time. He explains,

> When you just lock up and play rhythmic things together that are not planned, it sounds like you actually rehearsed it all, and it makes a rhythm section sound cohesive. One small example might be to anticipate the "and" of a phrase together with a drummer. Many drummers anticipate the first beat of a measure by playing two eighth-notes, accenting the "and" of four and the "and" of one of the next measure. When I do those kinds of things together with drummers, many are surprised and go, "Oh, yeah?" But I can only do that because I listen to drummers so much. The figures we play together are most likely to occur at the end of phrases, like four- or eight-bar phrases. That helps to define the form of the tune.

Within their constantly changing scheme of interaction, successive "punches" of pianist and drummer produce different mixes of on-beat and off-beat accents. From beat to beat, elements of their comping fig-ures either converge, reinforcing one another, or diverge, creating cross-accentuation schemes or interlocking patterns, one part's components occupying the space left by its counterpart. Throughout, drummer and pianist regulate these features of their interplay, adding momentum to the performance and contributing to its dynamism.

Equally crucial is the relationship between pianists and bass players, because they overlap in their function of interpreting the piece's harmony. The pianist and bassist work together to improvise novel variations on the basic chord progression of the song. Thus, the harmony produced by jazz players is rarely identical to the standard version displayed on the music, but it is more like a lively composite creation, the product of multiple, ever-changing interpretations of the progression. Enriching the basic structure in endlessly varied ways, players may choose to reinforce or complement each other at one moment, to diverge at another, interrelating different harmonic pathways. The effects of such decisions may require immediate accommodation across the parts. Barron explains,

> Buster Williams, or whoever the bass player is, may play a different bass note than I expect or play a chord substitution, I have to be able to hear that and, at the same time, hear whatever rhythmic pattern is played by the drummer. If the bass player changes the whole chord, then I have to be aware enough of where he's going to go with him, or I may change the chord, and he has to be cool enough to hear where I'm going.

As in the interplay between pianist and drummer, the pianist and bass player depend on their knowledge of each other's generation or style period and musical personality to anticipate the ideas their counterparts are likely to perform in particular sections of the composition. Moreover, artists may repeat a pattern periodically or hint at it through variants to set up the idea for simultaneous performance, or for motivic treatment amid complementary counterparts. A bass player may pick up a recurring melodic fragment from one of the voices within a pianist's chord line and incorporate it into a bass part, just as a pianist may pick up a recurring fragment from the bass line and harmonize it as a comping pattern. Melodic-rhythmic interaction is also common between them.

Completing the rhythm section's circle of interaction are exchanges between bass players and drummers. Chuck Israels explains,

> When I'm listening to the other musicians and thinking about the form of a piece, there are little things that arise which I have to negotiate. Suppose I'm coming to a bar in the piece in which I would normally play four notes. The chord progression at that point dictates to me that, in order to keep the four-beat quarter-note rhythm going, I can play either four roots of the chords or I could play two roots and passing notes in between them.

But suppose, just before I get to that bar, the drummer plays a pattern that suggests a quarter-note triplet feeling and I would like to latch onto that rhythmic feeling and play the pattern with him. That creates an instant problem because I had intended to play four notes to the measure and now I need six notes for the two triplets. Where do you find them? Sometimes, you can find them chromatically between the main chord tones or in a chromatic approach from either below or above the chord tones. Sometimes, you find them in an extra secondary dominant chord or in a pattern of thirds. Those are the tricky little problems that arise when you play with other musicians.

At the same time that they are collectively negotiating all of these aspects of the music, the rhythm section must also provide support for the soloist. Rhythm section players commonly require a period of time for their own internal adjustment before the soloist joins them. "Years ago you let the rhythm section start playing by themselves at the beginning of the evening," Jimmy Robinson observes. "If they were having any trouble, you just let them play to get the kinks out. After they'd got the feeling for one another and got themselves together, then the horns joined them." When experienced improvisers perform together, such adjustments can occur almost instantly. Just as often, however, musicians need a few pieces or even the better part of a set to lock into meaningful conversation and invite soloists into their interplay.

SOLOISTS AND RHYTHM SECTION PLAYERS

Although soloists join the performance as featured speakers and temporary leaders of the group's journey, they typically rely upon the rhythm section to provide signposts for the performance's direction. Many horn players listen specifically to the drummer's constant hi-hat cymbal for the beat. Others focus upon the swinging ride cymbal pattern that enhances their improvisations by providing, as Curtis Fuller puts it, a "smooth carpet" for them to "walk on," or in Paul Wertico's words, a rhythmic "drone to ride on." Representing another approach, veterans in Chicago taught Doc Cheatham "to listen to the bass" because it carries "the time and the harmony." As long as he focuses his attention on the bass during his solos, Cheatham admits, "I can't make too many mistakes." To gain his own bearings, Lou Donaldson also listens to the bass "for the harmonic pivot points" in chord sequences, which, he explains, help him "keep track of the changing tonal centers of pieces." If a piece is "highly rhythmic, I will play mostly off the bass rhythm."

The rhythm section commonly provides more than structural markers amid its multilayered backdrop of musical counterpoint. At times, rhythm section players interject punctuations and unique melodic figurations between the soloist's phrases in brief antiphonal response to them. As often, players offer simultaneous commentary; their comping patterns overlap or interlock with the soloist's figures, or anticipate their elements precisely, contributing cohesion to the performance. New lines of interpretation can occur to them in ongoing inspiration, as soloists hear and feel features of their ideas reinforced by their counterparts. Moreover, within the reciprocal relationships between soloists and supporting players, interesting ideas that originate in any part can influence others, leading to various kinds of imitative interplay. Lonnie Hillyer "plays well" with Leroy Williams because he can "draw from him." Hearing Williams play a tasteful rhythmic pattern in his drum accompaniment, Hillyer might "play it back to him." Conversely, Williams might hear Hillyer "play a certain rhythm and play it back." Art Farmer notices that to initiate a longer chain of events, a soloist sometimes performs "strong rhythmic patterns just to wake up the drummer" and then "tries to respond to whatever" the partner "does in reaction to that."

Describing this relationship from the drum chair, Williams explains that his role is "to keep the music swinging while embellishing what goes on around me. I'm constantly playing, feeding, and helping everyone, making each soloist sound as good as I can." Ronald Shannon Jackson elaborates from the same perspective:

> The role of the drum in Betty Carter's group was not just a time-keeping device. It was to accent what she was singing. She scatted and phrased the words of the songs with such finesse and style, with such rhythmic pull, that it was like the drum and her voice were one thing. Betty was very rhythmic, and she loved to play with the drummer with her voice. She used scat syllables to sing the same type of things I could play with my left hand on the drums. She'd sing along with what I was playing or improvise on top of it, and that would be like magic for the audience. We were still calling her "Betty Bebop" at that time because she could sing the same rudiments with her voice that you could play on the drums.

Michael Carvin once displayed the skillful drummer's ability to play the improvised lines of soloists along with them at a New York performance. Phrasing together with Walter Bishop, Jr., Carvin invented drum patterns that not only began and ended with the pianist's melodies, but also anticipated their accents (also see Monson, 1991, p. 38; Rinzler, 1988, p. 158). Within these phrases, Carvin sometimes duplicated Bishop's precise rhythmic figures and at other times, provided them with a rhythmic counterpoint. For further variation, he would switch to a steady swing pattern, periodically filling the rests between the soloist's phrases with a press roll.

Paul Wertico started honing such aspects of interaction as a drum student, already sensitive to the harmonic and melodic aspects of music, especially the changing directions and patterns of tension and release in a composed melody or in a soloist's improvisation. Wertico learned the essential lesson of responding to such changes by listening to figures played by drummers like Roy Haynes, studying their precise effects on the surrounding parts. There was a difference, for example, between "suddenly striking" the cymbal and bass drum together, which weighs the music down, and striking an open cymbal alone, which creates "a feeling of expanding space." With increasing sophistication in such matters, Wertico would guide his accompaniment by assessing drum set patterns for their likely musical and emotional effects on the performance. Accordingly, changes in the musical expression of the other group members also influence the drummer's choice of figures and their orchestration.

The soloist's relationship with pianists is equally important. "The piano player might just independently do something as part of the rhythm section that is attention-getting, something he is just directing at me," Lee Konitz points out. "If I hear the piano player play a figure, I'll stop for a moment and then react to that. I'll do something as a result of what he did. Or maybe the piano player does something that is a reaction to something I've just played. That's a surefire way of getting my attention."

Melodic invention is one aspect of this type of exchange. When John Lewis accompanies Milt Jackson's solos, Lewis does what Tommy Turrentine calls "sub-soloing. Instead of just saying, 'ching, ching, ching, ching,' he'll do that for a while and then play a little melody in octaves." Although such figures can stand simply as a counterpoint to the soloist's part, at times soloists incorporate them into their performances. Lonnie Hillyer was once performing with pianist Walter Davis when Davis played a pattern behind him that was "really wild, really outside" harmonically—"some godforsaken interval"—that Hillyer immediately "reached out and grabbed" for his solo. "I like that kind of spontaneity," Hillyer declares. The reverse can be equally exciting. Greg Langdon describes an early band whose phenomenal pianist could "pick up whatever the soloist played, either duplicating it or doing something like it instantly." Langdon had "never experienced anything like it before." Once learners have absorbed such conventions for sympathetic interaction, they soon begin to imagine responses of rhythm section players to their own improvisations, even when practicing alone.

The pianist's accompanying figures can provide either a general rhythmic impetus or precise rhythmic ideas. Patti Bown strives to provide "a foundation" for soloists by inventing "some kind of rhythmic pattern that would make it interesting for them to play and to work in and out of." Soloists express admiration for pianists who "have a way of comping that has a strong rhythmic feel. They will anticipate the beat a little, putting a little rhythmic push into it, adding life to the music" (Art Farmer). Vea Williams agrees. "I love pianists who enhance or let me feed off what they're doing. Good accompanists like Norman Simmons or Albert Dailey know how to let a singer sing," she explains. "They'll play things that will give you ideas on how to expand a phrase or how to string out a word in a spontaneous and unique way." This requires versatility as well as sensitivity in musical interaction. Freddie Greene praises Count Basie who, as an accompanist, "always seems to know the right thing to play . . . making the rhythm smooth . . . [and contributing] the missing things" (Shapiro & Hentoff, 1966, p. 305).

In addition to setting forth melodic and rhythmic options, pianists stimulate soloists through selected chord voicings. John McNeil explains,

> Ultimately, both soloists and pianists need to grasp each other's interpretation of harmony, one through chord voicings and the other through the melodic line. When you change the harmony a little in your solo and pianists hear it, then they should echo you a bit or play a chord voicing in such a way that it will complement what you've just played and spur you on to something else. Joanne Brackeen is one of my favorite pianists to play with. She doesn't use a lot of space, but she really listens well. She always plays things that go with the things that you play. When I play with her, I'm rarely conscious that she's there, except that everything sounds real good. We're just into the flow of it together.

In Art Farmer's view,

> The thing that really makes the music sound good is the way the pianists voice their chords. Some people leave you space and give you some freedom at the same time they're leading you in a certain way. I'll listen to how the pianist voices a chord, and I'll get an idea of what note would go well with it. I'll get an idea of what starting note to use for my solo.

Curtis Fuller adds that when Bill Evans plays "real pretty chords," their leading tones can be very suggestive, "opening up the soloist's ears." Wynton Marsalis comments similarly. Pianists "don't have to put every note in the chord," he declares. "To find the best possible choice is the thing; four notes can sound like a thousand if they're the right ones."

Finally, there are the mutual reactions of soloists and bass players. The bass player's contributions can be as critical as the pianist's in determining the harmonic complexion of the music. "If Harold Land and Bobby Hutcherson were playing a chord like a major seventh chord, they would voice it in fourths," Rufus Reid recalls. "The harmony was more open that way. If I changed the bass note I was playing, all of a sudden the sound of the whole chord would be different." In equally dramatic terms, a bass player who temporarily switches to a repeating pedal point, suspending a detailed representation of the progression for "a more general articulation of tonality"—perhaps the tonic or dominant of the piece's key—offers "the pianist and soloist considerable harmonic latitude" (Monson, 1991, p. 123). Similarly, when a bass player "takes the chord progression in a different way" than Tommy Turrentine expects, it can change his thinking and influence the course of his solo.

Besides praising bassists' imaginative harmonic concepts, musicians praise their time-feel or swing-feel, their sound, and the shapes of their lines. Kenny Barron describes the experience of performing with inventive bass players like Ron Carter, whose "rhythmic concept is different and...choice of notes sometimes can be very unusual...When the chord sequence itself isn't chromatic, he may find a chromatic line that will work and I'll say, 'Oh, yeah?'" Correspondingly, the dialogic improvisation of melodic-rhythmic elements is common between the bass and solo parts. Patti Bown likes "to have a bass player feed me some energetic ideas to play off of." Conversely, Lonnie Hillyer remembers Charles Mingus imitating things that the soloists played in his band, making "for a conversation." In addition to imitative interplay, soloists and bass players interact through regulating contrapuntal features of their parts. Chuck Israels generally appreciates a bassist's "contrary or oblique motion" in relation to a solo line, but acknowledges musical situations in which "sudden parallel motion becomes the very best thing to do."

This kind of interaction depends upon the improviser's keen aural skills and ability to grasp instantly the other's musical ideas. These talents represent the culmination of years of rigorous training begun in students' initial efforts to acquire a jazz vocabulary. Akira Tana elaborates,

> The goal is to mesh your sound with all the other instruments and to create a balanced group sound. I don't just mean this in terms of volume. I'm talking about balancing the figures you play with all the things that you hear coming from other instruments. As a drummer, I'm listening to the

rhythm section in relation to what the soloist is doing. I'm still learning to hear the whole group and all the individual instruments in relation to my own.

Saxophonist Lee Konitz also "wants to relate to the bass player and the piano player and the drummer, so that I know at any given moment what they are all doing. The goal is always to relate as fully as possible to every sound that everyone is making." Konitz reflects on the task and exclaims, "But whew! It's very difficult for me to achieve. At different points, I will listen to any particular member of the group and relate to them as directly as possible in my solo."

Although hearing everything over a musical journey represents the ideal, listening is typically a dynamic activity and performers continually adopt different perspectives on the musical patterns that surround them. Their constantly fluctuating powers of concentration, the extraordinary volume of detail requiring them to absorb material selectively, and developments in their own parts that periodically demand full attention, together create a kaleidophonic essence of each artist's perception of the collective performance. Moreover, as suggested above, improvisers sometimes deliberately shift focus within the music's dazzling texture to derive stimulation from different players. Walter Bishop, Jr. can "zero in on the bass player or the drummer, either one by himself or both together. Or, if the band's a quartet, I can listen in quadruplicate."

Amid the rigorous operations of listening and responding, the overlapping perceptions of all the players can potentially compensate for any individual's difficulties or divergent viewpoints and bring cohesion to the larger performance. The piano player might hear something in what the soloist is playing that the drummer does not hear at the time, but if the drummer hears the pianist's response to the soloist and he complements the pianist's idea, then what the drummer plays will also complement "the whole musical thought of the soloist" (Leroy Williams). Discerning audience members, as well as players, share in the exciting moments of instantaneous conversation across all the parts as performance interaction intensifies, producing such varied effects as a fleeting ripple of accents from player to player or the collective development of motives over an entire chorus (see Appendix).

INTERPRETING IDEAS

Exercising their skills of immediate apprehension, improvisers engage in effective musical discourse by interpreting the various preferences of other players for interaction, and by conveying their own personal pref-

erences. Sometimes they are familiar with their cohorts on the bandstand, and sometimes they play with artists of whom they know
practically nothing. By reputation, some horn players like to "converse
rhythmically when they solo; different things played behind them give
them ideas. Others don't like any of that. They just want straight time
played behind them" (Akira Tana). Tommy Flanagan makes similar distinctions. "Sonny Rollins doesn't need very much in the way of you
chording for him, because he covers the whole thing in his solos—he
plays the chords and the rhythmic part. Miles plays with a lot of spaces,
so that leaves more room for the rhythm section to play fills and to do
things as a whole." Calvin Hill contrasts two of his colleagues:

> George Coleman is a person who plays a lot of notes, a lot of rhythm and
> everything, so actually, all you have to do is to give him a cushion and just
> let him go. . . . But when you're playing with somebody like Pharoah Sand-
> ers who doesn't play as much, you can play a little bit more out front, a lit-
> tle more complex and with more activity because he uses the rhythm
> section more than somebody like George Coleman.

Experience over time greatly enhances musical cohesion, of course.
Specific knowledge of the concepts or approaches of different musicians—reflected in their recurring vocabulary patterns, the logic underlying phrase construction and motive development, and long-range
storytelling strategies—provides additional clues for fellow band members. Consequently, while attending to their own parts—assessing inventive material and selecting elements for development—performers must
constantly exercise musical "peripheral vision" to determine the course
their coperformers are taking. After a rhythm section becomes accus-
tomed to particular soloists, it can "follow their train of thought and
complement it," Akira Tana says. Curtis Fuller elaborates: "In Miles
Davis's band, 'Philly' Joe even learned to play little things to set Miles
up for his phrases. He'd play things before and after Miles's figures. Little things like that let you know the drummer is listening." In groups
that perform together frequently, players sometimes develop a core of
common patterns that they periodically reintroduce in performances to
stimulate interplay.

Having an attuned rhythm section mattered greatly to Miles Davis,
who, as Fuller reports, "also spent a lot of time getting the rhythm section to know how each other plays so that they could anticipate one
another." Kenny Barron discusses this process: As a pianist who prides
himself on being able to "adjust to almost anything that a drummer can
do," Barron strives not only to synchronize his comping figures with the
conventional accompanying patterns for drums described earlier, but to

"do different things with each drummer based on what [each does]." Watching a partner can be important in developing such rapport. A musician recalls a concert in which a young drummer "didn't take his eyes off the piano player the whole night," successfully anticipating the pianist's accentuation patterns from the motion of his arms.

As Fred Hersch points out, the constant stylistic features of a bass player can also shape the expectations of other band members and suggest different limitations for improvised interplay. "Sam Jones is a great bassist," Hersch asserts, "but he's fairly conservative. On waltzes, he'll play just one note at the beginning of each bar; on a ballad, he'll end up double-timing it usually. If he's playing a walking bass line behind you, the only thing he might do in reaction to what you've played is to introduce a substitute chord change, taking a slightly different harmonic route through the piece." In contrast, other bass players "will stop walking for a while and strum their basses, or play a constant pedal point, or play a counter melody, or change the rhythm."

Group members can eventually develop a series of musical signs that reveals one another's intentions. As implied earlier, the soloist might leave more space to invite greater activity on the part of the rhythm section. "Pharoah might play something and want the group to react to it," says Calvin Hill. "Like he'll play a little bit and rest, giving the group some time. Then he'll play a little bit more and rest again, giving the group some more time." Although soloists often deliberately leave space to encourage others, at times they may simply tire and require a short rest, or they may have a temporary lapse of imagination after completing an idea. "The give-and-take is ideal," Lee Konitz says, "so that·if you go down for a second, all you have to do is to keep quiet and let someone else play for a second. In that way, the music continues to grow." Akira Tana agrees: "If a horn player is playing a solo and in the middle of it, he lays out for a moment, the drummer should comp for him and chord for him, trying to inspire him and give him things that will boost him."

Additionally, the repetition of a phrase can suggest a motive for development on the part of other artists or the whole group. "If a piano player hints at a certain rhythmic figure behind the soloist throughout the chorus or during the first half of the tune, the drummer can keep time and comp simultaneously, either playing the same rhythmic figure as the pianist, or playing off of it, or playing against it," Akira Tana explains. "You can do the same thing with the soloist, too, answering his phrases, playing along with the things he states rhythmically, or playing variations on those things." As an alternative, rhythm section players can invite intensification of the music by repeating a big-band riff and leaving space for their counterparts to fill in with call and response exchanges (Monson, 1991, p. 252).

Beyond such overt musical suggestions are myriad subtler ones. An example would be the challenge Don Pate acknowledges when Roy Haynes "signals something to me just through a gesture in his playing." In Miles Davis's quintet with Tony Williams, a dramatic leap to the trumpet's high register on a downbeat was often a signal for the group to switch from a floating rhythmic feeling or a two-beat feeling to a precise four-beat, swing feeling. Similarly, Fred Hersch has learned to detect subtle messages in Art Farmer's trumpet playing:

> When I'm playing with Art Farmer, it's the same kind of thing. Art is very spontaneous. He listens to what you play behind him and you really play with him. When he plays something that I know I can feel from him, that means for me to do something. For example, when he'll go up to a high note and shake it, that means, "Okay. Come on up there with me." Or, when he will choose a series of very obtuse pitches in a line, that means, "Lay out." It doesn't mean, "Try to find me." It means, "I'm trying to lose you, so just let me play without you for a while."

As the group's enveloping mix of patterns emerge—at times dance-like, at times lyrical, at times speech-like—the powerful color of the revealed emotions also demands reaction. Improvisers immediately catch and follow up the feelings of despair or joy or any of the endlessly varied shades of meaning conveyed by the evocative timbres of the patterns' mixture. "The amazing thing about playing with Art [Blakey]," says Terrence Blanchard, "is that he has a way of tuning into inspiration that can draw an emotion out of you that you may have never experienced before" (quoted in Blakey, 1987). Curtis Fuller comments from the inside as music flows to him from another artist, "When you hear Paul Chambers play some frisky little thing behind your solo, it makes you feel frisky like that and it influences what you play."

Finally, the larger framework of a group's common tradition may provide allusions that prompt new ideas and influence the performance's course. When saxophonist Arthur Blythe plays "little phrases" that bring to mind another song for John Hicks, "I might use it," Hicks says, to play off the second song within the framework of the first. Lonnie Hillyer is also the kind of player who likes to quote different compositions in his solos. "A friend of mine says he always hears me quote from 'How Are Things in Glocca Morra?' Now, if I'm playing with a sensitive piano player, he might answer me with something related to 'Glocca Morra' in a rhythmic, melodic, or harmonic sense."

Musicians can also communicate by improvising patterns reminiscent of the characteristic interplay of renowned artists within historic bands.

Tommy Turrentine says, for example, that if, while formulating his solo, he hears the drummer play a figure "ka plum," reminding him of "something Max Roach played behind Fats Navarro," he "would think about the way Fat Girl played" and incorporate that "feeling" within his own performance. If the figure reminded Turrentine of "what Miles played with Max," however, then he might be inspired to perform a phrase by Miles Davis.

SHAPING THE LARGER PERFORMANCE

In their responses to other players, musicians typically seek to preserve a general continuity of mood. Beginning a solo, John Hicks listens to the "spirit coming from the whole group" to determine "a direction" for expansion that "contributes to the overall feeling." Toward such ends, soloists can draw inspiration from the general approaches or specific ideas of the musician who soloed just before them, selecting a common vocabulary pattern or tune quotation introduced in that solo. They often select the solo's final idea. Showing special consideration in this regard, Count Basie was known for "prepar[ing] an entrance for the next man" at the close of his own solos (Freddie Greene, quoted in Shapiro & Hentoff, 1966, p. 305). "If Sonny Stitt plays before me," Harold Ousley says, "I'll listen to the phrases that he plays, and they will give me ideas for related things that I can play. I might take the last phrase that he played and come in on it. Sometimes, musicians do this as a connecting point to their own solos." In such cases, soloists may simply treat the "connecting" figure as a fleeting transition, or they may treat it as a motive, transforming it according to the procedures by which they develop their own ideas.

When soloists "trade eights" or "trade fours," alternating short improvised phrases, they sometimes respond to the most general features of each other's phrases, for example, extending their contours gracefully to create such continuity between the parts that the resultant line sounds as if it were conceived by one mind. Other times, they adopt practices comparable to those described above, imitating or transforming, to varying degrees, the precise features of the previous player's ideas. As often, they combine such operations with their own ideas. Tommy Flanagan reflects on the piano duo albums he has made with Hank Jones and Kenny Barron:

> You don't know what the other player is going to play, but on listening to the playback, almost every time, you hear that you related your part very quickly to what the other player played just before you. It's like a message

that you relay back and forth. It happens at any tempo, whether it's very fast or whether you're playing a ballad. Or, if we're switching off every eight bars, there will be something in my eight bars that related to the last part of the soloist before me. . . . You want to achieve that kind of communication when you play. When you do, your playing seems to be making sense. It's like a conversation.

Because of the influence that improvisers often exert on those who follow, some band leaders deliberately vary the order of soloists from piece to piece. Featuring different players in the first solo position varies the potential influence each soloist has on the initial direction of the piece's interpretation and, over the course of a set, may vary the feeling or concept overall from piece to piece, as well. A leader may have assertive, self-sufficient soloists perform ahead of those who usually require an inspired model to reach their own potential. Sometimes, musicians unfamiliar with the piece may themselves decide to avoid the first solo to garner ideas for their own approach by studying the ideas of soloists who precede them (Harold Ousley).

Of course, improvisers can take the opposite musical tack when their cumulative sense of the performance suggests that a strong contrast would enhance its dramatic qualities. "If the music's been really hectic rhythmically, very rhythmic and loud," Calvin Hill says, "I might just be silent for the first four or eight bars" of the solo, "not play anything, or maybe play one note every three or four bars." Issues of professional image can also influence such decisions. One musician said that if the previous soloist had "really covered a particular thing well, like playing very high and very technically," the best strategy for avoiding an unfavorable comparison was to adopt "a different approach altogether." Toward such ends, the soloist might draw stimulus from such varied sources as musical ideas unrelated to the performance that "had been going on in my head earlier that day . . . [or even] a sound out in the street" (Buster Williams).

As often as not, musicians pursue a middle ground that satisfies their desire for both continuity and change by borrowing material from one another and transforming it. This is as true in the interaction between soloists as in their reciprocal exchanges with the rhythm section. Horn players can create new figures by adding their own notes to rhythmic patterns that they derive from the accompanying parts, perhaps by playing off of the drummer's accents—extracting a simpler pattern from the larger drum phrase—or by seizing a complex rhythmic fragment from the phrase for a template. "You can never know in advance of the situation what you will do at the time," says Leroy Williams when discussing these practices from the rhythm section's side.

Maybe the soloist will play a phrase, and you will feel like grabbing the phrase and taking it someplace else, doing something else with it. What makes creativity is playing half of this and half of that, interjecting your own thing into it. Or, you might let the soloist's phrase go by completely because it would seem too obvious to play it. The unexpected is as cool as the expected, at times.

Rufus Reid describes the multiple interpretations that improvisers can put upon one another's statements and the physical aspects of ideas that can affect their discussion within the group. Many times players "will play a certain rhythmic pattern, or melodic motive," he says, "and then I could play a portion of that motive intertwined in my bass line." In a live performance, the listener may not initially hear that "as a separate entity"; it is part of the continuous flow of the music. But if the performance is recorded, Reid says, a listener may "say, 'Wow, did you hear that?'" Reid might have used the pattern in his own solo four bars after it was introduced by the horn player, either imitating it "verbatim," or taking the rhythm of the phrase and adding something different harmonically. Reid finds it more interesting to take something from someone else and add a little bit to it. For example, a saxophone player might play things Reid never had "thought of playing" because of the different capabilities of their instruments. If the entire phrase is too difficult to execute with the bass, Reid might play a portion of the saxophone player's phrase and go on to develop it his own way.

Beyond sharing precise melodic and rhythmic material, musicians initiate and respond to change by regulating general features of their improvisations such as range and voicing. Contour is also an ongoing feature of interplay, as players anticipate and respond to the nuances within each other's evolving shapes, the distinctive "hills and valleys" of their creations. In contrapuntal schemes with endless possibilities, they formulate lines that, for example, run parallel to one another, or create contrary motion, or provide other kinds of contrast. Dynamic changes also come into play. If the soloist performs something dramatic that goes from soft to loud, Reid explains, it might inspire the rhythm section to do the same thing a few bars later. "And then, in turn, the soloist could turn around and play it loud to soft," he adds. Drummers sometimes follow a soloist even more closely. "If I'm playing very loud at a certain point in my solo—really hollering—and then I suddenly come off it and get soft, they will also back off with me," John McNeil remarks.

You can build and build, and then back off, and then come up again together. I like to do things like that because it's interesting for me to listen to. It's good when drummers stay under me, as opposed to over me, in terms of volume. And yet at some point, they can play right up to my level and just a little beyond to take me a little further. But if he does that and I don't take him up on it by playing any louder, then he should know enough not to push it too far. It's a give-and-take situation that way. I like a drummer to really roar in the back of me sometimes and it gives me a lot of support; but there has to be a balance.

Equally influential for the design of a solo are the relative rhythmic complexity and density of its accompaniment. These features allow the music to breathe and diversify. "Some piano players will let a few bars at a time go by without playing," Lonnie Hillyer explains. "That gives horn players room to establish their ideas." Similarly, Patti Bown "tries to leave space" within the framework of her comping patterns. "It's important to learn to play less," she cautions, "because it's possible to fill up every hole."

The composition's formal structure dictates, in part, the regulation of rhythmic activity and other interactive features. General collective goals, such as "accenting the endings of harmonic units," assist artists in anticipating and complementing the details in each other's parts (Rinzler, 1988, p. 157). So do shared expectations for events that typically occur at particular "location[s] within the time cycle." Typically, while the soloist extends phrases over principal harmonic section boundaries or highlights them by resting, rhythm section players define structural cadences through various combined operations in the last two bars of sections. They may, for example, increase their parts' rhythmic and harmonic density and tension, or expand their parts' range, then reverse such operations, returning to the tonic on the new section downbeat or just after it. Such events are made all the more dramatic when, at their onset, the pianist drops out of the performance, then rejoins to assist in creating a climactic peak. On the other hand, comparable aspects of group interplay can transcend formal units, occurring instead as sympathetic responses to evolving ideas in the various parts, creating unique designs in the process.

Rhythm section members sometimes steadily increase the intensity of their own activity over the course of the solo. "Working with Art Blakey taught me about how to build a solo," Gary Bartz recalls. "Art will build it for you, so you have to go along with him. He starts off nice and soft the first chorus and he builds the second chorus a little and by the time you get to the third chorus, he's bashing behind you. You have to build your solo on him, so you learn how to build a solo like that. It isn't necessarily that he plays louder each chorus," Bartz says, "but his playing becomes more intense each chorus, so you learn how to build the intensity of your solo each chorus." Art Farmer also acknowledges the give and take between the soloist and the supporting players. "If I would play with Horace Silver, I would learn something about drive," Farmer declares,

> because Horace was so strong on the piano. If I would play with Blakey, I would also have to play something interesting, something with life in it. If you played something dull, then it was just like you were in their way. Horace and Art were supposed to be playing background for you, but at the same time, they were really driving you and pushing you. And if you didn't respond, you might as well stop playing and let them go ahead without you. They didn't let you coast. You had to get into it.

Speaking from the drummer's viewpoint, Akira Tana observes that shaping a solo commonly includes a combination of strategies, "playing straight time, starting with a little interaction and building from there. You can develop a very nice tension sometimes when you have rhythmic figures going against each other," Tana explains. "You can keep up the tension over eight or sixteen bars and resolve it at the bridge of the piece. Or, you can keep it going over the tune's form for a whole chorus, or even beyond that, depending on how much freedom you have in developing your idea. You have to be very conscious of time and the form of the piece when you do this. It has to be in reason."

At one concert in which saxophonist Frank Foster subjected a melodic phrase to motivic variations of increasing rhythmic complexity and volume, drummer Billy Hart increased his part's volume and cross-rhythmic activity accordingly, culminating with a thrashing crescendo just as Foster restated the solo's motive in the saxophone's highest register and brought the performance to a climax. Immediately afterward, Hart created a huge swell of sound with a press roll, leading with a rapid decrescendo to a soft time-keeping pattern that prepared the next soloist's entrance.

When soloists create several climaxes over their performance's course, accompanists sometimes choose simply "to hold down the beat," stabilizing the music's foundation in relation to dramatic changes in the soloist's part. This was illustrated at a New York club in which soloist Walter Bishop, Jr. suddenly switched from streams of even eighth-notes to a repeated asymmetrical pattern, whose accents fell in progressively different places in relation to Michael Carvin's accompanying swing figure, creating varied schemes of rhythmic counterpoint. Instantly aware of the pressure between the two parts, both performers smiled as they sought to steady their components in the face of their growing tension, not knowing when they would find alignment. When after eight measures the patterns finally coincided, the two musicians laughed with enjoyment, and repeated the same sequence of events before Bishop, Jr. abandoned the asymmetrical figure and returned to his former groove.

As suggested above, improvisers must respond creatively to surprises that constantly arise during performances. Within the normal compass of events, unexpected turns occur everywhere: in the ever-changing details of each part and in the periodic large-scale changes in repertory programs and formal structures that guide improvisations. When the liberties that players take conspire with capricious turns of improvisation in a way that defies the expectations of the band, they are what Herbie Hancock likens, within Miles Davis's band, to the unpredictable course of conversations. "How many times have you talked to somebody and you got ready to make a point, and it kind of went off in another direction? . . . Maybe you never ended up making that point," Hancock says, "but the conversation just went somewhere else and it was fine. There's nothing wrong with it. Maybe you liked where you went. Well, this is the way we were dealing with music" (Davis, 1986). Such events occur typically when the natural flow of ideas conceived in performance leads a particular improviser outside the group's agreed formats or musical arrangements, and other players follow along. Ultimately, the flexibility with which musicians treat arrangements, whether subtly ornamenting or substantially altering their features, enhances the improvisatory spirit of performances.

To those unforeseen turns of event that form the normal basis for collaboration, errors in performance present yet additional challenges. Jazz groups simply treat performance errors as compositional problems that require instant, collective solutions—in some cases the skillful mending of one another's performances. Tactful responses not only mitigate musical errors, but can at times produce unexpected benefits for the entire group. Max Roach observes that "there are chances we all have to take when we're dealing with improvisational music and sometimes clashes occur between musicians. That's why there's so much skill and sensitivity required to make the music come off well. There are also times when a clash isn't bad," he says. "It can create a tension and something new can come of it. For example, if two players make a mistake and end up in the wrong place at the wrong time, they may be able to break out of it and get into something else they might not have discovered otherwise."

As Roach indicates, the skills by which performers share ideas during the routine course of improvisation are put to great test by error. Like exceptional visions that suggest new paths for exploration, problematic turns can ultimately provide dramatic, even welcome, contrast to the prearranged performance features, their effective solutions contributing uniqueness to the musical journeys of improvisers. In fact, among veteran performers, artists are known to deliberately introduce "musical problems" into the group's performance or to otherwise increase the risks they take in their own performances—ultimately increasing the possibility of challenging the other band members as well. To emphasize the value that he places on adventurous experimentation, Miles Davis would periodically encourage his band members to avoid their routine maneuvers. "I pay you to practice on the bandstand," he would exhort them (Davis, 1986). In a similar spirit, some leaders build extemporaneous interaction into performances—requiring musicians to rely heavily on their ingenuity and their sensitivity to one another—by limiting rehearsals and minimizing discussion about the music.

THE ONGOING INTERPLAY BETWEEN COLLECTIVE IMPROVISATION AND PRECOMPOSITION

In the final analysis, the spontaneous and arranged elements of jazz presentations continually cross-fertilize and revitalize one another. Precomposed background lines or riffs that add interest to the performance and, as musical landmarks, help soloists keep their bearings over a progression, also provide material that soloists can incorporate into their inventions. Conversely, supporting players, without external direction, can adopt a soloist's interesting phrase extemporaneously as the basis for a new accompanying riff. As artists absorb and share initially improvised patterns, repeating them as components of increasingly consistent routines, the patterns shift subtly from the realm of improvised ideas to that of arranged or precomposed ideas. These are common occurrences over a single performance. In the renowned interplay within the Creole Jazz Band, Joe Oliver would, at times, introduce a new break figure at the end of one chorus, and Louis Armstrong would instantly absorb it to perform it with Oliver at the break in the middle of the next chorus. Moreover, Oliver's cue to his partner was sometimes but a silent miming of an intended idea's finger pattern. Before the targeted break, Armstrong, translating the patterns into sound, actually composed a second part to the anticipated Oliver "lead" in time to "blend" with his (Buster Bailey and Louis Armstrong quoted in Shapiro & Hentoff, 1966, pp. 103–104).

From event to event, groups may preserve successful elements of improvisations within an arrangement's ongoing performance tradition. When playing through a composition together, singer Vea Williams and pianist Franklin Gordon sometimes "get to a place where the chords normally resolve a certain way," Williams says, and spontaneously "try something different from the way the tune's written. The other day, we were doing 'Come Rain or Shine,'" she recounts, turning to Gordon for the details of his accompaniment, "and we came to the place where you go from F7 to B-flat7 in the key of F or G minor." Gordon continues: "Instead of playing the F7th, I played B-flat half diminished going to the B-flat. It's a beautiful sound." Williams nods in agreement, adding, "And it's away from the melody. It gave me this surge, just this tremendous feeling. We talked about it afterward and decided that whenever we did that tune, we'd play it straight the first chorus and add the new chord the second or third time around because that made the music so fresh."

Larry Gray describes even more radical harmonic alterations during one performance with James Moody at the Jazz Showcase in Chicago. Feeling adventurous that evening, Gray decided to see what would happen if, in between the pivotal "signpost" chords of the blues, he pursued in his bass line harmonic pathways loosely associated with Coltrane's "Giant Steps." Moody instantly grasped Gray's intention and improvised his own solo along the same lines. Afterwards, he expressed his surprise and delight to Gray, and the two decided to adopt this approach during future blues performances.

Chuck Israels gives a similar interpretation of the way in which rhythmic features of a group's interplay enter arrangements. "There are cross-rhythms and other figures that the rhythm section players can catch from each other and find ways of playing together, like the triplet figures which 'Philly' Joe Jones, Paul Chambers, and Red Garland play together on Miles Davis recordings. Things like that are worked out. Some people in the band initially play it and somebody else says, 'Oh, that's good. Let's do that again.'" In fact, when Don Friedman once worked with "Philly" Joe Jones in a band with Chet Baker, Jones taught Friedman some of the "complicated rhythmic figures" he had performed with Garland, so that they, too, could play the figures together when he initiated them. Friedman recalls, "I used to hear that band with Miles live and it was fantastic to hear [Jones and Garland] play together because they had so many things worked out. They'd do all these great [rhythmic] hits," he recalls, that "would suddenly come out of nowhere," breaking up the music's "constant repetitive beat," providing "such a lift." Various features of "Philly" Joe Jones's interaction with Miles Davis also became classic routines, not only recreated by the artists themselves in performance, but adopted by other jazz groups as well.

Of course, routines iike those within Miles Davis's group can also develop among improvisers without any discussion. "Philly" Joe Jones remembers that, in general, when performing with Davis, "Miles would ask if we knew the tunes and we did, so we'd play them spontaneously each night. By playing the tunes every night in a certain way, it becomes an arrangement, actually a better arrangement than if it had been written out" (Jones quotation from Mansfield interview cited in Stewart, 1986, p. 187). A specific case is Roy Haynes's interaction with Sarah Vaughan during performances of "Shulie-A-Bop," in which Vaughan departs from her scat improvisation to introduce the other band members. The exchange that became a permanent feature of their rendition had its roots in an event during which, after hearing her acknowledge John Malachi and "Crazy" Joe Benjamin, Haynes decided that he would "set her up" for his own introduction. Anticipating the moment she would announce his name, he played a loud kick on the drums, then, hearing Vaughan call, "Roy," he interjected a few more kicks into the performance between "Roy" and "Haynes." Following her mention of his surname, he created an explosive drum response ending on their recorded version, with triplets that Vaughan immediately picks up to launch her own continuing vocal improvisation (Vaughan, video, 1991).

Musical parts conceived through group interaction may even assume independent lives as compositions. Guitarist John McLaughlin and violinist Shankar, of Shakti, would record their informal improvising. After evaluating the taped sessions, they sometimes extracted the most cohesive segments to combine and reassemble into original compositions and arrangements. As these representative cases demonstrate, collective interplay can lead players beyond the bounds of their initial plans and cause them to invent new musical forms that subsequently serve as vehicles for the group's improvisations. Such practices, reminiscent of the genesis of tunes in solo invention, reveal the perpetual interplay between formerly composed ideas and those conceived in performance. It is this dynamic reciprocity that characterizes improvisation as both an individual and a collective music-making process.

In this chapter, musicians speaking about their own experiences provide insight into the complexity and richness of musical interaction during jazz performances. As a multi-layered, dynamic activity, collective improvisation makes unique demands on artists, requiring them to respond instantaneously to the changing rhythmic, harmonic, melodic, and timbral features of their group's inventions. In this light, it is not surprising that the artists attach great value to finely honed skills of listening. Musicians cultivate this listening ability because it allows them to attend to the musical events flowing around them during performances and at the same time, add their own creative contributions to that flow.

In informing us about their experiences, artists also implicitly point up the misleading nature of popular conceptions of improvisation whose exclusive emphasis upon spontaneity suggests that improvisation entails "performance without previous preparation." In fact, it is the artists' training in the rigors of musical thinking and their mastery of a vast system of knowledge that enable them to respond artfully, as well as spontaneously, when improvising: to create individual musical parts that are meaningful in their own right, and at the same time, complementary to the group. As jazz musicians continually increase their store of knowledge, skill, and experience, they change the configuration of all three that they bring to successive jazz performances, ever-renewing the collective pool of ideas from which they fashion art. There is, in this sense, a lifetime of preparation behind the ideas artists conceive during improvised performances.

For a more elaborate treatment of these and other related issues, interested readers are encouraged to read *Thinking in Jazz* (Berliner, 1994), and in particular, to study its extensive musical examples. Transcribed from renowned jazz recordings, the work's large score segments bring to light many additional patterns of group interaction—allowing further analysis of the processes and products of improvised musical behavior.

APPENDIX

Intensified conversation across all the parts
Miles Davis, Red Garland, Paul Chambers, and "Philly" Joe Jones, "Blues by Five" (all excerpts $\downarrow$ = 176)

In *a*, intensified conversation takes the form of imitative responses to a single idea, the soloist's emphatic on-beat accent. In *b*, it involves a concentration of different kinds of exchanges: the near-simultaneous conceptualization of a melodic idea between the soloist and bass player, and sharing of identical or otherwise complementary pitches among soloist and accompanists as the players alter the progression. In contrast to choruses in which performers create relatively independent complementary lines or in which exchanges are fleeting, some choruses, as illustrated in *c*, are deeply embedded with responsive exchanges among different combinations of players. From the onset of the chorus, a recurring rhythmic component of the soloist's motive invites the pianist and drummer to perform a related, ongoing fill together. Meanwhile, the bass player sets up a blues figure in bar 90, then plays a variant of it in bar 93, prompting the pianist to absorb a prominent component of the figure into the lower voice of the piano part, rephrasing and harmonizing it. Subsequently, the soloist adopts the rhythm and gestural shape of the pianist's figure to create a variation on the cadential portion of his previous solo phrase. Finally, the pianist responds by combining the rhythm and tonal center of the soloist's idea (in the outer voice of the piano part) with a slight variant of the bass player's previous blues figure (in the inner voice of the piano part) to produce a fitting chorus cadence.

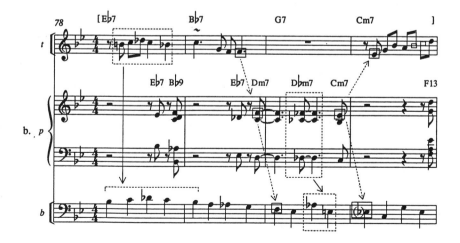

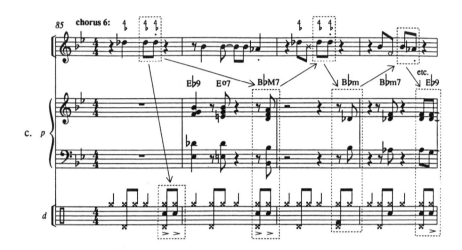

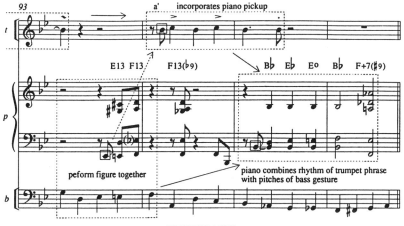

REFERENCES

Berliner, P. (1994). *Thinking in jazz: The infinite art of improvisation.* Chicago: University of Chicago Press.

Blakey, A. (1987). *Art Blakey: The jazz messenger.* Dick Fontaine and Pat Hartley. Grapevine Pictures, Central Independent Television and Channel Four (UK). Film, 78 minutes, 1987. Available as video from Rhapsody Films, Inc., #8016, 1988.

Davis, M. (1986). *Miles ahead: The music of Miles Davis.* Mark Obenhaus and Yvonne Smith. WNET/Thirteen and Obenhaus Films, Inc., in association with Channel 4 Television, London. Great Performances public television program #1303, 60 mins., Oct. 17, 1986.

Keil, C. (1966). Motion and feeling through music. *Journal of Aesthetics and Art Criticism, 24,* 337–349.

Kernfeld, B. D. (1981). *Adderley, Coltrane, and Davis at the twilight of bebop: The search for melodic coherence (1958–1959).* Ph.D. dissertation, Cornell University.

Monson, I. T. (1991). *Musical interaction in modern jazz: An ethnomusicological perspective.* Ph.D. dissertation, New York University.

Owens, T. (1974). *Charlie Parker: Techniques of improvisation.* Ph.D. dissertation, University of California at Los Angeles.

Rinzler, P. (1988). Preliminary thoughts on analyzing musical interaction among jazz performers. *Annual Review of Jazz Studies, 4,* 153–160.

Shapiro, N., & Hentoff, N. (1966). *Hear me talkin to ya: The story of jazz as told by the men who made it.* New York: Dover. (Orig. pub. New York: Rinehart, 1955)

Stewart, M. L. (1986). Player interaction in the 1955-1957 Miles Davis Quintet. *Jazz Research Papers, 6,* 187–210.

Vaughan, S. (1991). *Sarah Vaughan: The divine one.* Toby Byron and Richard Saylor. Toby Byron/Multiprises in association with Taurus Film, Munich, Video Arts, Japan, and Thirteen/WNET. American Masters public television program #604, 60 mins., July 29, 1991.

chapter 3

Musical Improvisation: A Systems Approach

Mihaly Csikszentmihalyi and Grant Jewell Rich
The University of Chicago

Dr. Csikszentmihalyi is best known for his seminal work on flow, *a mental state often associated with moments of highly creative activity. His systems view of creativity has been influential in conceptualizing the social and historical dimensions of creativity. In this chapter Csikszentmihalyi and Rich apply these concepts to the analysis of a series of extended interviews with the improvisational musicians Ravi Shankar, Oscar Peterson, and Gunther Schuller. These interviews are drawn from the "Creativity in Later Life" project, an extensive, multi-year study of 100 creative individuals, all of them over the age of 50. The 2-hour interviews cover a broad range of factors that can influence creativity, including social forces, mentors and parents, changes over the lifespan, and work habits (see Csikszentmihalyi, 1996).*

In addition, this chapter focuses on how improvisational creativity is similar to other forms of creativity, especially in two areas. First, Csikszentmihalyi has argued that scientific and artistic creativity cannot be studied as a purely individual, psychological process. Social, cultural, and lifespan influences play essential roles in creativity. Improvisational musicians are also subject to the influences of Csikszentmihalyi's systems model: person, domain, and field all contribute to the creative product. Second, many improvisational musicians report a state of peak experience that they describe as a "flow" state. In fact, one of the main reasons that musicians perform night after night is to attain this flow experience. It is this intrinsically motivating factor that keeps aspiring musicians playing through poverty, hard work, and unpleasant gigs.

The descriptions of flow in these interviews echo many of the comments quoted in Berliner's chapter. Jazz musicians experience flow through the musical conversation that proceeds onstage. Furthermore, the extra-psychological components of the systems model relate to themes in the chapters by Silverstein and

43

Monson, who focus on the role of culture and social context in performance, how culture influences musical and verbal conversations, and how the performance is interpreted.

Creativity research in recent years has been increasingly informed by a systems perspective. Starting with the observations of Morris Stein (1953), and the extensive data presented by Dean Simonton showing the influence of economic, political, and social events on the rates of creative production (1988), it has become increasingly clear that variables external to the individual must be taken into account if one wishes to explain why, when, and where new ideas or products arise and become established in a culture. A good example of this trend can be seen in the recent special issue of the *Creativity Research Journal* and the debate surrounding its lead article (Kosof, 1995).

FLOW AND THE SYSTEMS APPROACH

The particular systems approach developed here has been described before, and applied to historical and anecdotal examples, as well as to data collected to answer a variety of different questions (See Csikszentmihalyi, 1988, 1990b, 1996; Csikszentmihalyi, Rathunde, & Whalen, 1993; Feldman, Csikszentmihalyi & Gardner, 1994). In the present context, we shall apply this model specifically to musical improvisation.

The data for this chapter, extended interviews with three eminent musicians, are part of a larger project that includes nearly 100 interviews with creators in a variety of fields. This larger project, the Study of Creativity in Later Life, was published in the book *Creativity* (Csikszentmihalyi, 1996). For this chapter, the authors selected interviews with the world-renowned sitar player Ravi Shankar, the Grammy award-winning jazz pianist Oscar Peterson, and the Pulitzer Prize-winning composer Gunther Schuller.[1] The chapter extends the systems model of creativity, arguing that the same personal, social, and cultural factors apply to performance creativity as to other types of creativity, though the time frame of the creative process is abbreviated in a performance creativity domain such as musical improvisation.

Why Do We Need a Systems Approach?

Psychologists typically view creativity as a purely intrapsychic process. They assume that one can understand creativity by understanding the thoughts, emotions, and motivations of individuals who produce novelty. But in real life, the situation is more complicated. In a longitudinal study of artists, for instance, it became increasingly clear that some of the potentially most creative young persons stopped doing art and pursued ordinary occupations, while others who seemed to lack creative personal attributes persevered and eventually produced works of art that were hailed as important creative achievements (Csikszentmihalyi, 1988). To use just a single example, young women in art school showed as much, or more creative potential than their male colleagues. Yet ten or twenty years later, not one of the women had achieved recognition, whereas several of the men did. In jazz, while women vocalists from Bessie Smith and Billie Holiday to Ella Fitzgerald and Betty Carter have played prominent roles in the field (Friedwald, 1990), numerous and gifted woman instrumentalists have achieved less widespread success (Placksin, 1982). In an interview with one of the authors, the jazz pianist Dorothy Donegan discussed how her career took off after the deaths of Mary Lou Williams and Hazel Scott: "they only make one of us at a time" (Autumn, 1992).

The same situation holds in science. As Sir Francis Darwin said long ago, "In science the credit goes to the man who convinces the world, not to the man to whom the idea first occurs" (1914). New ideas in any discipline—from technology to religion—are dime a dozen; the question is, will they make a difference? And to make a difference, one must be able to "convince the world," and have the idea become part of the cultural heritage of humankind.

Confronted with this situation, one can adopt one of two strategies. The first one is the one articulated by Abraham Maslow (1963), which involves denying the importance of recognition. It is not the outcome of the process that counts, but the process itself. If a person re-invents Einstein's formula, he or she is as creative as Einstein was. A child who sees the world with fresh eyes is creative; it is the quality of the subjective experience that determines whether a person is creative, not the judgment of the world. But if creativity is to retain a useful meaning, it must refer to a process that results in an idea or product that is recognized and adopted by others. In practice, creativity research has always recognized this fact. Every creativity test, whether it involves responding to divergent thinking tasks or whether it asks children to produce designs with colored tiles, is assessed by judges or raters who weigh the originality of the responses. But we know that expert judges do not possess an external, objective standard by which to evaluate "creative" responses. Their judgments rely on past experience, training, cultural biases, personal values, and idiosyncratic preferences. Thus whether an idea or product is judged creative depends on the effect it is able to produce in others who are exposed to it. Therefore it follows that what we call creativity is a phenomenon that is constructed through an interaction between producer and audience. Creativity is not the product of single individuals, but of social systems making judgments about individuals' products.

A second strategy that has been used to accommodate the fact that social judgments are so central to creativity is not to deny their importance, but to separate the process of creativity from that of persuasion, and then claim that both are necessary for a creative idea or product to be accepted (e.g. Simonton, 1988). However, this stratagem does not resolve the epistemological problem. For if you cannot persuade the world that you had a creative idea, how do we know that you had it? And if you do persuade others, then of course you will be recognized as creative. Therefore it is impossible to separate creativity from persuasion; the two stand or fall together. The impossibility is not only methodological, but epistemological as well, and probably ontological. In other words, if by creativity we mean the ability to add something new to the culture, then it is impossible to even think of it as separate from persuasion.

Of course, one might disagree with this definition of creativity. Some will prefer to define it as an intrapsychic process, as an ineffable experience, as a subjective event that need not leave any objective trace. But any definition of creativity that requires an inter-subjective dimension will have to recognize the fact that the audience is as important to its constitution as the individual to whom it is credited.

An Outline of the Systems Approach

In addition to considering the individual who produces a new idea or product, we adopt a view that encompasses the environment in which the individual operates. We identify two aspects of the environment: A cultural, or symbolic, aspect that we call the *domain*; and a social aspect we call the *field*. Creativity is a process that can be observed only in the interactions between individuals, domains, and fields.

The *domain* is a necessary component of creativity because it is impossible to be creative—at least by the definition used here—in the absence of a symbolic system. Original thought does not exist in a vacuum. It must operate on a set of rules, of representations, of notations. One can be a creative carpenter, cook, composer, chemist, or clergyman only after the domains of woodworking, gastronomy, music, chemistry and religion exist. Without rules there cannot be exceptions, and without tradition there cannot be novelty.

Creativity occurs when a person makes a change in a domain, a change that will be transmitted through time. Some individuals are more likely to make such changes, either because of personal qualities, or because they have the good fortune to be well-positioned with respect to the domain—they have better access to it, or because of social conditions that allow them free time to experiment. For example, until quite recently the majority of scientific advances were made by men who had the means and the leisure—clergymen like Copernicus, tax-collectors like Lavoisier, or physicians like Galvani—men who could afford to build their own laboratories and to concentrate on their thoughts.

But changes will not be adopted unless they are sanctioned by some group entitled to make decisions as to what should or should not be included in the domain. These gatekeepers are what we call here the *field*. In physics, the opinion of a very small number of leading university professors was enough to certify that Einstein's ideas were creative. Hundreds of millions of people accepted the judgment of this tiny field, and marveled at Einstein's creativity, without understanding what it was all about. According to Tom Wolfe (1975) ten thousand people in Manhattan constitute the field in modern art. They decide which new paintings or sculptures deserve to be seen, bought, included in collections—and therefore added to the domain.

In creativity research the field usually consists of teachers or graduate students who judge the products of children or other students. It is they who decide which test responses, mosaics, or portfolios are to be considered creative. At every level, from considering Nobel Prize nominations to considering the scribbles of four year olds, fields are busy assessing new products and deciding whether or not they are creative—in other words, whether or not they should be included in a domain.

The systems model is analogous to the model that scholars have used to describe the process of evolution. Evolution occurs when an individual organism produces a *variation* that is *selected* by the environment and *transmitted* to the next generation (see Campbell, 1976; Mayr, 1982). The variation that occurs at the individual level corresponds to the contribution that a person makes to creativity; the selection is the evaluation of the field; and the transmission is the incorporation of the product into the domain. Thus creativity can be seen as a special case of evolution; specifically, it is to cultural evolution as the mutation, selection, and transmission of genetic variation is to biological evolution.

In biological evolution it makes no sense to say that a beneficial step was the result of a particular genetic mutation alone, without taking into account environmental conditions. Just as a genetically superior seed will not grow into a flower or a tree unless the conditions of the soil are just right, and unless there is enough rainfall to assist the process of germination, so a potentially creative individual will not be able to add a new idea to the culture without access to the information contained in a domain, and without the support and recognition of a field. Moreover, a genetic mutation that cannot be transmitted to the next generation is useless from the point of view of evolution. The same is true of a creative product, when the latter is seen as the form evolution takes at the cultural level.

Flow and the Creative Process

The systems model helps illuminate the creative process at both the macro and the micro level. At the macro level, it reminds us that historical examples of creativity are dependent on cultural knowledge and societal resources. For instance, it would be difficult to explain the great flowering of music through German-speaking Europe in the 18th and 19th centuries without reference to the small but affluent princely courts competing for new musical compositions; or to explain the history of jazz without reference to early Afro-American slavery followed by sudden urbanization (Kenney, 1993; Porter, Ulmann, & Hazell, 1993; Tirro, 1993).

At the micro level, the systems model suggests that the creative process involves a person's ability to innovate while interacting mentally with the rules or practices of a domain, and while keeping in mind the judgments and practices of the field (Csikszentmihalyi & Sawyer, 1995). A person creates music, for instance, by building on or by transforming a body of existing compositions, and doing so in a way that someone else—other musicians, patrons, critics, music historians, the public, or posterity—will find to be an acceptable improvement. And to convince others it is greatly advantageous to be able to anticipate their reactions.

But what is the phenomenology of this micro level of creativity—in other words, how does the person feel, how does he or she experience the process while it lasts? Perhaps the most salient experiential aspect of creativity is the enjoyment it provides. Artists and scientists remember moments of creativity as instances of "peak experience" (Maslow, 1971), or "flow" (Csikszentmihalyi, 1975, 1990a, 1996). It is true that all creative persons complain of the long periods of frustration and depression that often precede and sometimes follow such moments. After all, as Thomas Edison has been quoted as saying, creativity is indeed roughly 99 units of perspiration to each single unit of inspiration. Yet when the inspiration strikes, the quality of a person's life jumps to a level that is rarely found in normal life.

Why is the creative process experienced as an enjoyable, optimal experience? The flow theory helps to explain the reason. This theory holds that people will feel that what they are doing is enjoyable when a common set of conditions are present. These include: clear, specific goals; immediate feedback; a balance between the opportunities for actions (challenges) and the person's ability to act (skills). Given these conditions, a person will begin to focus concentration and forget personal problems, will begin to feel in control, will lose critical self-consciousness, will lose track of time, and eventually will begin to feel that whatever the activity is, it is worth doing for its own sake. This is primarily the reason why people are willing to engage in activities—such as sports, games, art, and music—that provide few conventional rewards like money or fame.

Musical improvisation, under ideal conditions, is an excellent vehicle for the flow experience. If the musician "knows" after each note what the next note should be, and then can immediately hear whether the note played was indeed the best that could have been chosen, it is an activity with clear goals and immediate feedback. If the musician can choose the right level of difficulty for his own level of skills, and then go a step beyond that, the criterion of balanced challenges and skills is met. Concentration, control, unself-consciousness, flexibility of time can all be achieved in the ideal musical session. And when all these conditions are present, the process of improvisation becomes intrinsically rewarding.

It is this intrinsic reward—the enjoyment one feels when performing at the highest limits of one's skill—that keeps musicians trying again and again to surpass themselves and extend the limits of the domain. It is this that keeps one persevering through the 99% of perspiration that might result in the single nugget of creative performance. Whether one will succeed or not depends on many other factors—on how well one has learned the domain, on how receptive the field is, and on many other personal qualities such as originality, boldness, and talent—but without enjoyment, the motivation one needs to persevere in the usually thankless process of innovation would be lacking.

Having described the systems model as a theoretical background for understanding creativity, and having shown how flow theory explains the motivation necessary to keep one's attention focused on the activity at hand, we now turn to a review of some interviews conducted with musicians whose ability to improvise has been recognized by the relevant field as worth including in the canon of the domain. From these interviews, we can better understand the dynamics and phenomenology of the creative process as it unfolds in musical improvisation.

THE INTERVIEWS: THREE IMPROVISATIONAL MUSICIANS

As part of a larger study of creativity in later life (Csikszentmihalyi, 1996), three highly eminent improvisational musicians were interviewed. These videotaped interviews each lasted approximately 2 hours, and were conducted at the musicians' homes. Each interview employed a semi-structured protocol based on the systems model, with an emphasis on flow experiences. While whole books could be written about each of these three musicians, for the purpose of this chapter a brief introduction to each musician will be sufficient.

Ravi Shankar, the sitar master and composer of Indian classical music, was born in Benares, India, in 1920. In the late 1960s, Shankar's relationship with the Beatles' George Harrison helped bring Indian music to the West. In his autobiography/lesson book, *My Music, My Life* (1968), he introduced both Indian culture and Indian music to Western audiences. In addition to his soundtrack work, which includes music for Satyjit Ray's renowned *Apu Trilogy* and for the more recent film *Gandhi*, he has worked with well-known Japanese classical musicians. Shankar has collaborated with eminent Western classical musicians as well. A few examples are his work with the flutist Jean-Pierre Rampal, with the violin virtuoso Yehudi Menuhin, and with the minimalist composer Philip Glass. Recently, the Indian government awarded him a grant to found a school and performing arts center in India, a goal he had been working toward for some time (Landgarten, 1992).

Oscar Peterson, the Canadian jazz pianist, was born in 1925 in Montreal. He has won Grammies, been named a companion of the Order of Canada, been awarded honorary doctorates, and been called, with Glenn Gould, the "most famous Canadian musician" (Lees, 1990). He is known as much for his solo playing as for his trios, and has collaborated with classical musicians, including the violinist Itzhak Perlman. His jazz compositions, such as those on *Canadiana Suite*, have been highly acclaimed, though he is more frequently associated with his technically flawless and creative interpretations of jazz standards (Blumenthal, 1995b).

Gunther Schuller, composer, conductor, author, and educator, was born in 1925. He is known equally for his work in classical music and in jazz. For example, in 1994, his classical composition, "Of Reminiscences and Reflections," won the Pulitzer Prize. A year later, in 1995, *Downbeat*'s International Jazz Critics Poll awarded the "Jazz Album of the Year" to Joe Lovano and Gunther Schuller's *Rush Hour*. In 1993, *Downbeat* awarded Schuller its Lifetime Achievement Award. In addition, his in-depth technical and critical histories of jazz, such as *The Swing Era: The Development of Jazz 1930–1945* (1989), are the standard works in the field. As a performer he played classical horn under Toscanini and jazz horn on Miles Davis' seminal albums *Birth of the Cool* and *Porgy and Bess*. He has composed music played by Ornette Coleman and by James Levine conducting the Chicago Symphony Orchestra. Finally, as its president, for ten years he led the New England Conservatory to its current status as one of the top music schools in the United States (Blumenfeld, 1995; Blumenthal, 1995a).

EVIDENCE FOR THE SYSTEMS MODEL: INTERVIEW EXCERPTS

In this section, interview excerpts from each musician will be considered one at a time in terms of a systems model of improvisation and optimal experience. In the final section of this chapter, the interviews and their themes will be explored together.

Domain

Contrary to what one might expect from its spontaneous nature, musical improvisation depends very heavily on an implicit musical tradition, on tacit rules (Berliner, 1994). It is only with reference to a thoroughly internalized body of works performed in a coherent style that improvisation can be performed by the musician and understood by the audience. Thus despite the relative youth of the art form, jazz musicians have deep respect for the tradition of the genre. In part this is because they realize that it is impossible to create new music unless one realizes what types of music have already been invented, and can incorporate this knowledge into one's repertoire where it might be expanded or transformed into something new. Similarly, classical Indian ragas (also an improvisational music) are deeply steeped in ancient standards of musical practice that change slowly over the years as musicians find new ornaments that enhance the "flavor" of the mode.

The domain of improvisation has important implications for creativity. A highly spontaneous art form, jazz is associated with a certain mysterious air and with an almost religious revelation (Berliner, 1994). Almost any stimulus may serve as inspiration or as a touchstone for further musical development. For instance, since in many senses the music is ephemeral, an aesthetic of jazz as an "imperfect art" (Gioia, 1988) has developed, which tolerates "mistakes" as minor blemishes to be expected as improvisers take risks and explore new musical territory. Indeed, empirical evidence from cognitive science suggests that behavior of experts differs qualitatively from that of novices in a given domain such as classical piano performance with regard to such variables as planning, anticipating future events, and even making "smart" errors (Rich, Palmer, & Drake, 1993). To use an error creatively, one must be trained in the domain; a child who has studied piano for only one year will be unlikely to make as creative use of his mistakes as would a professional performer in her fifties or sixties.

It is in this vein that Oscar Peterson describes change and innovation against a background of traditional expectations. Playing the jazz standard *My Funny Valentine*, for instance, a fortuitous change in meter may suggest an entirely new version of the classic—but only because the 3/4 beat is perceived as an alternative to previous performances in the repertoire.

> For me, it's always the way that that particular selection hits me. At that time. For instance, we may start playing it with the idea of putting it into the repertoire. And we'll just start playing, and all of a sudden we might go into 3/4, or somebody might—mistakenly even—go into 3/4, and I might turn around and say, "Wait, hold that for a second." And it triggers something within me, that this might work to a better advantage in 3/4 for us at that moment.

In what at first seems like a paradoxical statement, Peterson suggests that recorded jazz can be more open and less restrictive than a live performance. This is because one can adjust and fine-tune the recorded performance in a way that one cannot do in a spontaneous concert performance. But the fine-tuning is possible only with reference to the canons of the domain, which tell the musician if something didn't work out the way it was supposed to:

> It can really happen in both forums. The main thing is that you have a little more freedom on a record date because you can go back and say, "Well, that didn't work out the way we thought it would. Let's go back and redo it." You can't do that on the concert stage.

The malleability and flexibility of jazz is a hallmark of the genre. In Indian classical music, too, this flexibility allows for great creativity, by allowing novel combinations of different genres of music.

The fact that Ravi Shankar is an improvisational musician has had an enormous impact on the degree and nature of his success. It has allowed him access to a wide variety of musical fields. For instance, through improvisation Shankar was able to find common musical ground with the blues-based electric guitar rock of George Harrison of the Beatles. Thus, while many Western classical musicians were at a loss to understand, let alone participate in the world of rock and roll, a non-Western improviser was able to almost immediately join in a musical revolution. The flexibility in the domain of improvisation similarly allowed Shankar to perform with Japanese classical musicians (an improvised tradition) and to meld his music to a fixed visual track in the case of the Satyjit Ray films. By participating in a flexible domain, Shankar was able to gain access to a wider field of Western and non-Western critics and audiences, and thus achieve both greater creativity and greater eminence. Had he been a composer of fixed scores, like the traditional Western classical composers Brahms and Berlioz, the chances for the type of scope of his success would have been vastly diminished.

Gunther Schuller's work is exemplary of how the nature of the domain may determine the type of the creative product, and may even allow for the emergence of a new domain. Arthur Koestler (1964) suggests a "bisociation" theory of creativity: When two previously separate domains of knowledge are combined, a third, new domain is created. As a composer, Schuller has pioneered a new genre of music known as the "Third Stream," which combines the rhythms and instrumentation of jazz with modern classical movements such as serialism. Only by mastering both domains was Schuller able to create something truly new and innovative. As an example, Schuller recently recorded an album with the jazz saxophonist Joe Lovano that won *Downbeat* magazine's international jazz critics' poll. On this album Schuller has carefully composed and arranged compositions on which he allows room for spontaneous improvisation by Lovano. This dynamic between the fixed and the fluid helps explain the album's appeal. On Miles Davis's seminal jazz album *Birth of the Cool*, Schuller was involved in a similar project, but was a horn player rather than a composer. As in evolution (Campbell, 1976; Mayr, 1982), the production of variation is essential to improvisational creativity in that it allows a product (a new piece, a new instrumentation, a new style, a new phrase) to be selected and evaluated by the field, and, if successful, be transmitted to the next generation of performers and audiences.

In a performance tradition, where is the domain? In a music that is largely performed live, younger players and listeners might have difficulty accessing the themes and traditions on which the improvisation is based. One answer is that elements (or *memes*, to use the more generic term coined by Richard Dawkins to designate units of learned cultural transmission) such as favorite jazz tunes, styles, and altered chords are passed down orally via formal and informal meetings between younger and older musicians (Rich, 1994a). Berliner (1994) notes the importance of local record stores, musicians' hangouts, radio stations, and concerts for the same purpose. And of course most young jazz musicians encounter the illegal "Real Book," (no date, no publisher) at some point early in their careers. This book is a virtual road map to the domain of jazz, containing favorite jazz standards, often with altered jazz chords and sometimes with scale and transposition charts at the back of the book.

In addition to these cultural artifacts, the domain resides in the minds of experts. Gunther Schuller, who has written whole books on jazz history, carries an encyclopedic knowledge of many musical works, phrases, styles, and forms with him each time he sits down to compose. When he conducts, he is able to rely on his knowledge of the domain to help him through unexpected surprises such as the acoustics of the concert hall he is presented with, a section that misses a cue, and so forth. Oscar Peterson stresses the importance of learning from the masters so that one could both employ their techniques and repertoires and move beyond the older cohort of jazz players to create something new. A knowledgeable musician such as Peterson carries these "ways of the hand" (Sudnow, 1978) to the piano every time he plays. Each performance is a combination of the constraint of the genre (e.g., must be improvised, use a "standard" tune) and the freedom to create something novel and musically meaningful (Johnson-Laird, 1988; Sawyer, 1992).

When an especially successful addition is made during a performance, this novelty may enter the domain. For instance, many trumpeters have heard the effects Miles Davis was able to obtain from a special trumpet mute. In imitation of Davis they sought out the exact type of mute Miles used and began to employ it in ways inspired by the great trumpeter. In a similar way, when one performer records or becomes known for a performance of an obscure composition, other groups may decide to add the tune to their repertoire. Herbie Hancock composed the tune "Maiden Voyage," an excellent vehicle for extended modal funk improvisation. In recent years this tune has entered the repertoire of many groups, even at the high school level, and had been recorded many times, sometimes using instrumentation such as Hancock used, sometimes using smaller, larger, or different ensembles.

Field

At first it may seem that for improvisational music the field is largely irrelevant. Because the music most often is played live, with little opportunity for later evaluation, the input of teachers, mentors, "gatekeepers," peers, audiences, and patrons must have little effect on the music that is played. But a more careful analysis reveals that several representatives of the field evaluate performers and the music being produced.

For instance, in addition to the immediate comparison an individual performer makes between what he has played and what he would like to have played, the field for live performance consists of other band members, the audience of jazz lovers and novices in the club, the club owner, and perhaps any critics in the audience. Of course, should the performance be recorded, the field broadens to include musicians, jazz listeners, and professional critics who were not physically present at the time the improvisation was created. However, these listeners, too, determine whether or not the product is evaluated as creative or banal in that they may choose to buy many albums, or award the music many or few stars in a review, and so on.

The career of the Indian sitar player Ravi Shankar offers an excellent illustration of how the field evaluates potentially creative products. Shankar's relationship with his critics and audiences was vital to his success, and this relationship was different with musicians and non-musicians, with Western and non-Western audiences. For example, a performance by Shankar that was highly regarded by a Western rock concert audience—an audience that had never heard live sitar music before—might be considered just a run-of-the-mill performance by an experienced Indian music critic. Thus, the identical performance, performed in different contexts, could be considered either banal or tremendously creative. Shankar describes different critical responses:

> Having criticism from an American in New York or San Francisco or Los Angeles can be different than in Delhi or Calcutta or Bombay. Because there you expect much more knowledgeable criticism. . . .Words like it "was a grand performance," "a lot of excitement," and things like that don't really say much. But if the review is detailed and says such-and-such a part was really outstanding, this part wasn't the best—that is something which I think I can understand.

Critics and audiences operate with various degrees of understanding of the domain of music, and accordingly their opinions carry different weight in determining whether a performance is creative or not. As more specialized and knowledgeable representatives of the field, critics usually have a greater say in deciding whether a work will become part of the repertoire, and enter the domain; whereas audiences have a greater say in establishing the short-term popularity of the work.

If a certain historical period does not produce many creative works, it may not be because there are few creative musicians, but because the field is unable to respond positively to valuable new works. It is often the case that the potential creativity of a new piece is recognized only by a later generation of critics or audiences. On numerous occasions compositions that were later heralded as masterpieces were initially received as critical flops. In his *Lexicon of Musical Invective*, Nicolas Slonimsky (1965) cites highly disparaging reviews to such currently recognized masterpieces as Stravinsky's *Le Sacre du Printemps*, Beethoven's Ninth Symphony, and Tchaikovsky's First Piano Concerto.

Of course, one factor that seems to contribute to critical foresight and acumen is musical expertise. Gunther Schuller is in a special position to evaluate the importance of the field to creativity, since he is both a renowned composer and a jazz critic (e.g., Schuller, 1986). His inside knowledge of what is easy or difficult, ugly or beautiful, innovative or old hat, enabled him to lend early and crucial support to seminal, avant-garde musicians such as Ornette Coleman. While "violent rejection was almost unanimous from most traditional jazz artists" when Coleman made his debut on plastic saxophone in New York, some scholars felt that support from Gunther Schuller and the musician John Lewis were largely responsible for Coleman's success (Tirro, 1993, pp. 375–376). The systems model helps explain how an improvisation or composition may be considered trivial for many years before later being heralded as a masterpiece. Such a phenomenon occurs in other domains as well. For example, Mendel's experiments with the cross-breeding of pea pods could not be seen as path-breaking work until a few generations later, when its implications were realized in the context of a genetic theory of evolution that had not existed in Mendel's time. In cases like this it is more accurate to say that the work became creative only after its author died, and was not so during his or her lifetime.

Oscar Peterson discusses another aspect of the relationship between the field and the individual. There is some empirical evidence suggesting a statistically significant relationship between performer mood and audience reaction, at least when the audience has some musical expertise (Rich, 1994c). Peterson agrees that the more he enjoys playing, the more the audience enjoys itself. It is for this reason, he says, that he is a "selfish player."

> If you're not enjoying yourself, I don't believe the audience will. I think we have to give the audiences credit. For they know what they came to hear, and they know what they want to hear. And if for some reason you're not enjoying yourself, that transmits also. . . . If there's a certain amount of discomfort on the stage that transmits also.

When it was noted that the great trumpeter Miles Davis often played with his back to the audience, in what seemed to be open defiance of its importance, Peterson responded

> I think it's a lot easier if you want to play with your back to the audience to stay home and play for yourself. Then you don't have to worry about the audience at all. If that's the intent of your doing that. And I'm not downgrading Miles, I'm just saying that if that's the feeling behind it, that you don't want the audience to be involved, then play at home.

Of course, this is the point made by the systems model: With no audience—with no *field*—there can be no creativity. A musician might play with great passion alone at home, but without other musicians, audiences, and critics, it will be impossible to determine whether what was played was creative or not. In classical music, a famous illustration of this issue is the life of Charles Ives (1874-1954). His enormously original musical vision was almost left undiscovered as Ives headed the largest insurance agency in the country and worked on his music alone during evenings and weekends. At the time they were written, his pieces, inspired by the amateur performances of New England hymns and folk tunes he heard in his youth, were called "ugly" and "unplayable." It was not until many years after their composition that pieces such as the privately printed *Concord Sonata* was performed by John Kirkpatrick in 1939, and the Third Symphony was awarded a Pulitzer Prize in 1947 (Machlis, 1984).

Person: The Dynamics of Persistence and Enjoyment

An enormous number of genetic and personal experiential factors shape the individual musician. For instance, nature dictates that a pianist with large hands will have access to music that is physically impossible or prohibitive for a pianist with a smaller reach of fingers to play. Similarly, nurturing early exposure to a particular instrument or genre of music by a parent, older sibling, or a community organization such as a church, may introduce a potential young musician to a lifelong passion that might have been left untouched had the child been born to different parents in a different place or time (Rich, 1994a, 1994b, 1995). While there is a vast number of personal attributes that impact musical creativity, one pair of dynamically related attributes that were often mentioned by the musicians interviewed was—in Thomas Edison's terms—the importance of both perspiration and inspiration.

At first, determination and persistence may seem a surprising quality to mention. Because improvised music often seems so spontaneous and free, it might be thought that little struggle, effort, or resolve is needed to succeed in this domain. The interviews clearly show that this is not the case. Chance, environmental, and perhaps genetic factors have combined in the lives of each of the musicians interviewed to create a situation where an impasse had to be overcome. It was only through a determined struggle that the creative career could unfold over time.

For Ravi Shankar, this quality of resolve was evident when he was an adolescent, and his early decisions had clear implications for his later career. When asked if there had been a particular event that had significantly influenced the direction of his career, Shankar composed his thoughts and then began to think back to "a very much earlier age" and to his guru, "one of the greatest musicians of all time, Baba Alaudin."

By age 15 Shankar had been touring the world to great popular acclaim with his older brother's ensemble as both a sitar player and as a dancer. Baba joined the troupe occasionally, and at age 19, Shankar found he had to make a decision—he must either leave the troupe and return to India to study sitar seriously with Baba in a small village, or remain as a popular performer with his brother, but relinquish dreams of becoming a virtuoso sitarist. Shankar reports,

> And I was, being a young man, very experienced in many things and having had the best of things, it was a very difficult choice for me to make. To go into that remote village. No comfort—I was in an ordinary place with just a bed, I didn't have a chair even. And being in the West for all these years, to confront the mosquitoes and flies and lizards and cockroaches and even snakes, just going into the room sometimes. All that shook me up very badly, but I had determination, and I really decided. And I could overcome that.

A less determined young man might easily have remained a pampered dancer performing in five-star Parisian hotels. A less mature young man might have decided that immediate wealth and acclaim was more valuable than lonely years of isolated preparation and serious study of music. Had Shankar chosen to remain in Paris, it is unlikely that anyone would recall his name today.

While for Shankar conviction played an important role early in his life, the interviews with Peterson and Schuller show how personal determination might lead an individual to overcome serious obstacles later in life. Oscar Peterson, for instance, had suffered a major stroke about a year and a half before he was interviewed. The illness seemed to threaten his musical career. Peterson notes,

> It knocked me back and caused me a lot of mental anguish. I practically lost the use of my left hand. And it caused me some huge mental problems. But thanks to some wonderful therapy and a wonderful therapist, it also gave me a chance to see if there was still moral fiber inside of me to make myself come back. I wanted to know if I could get it back to the point where I would be confident enough and pleased enough with what I could do, to go out and face an audience again.

This is how Peterson describes the effects of his illness:

> It's quite debilitating. It's a frightening occurrence. Because you know if you stop to realize, over the years I've built up a certain amount of confidence . . . I've built up a certain amount of belief . . . in myself and what I could do sitting at the instrument. And then sitting there one day and not being able to play a simple tune because I couldn't get my hand to move is—very frightening . . . [I] went crazy! Oh, I bugged [my wife]. Caused her a bit of mental anguish. I was intolerable for a while. Because piano's been my life. And I guess will always be some part of my life. And the thought of not being able to talk to it the way I had been able to talk to it seemed incomprehensible.

In recovering his abilities Peterson seems to have uncovered several fundamental principles of flow, including the importance of a balance of challenges and skills which is necessary for deep enjoyment:

> I found out that when I couldn't play what I wanted to play, I could play within that restriction. And so the only way I can analyze it was that I had to learn how to possibly stretch that restriction as I played. And to stretch it to the point where my playing would increase. And that's the only way I can figure out that anything came about.

Eventually, his recovery progressed to the point where he pursued a new collaborative recording project with the classical violinist, Itzhak Perlman:

> Well, the project with Itzhak Perlman, believe it or not, came up. And I thought about it…seriously one night, and I said to myself . . . if I say "I can't do this," this might be throwing in the towel. So I decided that perhaps this would be the best forum in which to re-enter. Where there would be no huge audience. And so I decided to do the record date. And with the outcome of the date, and the fact that I *could* play, I then pressed it further and decided that I would do a concert. It turned out to be a small series of concerts, but noticeably, each one became a little more impressive.

An individual with less resolve might not have had the determination to painfully work toward regaining the skills Peterson lost at the time of his stroke. Mental toughness allowed him to pursue technical excellence in the domain of music until he was ready to subject his efforts to the field of what turned out to be receptive audiences and critics.

Sometimes even a devastating challenge, if overcome, may lead to a flow experience. For Gunther Schuller, the challenge was the grief of losing a spouse. His truly poignant words speak for themselves:

> One of the most recent experiences . . . was my piece that just recently won the Pulitzer Prize. Which followed a terrible period in my life. I lost my wife exactly two years ago to the day. Today is the anniversary of her death from cancer. . . . I realized, as I had already dimly realized before but it really came to me before in full force when she died, that everything that I had done in my life was for her. . . . And when she was gone, I suddenly couldn't work. . . . I could conduct, I could do things that were not based on my own creativity. But my own creativity suddenly came to an absolute standstill. And it was a horrifying experience. I was just totally blocked up. At times the thought came to me—will I ever compose again? I mean, I may be finished as a composer. And that whole thing took about 10 months, and I kept trying every once in a while and nothing came, absolutely nothing. It was like my brain was brain-dead. And then one

morning again—it was in October—I thought, well, I can't go on like this, I've got to try, and a certain musical idea appeared to me suddenly, and it is the beginning of that piece. And then I wrote the whole piece in five mornings, not five days. Not five days, but five mornings—it's a 16 minute piece. And the whole piece just poured out of me in about 20 hours. . . . The musical ideas came to me so fast that I could almost not keep up writing them, and I have certain shorthand methods by which I write down the music as fast as I can . . . there is nothing that is left out . . . and that went so fast and the joy and the excitement . . . the relief that I could compose again—that was such an overwhelming experience that there's no words for that. . . . And once it was finished it was finished, and then of course, then come the mundane aspects of getting a performance and all that—in this case the piece had been commissioned and I premiered it in Louisville with the Louisville Symphony, and then it turned out to win the Pulitzer Prize just by, by chance. So it comes in many different ways. But there again it was one musical gesture which was influenced by a somewhat similar gesture in a certain work—I'm not going to reveal which—by a certain composer that my wife and I particularly loved and loved to listen to together. The piece is called, you know, "Of Reminiscences and Reflections," because the piece is about our life together as musicians. . . . Hidden in the music there are certain allusions to certain very great pieces which we listened together to on records or in a performance that we consider unforgettable. The piece started out of one of these gestures that occurs in one of these pieces, so I guess as I keep talking about this, I guess I realize that inspiration comes in so many different ways.

As suggested earlier, and as the above quotation also indicates, musical composition and improvisation are ideal activities for peak experiences or flow to occur. Musicians may describe these experiences by using the word "flow" (Boyd & George-Warren, 1992), the expression "in the groove" (Keil & Feld, 1994), the phrase "caught up in the moment" (Berliner, 1994), or by employing other similar terms. In a conversation with one of the authors, the jazz pianist Denny Zeitlin, who has recorded 20 albums and is also a practicing psychiatrist, notes that he is well-acquainted with the technical details of the flow experience, and that the psychological construct accurately describes his state of mind while playing the piano (Zeitlin, personal communication). Each of the three musicians in this study stressed the importance of the intrinsic rewards they experience while performing.

Shankar, for instance, describes how he feels when playing the sitar:

I am very committed person when I perform. I know that I must try my best and be attuned in a way that I can give my best. And then I let myself go. . . . It takes a little time, some time. In the beginning, I am still conscious that I must give my best. Because our music is not a written-down music, it's not a fixed music. It's improvised totally. . . . Sometimes from the very first stroke I feel it is there. And then I let myself go. And then I become very introverted. And that is the best moment, or rather when the best thing comes out of me.

One reason the flow experience is important to creativity is that it encourages an individual to repeat the experience again and again. Of course if the experience is exactly the same, the person will soon tire of it and become bored. But by gradually increasing the difficulty or complexity of the task, flow may continue and expertise and creativity may occur in the improvisation.

The issue of enjoyment and its effect on practice is also discussed in this excerpt of the Peterson interview:

> **Interviewer**: Can you describe how you feel when you're playing something that you enjoy?
> **Peterson**: Ecstasy! . . . Sheer ecstasy. Because when you get something to the point where you can really execute it with all the emotion and intent that you feel within you, and you can project that, it's pure happiness. At least to me it is. . . .Because I think we're reborn as we play. I think when that happens, there's an enlightenment that takes place. And you start saying to yourself, "Well, I must have reached a certain level with that. Can I go on and continue? Can I make that continue in that vein?" Because it has that kind of impetus.
> **Interviewer**: What's kept you going, doing music since you were a child?
> **Peterson**: Interest. The love of it. Once I found out that I could play to some degree, it went in stages. The more I found out that I could play, the more I wanted to play. It's like anything else, I suppose. And I wasn't going around measuring my talent, so-called. It's just that I'd set certain goals for myself musically, and if I got to them, then I'd look for new goals. It was that simple. And along with the insistence of my dad that I learn certain things, and the help of other teachers, including my eldest sister Daisy, I started developing as a musician.

As with his recovery from his stroke, in this excerpt Peterson shows how a principle of flow—balance between challenges and skills—leads to the production of novel, creative ideas, and how enjoyment propels this process of increasing complexity forward.

Flow isn't enough—musicians must also earn a living, and in a highly competitive field such as music, an individual must consider the potential marketability of his product. All three of the musicians in this study are enormously successful, and interestingly all three discussed how they have de-emphasized the importance of the extrinsic rewards of the marketplace. Gunther Schuller is particularly eloquent on the issue of composing for intrinsic as opposed to extrinsic reasons:

That's how I make my living to a large extent [in music], and though I'm no Mozart, that's exactly what Mozart did, too. I mean, he wrote on command, on demand. And it's a very nice thing but of course it also has this other side to it, in that you then never get to write something that you might write just on your own. I mean, there is a piece that I've wanted to write for many, many years. And I've not yet written it because I have never had time to do it. Because I am so loaded up with commissions all the time. Sometimes as many as ten or twelve at a time. That all I can do is finish a piece and get to the next one and fulfill this demand. So the idea of saying "Now, wait a minute, let's throw all this stuff out"—I can't afford to do that really financially...what has happened, fortunately, is that occasionally somebody comes along and commissions the very kind of piece that I have wanted to write, so then that works very well. But . . . the enjoyment—enjoyment is almost too mild a word—the excitement of creating, this almost ridiculous process by which we put little black dots onto a piece of paper and they eventually take on a meaning, an acoustic life— that is so exciting in itself for me. And when I feel especially inspired and things are really going almost too fast, I almost can't write down fast enough the ideas that are coming to me. That is so incredibly exciting that I'm not enough of a poet to find words for that. I mean, it just sort of spills—spills out.

As Schuller makes clear, when intrinsic and extrinsic motivations coincide, the musician is particularly lucky—both finances and art may be satisfied. Moreover, the issue of commissions makes clear once again the importance of seeing creativity as the outcome of a systems process: the field (symphony orchestra, benefactor, arts foundation) selects a person (the composer or performer) to contribute to a domain (kind of piece commissioned, genre of piece). When the three elements of the systems model coincide, the person is likely to experience flow, as Schuller illustrates in the last excerpt. And if everything goes well, the resulting performance will be deemed worthy of inclusion among the exemplars of the domain, to be passed on to the next generation of listeners and performers.

DISCUSSION

The three interviews summarized in this chapter, when viewed from the perspective of the systems model, suggest a few conclusions that may seem counter-intuitive in terms of a commonsense view of what is involved in musical improvisation.

First, improvisational musicians are deeply steeped in at least one musical tradition. The sounds a musician produces are evaluated in real time with reference to this tradition, and the shape the improvisation will take depends on this dialogue between the unique performance and the template from which it was generated. Only after they internalize a musical idiom, and learn the relevant performance skills, can musicians perform spontaneous variations that can be appreciated, evaluated, and if they are truly exceptional, selected for inclusion in the canon of performance. In certain cases—and perhaps more often than one would think—creative improvisation involves the integration of two separate traditions, such as that of the Indian ragas with contemporary rock idioms.

Second, despite the seeming autonomy and even solitude of improvisational musicians, their performances are always collaborative products. The player internalizes not only a musical tradition, but inevitably also absorbs the tastes and preferences of his or her reference group—respected predecessors, peers, audiences, and critics. Each new pattern of sounds is the product of this collectivity represented in the player's consciousness, and is evaluated and elaborated in its terms. In addition, the actual interaction between the musician and the relevant others—peers, critics, patrons—is also always a part of the field of forces that determines the shape of the emerging music. Of course the musician must choose which of these forces to endorse or to oppose; the one option that is not open is to ignore them.

Third, the seeming spontaneity of musical improvisation often masks the enormous perseverance that is required to perform it well. To learn the musical skills requires years of dedicated discipline. In addition, inevitable tragedies—such as illness, the death of loved ones, economic hardships, lack of recognition—are likely to intrude on a musician's career. Without a great deal of resolve, such events may not only slow down creative output, but end it altogether.

While performance has not been a major focus of study for creativity research, the interviews in this chapter suggest that the processes that shape musical improvisation are similar to those processes that shape other forms of creativity. The same personal, social, and cultural factors that interact in musical performance also interact in other forms of creativity, such as biology and literature, that have been studied previously (Csikszentmihalyi, 1996). One difference between musical improvisation and many other types of creativity is the time frame. While a fiction writer or biologist may spend many months writing and rewriting a novel or setting up ever more precise laboratory experiments before publishing the results, the improvisational musician creates what Oscar Peterson calls "instant composition"; a performance is created "on-the-spot." Certainly many years of practice and diligent preparation occur prior to creating such an "instant composition," but the actual time frame of such a performance is usually only minutes. After the performance, unless it is recorded or is remembered, the improvisation vanishes forever. Furthermore, as an "imperfect art" (Gioia, 1988), the field of music critics and audiences may evaluate a musical improvisation using different aesthetic criteria than they would when evaluating a symphony or opera score that took many months to complete.

Given all these obstacles in the way of creative musical improvisation, one is left wondering how it ever takes place at all. The answer seems to be that the domain of music is one of those symbolic systems (some others being art, sports, literature, dance, religious ritual) that produces experiences worth having for their own sake; experiences that make living itself worthwhile. When the composition or improvisation goes well, the musician enters the state of flow, and the hardships and tragedies of everyday life become muted. Instead one feels that "incredible excitement" Schuller describes so well, and this is what justifies the difficult discipline the art requires.

NOTE

[1] Unless otherwise noted, quotations are from interviews by Grant Rich: Ravi Shankar, May 2, 1994; Oscar Peterson, September 20, 1994; Gunther Schuller, November 17, 1994.

REFERENCES

Berliner, P. F. (1994). *Thinking in jazz: The infinite art of improvisation*. Chicago: University of Chicago Press.

Blumenfeld, L. (1995, August). Joe Lovano: Jazz artist and jazz album of the year. *Downbeat*, 26.

Blumenthal, B. (1995a, March). Joe Lovano and Gunther Schuller. *Downbeat*, 20–23.

Blumenthal, B. (1995b, May). Oscar Peterson (cover story). *JazzTimes*.

Boyd, J., & George-Warren, H. (1992). *Musicians in tune: Seventy-five contemporary musicians discuss the creative process*. New York: Simon and Schuster.

Campbell, D. T. (1976). Evolutionary epistemology. In D. A. Schlipp (Ed.), *The library of living philosophers: Karl Popper*. La Salle, IL: Open Court.

Csikszentmihalyi, M. (1975). *Beyond boredom and anxiety*. San Francisco: Jossey-Bass.

Csikszentmihalyi, M. (1988). Society, culture, person: A systems view of creativity. In R.J. Sternberg (Ed.), *The nature of creativity* (pp. 325–339). New York: Cambridge University Press.

Csikszentmihalyi, M. (1990a). *Flow: The psychology of optimal experience*. New York: Harper & Row.

Csikszentmihalyi, M. (1990b). The domain of creativity. In M. A. Runco & R. S. Albert (Eds.), *Theories of creativity* (pp. 190–212). Newbury Park, CA: Sage.

Csikszentmihalyi, M. (1996). *Creativity: Flow and the psychology of discovery and invention.* New York: HarperCollins.

Csikszentmihalyi, M., Rathunde, K., & Whalen, S. (1993). *Talented teenagers: The roots of success and failure.* New York: Cambridge University Press.

Darwin, F. (1914). *First Galton lecture.* London: The Eugenic Society.

Feldman, D., Csikszentmihalyi, M., & Gardner, H. (1994). *Changing the world.* Wesport, CT: Praeger.

Friedwald, W. (1990). *Jazz singing.* New York: Macmillan.

Gioia, T. (1988). *The imperfect art: Reflections on jazz and modern culture.* New York: Oxford University Press.

Johnson-Laird, P. N. (1988). Freedom and constraint in creativity. In R. J. Sternberg (Ed.), *The nature of creativity* (pp. 202–219). New York: Cambridge University Press.

Keil, C., & Feld, S. (1994). *Music grooves.* Chicago: University of Chicago Press.

Kenney, W. H. (1993). *Chicago jazz: A cultural history.* New York: Oxford University Press.

Koestler, A. (1964). *The act of creation.* New York: Arkana.

Kosof, J. (1995). Explaining creativity: The attributional perspective. *Creativity Research Journal, 8,* 311–366.

Landgarten, I. (1992). Ravi Shankar: Avatar of the sitar. *The Beat.*

Lees, G. (1990). *Oscar Peterson: The will to swing.* Rocklin, CA: Prima Publishing & Communications.

Machlis, J. (1984). *The enjoyment of music* (Fifth Edition). New York: W.W. Norton and Company.

Maslow, A. H. (1963). The creative attitude. *The Structuralist, 3,* 4–10.

Maslow, A. H. (1971). *The farther reaches of human nature.* New York: Viking.

Mayr, E. (1982). *The growth of biological thought.* Cambridge, MA: Belknap Press.

Placksin, S. (1982). *Jazzwomen 1900 to the present: Their words, lives, and music.* London: Pluto Press.

Porter, L., Ullman, M., & Hazell, E. (1993). *Jazz: From its origins to the present.* Englewood Cliffs, NJ: Prentice-Hall.

Rich, G. (1994a). *How talented teenage musicians develop careers.* Roundtable paper presented at the Esther Katz Rosen Symposium on the psychological development of gifted children, Kansas City, MO.

Rich, G. (1994b). *The systems view of creativity and the study of creativity in later life: Lessons from Ravi Shankar.* Paper presented at the XIIIth Congress of the IAEA, Montreal.

Rich, G. (1994c). *The communication of emotion through improvised jazz piano performance: A cognitive science approach to the development of aesthetic sense.* Unpublished manuscript, University of Chicago.

Rich, G. (1995). *Village, sitar, guru: How a return from the road made a musician.* Paper presented at the Central States Anthropological Society, Indianapolis, IN.

Rich, G., Palmer, C., & Drake, C. (1993). *Developmental trends in music performance: Advanced child pianists plan more than beginners.* Poster presented at the Fifth Annual Convention of the American Psychological Society, Chicago.

Sawyer, R. K. (1992). Improvisational creativity: An analysis of jazz performance. *Creativity Research Journal*, 5, 253–263.

Schuller, G. (1986). *Musings: The musical worlds of Gunther Schuller*. New York: Oxford University Press.

Schuller, G. (1989). *The swing era: The development of jazz 1930–1945*. New York: Oxford University Press.

Shankar, R. (1968). *My music, my life*. New York: Simon and Schuster.

Simonton, D. K. (1988). *Scientific genius*. New York: Cambridge University Press.

Slonimsky, N. (1965). *Lexicon of musical invective: Critical assaults on composers since Beethoven's time* (Second edition). Seattle: University of Washington Press.

Stein, M. (1953). A transactional approach to creativity. In C. W. T. & F. Barron (Eds.), *Scientific creativity* (pp. 217–227). New York: J. Wiley.

Sudnow, D. (1978). *Ways of the hand: The organization of improvised conduct*. Cambridge: MIT Press.

Tirro, F. (1993). *Jazz: A history* (Second edition). New York: W.W. Norton and Company.

Wolfe, T. (1975). *The painted word*. New York: Farrar, Strauss, & Giroux.

chapter 4

What the Drums Had to Say—And What We Wrote About Them

David Henderson
University of Texas, Austin

This chapter was written while Dr. Henderson was in the field, engaged in a one-year study of music and culture in Nepal. This chapter describes his experiences as a learner of two Nepalese drumming traditions.

In the process of learning these drumming styles and becoming socialized into a community of traditional practice, he was forced to confront a range of issues that are central in contemporary performance studies: the place of tradition in modern performance, the reinterpretation and reproduction of tradition in current practice, the contrast between oral and written performance knowledge, and the relationships of both to musical tradition.

The distinctive contribution of this chapter lies in its close focus on the notational system for the drums, and how different the actual performances are. Henderson found that the notational system has very different meanings for a beginner and for an expert. The notation takes on an experiential depth for experts that already "know" how the piece is supposed to sound. Even though it originated as a shorthand way of describing existing performances, over the decades this shorthand has begun to influence how the musicians themselves think about a song. This is reminiscent of Silverstein's observation that lexicalization has a strong effect on the linguistic ideology, the beliefs of a language community about how they use language to do things, and the work of theorists of literacy and orality including Ruth Finnegan, David Olson, and Walter Ong. Henderson draws out the parallel implications of what "culture" is, what it means to represent a culture through a text, and how that text takes on properties distinct from the practice of culture itself.

Henderson also touches on issues of socialization, learning, and the place of the notated text in performance. His focus on the place of the text in performance is related to the poetics tradition summarized in Bauman and Briggs' chapter.

And his incorporation of culture into the analysis of performance shares much with Silverstein's chapter, in its analysis of how culture suffuses the most ordinary dyadic conversations.

The day before I left Austin, Texas, in January 1995 for a year's worth of fieldwork, I escaped for a moment from piles of boxes and overflowing bags to call Southwestern Bell and disconnect my phone service. In the course of our transaction, the woman who fielded my call asked if I wanted to have an automatic message give my new number. I told her, thanks, but I was off to Kathmandu, and the service operator, sitting in an office up in Waxahachie, exclaimed that she had just been listening to that song (you know, Bob Seger's tune from the '70s that goes, "Ka-ka-ka-ka-ka-ka-KAT, MAN, du...") the night before. After figuring out just where Kathmandu actually was and finishing up our transaction, she brought the call to a close by remarking that now whenever she heard that song, she'd think of me, and "when you're sittin' over THERE in katmanDU, don't forget to think of the PHONE lady!"

It's a long way from a jukebox in a Texas bar to these drums that I've been playing in the Kathmandu valley in Nepal, but this little bit of song really gets me where I'm goin' to; as I talk about two different kinds of drumming traditions here, I'm also thinking about what places mean to people, what culture is becoming, and who really cares about tradition in this country where questions of identity—national, ethnic, and personal—really have gone public over the past few years. If, for one woman in Texas, Kathmandu was just a wild place somewhere on the other side of the world, it is, for its residents, a city with multiple personalities. And these personalities now emerge out of an increasing consciousness of culture, not only in everyday life, but also in "cultural programmes,"[1] festivals, and song and dance shows for tourists. What used to just be lived, an anthropological "culture" hanging out in villages and neighborhoods waiting to be collected, now also is gathered into staged performances that often try to live up to artistic notions of "Culture"—a Culture where timing, presentation, and variety bear more weight that kinship, religion, and customs.

So here I am studying, with two teachers, both *navabājā*[2]—a collection of nine drums—and *tablā*—a pair of drums used in many South Asian musical genres—wondering just what I can say about creativity in performance when performance here is frequently a way of segregating culture and practice (*sanskriti* and *chalan*), when the stage is often a place to keep creativity out of performance by demanding that performers and organizers present finished products, prefabricated arrangements of culture and identity. These drums are things of culture, tangible icons or artifacts of identity that Nepalis can and will point to when you ask about Nepali culture or music. But the things that get put together to make up culture continually rearrange themselves in the words of people who care to have opinions about such things—which as far as I can tell is most everybody here. Many people told me when I got back here in early 1995 that to study real Nepali music I had to get out of the city, go out to the villages where culture could still be observed in its native environment. On the other hand, Newars, a large part of the population in the Kathmandu valley, were pleased that I was planning to do research on their musical practices in particular, since by and large they themselves confessed to not knowing much about Newar music, and saw their ignorance as yet another sign of how Nepali national culture has been eating away at distinctly Newar traditions. Other people were puzzled that I'd take *tablā* lessons, since *tablā* are a part of *śāstriya saṅgit*, classical music, which seems in recent years to be more of an Indian genre, and not essentially Nepali. While many poststructuralist anthropologists suggest that culture is not a seamless and monolithic entity, music still is imagined in practice (both in Kathmandu and back in Texas) to be fixed, appearing in particular places and times, incontestable proof of itself and the culture of its makers—that is, at least until one comes ear to ear with it and hears unexpected differences.

The rift between ideological culture and everyday practice, which sometimes divides creative products from the creative process, appears as a ragged gulf between the instruments I'm studying and the fluctuating contexts for music performance in the Kathmandu valley. Outside of my house and my teacher's house, I've heard *tablā* primarily in small concert halls populated mainly by tourists from Europe, Australia, and the United States. The *navabājā* are played in their entirety about once a year, and my teacher, Hari Govinda Ranjitkār, currently has only two students—his daughter and me. How can these instruments be more than relics, their music more than antiquated sounds that occasionally come to life in the present? Certainly people with good memories as well as those with good imaginations believe that performances were much more frequent in the past. Indeed, until about five years ago, the neighborhood-based *navabājā* group in which Hari Govinda played gave twenty-two performances every year.[3] Yet now people often find themselves stuck between describing what they do (a cultural definition of who they are) and what they used to do.

The two Nepali words for culture and practice that I stuck in parentheses earlier—*sanskriti* and *chalan*—have their own currency in what people have had to tell me about recent changes in music and life. *Sanskriti*, meaning culture or tradition, is tied by etymology to notions of ancient customs that still survive, particularly in ritual; related to the word for *Sanskrit*, one of the ancestors of the Nepali language, *sanskriti* is the word people sometimes use when they talk about what culture is. When people talk about what they do, however, they often use *chalan*— what I call "practice." *Chalan* is related to two common verbs in Nepali: *chalnu*, "move," and its causative form, *chalaunu*, meaning "make move." Although *chalan* is often translated as "culture," I interpret it as the part of culture that changes, the place to look for creativity, the everyday stuff that swirls around and never sits still long enough for its monograph to be taken. Cultural programs, classical music concerts—these are a new kind of *sanskriti*, performances of culture as Culture. Religious festivals throughout the Kathmandu valley are older and more widely recognized annual recreations of *sanskriti*.[4] Meanwhile, my music lessons, my conversations with people about music's importance in their lives—here is where people creatively engage with someone who sometimes knows exactly what they're talking about and sometimes seems to know nothing at all, a kind of *chalan* where people both perform their practices and explain them.

Certainly there are good reasons for moving this chapter offstage and into the various interactions between teachers, students, and ethnographers. None of these have to do with the music itself, for despite the proliferation of a Culture that capitalizes on fixed products, drumming performances are still usually elaborately crafted on the spot—partly improvised designs strung between the various performers and their audiences. But what captured my attention first was the hermeneutics of performance, the way teachers explicate the style, structure, and handling of various pieces in order to map out an array of possibilities before they ever are realized in actual performance. Working as both student and ethnographer, I confound some of my teachers' expectations and force them to explain things in novel ways. This is not, however, unusual. I imagine the history of music in Nepal as written explicitly around these kinds of juxtapositions, between people who know one way to play and someone down the street or across an ocean who knows another way. And I see the collaborations between people from different places, from houses of unique imaginations, to be very productive and provocative while also generating far-flung desires for exotic sounds: pianos carried by porters up to Kathmandu, drums shipped by air to France, rock music down the street from the royal palace in the 1970s, while *sitār* music floated through the palace itself. But this is not just a history of clangorous transaction or specifically of musical interaction, because beyond music, society in the Kathmandu valley is itself the product of many different human junctions: Newars, Brahmins, Chhetris, Gurungs, Sherpas, and Tamangs; tourists, merchants, foreign aid organizations, and household staff; Tibetans, Nepalis, Americans, and Indians all have played their riffs on Kathmandu. So, while I could look back at this chapter and think, well, this is just about how two men taught me how to play drums, I should also remark that much of what might be called culture in the Kathmandu valley—whether creative or uninspired, performed or dormant—comes directly out of a long and now accelerated interaction between many different kinds of people, while many reconstructions of culture in Nepal today are pulled out of an ethnically and geographically bounded past that perhaps never existed.

However, whether we speak of spurious cultures (Sapir, 1924/1966), imagined communities (Anderson 1983/1991), invented traditions (Hobsbawm & Ranger, 1983), or re-presentations and other uses of the past (Alonso, 1988; Brow, 1990), it should be clear that we are talking not so much about the sham of culture as about the ingenuity or insidiousness of the production or reproduction of culture. In Nepal, "culture" is a term that has congealed into a transparent film over identity, the immediate and most visible possession of any individual or group. Who someone is, what the nation is, what ethnicity is—each can be described as having a distinguished and distinguishable culture. This is the implicit legacy of the concept of culture: the terms of earlier ethnographic research in Nepal and elsewhere have slid across the seams of academic knowledge into wider labeling standards for self, ethnic group, city, and nation. In making ethnographic others, anthropology also revealed in its own words tactics for producing others, and while everyone continues to debate the value and validity of "culture," the term itself has become a widely used if somewhat nebulous prefix to modern life. Predicated on self-definition and extrapolated from world events, this cultural revolution in Nepal significantly but without explicit coordination finds Culture being put to work in the tourist industry, in party politics, in development projects, in nationalistic sentiment, in ethnic revival movements. Yet some Nepalis refuse to engage in overt projects of identification, and prefer exploring the possibilities of identity and community to fixing them. They are ethnographers in their own right, writing their own notions about us into their lives as we write about them into our books—or, as we write about us, as they write about them.

CULTURE AND THE DISTRIBUTION OF THE PAST

Shambu Prasad Misra is the stalwart 77-year-old master of a *tablā* tradition brought from Banaras by his family seven generations ago for the pleasure of kings, queens, and other sorts of nobility. He was his mother's eldest son in a vast household that spanned three generations and encompassed his father's several wives. Born in Naxal, just to the east of the royal palace, Shambu Prasad did not become especially interested in *tablā* or *śāstriya saṅgit* (classical music) until his twenties, when he began studying *tablā*, *sitār*, and voice, primarily from his grandfather. Soon he was playing alongside his father and grandfather at the scattered courts of royalty and government in Kathmandu.

Born into a Nepal that 19th- and early 20th-century writers—British, Indian, and French—described as a wild and remote Hindu mountain kingdom, Shambu has witnessed days and months of rapid change and years of shifting winds that have brought many people from Nepal, India, and elsewhere into Kathmandu, currents that also have brought Star TV with its videos of old Indian film songs and BBC with its neatly delimited world news into his sitting room. And as we sit there watching the news on Nepal TV before an early-morning lesson, we see politicians and students, taxi drivers and businessmen trying to make sense of the political changes that have emerged from a government in which the conflicting opinions of the Nepali Congress Party, the United Marxist-Leninists, and smaller parties have pushed public policy into new shapes or, occasionally, have halted productive dialogue entirely.

To the southeast of the parade grounds in Kathmandu sits Siṅgha Darbar, a vast collection of buildings and grounds that expresses architecturally the neoclassical flamboyance of the leaders of the Rāna period—a one-hundred-and-three-year era that began with Jang Bahādur Rāna's rise to power as prime minister alongside a weak king and against strong familial factions in the 1840s. Shortly after his rule began, Jang Bahādur travelled to Europe as one of the first state dignitaries from the subcontinent to make an official visit to England.[5] While there were some who feared that a year's absence would allow Jang Bahādur's reign to dissolve, in fact his power was reinvigorated when he returned enchanted with some of the styles, habits, and military tactics of Europe. In 1857, Jang Bahādur obtained a royal decree making the position of prime minister transferable along Rāna family lines, and when he died on a hunting trip in 1877, his brother, Ranoddip Singh, became the prime minister. The Rāna family continued to hold power until King Tribhuvan, with military support, founded "democracy" in Nepal in 1951, establishing voting rights and political freedom along lines that have been contested and revised through the 1990 revolution into the current day of party politics.

Siṅgha Darbar was built around 1903 by Chandra Shamsher Jang Bahādur Rāna, the prime minister from 1900 to 1929. Like most of the other palaces built by the Rāna family, Siṅgha Darbar is an example of what Boris (see p. 74) called "Kathmandu baroque" (Peissel, 1966, p. 26). I have focused on it for a moment here because its mid-century transformation from a palace of a thousand rooms to home of the *Rāṣṭriya Pañchayat* (National Parliament) of His Majesty's Government parallels the changes that have affected the everyday lives of some musicians. In the late 1940s, Shambu Prasad used to go to Siṅgha Durbar to play for Mohan Shamsher Rāna, then the prime minister. Today, Siṅgha Durbar houses various offices and ministries of the Nepalese state, including NTV (Nepal Television) and Radio Nepal, and Shambu still goes there frequently to perform on twice-weekly fourteen-and-a-half-minute radio spots of classical music.

Certainly, the venues of performance have changed for Shambu Prasad and other classical musicians in the Kathmandu valley. This also happened in India, where a performance tradition centered around the wealth of courts began to falter as the courts themselves began to collapse under the weight of British rule. However, in much of India the patronage of the courts began to be replaced by public support around the turn of the twentieth century as public concerts—and later All-India Radio and the film industry—were becoming viable entertainment just as an emerging middle class was developing a taste for the redistributed luxuries and relics of India's past.[6] Although Kathmandu is not unlike the earlier courts of Lucknow, Banaras, or Delhi in North India, for musicians certainly moved around through these cultural capitals and were lured from one to another, the reformation of the Nepali government in the 1950s led in different directions. The overthrow of the Rāna regime in 1951 brought more power to the kings—first Tribhuvan, then Mahendra in 1955, then his son Birendra in 1972. And these kings have dispersed state power in various ways, from Mahendra's vaguely democratic and supposedly traditional *panchayat* system to Birendra's apparent (yet never certain) relinquishing of most power to an elected parliament in the 1990 revolution.

While these events have grabbed a glossy page or a column of newsprint in the United States over the years, classical music has been looking for quiet new homes behind the headlines. In Kathmandu, what might be called an emerging middle class in the last twenty years has not prompted the reinvention of public concerts of classical music as happened around India in the early 1900s. When *śāstriya saṅgit* became the soundtrack for American and European imaginations of the East in the late 1950s with the efforts of Ravi Shankar, Ali Akbar Khan, and their Western patrons, it also became the predominant stylistic representative of Indian music. And although *śāstriya saṅgit* also exists in various forms in the other countries of South Asia, tourists from many places have come to Kathmandu and wondered if Nepal might not have a musical tradition to call its own. This inevitable linking of nation, nationalism, culture, and capitalism that sticks plastic dividers labeled

"India" or "Africa" or "Native American" between CDs in a bin in the Tower Records store in Austin, Texas, extends also to various places in Nepal, where *lok git* (folk/people's song) has become, for many people, the foremost musical heritage of the nation. At Radio Nepal, which began broadcasting in the 1950s, composers recognized the utility of folk music for creating a new form of national music that would appeal to the new radio audience stylistically, but would also express current themes and sentiments peculiar to life in Nepal. This music is called *adhunik git*, or modern ("dynamic") song.[7] The fusion of folk song with other genres continues today: rock singers make NTV videos for Democracy Day (*prajātantri divas*) out of various markedly indigenous film segments of people out working their fields or strolling around temples, and Kumar Basnet, a well-known singer and collector of folk songs, recently put out a cassette of older songs fused to a predominantly rock beat. Obviously, other musics are recognized and cultivated: recent Indian film music pops in and out of cassette players on buses struggling through crowded city streets; the new band, Prism, plays English-language rock songs at both a restaurant frequented by young Nepalis and one on the outskirts of Thamel, the tourist district; Nepali-language pop music appears on stage live at yet another cultural program at the Royal Nepal Academy. But in a country that builds its sense of culture and practice out of its imagined villages (cf. Pigg, 1992), *lok git* is the index of nation, the songs from the highlands that speak to an ideal of shared, if diverse, heritages. And partly because of this different sense of musical indexicality, because *śāstriya saṅgit* is thought of as an Indian and not a Nepali art, it has never become a widespread indicator of nationalistic prestige as it once was in India. But even if it doesn't thrive, it has dug itself into previously uncarved niches.

Although he says he's retired, Shambu Prasad still goes to the king's palace to perform or to teach music to the queen. He himself plays infrequently at evenings of *bhajan* (devotional) music and classical music at the Nārāyaṇ temple adjacent to the palace and at Kirātesvar in Pashupati (a vast temple complex to the east of Kathmandu) for monthly observances and for other religious holidays, but several of his children do perform regularly. Although he is still asked to judge music exams at the campuses of Tribhuvan University, a younger generation of *tablā* players headed by Hom Nath Upadhyay is much more active in formal education than Shambu has ever been. He does teach privately, and has taught many students from India and Nepal and a few from the United States.

But perhaps the best opportunities for performers of classical music come in hotels and concert halls constructed around tourism. Ever since Boris Lissanevitch, previously a dancer with Diaghilev's Ballet

Russe, opened the Royal Hotel in part of Bahādur Shamsher Jang Bahādur Rāna's palace (near the royal palace), classical music has served also as a condiment of fine dining in restaurants and hotels sprinkled with tourists and business people from, increasingly, most everywhere. Less often does classical music come as the main course. The Hotel Vajra, touted as something of an artist's or aesthete's retreat out under the afternoon shadow of the stupa of Swayambhu, west of town across the Vishnumati River, hosts evenings of classical music performances among its other offerings, and here Shambu will play on occasion with Danny Birch, an American *sarod* player who has lived and worked on and off here over the past twenty-one years. The owner of a music store near Durbar Square[8] rents out a hall in another of the old Rāna palaces behind her shop, and several performers and groups take turns playing there. Most of the audience at both of these places is made up of tourists, and fluctuates according to season: guidebook in hand, tourists come to Nepal especially to trek in the Himalayas, and come and go as the monsoon rains cease, the sky clears, and the nights fall more bitingly cool.

So through the husbandry of the tourist industry, classical music and *tablā* performance have been paired up with traveling consumers of culture to create performances that represent culture even as they produce it and are shorn from it. Although two hundred rupees, a common admission fee for these concerts, runs on both black and bank markets at around four dollars, it remains for many Nepalis a steep price. Not that it can't be paid: thousand-rupee tickets for rock concerts or cultural programs do sell. Partly, though, classical music concerts separate tourist from local by exploiting a touristic desire for culture—a desire for a vanishing culture lost amidst throat-scratching smog, vociferous vendors, and roving gangs of Nepali teens wearing Nirvana T-shirts and bell-bottoms. Many performers of *śāstriya sangit* play in hotels, restaurants, and concert halls almost every night, but not many other Nepalis come to listen, and don't particularly care to tread inside Oriental music boxes made primarily for the tourist trade.

CREATING AND RECREATING PERFORMANCES

Working toward a discussion of the spoken and written texts of drumming performance, I've pieced together a small part of the music scene of Kathmandu and a little of Shambu Prasad's life. But here I've run into an unexpected turn on creativity in performance. Just as much creativity comes not entirely within the performance, or even in teaching, but in finding or developing opportunities for performance. Most musicians, far from making a living on music alone, actively seek out new places for performances, new combinations of sounds, and new social connections. One of the more successful groups of musicians in Nepal is Sur Sudha ("clear/pure voice"), three classical musicians who have recorded songs recently for cassettes, CDs, and Nepali films. Prem Rāna "Autari" plays the *bāñsuri*, a transverse bamboo or wood flute; Bijaya Vaidya plays *sitār*; and Surendra Shrestha plays *tablā*. One of their cassettes, produced and recorded in Hong Kong, is called, "Images of Nepal" (1993). Of the five pieces on the cassette, three take their tunes from folk songs; the other two are more typical classical pieces. This is not unusual, as many classical performers from both India and Nepal now take folk songs or *bhajan*s (devotional songs) as the basic melodic material for one or several numbers on a concert program. These are sometimes called "light classical" (see Manuel, 1989, and Wade, 1995), and are short numbers that balance the much longer and more improvisatory, or more "classical," pieces. Yet no performer goes quite as far as Sur Sudha's other album, "Languages," which works the sonic dimensions of rock, jazz, and rap into their still predominantly classical mix. Unlike many Nepali musicians, Sur Sudha explicitly arranges its sound to fit the New Age market, working smooth timbres through the delay and echo effects that give New Age recordings their characteristic spatial depth. Despite the group's name, they don't claim to be making pure or authentic Nepali music. But while many would argue against their sound precisely because of its impurity and inauthenticity, few would argue that they have not creatively explored (some critics would say exploited) the possibilities for Nepali music outside of Nepal, in record bins and occasional concert tours.

One of the more unlikely concert tours was one that my *navabājā* teacher, Hari Govinda Ranjitkār, made in 1990 along with ten other Newar musicians and Gert-Matthias Wegner—a German ethnomusicologist who first studied with Hari Govinda in 1983. Hari Govinda has lived in the same neighborhood in Bhaktapur, the smallest of the three cities of the Kathmandu valley, for all sixty-one years of his life. Bhaktapur sits about ten miles east of Kathmandu, and over the past twenty years has been turned into a stronghold of urban traditions and culture at the same time that Kathmandu has been given up to the gods of progress and urban sprawl. West Germany's gift at King Birendra's coronation in 1975 was a binational development project to help restore some of the deteriorating buildings and water tanks, as well as implement some small-scale activities like building indoor toilets and establishing small craft industries. Even as a large and youthful portion of Bhaktapur's primarily Newar residents escape by trolley bus or minibus into Kathmandu by day to work in offices or to study, Bhaktapur itself has become a tourist's vision of medieval urban life, upset only by the squealing of an occasional motorcycle where one might hope to hear the creaking of a wooden pushcart. Veritably, just as the anthropologist Robert Levy imagined and described Bhaktapur as a stage upon which the "dance of life" takes place (1991), Bhaktapur has been turned into a sort of stage demarcated by toll booths at each road into the inner city where tourists are charged a fifty-rupee admission fee.

Actually, though, there's not a lot of hype to go with Bhaktapur's status as a UNESCO World Heritage site. The place does indeed look old, except for the San Miguel beer billboards atop narrow four-story mossy brick houses. But many tourists are unaware of the work that went into recreating Bhaktapur as a travel destination. Rarely, for example, do they realize as they gaze out from under the pagoda roof of the Cafe Nyatapola that the cafe itself is part of an old temple fallen down and refurbished into a restaurant as part of the Bhaktapur Development Project. But as they look out at the temple complex for which the cafe was named, it would not in fact be unusual for them to see some musicians accompanying a procession down the street or huddled on a pavilion nearby, for Newar music flourishes in the festivals that speckle the calendar. The frequency of performances has diminished somewhat, and instrumental ensembles common some years ago are now often replaced by brass bands playing a repertoire of Hindi film songs and Nepali folk tunes. Until recently, too, many performers of the older styles were older men. However, over the last decade, Gert-Matthias Wegner's life and work in Bhaktapur have helped reinvigorate some of the city's musical practices, and there are, for instance, many young men who have worked with him and learned to play the *dhimay*, a large barrel-shaped drum played with a thin bamboo stick in the right hand and with the palm of the left hand on the larger head.

Hari Govinda himself knows much of the repertoire of different kinds of drums.[9] The first instrument I learned with him was the *dhāh*, a narrower double-headed drum played, like the *dhimay*, with a stick in the right hand, albeit a heavier wooden stick used to strike the larger head, leaving the left palm to play upon the smaller head. And currently he is teaching me the *pachhimā*, a cylindrical drum thicker in the middle and played similarly to the *tablā*, with the right hand playing upon a smaller drum head, upon which a circle of black tuning paste is affixed, and the left hand upon the larger head, upon which a paste of wheat flour is stuck just before playing.

Like Shambu Prasad, Hari Govinda did not begin learning much of the *navabājā* repertoire nor that of any other instruments until he was in his twenties. When his grandfather was quite old, he and another drummer, just as old but also blind, realized that when they died, the *bhajan*

house in their neighborhood of Yāchheñ would be left with its collectively owned drums and no one to play them. It was at this time that
Hari Govinda and a few others of his generation began to learn the
words of the drums, the *boli* (speech)—the spoken syllables that represent each different drum stroke uniquely, yet not inconsistently, on each
different drum. Hari Govinda both plays and teaches with obvious rel-
ish, and remarked once during a lesson that he learned how to play the
instruments not only because it pleased him, but also because it pleases
bhagavān, god. Certainly, he does not make a living as a musician. Not
too long ago, performers were paid out of the collective funds of the
guṭhi—a neighborhood organization that sponsors performances for
religious festivals and holidays—or were paid by someone who would
hire them to play for a *pujā* (worship) on their behalf. These days *guṭhi*s
are less able to pay for musicians, and individual patrons are fewer, even
if a few musicians receive sporadic income from ethnomusicologists and
foreign students.

Income or not, religious festivals are still the main venues for performances of the kinds of drums that Hari Govinda plays. The various
drums can be played solo with the accompaniment of cymbals, sometimes with wind instruments like the double-reed *mahāli* or the *bāñsuri*
flute, but some of them, like the *dhimay*, are played predominantly in
ensemble. The repertoire for each kind of drum, though, is different,
with some overlaps, so that ensembles do not bring together a variety of
drums, but a number of players of the same kind of instrument. Some
performances have various performers taking turns. For instance, at *gāi
jātrā*, in August, families mount a photo of a member of the family who
died in the preceding year upon tall bamboo palanquins (*rathas*)
wrapped with cloth. Dancers and musicians lead the relatives, several of
whom carry the palanquin on their shoulders. The music consists of two
contrasting groups: one or several *dhāḥ* players accompanied by
bhuchhyāḥ and *sichhyāḥ* (large and small cymbals) alternating with a
lālākhiñ player accompanied by *jyāli* and *taḥ* (hand cymbals). While the
rhythmic patterns for each group are remarkably similar, the sound of
each group is unique—the former is raucously loud and energetic, and
the latter somewhat subdued but more resonant.

Aside from festivals, there are unexpected performances. In 1990,
Gert-Matthias Wegner traveled with Hari Govinda and ten other Newar
musicians to Europe for an international drumming festival, with drummers from Ghana, Brazil, Senegal, and elsewhere playing in France, Germany, and elsewhere. Like Jang Bahādur Rāna in 1851, Hari Govinda
traveled across the ocean and came back with tales of Europe: how clean
the streets were, how fantastic the concerts and buildings. While Jang
Bahādur refused to eat with Europeans for fear of losing caste, Hari

Govinda remarked that, unlike in Nepal, everyone in their group sat and ate together, the Newar drummers side by side with *mahāli* players— from whom they would not accept drinking water in Nepal—eating French bread and drinking steins of beer. Of the other drumming groups, Hari Govinda heard only a little and offered fewer opinions, although he did mention that when the group from Senegal played it was so loud he had to cover his ears. But more importantly, the organizers of the event drew a clear distinction between the various sounds on stage in their advertising: the French poster split the festival into modern and traditional sections, with a European percussion ensemble playing new compositions and the various world ensembles playing traditional music. As in a Nepali model of city and village (see Pigg, 1992)—where the village remains the source of traditional life while the city continues its ongoing march of development and industry—Europe appeared in promotional materials as the home of Culture, Progress, and Innovation, while tradition, quaintness, and culture continued unabashed in other countries, stuck in out-of-the-way places, a sort of global version of Raymond Williams' *The Country and the City* (1973).

Keeping these juxtapositions of people from disparate places in mind, I'll turn now to the syllables that make drumming intelligible and legible between teacher and student. These syllables can be a boundary between people who turn them toward different results and products— for instance, making clean transcripts for this chapter is clearly not the same as scratching down a few notes during a lesson, which is certainly not the same as having my teachers dictate entire compositions into a tape recorder. But what strikes me as I write is that these syllables can also be a ropeway that crosses the gap between different performative knowledges and produces a space in which drumming, and the pleasure of it, can be shared.

WORD IMAGES AND SOUND PRINTS

Example one: *pachhimā* composition, June 6, 1995.

dhāñ gheñ dra kha
dhāñ gheñ dra kha
dhāñ gheñ dra kha
tā dra kha tā ka
3
dhāñ dra kha tā ka
dhāñ dra kha tā ka
dhāñ dra kha tā ka
tā dra kha tā ka

———— 3
tā tiñ dra kha
di tā kha tā
kha tā dra kha
ta ka dhāñ ti ni

————
dhāñ gheñ ni
nā ka gheñ ni
4
dhāñ dhāñ dhāñ dhāñ

————
gheñ nā kha ti
ni nā kha tā
kha nāñ dra kha
ni nāñ dra kha
tā ti dra kha
di tā kha tā
kha tā dra khā
ta ka dhāñ ti ni
tā kā gheñ

This is a composition for *pachhimā* that Hari Govinda wrote down for me with a blue pen in Devanāgari script, on a long strip of paper about two inches wide. It is the piece that precedes everything, the *dhyaḥ lhāygu*, or "speaking to god" composition. Because I learned to transcribe *tablā* compositions back in Texas a few years ago, using more or less the same notational style in use in much of India and Nepal since the early 20th century, I adapted these habits to writing down *navabājā* pieces as well. So my own notation of this same piece in example two, copied in Devanāgari in a student's exercise book about eight by ten inches, looks something like my transcripts of *tablā* pieces.

Example two: same composition as above, June 6, 1995

X | X | *[...]*
[(dhāñ - gheñ - *dra kha*)₃ tā - *dra kha tā ka*]₃
[(dhāñ - *dra kha tā ka*)₃ tā - *dra kha tā ka*]₃
X | X | *[...]*
tā tiñ - drakha di tā kha tā | kha tā dra kha taka dhāñ ti ni |
(dhāñ - *gheñ ni nā ka gheñ ni*)₄₊ dhāñ - dhāñ - dhāñ - dhāñ - ₊|
——————➤
gheñ nā kha ti ni nā kha tā | kha nāñ dra kha ni nāñ dra kha |
tā ti - drakha di tā kha tā | kha tā dra kha taka dhāñ ti ni |
tā - kā - gheñ - ——

Both of these styles of notation, like all written representations, convey some information while requiring other pieces of knowledge to fit them together. My transcript attempts to represent timing partly by marking out beats and parts of beats, and also by showing how beats are ordered into a regular pattern, into what a pianist or a musicologist would call "rhythm" and "meter."[10] A *tablā* player or a middling music theory student could recreate a performance of sorts out of my transcription, but the student could only guess what the syllables represented. Hari Govinda's transcript demands more of a working knowledge of the repertoire: it indicates groupings of strokes and structures the piece into four sections (not shown in my transcript) but doesn't indicate the rhythms—the durations between strokes. Written transcripts of the drumming repertoire in Bhaktapur are, of course, just one component of learning to play an instrument, and not an essential part. Many performers have learned without writing down any of the pieces they learn, since a transcript only reinforces the oral mnemonics of these syllables. Instrumental performance does not exist in unmemorized form: Hari Govinda one day jokingly evoked a picture of me drumming at a festival, trying desperately to keep my copy book open in front of me. His transcript is merely a reminder of the sequence of drumming strokes. Having learned the piece implies that if I just listen to the syllables on the page, I will remember the rhythms to read into them. In the limited forms in which they are used in Bhaktapur, drumming transcripts give the words of the drums—their *boli* or speech—but not their way of speaking or their tone of voice except in very small ways.

However, while transcripts have limited utility in Bhaktapur for the essentially oral tradition of drumming instruction, Gert-Matthias Wegner, in his continuing work on the various Bhaktapur drum repertoires, has provided written records of many of the performance traditions, records that can be useful in teaching or studying.[11] Indeed, when I started learning *dhimay* from Hari Govinda, he pointed out that I would just need to have a few lessons to learn the different strokes for the drum, and then I could learn simply by reading the compositions in Wegner's book (1986).[12]

Example three: dhāḥ/dhimay lesson, March 14, 1995

ab dhāḥ	now then, the dhāḥ,
sabai siddhiepachhi	after finishing everything
dui-chār din āunus mā	come two, four days I'll
sikāunchha	teach, you, playing over there, if you
tapāiñ ya tyahāñ bajāuna heri	look, look (at Wegner's book) it will
heri bhāe āuñchha	come.

yo pher*idhā ḥ* bhannus nā *yo dhā ḥ ko* ho
tapāiñ sabai āepachhi
āh

ani
tapāiñ yahāñ das mahinā basnuhunchha
ho ki? āh
mā dui-chār din yahā āunus a mā
dhimay pani hāvas
alikati bajāe tapāiñ sabai āuñchha āh

bhujchha ani
tyo yo heri heri
āuñchha
ani amerikā jāne belāmā
yaso herdai bajā ū dai
yaso herdai ba...nā
tyasai āuñchha

this *say that* dhāḥ *again?* this dhāḥ's
(music) *yes* after it all comes to you,
uh-huh

then....
you're staying here ten months,
right? *uh-huh*
I....come here two, four days, and I'll
also (teach) dhimay.... *sure*
after playing just a little all of it will
come (to) you, *oh*
make sense. then,
looking at that, this (book), it'll
come.
then when it's time to go to America,
just looking, playing,
just looking, pla...so
in that way it will come.

Hari Govinda gets his copy of the book out occasionally to show people the pictures of him in it, rarely to use the transcripts. I'm taking my copy back to the United States so I can learn the compositions there, since I'm running out of time here. But the question remains: what can all these different transcripts mean to their various audiences?

First, how should you respond to these syllables, what should your body be doing? Essentially, these syllables serve to unite otherwise disparate sensory realms of the body, synesthetically reinforcing the movements of the hand with the feel of the tongue saying the accompanying syllables, and with the perceptually simultaneous sound of the strokes and the syllables that represent them, and, sometimes, with the sight of the syllables on the page. The syllables themselves are onomatopoeic words for the sound that each particular drum stroke makes, and thus are slightly different for each slightly differently voiced kind of drum. So what an uninformed listener hears in a performance is just the sound of the drum, but the performer is actually drumming at a point of contact between all these dimensions of playing, each of which is preserved and promulgated in the senses in a network of overlapping representations. During a performance, a drummer might also hear the syllables that human voices substitute for drum voices, feel his tongue wanting to say them, sometimes notice his hands going in a particular direction without having been moved by a noticeable thought, and see images of the written notes passing before his mind's eye on an invisible page. At least I see these images frequently enough, along with after-images of Hari Govinda animatedly reciting and playing these licks. I doubt many other performers see the syllables in quite the same way I do, and I'm not sure how to ask. I wonder if this makes a difference in my playing.

This expression of one kind of sensation in terms of another, or synesthesia (Merriam, 1964, pp. 85–101), clearly also extends to linguistic dimensions, or "intersense modalities," of both *tablā* and *navabājā* performance. For example, both Shambu Prasad and Hari Govinda have explained musical structures using visual and kinesthetic metaphors. Each of the separate *pachhimā* pieces that follow the *dhyaḥ lhāygu* has an above (*māthi*) and a below (*tala*). In the Newari language, these sections are called *chhinā* and *nhyāḥ*. *Chhinā* comes from the verb, *chhine*, which means to feel at ease, or comfortable: The *chhinā* is relatively slow and, because it is often repeated, comes easily to the hand. *Nhyāḥ* comes from the verb, *nhyāye*, meaning to move forward. Not only does this section carry the performer forward toward the end of the piece, it also is a section where the performer often increases the speed of the piece little by little until it becomes hard to play—a move toward virtuosity valued by performers and audience alike. So while in Nepali Hari Govinda explains how to go from a visually static top to bottom, the Newari terms for these sections incorporate a dynamic aspect as well. Many of the compositions also share identical or similar lower sections. Provoked by my incomprehension, Hari Govinda explained the structure of the pieces as like a hand: Each *chhinā* like a finger, its own unique appendage, yet attached in similar ways (he said as he traced lines down through his palm) to identical lower sections—all the fingers sharing one wrist, one forearm. Again, the visualization moves from top to bottom; as he explained this imagery, Hari Govinda held his right arm up in front of him and traced the paths of the compositions downward.

Both of my teachers combine the visions embedded in names and texts with both habitual expressions and novel images inspired by the moment. While Hari Govinda frequently directs me through a piece in terms of its *māthi* (above) and *tala* (below), he concocted the image of the hand as a response to my failure to read his other maps. Likewise, Shambu Prasad uses a wealth of metaphor wrapped around the iconic names of kinds of compositions. (These names are in use throughout much of north India as well: A *gat* means a style of walking, a *ṭukḍā* is a piece of something, a *chakradār* is a wheel [Gottlieb, 1993, pp. 32–59]). He frequently describes learning to play the *tablā* as like climbing a mountain; it requires persistence and effort to reach the *śikhar* (summit or peak). Or it is like pedestrian motion: You must learn how to walk before you are able to run. He produces other images on the spot. Yesterday he was telling me that there are two ways of playing a riff that goes, "te re ki te ta ka." In one, there is one fluid but irregular motion that moves from right hand to left to right to left; this is the "pure" version. In the other, there are two identical halves that can be played very rapidly and continuously, this is the "chemical" version. Shambu explained that he was thinking of two different kinds of pearls, and I immediately remembered seeing a short clip on a Nepal TV documentary a few weeks before that showed natural pearls being harvested in Japan and cultured, or "chemical," pearls being manufactured.

A moment ago I said that a music theory student might be hard put to decipher the syllables of my transcription. Despite the vast differences between what Shambu Prasad and Hari Govinda have taught me, their repertoires on disparate instruments share what I consider a system of syllabification. Let me give a quick lesson here.

You're sitting cross-legged on the floor, a *tablā* in front of you. There is a large metal or clay bowl-shaped drum under your left hand, a black circle of tuning paste a little off-center away from you on the skin of the drum head. Your right hand covers a short wooden cylindrical drum, also with a circle of black tuning paste in the middle of the drum head. If you're left-handed, like Shambu Prasad, you can reverse the drums, although I don't. Now, balance your right hand on your ring finger, which itself rests lightly on the near edge of the black spot. Raise your index finger and strike the drum quickly on its edge; this gives you a high-pitched, "tā," sometimes called "nā." Now strike the drum in the space between the edge of the drum and the tuning paste: this is a lower-pitched "ti" or "ni." Pick up your hand a little and hit the edge of the drum with your slightly curved palm: "tiñ" or "diñ" is the sound's name. Tap the black spot in the middle with your index finger: "te." With the other three fingers do the same thing. Alternate between these three fingers and your index finger: "te te te te..." Now try the left hand—just two basic strokes. Rest the heel of your hand just behind the tuning paste and hit a point just above the tuning paste with the tips of your second and third fingers: "ghe." Keep the heel of your hand where it is but raise the rest of your hand flat and slap the drum: "ka." Put your left hand's "ghe" together with each of the right hand strokes, and you'll get, in order, "dhā," "dhi," "dhiñ," and "dhe." Like lungs that gives a little more air to aspirated consonants, so the left hand takes the unaspirated syllables of the right hand drum and adds a deeper breath of sound to it.

And what about the *pachhimā* and Hari Govinda out in Bhaktapur? Now you've got in front of you a cylindrical drum that bulges in the middle; the large end of the drum, upon which you've just flattened out a circle of flour paste, is by your left hand, and the small end, with black tuning paste, on your right. Starting with your left hand: To get "gheñ" you hit the drum with your curved palm toward the rim near you; the sound is similar to "ghe" on the *tablā*. Hitting the drum with a flat palm across the surface of the drum gives you "kha" or "ka." Now for the right hand: "tā" is just like "tā" on the *tablā*, although your hand is now held vertically from the floor rather than parallel with it and perches on your little finger. "Ti," sometimes "ni" or "ji," is played like "tiñ." "Ta" is the same as "te." "Dra" is a new stroke, played by rolling the fingers from ring finger forward across the center of the black spot. Now put "gheñ" together with "tā": "dhāñ." With "ti": "dhi." With "ta": "dhe." Were you to go through a few more instruments, you would find that the names for the strokes played on the larger head of a drum (or the larger drum of a pair) sound alike, but with subtle differences in intonation, and likewise for the syllables used to represent the strokes on the smaller head (or the smaller drum of a pair). And combinations work similarly, an open stroke on the larger drum head prefixing "dh-" to the vowel sounds that distinguish the strokes on the smaller drum head from one another.

With this, you might now be able to start to read the transcriptions, slowly, with your hands as well. But this is still a book, and there's no secret compartment in the back with a cassette recording of the *dhyah lhāygu* for *pachhimā* squirreled away inside it. What does it sound like? Neither my transcription nor Hari Govinda's takes all the sounding dimensions, much less the visual or tactile dimensions, and tries to arrange them spatially. Indeed, what would I get if I transcribed more of a *dhyah lhāygu* that I recorded Hari Govinda speaking and playing during a lesson?

In example four below, these written syllables still drain some of the fluidity out of performance; the oral imagination that strings these sylla-bles together through nuances of pitch, dynamics, and pacing becomes fixed in graphic representations of those dimensions. But I have tran-scribed some of the things that I might otherwise not notice.[13] Hari Govinda emphasizes the shape of a repeated line most emphatically in the first enunciation of it, using variations in pitch and volume, even while his drumming remains mainly unvaried. This performance runs differently from the other two transcripts; the penultimate line of this transcript contains a pattern repeated three times rather than four, and the last line condenses the last section somewhat. More crucially, the last line along with the line beginning "tā tiñ - drakha" appear as structur-ally significant passages for the performer, emphasized vocally through volume, dynamics, and pitch. (The last line is also preceded by an increase in speed.) What even this transcript demands, however, is a vir-tuosic reader, someone to perform the words and gestures partially evi-dent on the page. In making this transcript of Culture, I have had to rinse it of culture and establish my own arbitrary system of representa-tion using recognizable practices of written culture in the United States. Hari Govinda puts these differences of transcribing in succinct terms: "We don't understand this, but you all do."

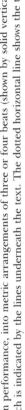

FIGURE 4.1.

Example four: *pacchimā* composition, June 16, 1995

Beats (about three per second) are indicated by the numbers at the bottom.
Beats are divided, in performance, into metric arrangements of three or four beats (shown by solid vertical lines).
Relative spoken pitch is indicated by the lines underneath the text. The dotted horizontal line shows the tonal center.
Relative volume of the spoken syllables is indicated by the size and case of print.

*"Three times.   Then…"
**"Speaking to god."

THE WORDS OF DRUMS AS TOLD TO PENS AND TAPE RECORDERS

I've raised questions of what and how written transcripts mean to their different authors and readers partly because it seems that transcripts relate to their performances more or less as Culture—which I described earlier as an artistic representation of culture—relates to culture in Nepal. Transcripts do not replace those things they are transcriptions of, yet they are often turned around and used as models upon which to base originals. And teaching and learning brings both model and original so close together that they look like rough copies of one another.

Transcribed drumming syllables refuse to say as much in print as they do in speech. Nonetheless, Hari Govinda encourages me to make full use of my written texts. Instead of teaching me *dhimay*, he tells me to read Gert's book; instead of overwhelming me with new *dhāḥ* pieces, and worrying that I would get stuck (*alamāl hunchha*) trying to remember a wealth of compositions, he suggested back in May that I write down several pieces just before I left so that I could take them with me to practice in the United States when I have more time. This is in stark contrast to something that Shambu Prasad told me during a *tablā* lesson in March. That morning he was teaching me some *pāltas*— variations of a basic pattern that I had already transcribed. As I started to write down some of these variations, Shambuji stopped me and said, no, these shouldn't be written down, they should be put in my heart, my mind, my brain, my hands. *Tablā* pieces are meant to be played extemporaneously, and this is only possible after I have taken them fully into myself.

A brief note of comparison. *Dhāḥ*, *dhimay*, and, to a lesser extent, *pachhimā* performances are essentially combinatorial. Because drummers often play in ensemble—for example, eight *dhimay* players accompanied by two or three *bhuchhyāḥ* (cymbal) players—they assemble relatively large blocks of sound, long strands of syllables that can be liberally repeated. Drummers usually do not lay out an entire performance beforehand, but dovetail one piece to another relatively smoothly on the spot. While the group is playing one piece, one performer (usually an older, more experienced musician) will initiate a new pattern and the rest, watching and listening to his drum, will shift quickly into it. The patterns will overlap somewhat, but the variations within each pattern are slight. But how do performers combine these pieces as they move through the city? Drummers perceive their own creativity in arranging sound to be more or less infinite, confined mainly by the extent of their repertoire.

Example five: Dhāḥ lesson, April 11, 1995 (Hari Govinda Ranjitkār)

tyo   that,
yaso   like this:
"ghe-ne-tā-ghe-ne-tā-ghe-nā-   play*"ghe-ne-tā-ghe-ne-tā-ghe-nā-gheñ*
gheñ tā tā ghe ghe-ne-tā-ghe-ne-tā-ghe- tā tā ghe ghe-ne-tā-ghe-ne-tā-ghe-ne-tā"
ne-tā" bajaune
                    ani yahāñbāṭa   and from here
yaso   like this:
kun gāu?   which one should (we) go to?
hāmi "ghe dra ghe tā ghe" jāu ki   should we go to *"ghe dra ghe tā ghe"* or
"ghe tā ghe ghe"mā jāu ki   go into *"ghe tā ghe ghe"* or
"gheñ gheñ tā gheñ tā ka" yata jāne   we could even go, go to *"gheñ gheñ tā*
jāepani hunchha   *gheñ tā ka"*
yaso   like this.
kun āuñchha tyo jāne   whichever one comes,
                                                            that's where to go.

pheri āuñdaina   (if) again it doesn't come (to you)—
"ghe-ne-tā-ghe-ne-tā-ghe-na-gheñ   *"ghe-ne-tā-ghe-ne-tā-ghe-na-gheñ*
tā tā gheñ"·tyasmā āune   *tā tā gheñ"*—come there.
yaso bhanera   having said it like this,
"ghe dra ghe tā gheñ tā tā tā"...u...   *"ghe dra ghe tā gheñ tā tā tā"*...uh...,
yahiñ jāne tyasobhāe   then in that case go here.
yahāñ manmā ke chha·yaso....   what's here in (your) heart-mind,
                                                            that's how (to play).

Learning, then, consists of practicing and memorizing these sequences of drum strokes until they can be done almost unconsciously, for the goal of performance is a flawless and uninterrupted cycling and recycling of pieces—sometimes coming back to a segment, sometimes using a bridging pattern between larger structures, never stopping to decide what comes next. And though these sequences must be skillfully manipulated and arranged out on the streets, taking shape around where crowds throng and where temples sit, they first must be learned one at a time.

Example six: Dhāḥ lesson, March 21, 1995

saphā garne ani aru lekhne   clean (this piece) up, then write
aba dherai lekhne   another; now (if you) write many:
u-yahi-u-yahi-u-yahi āh   there-here-there-here-there *oh*
almal hunchha   (you'll) get stuck,
ani saphā garnus nā   so please make it clean.

Otherwise the sequences may run into one another and contaminate each other. Instead of discrete performed pieces put together in endless ways, I would have strands of one piece tied onto bits of another.

In contrast to these combinatorial styles, *tablā* performances are permutational. Playing in alternation with a melodic instrument such as *sitār* or *sarod*, a *tablā* player will take a short pattern that extends over one or two turns of a rhythmic cycle, or *tāla*, and spin new patterns out of that original, sometimes returning to the original but often moving from one permutation of it into the next. Yet despite Shambu Prasad's insistence that I learn *tablā* compositions by heart so that I might be able to put them through an infinity of improvisational turns, he also insists that I write down the compositions that he teaches me exactingly, demarcating drum strokes, rhythm, and meter (*tāla*). Otherwise, if I came back to these pieces months or years later, I might not be able to recrate precisely what Shambu taught me.

The first *kāydā*, or basic pattern, that Shambu taught me in February moves quite simply in Devanāgari script across the page of my exercise book:

Example seven: *tablā* composition, February 19, 1995

dhā dhā te ṭe dhā dhā tu nā | tā tā te ṭe dhā dhā tu nā |
X   2
dhā dhā te ṭe dhā dhā tu nā | tā tā te ṭe dhā dhā tu nā |[14]
0   3

This pattern is followed by eight *pāltas*, or variations, and a concluding *tihāi* (a variation played three times in rapid succession) in my book; these Shambu gave to me as models intended to teach me ways of improvising variations of my own (cf. Berliner, this volume).

Example eight: *pālta*, February 19, 1995

no. 2
dhā dhā te ṭe dhā dhā te ṭe | dhā dhā te ṭe dhā dhā tu nā |
tā tā   te ṭe tā tā   te ṭe | dhā dhā te ṭe dhā dhā tu nā |

This simply repeats the first two beats twice, filling up another four-beat segment of the *tāla*. Here's a somewhat more elaborate permutation:

Example nine: *pālta*, February 19, 1995

no. 8
dhā dhā dhā te ṭe te ṭe dhā | te ṭe   te ṭe dhā dhā te ṭe |
dhā dhā dhā te ṭe te ṭe dhā | dhā dhā te ṭe dhā dhā tu nā |
tā. . . .

Now it's September, and as we improvise similarly on more complicated patterns during our lessons, there is a tight net of leading and following, speaking and playing, following the early model and deviating from it, that holds us together from the initial *kāydā* to the concluding *tihāi*. And Shambu continues teaching, showing me how to weave one variation into another twisted loop of it and back again to touch briefly on the initial form before moving in another direction, always drawing on the written, spoken, and performed memories of this pattern and its variations, other patterns, and their variations.

There are other differences between Shambu Prasad's teaching and Hari Govinda's. I came to Shambu Prasad having already studied *tablā* a little in Texas. In *śāstriya saṅgit* throughout South Asia, there is a relationship between teacher and student that implicitly assumes the student will follow the teacher's words to the letter. *Tablā bol*s, the ways the drums speak, had been codified and standardized early in the 20th century. (In *navabājā* performance traditions in Bhaktapur the syllables used differ slightly from one neighborhood to the next.) However, what I learn is mine to elaborate upon as I will, always with the understanding that my compositions come directly from Shambu Prasad, unmediated by any differences of transcription or anomalies of style.

I've juxtaposed these two teaching styles here in part to argue against the idea of text—the autonomous written work—and to argue for writing and reading as performative arts that vary widely in technique, method, and style from place to place. Through my own text I have woven the notion that as culture itself becomes more like a text (more a script for everyday life than an interpretation of it), or as Culture gets substituted as an emblematic recollection of "culture," the word begins to talk to itself in unusual ways. That is, culture and its various representations start to bleed into one another, enough so that it's sometimes hard to tell which was the text and which was the experience upon which the text was based. Insights into the "invention of tradition" also indexed a concurrent postmodern debate about the relations between text and experience (which itself stems from early hermeneutics), yet while we foregrounded the performative and creative nature of such inventions, we failed to articulate how the texts and experiences of "real" traditions are brought together in equally novel and continually meaningful ways. And what I find in these transcripts of drumming traditions in Kathmandu is not a condensed version of performative knowledge. Knowledge—of drumming, of teaching, of culture—resides not in texts but in the ongoing (written, read, or spoken) performances of texts, and in the arts of memory that turn these brief transcripts into visions of a way of doing things and communicating experience.

Which brings me back to the phone lady in Texas, offering to keep me communicating across new telephone lines. Such brief encounters with strangers transpire here in the Kathmandu valley as well: urban ethnography, for me, means mainly that I have to weave in and out of traffic, hit the streets, walk a few miles every day in thinning sandals, to get to the people who fill in the gaps in research and sociability, and on the way between places there are strangers curious about far-away places and their light-skinned travellers. If culture used to be the threads that held a community together, it is now also the undulating design that people locate themselves in as they attempt to thread communities together across variable distances. And the sense that emerges out of these unfinished patterns is that it is in small activities—those that can't be pulled out of ethnographic space and aligned into an objective distance—that the pleasures vibrant in creating community pull us into a community, wherever it might be—Kathmandu, Austin, or somewhere in between.

ACKNOWLEDGEMENTS

Hari Govinda Ranjitkār as usual had an impeccable sense of timing in giving me a three-week reprieve from my lessons in June and July, 1995, so that he could go out and do some fieldwork of his own, planting rice, leaving me to assemble parts of my work. Both he and Shambu Prasad Misra were gracious teachers who always took my questions to heart even though I couldn't quite explain what this chapter was going to look like. Danny Birch and Gert-Matthias Wegner read and commented on the first version of this chapter; Sarmila Maharjan, Suresh Ranjit, Nanda Kulu, Bina Shrestha, and Jyoti Basnet kept me going with tea and conviviality. Melissa Kwee and Joshua Callaghan, Fulbright students in Nepal during my stay there during 1995, helped by thinking about similar things in very different zones of activity: Melissa working with elite Gurungs on their own turf and Joshua filming porters and splicing up some interesting juxtapositions both in talk and on videotape. Calla Jacobson yielded up her computer for my writing during her final frantic days of research, and continues to remind me through her work that there are Nepals out there other than the ones with which I'm familiar. And Penny Walker, the executive director of the United States Education Foundation in Nepal, let me take time to write instead of doing more of the research that a U.S. Department of Education Fulbright scholarship brought me here to do.

NOTES

[1] Cultural programs are the Kathmandu equivalent of variety shows, frequently sponsored by organizations founded upon a sense of shared culture or

ethnicity among its members. A typical cultural program has ethnic dances, Hindi film songs, comedy, pop songs, and folk songs packaged together to appeal to a wide audience and particularly to youth.

[2]In transliterating Nepali words I have, throughout this chapter, either followed standard practices (see Schmidt, 1993) or used transliterations common in the Kathmandu valley for some people and places.

[3]Gert Matthias-Wegner predicted the decline of the *navabājā* (also known as *navadāphā* in the Newari language) long before I mentioned it here—see his 1987 article, "*Navadāphā* of Bhaktapur."

[4]Except, for instance, at the first annual Lalit festival (in Patan, just south of Kathmandu), a cultural program disguised as a street festival, a weeklong collection of events and displays in April, 1995, and touted by its organizers as providing "A Continuing Impetus To Conservation Of Our Living Heritage."

[5]For an account of Jang Bahādur Rāna's visit to England and France in 1850-51, see Whelpton 1983.

[6]Nayar 1989 gives a history of this period written around the work of one man, the musician and musicologist V. N. Bhatkhande.

[7]Kishor Gurung, whose father, Ambar, is one of the most productive and esteemed composers of *adhunik git*, has written an excellent brief history of recent Nepali music in the introduction to his book, *Ghantu: A Narrative Ritual Music Tradition as Observed by the Gurungs of Nepal* (1992/1996).

[8]Durbar Square is an array of temples clustered around the old royal palace, which itself is a juxtaposition of Newar, Nepali, and European architecture originally built in 1768 by the first king of Nepal, Prithvi Narayan Shah.

[9]For a more detailed description of the various drums and their repertoire, see Wegner 1986, 1987.

[10]A number of hand strokes in one beat are joined together by an underline, which in my handwritten transcript is actually a bowed line strung under the beat from its beginning to its end. Measures (the repeated rhythmic cycles of the meter) are separated by slashes, and the occasional X and | above the drum's words show the strong beats (X) and lesser beats of a measure—those that are accented by the accompanying *sichhyāḥ* (cymbal) player. The arrow indicates a gradual increase in speed, and the subscript numbers show the number of times a bracketed passage should be repeated.

[11]Gert uses an idiosyncratic notational style developed by his *tablā* teacher for the transcription of folk drumming.

[12]In this and other quotes from my lessons, my own words are distinguished from Hari Govinda's by italics or by reverting to the normal typeface.

[13]Likewise, I have transcribed most of this chapter in the present tense, emphasizing the immediacy of what any student learns. Especially in performance, both moments of lucidity and moments of futility are likely to disappear with practice as initial transcripts begin to take physical shape.

[14]Here, the *tāla* is a sixteen-beat pattern divided into four groups of four. X denotes *sam*, the first beat of the cycle; 2 the first beat of the second group; 0 shows *khāli*, the first beat of the third group, an "empty" group where often just the right hand and closed strokes ("kha") of the left will sound; and 3 is the first beat of the last group.

REFERENCES

Alonso, A. M. (1988). "The Effects of truth: Re-presentation of the past and the imagining of community." *Journal of Historical Sociology 1*, (1), 33–57.

Anderson, B. (1983/1991). *Imagined communities: Reflections on the origin and spread of nationalism.* Revised and extended edition. London: Verso.

Brow, J. (1990). "Notes on community, hegemony and the uses of the past." *Anthropological Quarterly 63*, (1), 1–6.

Gottlieb, R. S. (1993). *Solo tabla drumming of north India: Its repertoire, styles, and performance practices.* Delhi: Motilal Banarsidass.

Gurung, K. (1992/1996). *Ghantu: A narrative ritual music tradition as observed by the Gurungs of Nepal.* Kathmandu: United States Information Service.

Hobsbawm, E., & Ranger, T. (Eds.) (1983). *The Invention of tradition.* Cambridge: Cambridge University Press.

Levy, R. I., with the collaboration of Kedar Rāj Rājopādhyāya (1991). *Mesocosm: Hinduism and the organization of a traditional Newar city in Nepal.* Berkeley: University of California Press.

Manuel, P. (1989). *Thumri in historical and stylistic perspectives.* Delhi: Motilal Banarsidass.

Merriam, A. (1964). *The anthropology of music.* Evanston, IL: Northwestern University Press.

Nayar, S. (1989). *Bhatkhande's contribution to music: A historical perspective.* London: Sangam Books Limited.

Peissel, M. (1966). *Tiger for breakfast.* New Delhi: Time Books International.

Pigg, S. (1992). "Inventing social categories through place: Social representations and development in Nepal." *Comparative Studies in Society and History 34*, (3), 491–513.

Sapir, E. (1924/1966). "Culture, genuine and spurious." In *Culture, language, and personality,* edited by David G. Mandelbaum, 78–119. Berkeley: University of California Press.

Schmidt, R. L., (Ed.) (1993). *A Practical dictionary of modern Nepali.* Delhi: Ratna Sagar P. Ltd.

Sur Sudha. (1993). *Images of Nepal* (Cassette Recording No. 5234.333.003). Hong Kong: Schtung Music Ltd.

Sur Sudha (n.d.). *Languages* (Cassette Recording No. 5234.333.003) Hong Kong: Schtung Music Ltd. SCH 234.333.01.

Wade, B. (1995). Review of Manuel 1989 (ibid.). *Ethnomusicology 39*, (1), 129–32.

Wegner, G. (1986). *The Dhimaybaja of Bhaktapur: Studies in Newar drumming I.* Nepal Research Centre Publications No. 12. Wiesbaden: Kommissionsverlag Franz Steiner Gmbh.

Wegner, G. (1987). "Navadāphā of Bhaktapur: Repertoire and performance of the ten drums." In *Heritage of the Kathmandu Valley,* edited by Niels Gutschow and Axel Michaels, 471–488. Sankt Augustin: VGH-Wiss.-Verl.

Whelpton, J. (1983). *Jang Bahādur in Europe.* Introduction by Rishikesh Shaha. Kathmandu: Sahayogi Press.

Williams, R. (1973). *The country and the city.* New York: Oxford University Press.

chapter 5

What's Sound Got to Do With It?: Jazz, Poststructuralism, and the Construction of Cultural Meaning*

Ingrid Monson
Washington University

Dr. Monson draws on linguistic anthropology and poststructuralist theories of discourse to present a novel perspective on jazz improvisation. Her empirical work is in the ethnomusicological tradition, focusing closely on musical transcripts of live jazz performances. Her analyses are novel in that they focus on musical interaction during performance. Monson's focus on interactive processes during performance allows her to draw parallels between various African-American musical genres and with the discursive practices of the African diaspora.

In this paper, Monson uses a relatively accessible musical example, the shuffle rhythm, common in blues, jazz, and gospel. She builds on this example by drawing on the theoretical work of Silverstein (this volume) on the pragmatic and metapragmatic functions of language. In the same way that Silverstein argues that formal linguistics, by focusing on the referential properties of language, has neglected the importance of context and indexicality in language use, Monson argues that formal musical analysis, focusing as it does on segmental formalization, abstraction from context, and structural analysis, also has neglected the importance of musical contexts and of the relations between musical forms and their context of performance. For example, the shuffle rhythm, when performed before a knowledgeable audience, has indexical qualities in that it invokes memories of all of the past performances, performers, and time periods in which the shuffle rhythm was common. This focus on the pragmatics of music allows her to

---

*Some passages of this article appear in Monson, 1996.

explore how musical interaction and social interaction overlap and intertwine in performance.

In this chapter, Monson develops this linguistic metaphor for jazz performance, focusing on the rhythmic dimensions of musical performance. Monson refers to the rhythmic feel as the groove, and demonstrates how it is established through an interactive, improvisational process. But at the same time, Monson is concerned with how music and language are different, and with the limitations of the discourse metaphor as applied to musical performance. By focusing on the performed, contextualized nature of sound, as distinct from text or writing, Monson identifies some limitations of poststructuralist approaches such as those of Foucault and Derrida.

In her focus on the lived experience of performance, and the related critique of this version of poststructualism, Monson comes close to the phenomenological perspective articulated in Crease's chapter. Her focus on musical interaction during performance shares much in common with Berliner's chapter, and is paralleled by Sawyer's chapter on verbal improvisation in theater.

This article addresses several interrelated problems that center around the question how does sound itself participate in the construction of social and cultural meaning? I am interested in exploring the ways in which musical sound is both discursive and non-linguistic, the way in which these discursive and non-linguistic aspects of sound interact, and what implications these issues might have for contemporary debates in social and cultural theory in anthropology and ethnomusicology. With jazz improvisation as a point of departure, I hope to reconcile aspects of practice theory, with parts of postmodern and poststructuralist theories of discourse as they pertain to thinking about music as a cultural practice. My thinking owes a great debt to linguistic anthropology, especially work that has stressed language as a medium of social construction and interaction. We'll move from musical examples, to the pragmatic/creative implications of these examples, and finally to the social theoretical implications of these specifically musical processes.

THE INDEXICALITY OF GROOVE

I'd like first to introduce a family of rhythms common to several genres of African American music including jazz, blues, and gospel. Musicians call them shuffle rhythms and Figure 5.1 presents musical notation for several versions of them. Shuffle rhythms are triplet-based and it is up to the players in any given ensemble to decide how to realize a shuffle feeling at various tempos. Line two presents the rhythm most commonly

1. Guy, Buddy. "My Time After While." *The Best of Chess Blues. Vol. 2.*
    Recorded: Chicago, 1961. Chess CHD-31316.
2. Franklin, Aretha. "What A Friend We have in Jesus." *Amazing Grace.*
    Recorded: Los Angeles, January 14, 1972. Atlantic SD 2-906.
3. Mingus, Charles. "Wednesday Night Prayer Meeting." *Blues and
    Roots.* Recorded: New York, February 4, 1959. Atlantic SD-1305.
4. Davis, Miles. "All Blues." *Kind of Blue.* Recorded: New York, April
    22, 1959. Columbia PC 8163.
5. Coltrane, John. "Greensleeves." *Africa Brass.* Recorded: New York,
    May 23, 1961. Impulse! MCAD-42001.

FIGURE 5.1.   A Listening Tour

understood as a shuffle; the middle eighth note is dropped from the triplet. Line three alternates a quarter note with the triplet motion, creating the rhythm that is commonly know by jazz players as the standard "ride-cymbal" beat. Line four presents the same rhythm in its more usual notation as a quarter and two eighth notes (jazz musicians play it like line three, however). Line five elaborates line one by doubling the middle eighth note of the tuplet, creating a rhythm that circulates widely in jazz, blues, and gospel. These rhythms are ubiquitous in African-American popular musics, but are used very flexibly.

One way to appreciate this flexibility is to listen to several music examples featuring line five of Figure 5.1. One such sequence of performances would move through the listening tour suggested at the bottom of Figure 4.1. Buddy Guy's "My Time After While" (1961), Aretha Franklin's "What a Friend We Have in Jesus" (1972), Charles Mingus's "Wednesday Night Prayer Meeting" (1959), Miles Davis' "All Blues" (1959), and John Coltrane's "Greensleeves" (1961) all use line five as a time-keeping rhythm, but generate very different musical textures and emotional effects. One key to understanding the shuffle as a family of interrelated rhythms is to notice that within these performances the time-keeping rhythm is often combined with bass lines and piano accompaniments that stress alternate versions of the shuffle. In Buddy Guy's performance, the bassist plays a bass line in the rhythm of line two and the piano accompanies in the rhythm of line one, while the drummer keeps time on the cymbal in the rhythm of line five. Aretha Franklin's "What a Friend We Have in Jesus" features the same distribution of rhythms, but with more variations in the bass part—two-beat and walking bass lines in addition to line two. Davis' "All Blues," uses lines five (cymbal) and two (bass) in combination, but to play in 6/8 rather than 4/4. There are two broader points to take away: (a) Musicians can combine many different layers of the shuffle family, and (b) aural knowledge and recognition of the various shuffle rhythms serve both to organize the interaction of improvising musicians and provide audiences with a way *in* to the genre and emotional feeling of the performance.

Indeed, hearing the examples in succession will teach the listener not only the rhythm of line five but several possibilities for bass and comping parts. The listener begins to recognize the set of rhythms and accompaniment parts that define several types of shuffle feels in blues, gospel, and jazz, and when listening to other examples of African-American music the hearer may be reminded of some of them. The listener familiar with African-American music may recognize how common the rhythm of line five is in gospel music, and may be reminded of the African-American church, which in turn may evoke a "down-home" feeling that might be associated with a church experience from childhood, or that may be remembered from a film or TV representation. By the time one finishes listening to these examples, in other words, the rhythmic pattern has ceased to be a self-contained abstract rhythm that functions only in the present, and has become one that may allude to prior performances or may suggest several other possible interlocking complementary layers that can be played by an ensemble. Since several individuals combine their efforts to produce these layers, the interacting and interlocking musical roles simultaneously articulate social relationships between collaborating players.

The musical roles within the ensemble are hierarchical in the sense that the soloist has certain musical rights and expectations that are different than those of the accompanying players. The accompanying players may vary their parts, interject improvisatory commentary as seems appropriate, but they're not supposed to "interfere" with the soloist by deviating from their accompaniment functions so drastically that rhythmic feeling collapses. Jazz ensemble members take turns being the soloist, of course, but even within the soloist role, a musician may choose to sometimes play more like an accompanist—perhaps temporarily suggesting to the other players that it might be a good time for them to embellish their parts more freely. In other words, there is a lot of give-and-take with these roles in the performance process.

This active type of playing, which takes place through individual aural monitoring and is combined with the interlocking organization of the parts and people who play them, is something found widely throughout the music of Africa and the African diaspora. While the content of the interlocking layers varies greatly (as well as the social contexts in which they are heard), at the level of interactive processes there is more continuity than disjuncture. Despite its ubiquitousness and the centrality of music as a cultural discourse in the African diaspora, there has been relatively little theorization of interactive musical processes. A recent interest in the problem, however, can be seen in Christopher Waterman's (1990) work on Yoruba music, which has suggested a practice-centered approach to musical and cultural processes, Paul Berliner's (1994) work on jazz improvisation, and Jocylene Guilbault's (1993) work on zouk.

The work of linguistic anthropologists in theorizing the problems of language in use, language, and cultural context has been crucial to extending my thinking about interaction and improvisation, especially the work of Michael Silverstein (1976, 1993; see also this volume) and Bill Hanks (1987, 1989, 1990). For during the act of musical performance the process and functions of improvised interactiveness have much in common with what has been talked about under the rubric of the pragmatic and metapragmatic functions of language. The utility of this perspective in music has to do with approaching the perennial problem of the relationship of formal structures to contextual and cultural issues. I have taken as a point of departure Silverstein's ideas about the indexical or context signaling aspects of language. To briefly review his classic article, "Shifters, Linguistic Categories, and Cultural Description" (1976), Silverstein has argued that the categories of formal linguistics were designed to describe only the referential function of language, despite the fact that "the sign modes of most of what goes on in the majority of speech events are not referential" (p. 15). To illustrate how the referential functions of language are context dependent in even the most mundane, everyday speech events, Silverstein cited the contextual presuppositions of a verbal statement in the past tense. To assert that something happened in the past presupposes the time of the present verbal statement as a point of comparison against which the time of the past is estimated. Another example of a context dependent index are the so-called "deictics"—this/that, these/those—whose meaning depends on the location of the speaker that is using them. Both examples fall under the linguistic category of "shifter" (aka indexical denotational form), for which "the reference 'shifts' regularly, depending upon the factors of the speech situation" (p. 24).[1] Indexicality, for Silverstein, is present in any sign (regardless of whether it is also involved in iconic or symbolic modes of signification) in that "each signal form indexes its own context-of-occurrence," either presupposing something about the context or creating (that is, entailing) an expectation (p. 36).

In music the traditional objects of analysis have been the parameters of musical sound most amenable to Western notation: pitch, rhythm, counterpoint, harmony, and their combinations, relations of inclusion, structural properties, and architectonic shapes. These features of musical structure, and the categories in which they have been analyzed in the most widely known schools of music theory, I would argue, are analogous to the "referential function" about which Silverstein speaks. They are those features of a musical text that lend themselves most readily to segmental formalization, analytic systematization, abstraction from context, and structural analysis. That these same musical features may *simultaneously* participate in more pragmatic (indexical) musical functions is a point I wish to emphasize. Just as Silverstein has argued that semantics are contained by pragmatics, I would argue that formal structures in music are likewise contained by musical pragmatics.

I have been interested in the indexical aspects of music as they occur in jazz improvisation. The traveling shuffle rhythm, or a melodic quotation or allusion, provide an illustration of a context presupposing indexical; once we know the pattern, we can recognize it in new examples, and associate it with the versions of the rhythmic feel we have previously heard. Hence the rhythm points to other performances one might have heard. A listener may then additionally associate it with the church or the blues, or other extramusical contexts and emotions with which it has been linked through social use. This is the sonic equivalent of intertextuality and I have chosen to call it intermusicality to highlight the way in which sound itself can function in this capacity. Stated differently, the intermusical moment of *recognition* points to the capacity of music to establish a point of spatio-temporal reference relative to its context of occurrence through aural means.[2] In contrast to some work in music, therefore, I am arguing that music has the functional equivalent of a past tense and that this indexical, intermusical capacity is crucial to thinking about the constitution of social meaning through music (Abbate, 1991; Nattiez, 1990). The difference in the musical context is that the "pastness" does not function as a formal feature of the musical code, but takes place through the social experience people have using it.

More crucial to the issue of jazz improvisation is the interactive construction of the musical surface, or the "interactional text, " as Silverstein terms it (see Silverstein, this volume). This process makes use of context-entailing indexicals (as well as presupposing ones), for entailing indexicals set up a feeling of expectation, often through metrical or harmonic means. Silverstein asks how it is possible that a complex coherence, or "interactional text," can be constructed through language in interactive real-time use. Central to the answer is his notion of *metapragmatics*, the idea that the indexical aspects of any sign are themselves framed or structured by higher order pragmatic functions—that is, by linguistic signs functioning metapragmatically. Metapragmatics is thus concerned with the way in which pragmatic events develop certain kinds of coherence through time. To put it another way, there must be some way or ways in which various indexical moments in a musical performance are shaped into recognizable musical events, such as a solo with a beginning, middle, and end with appropriate intensification from the ensemble (see Sawyer, this volume).

I would argue that one of the most significant metapragmatic framing devices in jazz improvisation is the rhythmic feel (or groove), which is itself established by the interactive relationships among members of the rhythm section.[3] It is one sort of interactional text within the ensemble that is dynamically interrelated to an additional interactional text established between the rhythm section and the soloist.[4] In other words, those interacting drum, bass, and comping parts discussed above serve to establish a musical context in which the hierarchically more important interaction—between the soloist and the ensemble—can take place. In other words, I am arguing that the rhythm of line five in Figure 1, in addition to being a structurally definable figure, functions metapragmatically to shape interactional possibilities within the ensemble. The relative stability of the various shuffle rhythms and their combination relative to the soloist thus serve to shape the improvisational possibilities and direction of the improvising soloist at any given time (although I must emphasize that it's not a one-way street). In Silverstein's terminology, these "feel defining" musical layers of the ensemble *regiment* the local indexical musical processes. Unfortunately "regiment" isn't a word that works well with the ethos of jazz, so I prefer to say "shape" or "condition." This process of setting up expectations and subverting or confirming them is absolutely central to the interactive performance practice of jazz improvisation.

An important point to remember is that throughout the musical interaction, the establishment, consolidation, or liquidation of human relationships among participating players (not to mention audience members, or the complications introduced by songs with verbal texts) is operative at all levels within the interactive musical process, for the interacting parts are simultaneously interacting groups of human beings. The intersection of all of the interactional roles and musical framing devices contributes to the way in which interactionally produced musical performances develop their emergent forms. I would like to emphasize that these interactionally produced events structure both musical and social space.[5]

THE PHENOMENOLOGY OF SOUND AND THE DISCOURSE OF MUSIC

In the jazz ensemble there is a great deal of agency taking place through the medium of musical sound. Players are constantly doing something with their musical utterances, responding or not responding to particular musical events in the flow and finding that what they play may have both intended and unintended consequences to other players and audience members, as well as to the space of participation (or lack thereof) that is created in the process. But the ability to take a kind of social action through music also turns on the discursive (or relational) possibilities of sound; the intermusical associations it engenders that are dependent on the heterogeneous cultural listening experiences of the audience and other musicians, as well as the expectation-creating possibilities of various socially established musical contextualization cues.

I have argued elsewhere that these discursive dimensions of music are extremely important in understanding how sound participates in the construction of a sense of a cosmopolitan identity for both African Americans and non-African Americans and how a sense of participating in "blackness" through music also operates in this way (Monson, 1994). When several of the musicians with whom I worked made the point that "the music speaks for itself," I argued that they did not mean that music is autonomous from the social world, but that one needs to understand its discursive relations to get through to the deeper cultural and spiritual meaning of a performance. Not everyone, from their perspective, might be attuned enough to the musical contexts informing jazz improvisation to get the message.

The "message" here is not a direct and unmediated one, but filtered through the indexical relations of audible musical discursivity and the heterogeneous listening experiences of its hearers that link it to broader cultural and political contexts. When I first became aware of the concept of "discourse" it was through the literatures of sociolinguistics and linguistic anthropology of the 1970s and 1980s, and it contained much work concerned with the microanalysis of language use in face-to-face conversational interaction (Duranti, 1992; Goffman, 1986; Gumperz, 1982; Gumperz & Hymes, 1986; Labov, 1969; Levinson, 1983; Moerman, 1988; Ochs, 1988; Schieffelin, 1990). Two important aspects of this work were finding that the intelligibility of face-to-face conversation was extremely context-dependent, and that transcripts of spoken language were anything but transparent windows on human consciousness. I later encountered the more general notions of discourse and writing in the works of Foucault and Derrida, which have directed attention *away* from the micro-issues of interaction and *toward* the macro-issues of ideology, social construction shaped by hegemonic discourses, the dispersion of human subjectivity, and the importance of representation. While discourse-centered approaches to anthropology, in this broader sense, have contributed invaluably to theoretical, ethical, and methodological developments within the field, I would like to suggest that there are some limitations to this approach which are made particularly visible in their application to music as a cultural discourse. And it is the nonlinguistic aspects of sound that seem to be causing the biggest theoretical problem.

It is commonplace for ethnomusicologists and musicologists to notice that most of the influential cultural studies works on popular music don't really talk about music, certainly not its sound. Where is the music in Dick Hebdige's *Subculture* (1979), for example, or in Paul Gilroy's first book (1991), or in Lawrence Grossberg's work on rock and roll (1990), and almost all of the work on Madonna (Schwichtenberg 1993)?[6] These works have contributed a great deal to an understanding of the consumption side of popular music, its participation in representations of race, gender, and class, its importance in articulating identities of all kinds, the power relationships within the music industry, its importance in consolidating various kinds of youth movements, all of which have been tremendously understudied topics in traditional musical scholarship. But there has been very little that has asked, to paraphrase Tina Turner, "What's Sound Got to Do With It?"

I would like to suggest that this omission is only partly attributable to the technical difficulties of representing music, the musical incompetence of the writers, or the fact that lyrics are easier to think about. Rather I think there has been, in addition, a theoretical problem created by an overly broad application of the metaphors of discourse and writing to music. *Discourses*, in Foucault's framework, are broad epoch-defining configurations of ideas that shape and limit the possibilities of being human in particular historical periods, and he directs his attention to meta-level inquiries rather than toward the way in which language itself mediates everyday social activities and experience. One of the most widely circulated ideas of Foucault has been that social discourses "systematically form the objects of which they speak" (Foucault, 1972). Derrida expresses a similar concept by arguing that there is no "presence" anterior to signification processes (Derrida, 1982). While the metaphorical application of discourse to nonlinguistic phenomena such as music has been widely established, it remains true that in the process of theorizing, both authors primarily had Western written texts in mind. The problem when we try to compact music into this framework can be illustrated through one of Derrida's formulations. In his essay entitled *Différance*, Derrida gets much figurative mileage out of stressing that in French one cannot "hear" the difference between the word spelled with an "e" or an "a;" The conceptual difference between the terms, he emphasizes, emerges only in *writing*. In music, I would argue that the situation is usually just the reverse: that difference is "heard" primarily through the physical presence of sound, not in its various written representations. It begs the question to argue that the recording of music on CDs is a mode of writing by virtue of its creation of something repeatable, for so much of the metaphor of writing in the Derridean position is dedicated to questioning the importance of the phenomenal world. My point is to question the overuse of metaphors of writing and discourse in poststructuralist thinking, and to suggest that when used in reference to music, they can lead inquiry away from the relational or discursive peculiarities of music. For example there is a famous duet between Eric Dolphy and Charles Mingus (1960) on *What Love* that sounds like an iconic representation of a conversation—two people having an discussion. If I were to transcribe the notes of the performance and play them on the piano, they wouldn't sound very much like the conversation on the recording; for it is the relatively non-notatable timbral and dynamic inflections produced by the players that are the principal means of communicating the iconicity. Various visual mappings of waveforms now available on computer are not likely to do much better in communicating the iconicity, either. These timbral and dynamic inflections, as Gumperz might argue (1982), signal how the notes should be interpreted, and are not restricted to iconic examples such as this one.

I am arguing that the phenomenology of sound is extremely important to the *way* in which music is discursive, and cannot be bracketed off as external to signification processes. While the physical aspects of sound are "nonlinguistic," they very quickly become implicated in indexical discursive processes, such as intermusicality, and may in turn be commented upon by audience members with words. There is a constant interplay between music, discursivity, language, and representations thereof that takes place when human beings make and listen to music that needs to be theorized with its own peculiarities in mind. I am using "discursive" here to mean the kind of relationalities that can be established through the various modes of human communication (principally language, music, visual images, and bodily movement). While I don't particularly like language suggesting itself as the general model of relationality, I think the word "discursivity" in this general sense is here to stay. Derrida's use of "writing," however, is more problematic.

The line of argument in Derrida that values writing over speech, and grounds the decentering of the subject, may make sense in the context of debates in Western philosophy, but I would argue it has done considerable violence to understanding the ways in which music as a sonic phenomenon and human agency participate in the construction of social and cultural meaning. For some writers, there has been a principled avoidance of engaging with musical sound, or ethnographically collected opinions, which has been predicated on a suspicion that phenomenology of any kind will lead the writer into the traps of essentialism or otherwise into presuming the transparency of the human voice. Musical scholarship has had an additional fear that representations of music (such as musical transcriptions) are inherently formalist, reifying, and decontextualizing—a fear that has never seemed to worry those who write about written texts.

The poststructuralist decentering of the phenomenal world, in which even the body has been argued to be discursively produced, is the relevant context for how we might read Grossberg's statement that "one cannot approach rock and roll by using anyone's experience of it, or even any collective definition of that experience" (1990, p. 113). Lived experience is deprecated here and phenomenal reality is not so important as its mass representations, politics, and ideologies. This position, it seems to me, constructs a rather exalted role for the intellectual, since one is absolved of worrying too much about the phenomenal world or individual agencies, and is free to theorize at will. Indeed, a conviction about spoken language grounds Gayatri Spivak's position (1988) that it's point-less to document so-called native voices. The problem, she argues, is "phonocentrism" or "the conviction that speech is a direct and immediate representation of voice-consciousness and writing an indirect transcript of speech" (p. 212). Speech from a living human being (or musical notes from a horn), in this framework, become a metaphor for an unmediated concept of the individual, for essentialism, and for a romanticized "othering" of oppressed people.[7]

Yet, as we have seen, linguistic anthropology and sociolinguistics (with its emphasis on how language mediates social experience) have long since abandoned any idea of the self-evidence of speech (transcribed or not), and the transparency of individual voices independent of their construction in social and cultural contexts. Derrida's and Spivak's quarrel is actually with a concept of speech and voice that antedates that developed by linguists whose work I have talked about (e.g., Duranti, 1992; Hanks, 1987, 1989; Lucy, 1993; Ochs, 1988; Schieffelin, 1990; Silverstein, 1976, 1993). By the late 1970s, Austin's concept of the performative and its presumptions about intentionality was beginning to be deeply critiqued by several linguists (see Silverstein, 1979). Those who still carry on Derrida's objection to Austin's intentionality, which was perhaps timely when it was first written, it seems to me, are beating a dead horse.

Indeed, Silverstein's work implies that the mutually constituting indexical properties of human discourses are operative from the most micro level of interpersonal interaction to most macro level of metadiscursive textual speculation and ideology. From this perspective, there is simply no reason to imagine that engaging with what someone "says" (or "plays") is any less significant from a social constructionist (and representational) point of view than engaging with the macro-theoretical and ideological speculations of Foucault or Derrida. In other words, I question the opposition between social constructionism and lived experience that is frequently drawn (or presumed) in deconstructionist cultural interpretation. I would argue that thinking about the multifaceted social production of human beings and their social and cultural worlds need not be at the expense of human agency.

MUSIC AND CULTURAL PRACTICE

I am suggesting that to reject the deconstructionist perspective on speech, voice, (and by extension, sound) is to reject the idea of subjects so overdetermined by hegemonic ideologies that they are unable to speak or take action on their behalf. To reject the position on speech and agency, however, is not to foreclose a partial reconciliation between practice theory and poststructural conceptions of discourse. Like Hanks (1987) I like to think of discourse genres (linguistic and non-linguistic) as modes of action, indexically situated within a historical context, and as emergent, with people necessarily improvising upon them in social practice. If we think of actors or groups of agents consciously or unconsciously partaking of particular overlapping cultural discourses while negotiating their social statuses and positions—all conditioned, of course, by the restraints of hegemony—I think we might find a way of beginning to take what has been most useful and stimulating in recent social theory and to apply it to particular cultural problems. Interdisciplinary work on music and popular culture cannot afford to pretend that sound is not an active participant in the shaping of cultural meaning and human subjectivities, however peculiar its phenomenological discursivity might be, and however much music is simultaneously involved with other overlapping discourses such as gender, race, and class. We need rather to invent ways to get at the power of sound and the ways in which it shapes and is shaped by other cultural practices.

This phenomenological discursivity of music, I think, has much to do with the creation of emotion through music, or what Arjun Appadurai (1993) has called communities of sentiment, as well (see also Crease, this volume). Many of the non-notatable aspects of jazz improvisation including tone color, phrasing, dynamics, rhythmic coordination, and intensity are among the seemingly ineffable physical qualities that produce emotional reactions in listeners. Physical sounds may produce visceral reactions, but these reactions are immediately implicated in processes of discursive and cultural interpretation, which may result in the attachment of an emotional label to the "feeling." These reactions must be historicized despite how easily recordings make the dislocation of a performance from its historical contexts of production.

CONCLUSION

I'd like to finish by offering a coda that elucidates the limitations of having taken jazz improvisation as my point of departure, that considers the possible methodological implications of the position taken here, and lastly one that indulges in the opportunity to suggest that for some aspects of cultural theory, a musical metaphor might be more powerful than a linguistic one.

First, I have overstated my case for the importance of sound as cultural discourse in direct proportion to the centrality of instrumental and vocal sound in jazz as compared to other genres. Once music with texts is introduced, the problem becomes elucidating the relationship of words to the sound of the voice, as well as to non-vocal instrumental sound. There is a shifting balance between words, voice, and instruments that varies greatly cross-culturally. In many West African musics, for example, the boundaries between language and music are much blurrier, since speech may literally be spoken through instruments, most usually drums. In this case the tonal aspects of speech and music must be addressed, not to mention the relationship of both types of sound to the nonlinguistic discourse of dance. In some musical traditions and genres, however, sound may be quite secondary to its function of carrying text, as for example, in Quranic chant, which is not even considered to be music by culture bearers. Another example can be found in the Japanese Zen Buddhist practice of shakuhachi playing. While sound and music may seem centrally important to Westerners listening to the shakuhachi, more important to Zen Buddhist practitioners is the function of sound in gaining control of the breath. The shakuhachi and its performance genres traditionally have been considered spiritual tools, more than musical phenomena, despite their inclusion in concert performance settings. Thus my focus on sound is not intended to elevate sound unilaterally to an importance it may not possess cross-culturally. Rather, I mean to suggest that insofar as it is present in cultural practices, its role, relative importance, intersection with other communicative mediums, and the way in which it indexes broader cultural discourses ought to be assessed.

Methodologically, I would argue that issues of sound and agency are interrelated in the sense that intersubjective and historical research remain crucial to cross-cultural musical scholarship, however vexed by the inherent asymmetries in power relationships between the studiers and the studied. The neglect of history in work on popular music I find particularly disconcerting, since sweeping generalizations about race and African-American music have been made in apparent blissful ignorance of the ways in that cultural studies work reproduces some well-established pitfalls in the jazz literature. To engage in data-driven research, I would argue, is not the equivalent of presuming that socially constructed facts are a transparent window on reality.

Finally, I cannot resist the opportunity to suggest that a musical metaphor might be just as useful to social analysis as the ever-present linguistic ones. If we took the interlocking pragmatic and metapragmatic layers of the improvising ensemble as our metaphorical image for cultural heterogeneity, for example, we might be able to sustain the polyvocality everyone has been looking for more easily. What if global cultural processes were the rhythmic feel we were looking at? What if we thought of global cultural processes as practices and ideologies that may or may not be coordinated at any particular moment in time, that may, in other words, sometimes come into an interaction that produces a coherence, some times not? What if we thought of some layers providing a great deal of continuity, while others (at the same time) might be providing great tension and radical departure? If we recognized that the layers which provide continuity or change can trade places from moment to moment, then perhaps we could move away from the dichotomous understandings—us/them, heterogeneity/homogeneity, modernism/post-modernism, structure/agency, radicalism/conservatism—that continue to plague our discussions. There are a lot of partially overlapping grooves out there, none of which has a "monopoly on the truth" (Rosaldo, 1993, pp. xviii–xix).

This concept of "grooves writ large" is purposely meant to underscore the relevance of music and its organization to the "reshaping of social analysis," to borrow Renato Rosaldo's image (1993). It suggests that grooves (as well as the people who make them) may have much to contribute to streams of thinking that have had great difficulty incorporating non-linguistic discourses in a more than peripheral fashion.

NOTES

[1] There are also nonreferential linguistic indexes that describe something about the structure of a speech event, but contribute nothing to the propositional value of a statement. Linguistic tokens that, for example, indicate the gender of a person speaking or indicate a relationship of deference between speaker and addressee are examples of such nonreferential indexes (Silverstein, 1976, pp. 30–31).

[2] The quotation or allusion is semiotically an "indexical icon": a quoted musical phrase "points to a prior performance" through a musical phrase that resembles (is an icon of) a passage in the prior work.

[3] Silverstein, drawing upon Roman Jakobson uses the word *renvoi* to distinguish the literary sense of reference or allusion, from the formal linguistic sense of reference (1993, p. 51).

Remember that the establishment of the rhythmic feel includes the establishment of the harmonic context as well.

[4] In this example I am presuming the typical piano, bass, drums, plus horn soloist configuration. In the case of a solo from one of the rhythm section members the numbers of interactive layers establishing the groove would be reduced, but the fundamental idea that there *may* be multiple interactional layers at any given time remains.

[5] See Hanks, 1990, for an intriguing and suggestive discussion of the way in which language deictics structures social space among the Maya.

[6] McClary (1990) begins her chapter on Madonna by lamenting the lack of attention to Madonna's music.

[7]I do not mean to imply that Spivak always uses speech in this sense, nevertheless, it is most often the work of J. L. Austin and John Searle that she and Derrida have in mind when they critique the self-presence of speech. Spivak also raises the issue of "distancing" in knowing the self: "post-structuralist theories of consciousness and language suggest that all possibility of expression, spoken or written, shares a common distancing from a self so that meaning can arise—not only meaning for others but also the meaning of the self to the self" (1988, p. 212). For the best developed arguments for the discursive construction of the subject, including her body, see Butler, 1990, p. 1993.

REFERENCES

Abbate, C. (1991). *Unsung voices: Opera and musical narrative in the nineteenth century.* Princeton, NJ: Princeton University Press.

Appadurai, A. (1993). Topographies of the self: Praise and emotion in Hindu India. In L. Abu-Lughod and C. A. Lutz (Eds.), *Language and the politics of emotion* (pp. 92–112). New York: Cambridge University Press.

Berliner, P. (1994). *Thinking in jazz: The infinite art of improvisation.* Chicago: University of Chicago Press.

Butler, J. (1990). *Gender trouble: Feminism and the subversion of identity.* New York: Routledge.

Butler, J. (1993). *Bodies that matter: On the discursive limits of "sex".* New York: Routledge.

Coltrane, J. (1961). Greensleeves. On *Africa Brass* [Record]. New York: May 23, 1961. Impulse! MCAD-42001.

Davis, M. (1959). All Blues. On *Kind of Blue* [Record]. New York: Columbia CK40579.

Derrida, J. (1968/1982). Différance. In J. Derrida, *Margins of philosophy* (pp. 1–27). Chicago: University of Chicago Press.

Duranti, A., & Goodwin, C. (Eds.). (1992). *Rethinking context: Language as an interactive phenomenon.* New York: Cambridge University Press.

Foucault, M. (1969/1972). *The archaeology of knowledge and the discourse on language* (A.M. Sheridan Smith, Trans.). New York: Pantheon Books.

Franklin, A. (1972). What a friend we have in Jesus. On *Amazing Grace* [Record]. Los Angeles: Atlantic SD 2-906.

Gilroy, P. (1987/1991). *"There ain't no black in the union jack": The cultural politics of race and nation.* Chicago: University of Chicago Press.

Goffman, E. (1974/1986). *Frame analysis: An essay on the organization of experience.* Boston: Northeastern University Press.

Grossberg, L. (1990). Is there rock after punk? In S. Frith and A. Goodwin (Eds.), *On rock: Rock, pop, and the written word* (pp. 111–123). New York: Pantheon Books.

Guilbault, J. (1993). *Zouk: World music in the West Indies.* Chicago: University of Chicago Press.

Gumperz, J. J. (1982). *Discourse strategies.* New York: Cambridge University Press.

Gumperz, J. J., & Hymes, D. (Eds.) (1986). *Directions in sociolinguistics: The ethnography of communication*. Oxford: Basil Blackwell.

Guy, B. (1961). My time after while. On *The Best of Chess Blues. Vol. 2* [Record]. Chicago: Chess CHD-31316.

Hanks, W. F. (1987). Discourse genres in a theory of practice. *American Ethnologist, 14*, 668–692.

Hanks, W. F. (1989). Text and textuality. *Annual Review of Anthropology, 18*, 99–101.

Hanks, W. F. (1990). *Referential practice: Language and lived space among the Maya*. Chicago: University of Chicago Press.

Hebdige, D. (1979). *Subculture: The meaning of style*. New York: Methuen.

Labov, W. (1969). *The logic of nonstandard English*. Monograph Series on Languages and Linguistics. Washington, DC: Georgetown University.

Levinson, S. C. (1983). *Pragmatics*. New York: Cambridge University Press.

Lucy, J. A. (1993). Reflexive language and the human disciplines. In J. A. Lucy (Ed.), *Reflexive language: Reported speech and metapragmatics* (pp. 9–32). New York: Cambridge University Press.

McClary, S. (1990). *Feminine endings: Music, gender, and sexuality*. Minneapolis: University of Minnesota Press.

Mingus, C. (1959). Wednesday night prayer meeting. On *Blues and Roots* [Record]. New York: Atlantic SD-1305.

Mingus, C. (1960). Charles Mingus presents Charles Mingus. On *Charles Mingus Presents Charles Mingus* [Record]. New York: Candid BR-5012.

Moerman, M. (1988). *Talking culture: Ethnography and conversation analysis*. Philadelphia: University of Pennsylvania Press.

Monson, I. (1994). "Doubleness" and jazz improvisation: Irony, parody, and ethnomusicology. *Critical Inquiry, 20*, pp. 283–313.

Monson, I. (1996). *Saying something: Jazz improvisation and interaction*. Chicago: University of Chicago Press.

Nattiez, J. (1990). Can one speak of narrativity in music? *Journal of the Royal Musical Association, 115*, 240–257.

Ochs, E. (1988). *Culture and language development: Language acquisition and language socialization in a Samoan village*. New York: Cambridge University Press.

Rosaldo, R. (1993). *Culture and truth: The remaking of social analysis*. Boston: Beacon Press.

Schieffelin, B. B. (1990). *The give and take of everyday life: Language socialization of Kaluli children*. New York: Cambridge University Press.

Schwichtenberg, C. (Ed.). (1993). *The Madonna collection: Representational politics, subcultural identities, and cultural theory*. Boulder: Westview Press.

Silverstein, M. (1976). Shifters, linguistic categories, and cultural description. In K. Basso and H. Shelby (Eds.), *Meaning in anthropology* (pp. 11–55). Albuquerque: University of New Mexico Press.

Silverstein, M. (1993). Metapragmatic discourse and metapragmatic function. In J. A. Lucy (Ed.), *Reflexive language: Reported speech and metapragmatics* (pp. 33–58). New York: Cambridge University Press.

Spivak, G. C. (1988). *In other words: Essays in cultural politics*. New York: Routledge.

Waterman, C. A. (1990). *Jùjú: A social history and ethnography of an African popular form*. Chicago: University of Chicago Press.

part II

Creativity on Stage

chapter 6

The Creative Decision-Making Process in Group Situation Comedy Writing

Steven R. Pritzker
University of Southern California

Mark A. Runco
California State University, Fullerton

Mr. Pritzker worked as a situation comedy writer and producer for many years before beginning his graduate study in creativity research. Dr. Runco is the editor of the Creativity Research Journal, *and has played an influential role in the resurgence of creativity studies in the last 10 years. In this chapter, Pritzker and Runco examine collaboration in situation comedy writing. An episode is created by a group of 5 to 10 writers, executives, and producers. The episode is worked out scene-by-scene, and then one or two people are assigned to write the script. It's common for writers to improvise dialogues in these meetings that then are written into the script. The first few drafts of a script are reviewed by the group, and frequent revisions are the norm. Rewriting continues through the five days of rehearsal, up to the final taping. Thus the rehearsals themselves are a part of the creative process, with actor's spontaneous improvisations sometimes entering the next draft of the script.*

This chapter demonstrates that writing, which so many people associate with a solitary, inspired individual, can be a highly interactive, collaborative, group activity. Collaborations among writers, and rehearsals with the actors and show executives, contribute to the final product. Although the final broadcast show is performed from a script, this script represents only one possible endpoint of fixity in a fluid, dynamic process.

This chapter could be read in combination with Sawyer's chapter on improvisational theater, since writers and actors use improvisation to develop script ideas.

In its focus on collaboration and participation in creative groups, this chapter overlaps with Baker-Sennett and Matusov's chapter.

I n this chapter we look at the dynamics that influence the group decision-making process in situation comedy writing. The focus on writing may suggest that the concern here is on the processes underlying
performance, but much of the work in this field requires improvisational
performances. Ideas for scenes and jokes, for example, are tossed
around and dialogue suggested, then built upon by others. In this chapter we evaluate data that were collected from a group of Writer-
Producers. They were asked to describe both positive and negative professional experiences with comedy writing. Characteristics of writers
and studio and network executives are described, and dimensions of
leadership that can contribute to encouraging creative participation or
cause writers to shut down are identified. We conclude that the current
system may produce some good results but it is extraordinarily costly in
both monetary and human capital. Suggestions are offered for improving the process, and several future research possibilities are proposed.

COLLABORATIVE CREATIVITY

There is growing recognition that increasing creativity is an essential
goal for both individuals and organizations (Higher Education and
Goals 2000, U.S. Department of Education, 1993). Simply put, there is a
need to learn as much as possible about the creative process so students
and workers can receive the tools they need to work effectively. This
chapter represents our effort to learn from the creativity of a special
group of professional writers.

Situation comedy writers work in a collaborative group assembled to
write a specific show. Much of the work involves improvisation as ideas
for scenes and jokes are tossed around and dialogue suggested, then
built upon by others. More will be said below about the improvisation
involved.

Research on creativity and writing has primarily focused on the individual writer (Barron, 1961, 1972; Kellogg, 1994). Studies of collaborative writing seem to be nonexistent, other than a few biographies of
playwrights who wrote with others, such as George S. Kaufman
(Meredith, 1974), and screenwriting teams such as Billy Wilder and I. A.
L. Diamond. One possible explanation for this lack of research is that
collaborative writing was not that common until recently. Although
many screenplays had shared writing credits, most often these writers

worked at separate times on scripts and may have never even met each other. Collaboration appears to be common only in the musical theater, where writing teams such as Rodgers and Hart (Marx & Clayton, 1976), Rodgers and Hammerstein (Nolan, 1978), and George and Ira Gershwin (Rosenburg, 1991) worked.

Biographies of these teams indicate that these collaborative partnerships were as complicated as marriages. The Gershwins, for example, seemed to get along very well, while Richard Rodgers and Lorenz Hart gave the impression of opposite personalities with inharmonious work habits. Rodgers was quoted as saying

> When the immovable object of his unwillingness to change came up against the irresistible force of my own drive for perfection, the noise could be heard all over the city. Our fights over words were furious, blasphemous and frequent, but we both knew that we were arguing academically, and not personally. (Nolan, 1978, p. 88)

Hart probably took it very personally when his partner broke up the team to work with Oscar Hammerstein. Rodgers and Hammerstein became an enormous commercial and creative force in the theater; Hart died from alcoholism.

George S. Kaufman (Meredith, 1974) had an outstanding track record in theater, writing and directing numerous hit plays. He worked with a variety of partners, among them the famous author Edna Ferber. Their relationship was complicated and difficult, filled with fights that typically ended with Kaufman walking out the door. However, there were also moments of great creative energy. To give one example, Ferber once described the excitement of finally finding the solution to a problem:

> Suddenly the difficulties that always before had bested the plan of the play seemed to melt away. We warmed to the idea, we sparked, we became excited about this scene, this character, we began to interrupt each other, to argue, we were both talking together and walking up and down the room, gesticulating in each other's faces, acting out a bit as it came to one or the other of us. It was fine, it was exhilarating, it was glorious fun. (Meredith, 1974, p. 483)

These biographical studies indicate that writing partnerships are complex relationships, charged with emotion. No two people always see things the same way, and there is no one clear right answer, so collaborative writing seems destined to have enormous highs and lows.

If things are complicated with two people, what happens when you have collaborative writing with teams of 5 or even 10 people? Are there any interactions that seem to enhance or diminish creativity? How are conflict and risk handled within the group? How do individuals perceive the way the group works and their part in it? What do they see as promoting creativity? These questions are addressed in this chapter.

GROUP DECISION MAKING

Most important decisions within corporations and military and government organizations are made by groups or teams. Dickinson, Converse, and Tannenbaum (1992) define a team as a "distinguishable set of two or more people who interact, dynamically, interdependently, and adaptively toward a common and valued goal/objective/mission who have each been assigned specific roles or functions to perform and who have a limited life-span of membership." A variety of virtues for groups have been proposed by researchers. Laughlin and McGlynn (1986) asserted that small groups are better at inductive reasoning, for instance, and Sniezek (1992) concluded that groups lead to a feeling of confidence when decisions are made in uncertain conditions. Stasser (1992) pointed out that individuals in groups can share the task of recalling facts, and each member may be able to offer unique information, and recently Rubenson and Runco (1995) suggested that teams put individuals in a position in which conflicts can lead to creative insight.

In industry, groups are formed for problem-solving and management tasks; however, the notion that groups perform better than individuals is not necessarily supported by research (Cannon-Bowers, Oser, & Flanagan, 1992; deCock & Rickards, in press). A number of negative circumstances and situations have been identified that can interfere with effective group decision making. The *free rider effect* occurs when one or more less able members of the group decide to leave the work to more talented, highly motivated team members (Kerr & Bruun, 1983). In order to avoid the *sucker effect*, the higher functioning members may choose to work less (Kerr, 1983). *Social loafing* occurs when people relax because they do not feel individually responsible for the success of a project. They seem to feel that if they relax it will not really be noticed.

Jackson and Padgett (1982) looked at social loafing in creative collaboration by examining the work of John Lennon and Paul McCartney. Early in their career, these two took joint authorship whether they wrote songs individually or together. It was only much later that Lennon revealed how each song was composed. The songs they wrote together early on were more successful than the ones they wrote individually. After 1967, they started publicly identifying which songs were written individually or in collaboration. The result was that the songs they wrote together were significantly less popular than those from the earlier years. Jackson and Padgett attributed this decline to social loafing. Ancona (1987) reviewed other potential problems, including group polarization (Mosovici & Zavaloni, 1969), decision biases (Tversky & Sattath, 1979), solution-mindedness—the bias seen when persons concur on a solution very early in the process (Hoffman & Maier, 1964)—and the dominance of verbal but inaccurate group members (Hoffman & Clark, 1979).

One problem with analyzing group decision making is the large number of variables involved. These include composition of the groups, nature of the tasks, personal interactions, leadership issues, norms, roles, physical, social and temporal environments, culture, conflict, and outside influences (Levine & Morland, 1990). Streufert and Nogami (1992) pointed out that decision making involves "bringing together of preintegrated information about the task, observed events, external forces, member and team preferences, goals and more to produce an action." Other problems arise because there are so many different types of groups, many with their own task, structure, and goals (Cannon-Bowers, Oser, & Flanagan, 1992). Yet more complications arise because many of the variables change from one moment to the next. A decision that is productive at one point may be disastrous when conditions are different. Some variables may never be factored into models because they are outside the available knowledge base. Even though there has been empirical research, a model that can reliably improve the results of group decision making has not been developed.

At present, most creative work is probably being done in conditions where there is at least some group interaction. Recent qualitative studies (e.g., Sawyer, 1992) suggest that group creativity is a type of symphony where the conditions, leadership, and individual characteristics all interact. However, much of what really happens remains an intriguing mystery. In the remainder of this chapter we look at the dynamics that influence the group decision-making process in situation comedy writing.

BACKGROUND AND SETTING

Situation comedy is defined as a series of 30-minute television episodes with approximately 22 minutes of entertainment each week. These 22 minutes are broken into two acts. Usually an episode has a story that is resolved within that same episode. Most situation comedies are shot with a live audience on a studio stage.

Situation comedy writing requires that many decisions be made in a very short time. These decisions involve elements in the script, including humor, story construction, character, and dialogue. Suggested dialogue exchanges between writers often build on each other and then are included in the script. This kind of writing is, then, more than preparatory work for performances. It can be a kind of performance itself, and one that is frequently improvisational.

There is a definite hierarchy within the production staff, with the Executive Producer at the top. This position, sometimes referred to as Show Runner, is filled by one to three people. Traditionally Show Runners have actually created the show by writing and producing the pilot script. However, in recent years, as more stars have come from stand-up comedy, they have taken on more power. In many cases (e.g., *Roseanne, Grace Under Fire,* and *Ellen*), the original creator is no longer with the series.

Key staff members are given titles such as Co-Executive Producer, Supervising Producer, and Producer. Almost all of these people are hired because network and studio executives believe they have writing ability. They may participate in other production functions, but their primary job is writing. At a lower level are additional writers with titles such as Executive Story Editor, Creative Consultant, and Program Consultant.

The atmosphere around situation comedy may appear to be casual, but everyone is aware that they are playing in a high-stakes game. Although most staff do not start work until 10 a.m., many nights they do not leave the office until 7 or 8 p.m. Rewrite and show nights can extend to midnight—and beyond. The work is often demanding, and time pressures mount as the season grinds on. Writing starts in May when new shows are announced. It usually ends in March.

Most conceptual work is done in groups. Stories are worked out scene by scene and then written by one or more people. Usually these are staff members, although on occasion an outside writer is employed. Notes are given by staff members after a story is turned in, and then once more after a first draft. Even after the second draft, a script may go through a number of revisions before being prepared to be read by the cast for the first time at what is called a "table reading." The last revision is called "the final polish" and is often done by the Executive Producer with a few key staff members.

The table reading takes place on the stage. It is very important because network and studio personnel are there. Reaction to this reading often sets the tone for the week so great care is taken to make the script as funny and sharp as possible. Additional rewrites take place throughout the 5 days of rehearsal until the show is finally taped or filmed. Run-through performances with the actors give producers an idea of how well material is "playing." A kind of improvisation is common at this point because changes can be tried out on the spot or notes made where improvements are needed.

METHODOLOGY

Interviews were conducted with four writer-producers: Burt and Jim work as a team, whereas Karen and Lynn primarily write alone. Each interview was conducted by the first author of this chapter. Table 6.1, below, presents the questions used in the interviews. He knew these people personally for many years so they all were aware that he had spent 20 years as a writer-producer of situation comedies. The first author had experienced almost everything they related, and they spoke to him as someone who had "been there." They were open with their personal feelings about themselves and the individuals with whom they had worked over the years.

Initial interviews of approximately 2 hours were transcribed and coded. These semi-structured interviews were designed to understand as much as possible about each person's perceptions of collaborative writing. Follow-up interviews were conducted to validate perceptions.

Some questions given to the writer-producers were based on a decision-making model developed by Driver, Brousseau, and Hunsaker

TABLE 6.1. Interview Questions and Topics

—If I watched you prepare a story, what would the process be?
—What would I see you doing?
—Describe the physical setting.
—How many writers would be there?
—What factors are you considering?
—How would you describe the way decisions are made?
—How do you feel the group works in terms of personalities?
—How much attention do you pay to that?
—How do you know when a creative decision is right?
—Describe some of your feelings while going through the process.
—How do you see the various people in the room and their roles?
—How is conflict handled within the group?
—What has been your experience in terms of Show Runners whom you consider good and bad, and why?
—Describe your relationship with studio and network executives.
—What do you see as the various phases that occur during the writing of a script?
—Do you see different dynamics occurring during the final rewrite?
—What do you think helps promote or discourage creativity?

(1993). We will use interview material at various points in the remainder of this chapter to highlight different features of this model, especially the individual's *decision style*.

Additional data were collected by taping story conferences and later reviewing these to confirm statements made during interviews. Three of the four interviewees reviewed a complete draft of this chapter.

RESULTS OF INTERVIEWS

The Show Runner's need for control is a key factor that emerged from our interviews. All writers agreed that the most important single element in creative decision making for a situation comedy is the temperament and style of the Show Runners who are the Executive Producers of the show. They set the tone for the show in terms of creative choices and level of participation for staff members. Show Runners have a great deal of latitude in the way they choose to run a show.

Karen tartly summed up the situation, saying, "Play to win—that's the only rule. Be a sociopath, be an asshole, pretend you're a nice guy and then reveal you're a sociopath. It doesn't matter—just keep making money for everybody." In television, success is the key ingredient.

Actually, most Show Runners probably do not fall into this category. They recognize they need the help of staff producers and writers because there is so much work to do. Show Runners are responsible for making final decisions on the script but they are also concerned with every other aspect of the show. They need to deal with the actors, director, casting director, and studio and network executives; and handle production details such as logistics, sets and wardrobe, budget, and post-production (which includes editing, music, and sound).

Every informant could identify negative and positive experiences they had had with Show Runners. One of the key factors determining the quality of experiences with Show Runners was the amount of control the Show Runner exercised over the decision-making process. Burt described an extremely controlling Show Runner he worked for at an earlier stage of his career:

> He's a very creative guy, but based on that experience we were under the impression that an Executive Producer dictated the show and everybody else threw in jokes every now and then. It was extremely impressive but we've since learned the important lesson about the collaborative process— that it's not the best thing to shoot from the hip all the time. You sort of end up being a notetaker and stenographer. He relied on us as much as he relied on anybody, but it was still sort of holding his hat. Somebody

described it as like Al Capone, who would always take 12 people to watch him get a haircut.

Control and its antithesis, autonomy, have been associated with creativity in the previous organizational research of Amabile (1989), Runco (1995; Nemiro & Runco, in press), and Witt and Boerkem (1989).

Writers need to feel things are moving forward, and if they don't, they can become frustrated and angry. Taking a great deal of time is not necessarily viewed as leading to better creative solutions. Timing is very important in situation comedy, as in other creative domains, but it may be that it is mostly a matter of giving the creative personnel the freedom to work at their own pace, rather than necessarily working quickly or working slowly.

A Show Runner with top credits proved a disappointment to Burt, who skewered him in the following hypothetical example of what might happen if they were trying to create a story about two boys competing for a job in a restaurant:

> We would start off—there would be a discussion about whether they would go out to eat in a deli or Italian restaurant. And then he would say, "Maybe it shouldn't be a restaurant at all." And then the whole story would be forgotten, "No, no—we can't do this story at all." Then somebody would say, "How about a Chinese restaurant?" "Oh yeah, okay, that would work if it's a Chinese restaurant." So we would spend days and days hashing out every little detail of the story.

Show Runners need to work carefully to provide an atmosphere in which writers feel free to say what comes to mind without feeling they will be judged harshly or ignored. Satisfying experiences occurred when staff felt their work was appreciated and acknowledged by a decision maker they respected. This was represented by Show Runners who knew what they wanted and were willing and able to integrate their staff's work into the final product.

When the atmosphere in a work room is right, a sense of excitement and participation is experienced by everyone. It is a palpable feeling. Successful creative collaboration merges ideas, and the expression "the whole adds up to more than the sum of its parts" applies perfectly. It is a more creative and funnier script because of the process.

Lynn supported this in her description of the writers' room on an extremely successful Emmy winning show:

> That was an amazing feeling, that there was no pecking order. If you walked into a room where everybody was meeting, you wouldn't really know who was the writer; you wouldn't really know who was the Executive

Producer; you would just see a lot of people trying. It was more of a group thing—somebody having an idea and somebody else in the room adding to the idea and "How about this?" "How about that?" It was healthy competition and a camaraderie thing, and you would get the laugh and you'd feel really good if you got the laugh and everybody's talents were being used.

Although things may have appeared very democratic, audiotapes of these Show Runners working on a story conference indicate that they were clearly in charge of the session. However, they carefully listened to everyone's input, and when they rejected it, they did it very tactfully. The sense of equality was achieved by giving respect to writers' ideas and making the construction of the story a genuinely collaborative session.

THE AGONY AND ECSTASY OF COMEDY WRITERS

Why are inclusion and respect so important to comedy writers? Perhaps they tend to be sensitive individuals who developed humor as a survival tool early in life. Wallace (1991) discussed the sensitivity of writers of fiction, and writers of situation comedy may be the same. Certainly they have struggled through a very competitive gauntlet to get into show business, and because their job security is usually extremely tenuous, they are almost always concerned about how they are doing.

Trying to be funny provides instant feedback. In a free-flowing situation, lines may be suggested without self-censorship by the writer only if he or she feels that they will not pay too big a price for failure (cf. Rubenson & Runco, 1995). To make matters worse, the level of creativity an individual will have on any given day is unpredictable. Like an athlete, some days they may be "in the zone" where everything they say gets laughs, or they may be "cold as ice," missing time after time. On those occasions, writers may question if they have permanently lost their ability. Burt made it a point to laugh at lines pitched even if he didn't plan to use them. He did this because he recognized the dangers of allowing his staff to feel alienated. His partner Jim also was very careful about rejecting material:

> I've found that if there's too many negative influences, then people just start to shut down. And so there's a reason to be a little more positive, not to say no to everything—to let things play out and to listen to them. You encourage people to speak up with their ideas rather than holding them in because they're afraid it's going to get shot down.

A sense of camaraderie is important to many writers, but at the same time a need for personal validation and acceptance can be tied to the work. Karen mentioned that she always felt different from other people because of her constant sarcastic and humorous remarks. When she got a job in situation comedy, she found a place where she finally felt she belonged.

Working on a show requires writers to spend many weeks in a room together, sometimes working very late at night. The nature of the process seems to create an intense sense of intimacy, where people reveal a great deal of personal information. Karen related

> You find out a lot of what goes on with men sexually. There's volumes on that. Many of these situations men get to know you or me better than their own wives and vice versa. It's also quite interesting because a lot of times you never even see these people again or talk to them. But you know stuff they'd probably never in a million years ever tell you.

It seems that part of the reason many writers may be very sensitive to criticism is because they feel they put so much of themselves into their work.

Part of their motivation to write is based on the willingness to use personal experiences to enlighten and communicate with others. For example, Burt described a scene he inspired between a grandfather and a 6-year-old boy:

> The grandfather, in his way, was trying to say: "I'm never going to see these things but what I have up here (indicating head), I'm going to pass on to you. If you want to be a stock car driver like I was, I'll fill your head with everything I know." And [tears forming], it touched me a lot because it was a scene I never got to see between my father and my son. Maybe it reached somebody somewhere—some guy my age is estranged from his father somewhere, and who knows—we're not trying to heal the world with those things but that's a little bit of why.

The desire to somehow capture the essence of a moment keeps writers working despite the high failure rate in the business. The lows may be low but the highs are higher. Lynn described this feeling:

> I love writing something that satisfies me. I just love it. It's a place to have your ideas and your sense of humor and your take on life seen. Performed and then seen. Particularly when the actors are good, you get back so much. It's enormously satisfying. There's a oneness with . . . There's a kind of spiritual feeling of a oneness with the person who's performing. You understand them and they understand you, and the audience understands what it is that delights you and they're delighted by it. It's deeper than a laugh—it's a joy.

After a long contemplative pause, Lynn (referring to our interview) asked, "Do I get paid for this?"

There's the mutual recognition that everybody's bonded by going through many of the same emotional experiences. It may parallel what Garfield (1980) said about the "mutual congratulations" felt when several persons grasp the humor of a pun.

When feelings run this deep, it is not surprising that rejection can create resentment and anger. Arguments about behavior can get passionately out of hand because two writers are arguing over what is "the truth," which almost always is a subjective matter. There is a scene in the movie *Tootsie* that illustrates the tendency for things to get out of hand. Dustin Hoffman plays an actor who is fired from a commercial. Wearing a tomato suit, he explains to his agent that he was arguing with the director because he asked him to do something he thought was out of character: "A tomato would never do that."

Writers who feel rejected and frustrated may redirect their anger inward on themselves and become distraught or depressed. Or they may retaliate with passive-aggressive behavior toward the Show Runner. The Show Runner who made decisions slowly was openly mocked by his staff. Comedy often expresses anger in either subtle or explicit ways, and it is not surprising that the field tends to attract angry people. Conflicts do not necessarily occur on every show, but they are far from infrequent. Resolution of conflicts sometimes occurs by executives firing a Show Runner and locking him out of the studio. This contributes to an atmosphere in which almost nobody feels safe or secure. It is usually announced that the departing Show Runner left because of "creative differences," which frequently is a euphemism meaning "they lost the power struggle."

RELATIONSHIPS WITH STUDIO AND NETWORK EXECUTIVES

Studio and network executives can have an impact on the creative process by giving notes that encompass their reactions to scripts, cast readings of the script, run-throughs, and tapings. Writers said they understand these executives work for organizations that fund their work, and thus they have a right to be there. They also noted that on occasion, an executive may provide a different perspective that is helpful. However, for the most part executives were described in very negative terms. An executive is in effect "the boss," and it's not surprising or unusual that some resentment might be expressed. We can cite the divergent perspectives hypothesis here, for this explains common differences in perspective. Runco and Chand (1994) applied it directly to creativity and differences between judgments held by creators and by those offered by others. Runco and Smith (1992) reported empirical data showing differences between intrapersonal judgments and interpersonal judgments about the originality of ideas.

Still, the depth of disdain expressed by the writers in the present study and the "them vs. us" feeling was quite consistent and remarkable. Executives were seen as aliens who did not understand the writing process and so made suggestions that did not make sense. Resentment at executives' interference was compounded by the fact that they gave their notes and then disappeared, leaving the writers feeling like the foot soldiers on the front line, the people who really do the hard work.

Writers differentiate themselves from nonwriters. They feel that writers share a common language and bond, because they are the ones who face the blank page. Lynn summed up the resentment:

> The problem is that, if you're a nuclear physicist, your next-door neighbor doesn't say "Hey, Joe, you know that e=mc squared thing you're always talking about. My nephew thinks it should be e=mc cubed. Just an idea." But everybody has ideas about what comedy should be or what scripts should be or what things they see on television should be, so network people and studio people feel that they can say, "Oh, this character should be more this." Everybody and his brother—your aunt and your butcher—feels totally confident to be able to comment on stuff. And if they work for a network or a studio, well, hell, they have opinions, too—which they call notes.

There is also distrust of the motives of the executives. They are seen as having a different agenda, with their primary objective being their own survival. They want to give the illusion that everyone is on the same team, but many feel that if there are any problems that threaten an executive's fragile sense of security, he or she will instantly abandon the Show Runner. Although an occasional note may be useful, executives take no responsibility if their suggestions do not work. Burt put it this way:

> You can have a congenial relationship with them but you've just got to bear in mind that your best interest is not what they have at heart. I mean, you can take input from people. People have good ideas; you appropriate them, but ultimately the show's your responsibility and if you do something they disagree with and it works—then it's their idea. *Seinfeld* is a great example. The network said, "We have nothing here. No one gets this show. This is a disaster." And suddenly it's a big hit, and now it's fresh and innovative and every executive's hanging around the set getting their picture taken.

THE CREATIVE DECISION-MAKING PROCESS

All the writer-producers indicated that there are many people who have an influence on the creative decision-making process even though they aren't in the room. Show Runners must consider the parameters of the series and audience expectations as they develop stories. They must anticipate reactions from actors and executives. When it comes to the story itself, they need to be aware of the structure of the series and keep the action of each character consistent. They need to develop stories that move forward, have an interesting opening, a solid act break, and have a solution that is satisfying. On top of that, it should be funny enough to keep a live audience laughing. They must monitor the staff reaction and try to keep things moving. They need to be aware of the story they are working on and the story of what is happening in the room so that members of the team stay active and feel included. Obviously this can be a taxing process, and there is no question that fatigue and stress add to the pressure of the job as the season progresses and there is less time to work on each show. As Burt explained, this fatigue can lead to creative compromise:

> We're all guilty, I know I'm guilty, of when you get tired, you get lazy. Then you're not being creative because say you just pound your head against the wall for another couple of hours at two in the morning or you know this little bit that you saw on another show that you could translate into your characters and it'll work fine and get you out of here. One of the most difficult things to do when you get tired is to keep up the good fight.

Lynn pointed out that's one of the reasons creative collaboration is essential to situation comedy—there is so much work to do.

Rubenson and Runco (1995) suggested that somewhat heterogeneous groups will be optimal for creative work. With this in mind, and given what we just said about the huge amount of work to do in situation comedy, we were not surprised that the ideal team was seen as a mix of players with special strengths. Some writers are better at constructing stories, others write characters well, and there are writers who are great joke writers. A joke specialist often comes in on the last major rewrite to "punch up" the show.

Occasionally everything comes together and a memorable series emerges. Lynn described it this way: "All the odds are against it. It is somewhat of a miracle. It has to be the right people at the right place at the right time with the right idea."

CREATIVE DECISION-MAKING STYLES

Driver, Brousseau, and Hunsaker (1993, p. 3) developed a decision-making model based on two factors:

- *Information use*: the amount of information actually considered in making decisions.
- *Focus*: the number of alternatives identified when reaching decisions.

These two factors are not interdependent. When making a decision, an individual may use a great deal of information and generate only a few alternatives, or use very little information and generate many possible choices.

The amount of information needed to make any single decision may change depending on variables such as time pressure, the importance of a decision, and how complicated it is (see Figure 6.1). These range along a curve from *satisficers*, who make a decision as soon as they

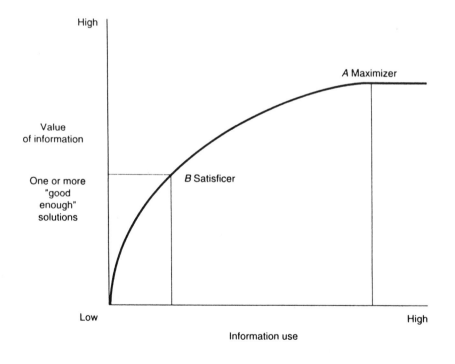

FIGURE 6.1.   Styles of Information Use

believe they have the minimum amount of information necessary, to *maximizers*, who wait to gather all the information they can before choosing a course of action. A satisficer who has made a decision can become very frustrated in dealing with a maximizer who wants to keep gathering information, and vice-versa.

The appropriate style varies according to the nature of the job. An aircraft designer needs to be a maximizer if the design must reflect all possible contingencies. A pilot who must make decisions rapidly needs to be a satisficer.

People also develop patterns in the number of alternatives required to make a decision. At one extreme, somebody who is unifocused generates only one viable solution to a problem and wants to implement it. At the opposite extreme, multifocused people develop many different alternative solutions which they want to carefully consider. Unifocused executives believe multifocused people are indecisive and wishy-washy. Multifocused people see unifocused people as narrow-minded and inflexible.

Driver developed an instrument designed to measure an individual's typical information use and focus. He defined five styles based on research with over 20,000 individuals, including at least 6000 managers and 6000 MBA students.

The five styles are

- *Decisive*: They make decisions quickly with minimal information and stay with their plan.
- *Flexible*: They make decisions rapidly but also change quickly as they get additional information. They like to keep their options open and tend to select social occupations.
- *Hierarchic*: They use a maximum amount of information to analyze and develop a specific, detailed plan which they feel confident is the best possible solution.
- *Integrative*: They use a maximum amount of information and generate as many options as possible as they search for the best solution. Plans are always open to change. They tend to prefer investigative occupations.
- *Systemic*: They use a maximum amount of information like an integrative and then make a decision through careful analysis like a hierarchic. They tend to see the big picture and try to solve different problems that are connected.

In Driver et al.'s (1993) theory of work patterns, each style has strengths and weaknesses, and different situations require different styles. Decisive and flexible styles work best where there is a limited amount of time available, which is often the case in situation comedy writing. The other styles are more effective when problems are more complicated. However, people with the integrative style often value creativity and exploration. Driver et al. further differentiate between an individual's *role style*—the style people think they *should* use—and their *operating style*—the way they actually make decisions. People aren't always aware of how they make decisions.

We asked the writer-producers several questions that we adapted from (a) a questionnaire about Background Factors Relating to Role Style (questions concerning national culture, social class, religion, parental values, emotional climate, and family size); (b) the Self-Concept Checklist; (c) the Role Style (preferred organization form, office appearance, personal appearance, formal communication preferences); (d) Biographical Factors Relating to Operating Style (Family size, birth order, parent style and beliefs; (d) education level and type of extracurricular activities; (e) community size and the number of communities lived in and job pattern; and (f) Style Perception Checklist (occupational task preference, project pattern, pace, planning, creativity use). Results were discussed with each individual, and they agreed that the styles attributed to them seemed accurate.

Results

Burt

Burt's Role Style	Decisive	Flexible	Hierarchic	Integrative	Systemic
Background Role Style	3	0	1	2	0
Self-Concept Role Style	6	3	0	4	0

Burt and his partner Jim are both about 40 years old. They were hired 5 years ago as term writers. At the time they got that offer Burt was a well-established television executive. He decided to take the big gamble of becoming a writer. His risk has paid off. He and his partner have been promoted almost every year and were recently appointed to the job of Show Runners.

At the time of the interviews, they had just finished their first 10 shows. Burt's role style is clearly decisive with an integrative backup style. This is consistent with his background.

Burt's Operating Style	Decisive	Flexible	Hierarchic	Integrative	Systemic
Background Operating Style	3	1	2	4	0
Style Perception Operating Style	8	2	2	0	0

Burt perceives his own operating style as strongly decisive, and he prefers working with decisive executives. For example, he spoke about his frustation with a former boss whom he felt was too slow to make decisions: "He was extremely deliberate in his thinking. We would spend days on a story and agonize over every little beat of every little thing that happened. I felt that this fool—in addition to the show not coming out well—I felt my own personal growth curve had been tamped."

Although Burt thinks of himself as decisive, his operating style is far more intuitive and flexible:

> **Interviewer**: How do you recognize something good when you hear it?
> **Burt**: For me, it's a very emotional thing. I get a little—I can just tell. I get happy on the inside or I get sad.
> **Interviewer**: Is it a physical feeling?
> **Burt**: Yes, yes, very much so.
> **Interviewer**: Literally?
> **Burt**: Literally my heart jumps or it sinks. That's how I would describe the feeling. If there's something that sparks, I get an adrenaline rush. You can be sitting there and sometimes a story conference can be a very enervating experience. People just—it can be the most deadly thing in the world and somebody hits something and it can just be fun. It's like hooking a yellow fin or something. It's an exciting moment.
> **Interviewer**: Have you ever hooked a yellow fin?
> **Burt**: (sounding totally unbelievable) Yes, I have. (Interviewer laughs) Not a yellow fin, a yellow tail. It was a yellow something. (Interviewer laughs) A safety vest.

Burt fits the description of a flexible to a tee—he is fast, intuitive, opportunistic, adaptable, entrepreneurial, likable, and uses a great deal of humor.

Jim

Jim's Role Style	Decisive	Flexible	Hierarchic	Integrative	Systemic
Background Role Style	1	3	1	0	0
Self-Concept Role Style	8	2	2	0	0

Jim's perceived role style is strongly decisive, which doesn't fit with his background role style. It also doesn't fit with his role in the partnership where he is more likely to let Burt take the lead in running the table or dealing with studio or network executives.

Jim's responses are the opposite of Burt's lightning-like answers. He took short and long pauses before answering questions, making sure he knew what he was going to say. His tendency trying to solve a script problem is to "take time to reflect. I feel for myself that definitely makes a difference as to how much time I have to sit with an idea."

His perception that he is decisive doesn't seem congruent with the way he appears or his description of his work process.

Jim's Operating Style	Decisive	Flexible	Hierarchic	Integrative	Systemic
Background Operating Style	2	3	3	1	2
Style Perception Operating Style	1	4	1	4	2

Jim's operating style is much different, with integrative primary and flexible as a backup. There is very little decisive in his actual operating style. Here is his description of a collaborative story conference:

> We benefit from a number of people sitting around a room collaborating, feeding on each other's energy, building on each other's ideas. That will really help a story. I suggest A, somebody else suggests B, or maybe there's a synthesis of C that really works well for the story we wouldn't have arrived at except that there were a number of people participating.

Clearly he is far less emotional and more integrative about the process than his partner. While looking for a story idea in a group situation, he said: "I'll give Burt the lead on these sorts of things if he wants to explore an area that I don't think is particularly fruitful. I'll say why I don't like it, but I don't want to shut down the whole process."

Jim confirms his integrative style when he describes what happens when he feels others aren't accepting his ideas: "You have an opinion, they disagree with it, you just tend to shut down or check out until you find a new way to join in."

Jim also displays some flexible traits. He is willing to talk about things up to a point, but if the conversation goes on too long, he's ready to move on:

> I've been with people who don't seem to exhibit an opinion one way or the other and the conversation is endless. It's more helpful to know what the leader in the group is looking for. You still have the sense of moving in a particular direction, even if it's chosen by the leader, than indecision or non-movement.

Burt and Jim's Partnership

In their own eyes, Burt and Jim's partnership is based on having complementary strengths. Burt is the one who is more likely to run the table because he is seen as quicker to make decisions and more comfortable at the helm. Jim is recognized by Burt and himself as someone who takes time to reflect on things and improve them.

The factor that in the long run may cause problems in their relationships is Jim's perception of his role style as extremely decisive. One of the authors mentioned to Burt that if Jim feels he is being shoved out of the limelight too much, it could possibly damage their partnership. Burt responded that they had been talking about that subject recently and that they are going to try to divide up their duties so Jim has more visible responsibility in the hope that they can keep their partnership running smoothly.

Karen

Karen's Role Style	Decisive	Flexible	Hierarchic	Integrative	Systemic
Background Role Style	3	1	1	1	0
Self-Concept Role Style	4	1	4	3	0

Karen's background suggests she would prefer a decisive role style. Her self-concept is a combination of decisive and hierarchic. This is described as a very tough style with "little tolerance for any behavior that strikes them as vacillating or confused or as indicative of partial commitment to goals" (Driver, et. al., 1993, p. 51).

Here is Karen's description of a recent experience as a producer:

> My last show, everybody was at least 20 minutes to a half hour late. They'd breeze in. One gal came in with a package—she was always getting cassettes from the Morris Agency. What she was reviewing, God only knows. Nobody had time to sit and do the project at hand because they were too busy engineering future projects or ongoing projects or God knows what else. It seems like everybody was on their way to becoming the next thing without actually spending time being this thing. We have a show to write here, folks!

Karen has worked on some excellent shows but she hasn't found much satisfaction. "My dream was to work with people I respected and I was disappointed every single time."

Karen's Operating Style	Decisive	Flexible	Hierarchic	Integrative	Systemic
Background Operating Style	2	1	3	2	2
Style Perception Operating Style	3	1	2	5	1

Although her operating style is integrative with a decisive backup, Karen's interview clearly indicated that she prefers a decisive boss. "Sometimes the Executive Producer will take up an hour looking for the right line. Nothing will suck the energy out of a room faster." She prefers a Show Runner who doesn't allow "endless debates about what should go in what shouldn't go in the script." After a while, it's "we're movin' on."

At the moment Karen is somewhat bitter because in her eyes her career is not going well. She seems obsessed with where it went wrong: "I think the conclusion I've come to was my biggest sin was not getting a show on the air. I could have gotten away with anything and no one would have cared."

Lynn

Lynn's Role Style	Decisive	Flexible	Hierarchic	Integrative	Systemic
Background Role Style	2	1	2	2	0
Self-Concept Role Style	2	3	2	5	0

Lynn's dominant role style is integrative with a flexible backup. She strongly exemplifies both the advantages and disadvantages of this style. She is a good listener, sees the big picture, is extremely creative, empathetic, informed, and open. She is very slow in her work and hates deadlines. "We had 6 weeks to write a script and our pay depended on if we finished it in 6 weeks. That was a terrible pressure situation and in a lot of cases, the pressure just made people incredibly nervous." Many writers would consider 6 weeks a long time to write a script.

Lynn's Operating Style	Decisive	Flexible	Hierarchic	Integrative	Systemic
Background Operating Style	3	3	0	2	1
Style Perception Operating Style	2	3	0	6	1

Lynn's background matches her style perception. Like her role style, she is integrative with a flexible backup.

Lynn has been a professional writer for 30 years. She has won Emmys, but at the time of our interview had been out of work for over a year. Yet she still is able to say: "I love writing something that satisfies me. I just love it."

She operates on a very intuitive level. As both a writer and a Show Runner, she valued working with others to achieve a goal most highly. Here is her description of an enjoyable egalitarian writing experience:

> That was an amazing feeling, that there was no pecking order. If you walked into a room where everybody was meeting, if you didn't know who was what, you wouldn't really know who was the writer, you wouldn't really know who was the Executive Producer, you would just see a lot of people trying.

This people-oriented approach surfaces everywhere. The most satisfying aspect of her work is to capture the essence of a moment so people experience "the mutual recognition that everybody's bonded by going through a lot of the same emotional experiences."

Overview

All four writer-producers agreed on specific characteristics they felt made a good Show Runner. These qualities included the following:

- *A willingness to include others in the decision-making process.*
- *An ability to keep decisions moving along at a pace that isn't too slow.* This suggests the most desirable bosses combined a somewhat integrative style with a decisive backup style. When Show Runners were perceived as overly dictatorial or indecisive, their staff became extremely unhappy. Writers who felt rejected and frustrated sometimes turned their anger inward on themselves and became distraught or depressed. Or they retaliated with passive-aggressive behavior toward the Show Runner.
- *A nonjudgmental atmosphere.* Creativity and comedy need a free, open atmosphere in order for writers to feel safe enough to express themselves. Karen summed it up: "Comedy is like getting naked. You cannot write when you're feeling uptight." Show Runners who reacted negatively when people pitched ideas created a tense and uncomfortable atmosphere.
- *Coolness under high pressure and time constraints.* Because the demands of the job are so stressful, Show Runners need to be able to handle pressure, which can create tremendous fatigue as the season wears on. There are often serious conflicts when styles collide under these pressure-cooker conditions.

CONCLUSION

We started this project expecting the bulk of the answers to focus on specific factors in the writing process, such as plot and humor. What emerged from the interviews was clear evidence that the creative decision-making process is embedded in a culture and environment that influences the writing process. Others have noted that a major problem when analyzing group decision making is the large number of variables involved (Levine & Morland, 1990; Nemiro & Runco, in press). That certainly applied to the present project. Fortunately a number of the observations shared by the writers interviewed were cogent and provided an initial framework for examining the creative collaborative process in writing.

As should be clear from our discussion, the job of Show Runner encompasses a number of activities and abilities that have nothing to do with writing—constructive criticism, collaboration, and decision-making. Yet people are promoted to Show Runner because of their writing ability. One problem that may result was noted by Perkins (1981) when he pointed out that it is one thing to criticize but another to produce. Runco and Chand (1994) applied similar logic to explain why some creative persons may not be good judges of the creative work of others. They cited research (e.g., Runco, McCarthy, & Svensen, 1992) showing professional artists to be questionable judges. These differences are pertinent because a good writer might not be all that capable of doing the other things a Show Runner should be doing.

Some organizations have become aware of the dangers in assuming a competent individual can easily learn a new job "on their feet," and they now supply training to cope with their new responsibilities. In an industry where success is a rare and valuable commodity, and millions of dollars are spent on every show, it makes sense for studios and networks to consider investing in teaching their new Show Runners skills they will need to be effective.

The respondents gave clear indications of the areas that they feel are important. These include communication skills, developing a positive environment, keeping the pace of decisions moving along, including the staff in decision making, and recognizing the needs of individual members of the team. Another area that demands improvement is the relationship between studio and network executives and Show Runners. Many executives are viewed as incompetent outsiders because they give advice to professionals without understanding what they are doing. It is like hiring a surgeon and then telling him or her how to operate on you—it makes no sense. This tradition probably dates back to the early days of movies when the owners hired writers and producers and told them what to do. In his book about ABC, NBC, and CBS, Auleta (1991) concluded that the networks were largely out of control of the new owners who had just bought them. Yet every time it seems that networks are about to be forced to change, the economy improves and advertising revenue bails them out. Two of the three networks have once again become very profitable. However, as competition in TV increases, networks will eventually be required to develop a higher success rate in order to maintain their present profitability. They need to experiment with new ways of doing things. NBC has already shown a willingness to change by breaking the tradition of segregating executives into strict categories of comedy and drama.

There are two possible ways to improve liaisons with Show Runners. One is to hire writers or people who have demonstrated knowledge of the writing process to become executives. The second is to have executives learn more about the writing process. If their suggestions to Show Runners are more knowledgeable, they might be seen more as allies than as the enemy. The result could be a much healthier relationship, which might help relieve a small part of the stress the Show Runner experiences. It is evident that Show Runners are under an incredible amount of pressure, which can ultimately lessen their effectiveness and the quality of the programs they manage. Perhaps Show Runners could be provided with support they trust so they can deal with staff problems with less stress for everyone involved. If there are sports psychologists, why not show-business psychologists?

Studios and executives might consider new ways to staff shows. Besides the addition of a business psychologist, as we just proposed, another example is to have multiple Show Runners with their own smaller teams producing fewer episodes of the same series. What the research in this chapter makes clear is that there is a great deal of pain and uncertainty in the production of situation comedy shows. Some of it can no doubt be avoided.

Future studies could answer a number of questions, some with qualitative and some with more traditional quantitative research. Are there differences between Show Runners on the exceptionally good programs and the weaker shows? Runco (1995) found the most creative artists in a large organization to be the least satisfied—is the same true in comedy writing? What are the elements involved in keeping a writer's room energetic and productive? What is the cognitive process writers experience when they are collaborating in a group? Does a happier, less stressed staff produce better creative work? Can productive and effective studio or network management be accurately predicted?

This chapter offers a first glimpse at a system that has produced some good results but is extraordinarily costly in both monetary and human capital. When creative talent is wasted because conditions are not favorable, both the individual and society suffer. We need to understand more about creativity and the factors that contribute to nourishing it. Researching and understanding more about the creative decision-making process in situation comedy writing could have implications for other potentially creative collaborative efforts (cf. Abra, 1993), including those in education, industry, and government.

REFERENCES

Abra, J. (1993). Collaboration in creative work. *Creativity Research Journal, 7*, 1–20.

Amabile, T. M., & Gryskiewicz, N. D. (1989). The creative environment scales: Work environment inventory. *Creativity Research Journal, 2*, 231–253.

Ancona, D.G. (1987). Groups in organizations. In C. Hendrick (Ed.), *Group processes and intergroup relations* (pp. 207–230). Newbury Park, CT: Sage.

Auletta, K. (1991). *Three blind mice: How the TV networks lost their way.* New York: Random House.

Barron, F. (1961). Creative vision and expression in writing and painting. *The creative person* (pp. II-1-II-19). Berkeley: University of California.

Barron, F. (1972). *Artists in the making.* New York: Seminar Press.

Cannon-Bowers, J. A., Oser, R., & Flanagan, D. L. (1992). Work teams in industry: A selected review and proposed framework. In R. W. Swezey & E. Salas (Eds.), *Teams: Their training and performance* (pp. 355–77). Norwood, NJ: Ablex.

deCock, C., & Rickards, T. (in press). In M. A. Runco (Ed.), *Creativity research handbook* (vol. 1). Cresskill, NJ: Hampton Press.

Driver, M. J., Brousseau, K. R., & Hunsaker, P. L. (1993). *The dynamic decision maker.* San Francisco: Jossey Bass.

Ferber, E. (1963). *A kind of magic.* Garden City, NY: Doubleday.

Garfield, E. (1980). The crime of pun-ishment. *Current Contents, 27*, 3–7.

Hoffman, L. R., & Clark, M.M. (1979). Participation and influence in problem-solving groups. In L. R. Hoffman (Ed.), *The group problem solving process: Studies of a valence model,* (pp. 82–97). New York: Praeger.

Hoffman, L. R., & Maier, M. R. F. (1964). Valence in the adoption of solutions by problem-solving groups: Concept, method and results. *Journal of Abnormal and Social Psychology, 69*, 264–71.

Jackson, J. M., & Padgett, V. R. (1982). With a little help from my friend: Social loafing and the Lennon-McCartney songs. *Personality and Social Psychology Bulletin, 8*, 672–77.

Kellogg, R. T. (1994). *The psychology of writing.* New York: Oxford University Press.

Kerr, N. L. (1983). Motivation losses in small groups: A social dilemma analysis. *Journal of Personality and Social Psychology, 45*, 819–828.

Kerr, N. L., & Bruun, S. I. (1983). Dispensability of member effort and group motivation losses: Free rider effects. *Journal of Personality and Social Psychology, 44*, 78–94.

Laughlin, P. R. & McGlynn R. P. (1986). Collective induction: Mutual group and individual influence by exchange of hypotheses and evidence. *Journal of Experimental Social Psychology, 22*, 567–89.

Levine, J. M., & Moreland, R. L. (1990). Progress in small group research. *Annual Review of Psychology, 41*, 585–634.

Marx, S., & Clayton, J. (1976). *Rodgers & Hart: Bewitched, bothered and bedeviled.* New York: G.P. Putnam's.

Meredith, S. (1974). *George S. Kaufman and his friends.* Garden City, NY: Doubleday.

Moscovici, S., & Zavalloni, M. (1969). The group as a polarizer of attitudes. *Journal of Personality and Social Psychology, 12*, 125–35.

Nemiro, J., & Runco, M. A. (in press). Creativity and innovation in small groups. *Creativity and Innovation Management*.

Nolan, F. (1978). *The sound of their music: The story of Rodgers and Hammerstein*. New York: Walker & Company.

Perkins, D. (1981). *The mind's best work*. Cambridge: Harvard University Press.

Rodgers, R. (1975). *Musical stages: An autobiography of Richard Rodgers*. New York: Random House.

Rosenburg, D. (1991). *Fascinating rhythm: The collaboration of George and Ira Gershwin*. New York: Dutton.

Rubenson, D. L., & Runco, M. A. (1995). *Creativity and Innovation Management, 4*, 232–241.

Runco, M. A. (1995). The creativity and job satisfaction of artists in organizations. *Empirical Studies of the Arts, 13*, 39–45.

Runco, M. A., & Chand, I. (1994). Problem finding, evaluative thinking, and creativity. In M. A. Runco (Ed.), *Problem finding, problem solving, and creativity* (pp. 40–76). Norwood, NJ: Ablex.

Runco, M. A., McCarthy, K. A., & Svensen, E. (1994). Judgments of the creativity of artwork from students and professional artists. *Journal of Psychology, 128*, 23–31.

Runco, M. A., & Smith, W. R. (1992). Interpersonal and intrapersonal evaluations of creative ideas. *Personality and Individual Differences, 13*, 295–302.

Sawyer, R. K. (1992). Improvisational creativity: An analysis of jazz performance. *Creativity Research Journal, 5*, 253–263.

Sniezek, J. (1992). Groups under uncertainty: An examination of confidence in group decision making. *Organizational Behavior and Human Decision Processes, 52*, 124–55.

Stasser, G. (1992). Information salience and the discovery of hidden profiles by decision-making groups: A "thought experiment." *Organizational Behavior and Human Decision Processes, 52*, 156–81.

Streufert, S., & Nogami, G. (1992). Cognitive complexity and team decision making. In R. W. Swezey & E. Salas (Eds.), *Teams: Their training and performance* (pp. 127–151) Norwood, NJ: Ablex.

Tversky, A., & Sattath, S. (1979). Preference trees. *Psychological Review, 86*, 542–73.

Wallace, D. (1991). The genesis and microgenesis of creative insight. *Creativity Research Journal, 3*, 41–50.

Witt, L. A., & Boerkem, M. N. (1989). Climate for creative productivity as a predictor of research usefulness and organizational effectiveness in an R&D organization. *Creativity Research Journal, 2*, 30–40.

chapter 7

Creativity in Ubakala, Dallas Youth, and Exotic Dance*

Judith Lynne Hanna
University of Maryland

Dr. Hanna is an anthropologist. She has written numerous books, including To Dance Is Human: A Theory of Nonverbal Communication; Dance, Sex, and Gender; *and* The Performer-Audience Connection: Emotion to Metaphor in Dance and Society. *In addition to her academic research and teaching, she has been a dancer, an arts consultant, and a civil servant specialist at the U.S. Department of Education. She begins this chapter by presenting a framework for the analysis of creativity in dance, defining dance as a form of human behavior. She summarizes the symbolic devices that are used in dance worldwide, and the ways that meaning is encapsulated in dance.*

Dr. Hanna then applies this framework to data that she has gathered in three different ethnographic studies, to demonstrate how creativity in dance relates to the cultural, social, and economic context, to the symbolic norms of the dance genre, and to the goals of the individuals participating in the dance. These genres include the Nigerian dances of the Ubakala Igbo, the spontaneous, self-created playground, classroom, and hallway dances of African-American children in a desegregated elementary school in Texas, and exotic dance in urban America. Using these examples, Dr. Hanna is able to show how individual creativity, in each case, works within a complex set of situational factors, and how dance is a symbolic medium where individuals creatively negotiate meaning and context.

These themes are found in many of the other chapters in this volume, particularly those that focus on stage performance, including the three chapters on musical improvisation and Sawyer's chapter on improvisational theater. At a theoretical level, Hanna's focus on the importance of the body in dance meshes well with Crease's phenomenological focus on performance.

---

*I appreciate the helpful comments of R. Keith Sawyer.

INTRODUCTION

I n this article, I will illustrate creativity in dance by drawing on my fieldwork on (a) the dances of the Ubakala Igbo of eastern Nigeria, (b) children's self-created dances in a desegregated school in Dallas, Texas, and (c) exotic dance (adult entertainment), in Seattle, Washington, and other sites nationwide. As an anthropologist, I draw upon psychobiology, cultural anthropology, and sociolinguistics to understand creativity. I try to show how psychobiological and sociocultural factors combine in performance.

From a multicultural perspective, dance can be conceptualized as human behavior composed of purposeful, intentionally rhythmical, and culturally influenced sequences of nonverbal body movements. The movements are other than ordinary motor activities, the motion (in time, space, and with effort) having inherent and "aesthetic" value (i.e., notion of appropriateness and competency held by the dancer's culture) and symbolic potential. Purpose is from the dancer's perspective, usually shared by the audience members of the dancer's culture.

This concept of dance (Hanna, 1987) recognizes a dancer's purpose may be to play with movement itself, to provide an emotional experience, or to conceptualize through movement. Both individual creativity and the dancer's cultural influences are integral to the concept. By culture I mean the values, beliefs, norms, and rules shared by a group and learned through communication. Members of the group acquire cognitive or mental "maps" enabling them to act appropriately and to interpret what they view.

Culture affects who dances what, why, how, when, where, with, and for whom, and the audience's role. Moreover, culture shapes what are permissible gestures, locomotion, and postures with different body parts in time and space and with effort, how these dance elements are interpreted, and the embedding of meaning in different devices and spheres of encoding movement. Time elements of dance include tempo, momentum, duration, accent, and meter; spatial include the body moving to create level, design, focus, floor patterns, and body shape. Effort refers to the potential for activity or passivity, strong to gentle force, and other movement qualities. When dances share characteristics within a tradition, a dance form or genre results.

There are at least six symbolic *devices* for conveying meaning that may be utilized in dance.

1. A *concretization* is movement that produces the outward aspect of something. For example, Ubakala warrior dances display advance and retreat battle tactics. Ubakala women mimetically cradle an infant in the dance-plays celebrating birth.

2. The *icon* represents most properties or formal characteristics of something and is responded to as if it were what it represents. Illustrative is a Haitian possessed by Ghede, god of love and death, who manifests his presence through dance and whom the Haitians treat with genuine awe and gender-appropriate behavior as if he were the god.

3. A *stylization* encompasses arbitrary and conventional gestures or movements. In their dances, Ubakala youth move the pelvic girdle and upper torso vigorously to highlight secondary sex characteristics and their potential for fertile marriages; women symbolize fertility stylistically with torso undulations and hip shifts to mark a woman's elevated prestige and status with the birth of a child (rebirth of an ancestor).

4. A *metonym* is a motional conceptualization of one thing representing another of which it is a part, or with which it is associated in the same frame of reference. As specialized cultural motion, Ubakala dance is metonymical to the motion of life and the Ubakala ethos of action. The processes of reproduction and recreation in the human-supernatural cyclical pattern of reincarnation merge, and the ancestors continue their existence in the dancers' bodies.

5. The expression of one thought, experience, or phenomenon in place of another that it resembles to suggest an analogy is a *metaphor*, the bringing together of different domains in often unexpected and creative ways. Among the Ubakala, dancing to celebrate the birth of a child serves as a metaphor for safe passage to different villages, achieving wealth and prestige, and fruitful parent-child and husband-wife relations. In the past, one obtained protection to visit and trade in villages other than one's own through marriage. Strangers were liable to be captured and sold into slavery or buried to accompany a prestigious deceased individual in the journey to the ancestor world. The dance for the newborn celebrates an increased labor force and the potential for wealth. Furthermore, the dance confirms family bonds: A parent properly cares for a child so the child may in turn play a reciprocal role in the parent's old age, second burial, and reincarnation (requiring the child's marriage and procreation). The dance is a vivid metaphor of the unity of lineage, past and present. Contrastive movement patterns are metaphors for distinct social and biological roles. When the women are the life-giving mothers, they dance slowly in circles with fluidity. When the men are the life-taking warriors, they dance rapidly in lines with tension.

6. An *actualization* is a portrayal of one or several of a dancer's usual roles. This device occurs, especially in theatrical settings without rigid boundary between performer and spectator, when dancers

express their own sexual preferences through dance and the audience member accepts or rejects the dancer.

The above six devices for encapsulating meaning in dance seem to operate within one or more of eight *spheres*:

1. An example of the meaning of dance being in the dance *event* is when Ubakala attend a dance to signal sexual or marital availability and to find partners, dancing itself being incidental.
2. The meaning of dance may be in the sphere of the total human *body in action*, as in female or male self-presentation or spectator watching. Ubakala believe a person's value and behavioral characteristics are revealed in the dance.
3. The *whole pattern* of the *performance*, which may emphasize structure, style, feeling, or drama, may be the locus of meaning for participants and observers.
4. Meaning may be centered in the *sequence of unfolding movement*, including who does what to whom and how, in dramatic episodes.
5. Specific *movements* and how they are performed may carry meaning. Illustratively, an Ubakala male dancer brandishes a machete to celebrate victory. A female dancer cradles an imaginary child to celebrate fertility. Youth vigorously shimmy the upper torso and rotate the pelvis to direct attention to pubescent body changes and potential fertility.
6. The *intermesh of movements* with other communication modes such as speech or costume may be where meaning lies. Ubakala dance into a circle as they sing "Ubakala, we are coming. Eh! I am coming, peace be with you as we come together. . . . Praise to the woman expert in bearing children."
7. Meaning may be in the sphere of dance as a *vehicle for another medium*, like dance serving as a backdrop for a performer's poetry or rap recitation.
8. The sphere of meaning may be centered in *presence*, the emotionality of projected sensuality, raw animality, charisma, or "the magic of dance."

In the ontology of a dance, a dancer translates experience or understanding from one or more systems of signs to another. The dancer's body is a sign at the same time that it is a medium through which one thing signifies something else to a viewer. Effective communication, of course, depends upon shared knowledge between dancer and audience and the interplay between the skill of dance expression and a sensitive perception.

Acquisition of Dance

Knowledge of dance is passed from one generation to another through such means as (a) direction, (b) modeling (providing illustration for observational learning), (c) supervised practice and coaching, and (d) enabling discovery (creating situations in which the student manipulates material in response to a problem, such as how many ways you can turn).

Individuals also learn on their own. They may gain inspiration from (a) their environment—home, street, school, TV, film, or clubs, (b) other dancers, and (c) their dreams and other personal experience.

Dances, and their various components, may be imposed by individuals or groups, be borrowed voluntarily, be an elaborated creation, or be independently invented.

Creativity

Creativity, with the implication of imaginativeness, originality, and novelty, is any idea or practice that is perceived by people to be new (Runco & Albert, 1990; Gardner, 1993). Creativity in dance may be part of a problem-solving process. Dancers may be inspired to be creative, usually in response to mood, music, and audience reaction (Hanna, 1983). Creativity may involve the manipulation of elements of movement; who participates when, where, and why; body parts used and emphasized; costume; staging; and the means of encoding and decoding meaning. Even in a set rehearsed dance, the performer has leeway for creativity in how it is performed.

For creative innovations to spread, they are usually introduced by a notable example and publicized through performance at a notable event or the media. Impediments include laws and social and moral standards in addition to styles too dissonant from expectations (Meyer, 1967).

Psychological processes that generate creative dances are the same ones that generate creative verbal communication in speaking and writing. Dance, indeed, bears similarities to verbal language. Both require the same underlying faculties for conceptualization, creativity, and memory. Both have a vocabulary (steps and gestures in dance), a grammar (rules for putting the vocabulary together), and a semantics (meaning). Dance, however, assembles these elements in a manner that more often resembles poetry, with its multiple, symbolic, and elusive meanings, than it resembles prose, which is more explicit and literal. Dance is not, as conventional wisdom has it, a universal language—there are distinct languages and dialects of dance. Most Americans, for instance, do not understand the *mudras* (symbolic gestures) of classical Indian dance.

Structuralists like Jean Piaget, Noam Chomsky, and Claude Lévi-Strauss assume that the mind operates according to specifiable rules that may be out of awareness. These determine the use of the body, and hence the characteristics of the dance. Several other scholars recognize the human ability to select various kinds of symbol systems within established traditions and conventions. Consequently, a "new" work can only be understood in relation to what prevails. Studies of creative people in the United States suggest that they remember, notice, recognize patterns, apprehend a thing or situation objectively, are flexible, spontaneous, vigorous, and open to advice (Perkins, 1981).

Most interactions among people display improvisational elements, and dance is usually a social interaction. Dancers creatively construct meaning and identity in response to the dynamics of culture (Hanna, 1988c). Creativity leads to new nonverbal configurations in which the dancer (often the same person as the choreographer or dance maker) makes symbols, intentionally or otherwise, on and with the body. Dance makers are influenced by their contemporaries; the institutional settings that provide for the creation, distribution, and evolution of dance; and audience reaction. A people's basic cultural assumptions and orientations, the proscriptions and prescriptions—as well as the seeds of their destruction or alteration—emerge in the dance mode of communication. Dancers may rebel and offer alternatives to the status quo. The cultural terrain is often marked by contestation and struggle, a polarity between those who embrace and those who fear the imagination and intellectual growth.

In Appendix A, I have presented movement categories and in Appendix B, a semantic grid, which can be referred to during the following discussion of three forms of dance: Ubakala, children's, and exotic.

DANCES OF THE UBAKALA IGBO OF NIGERIA

Dance among the Ubakala Igbo of Nigeria is a language of persuasion and control. Its performance not only reflects what is but also suggests what could be.

Values Conveyed Through Dance

The Ubakala refer to their dance as *nkwa*, which in Igbo can mean a "play," a "drum," a "dance," a set of dances, or any combination of these. Highlighting sex, gender, life, and death, dance serves as a vehicle through which paradoxical, contradictory values and organizing principles of social life can be expressed, taught, and mediated (Hanna, 1987, 1988a, 1988b, in press-c). The dance medium is similar to television news and commentary. Dances are held on the periodic market days that the Ubakala are expected to attend. As a result, many of the dances have a captive audience.

The fundamental and contradictory values of the Ubakala guide social behavior. However, the pursuit of one part of an antinomy to the exclusion of another creates social drama. In such a context, the dance is used to adjust imbalances and work through the dialectics of social life. This is especially true for the women and youth groups who are excluded from formal, society-wide, decision-making structures.

These dances symbolically represent five basic principles that seem to suffuse Ubakala life: (a) fertility and continuity, (b) egalitarianism and orientation toward competitive achievement, (c) innovation and group advancement, (d) respect for seniority, and (e) reciprocity. From another perspective the dances are continuity, competition, innovation, respect, and reciprocity. The *nkwa* contributes to the ordering of social relations through communication in song text and dance themes about the limits and contours of social roles; through the participation criteria for different dances; and through the correlations of movement style and structure, music, and costume to social roles. A few examples of these stimuli for creativity follow.

Fertility and Continuity

The importance of fertility and continuity are conveyed through dances that celebrate birth and death. The traditional performances for birth are also used in other contexts, such as the building of a hospital, the welcoming of a newly graduated barrister, or the celebrating of Christmas.

Women often create movements and song texts based on current events to promote established social roles. In "Onu Ahula Onye Ije?" ("Have You Seen a Traveler?") the women present a paradigm of behavior in gesture and song. A young married woman takes a short journey going about her business, and is confronted by a rather bold, unknown young man. She bids him let her go, threatens to tell her husband, and in fact speaks with the voice and authority that her husband gives her. The dance is designed to educate young women; the assumption is that when the lesson is remembered, marital stability will not be disrupted because the wife will know how to be faithful.

Egalitarianism and Orientation Toward Competitive Achievement

Perceived violation of these values catalyze creativity. The most notorious case of dance as a medium of "lobbying" is the 1929 "women's war" in which a creative dance was the vehicle for protest against the British colonial rule that eroded the traditional egalitarianism and competitive achievement. In 1923, the British government introduced taxation, which was applicable solely to men. Late in 1929, women incorrectly believed that this tax was to be extended to them. They viewed taxation as an infringement upon their economic competitive patterns, having begun to amass considerable wealth through the growing trade in palm kernels, a woman's crop.

Since women had not become representatives of the colonial government, as Nigerian men had, they did not see the benefits from the imposition of taxes. Indeed, the British had appointed chiefs who were no longer responsible to the people. So the women "sat on a man," which usually worked to resolve conflicts; the government representative was kept from sleeping and carrying out his usual tasks as the women danced and sang all night outside his house. They quickly improvised songs to meet the situation. However, the communication went unheeded, and the women went on a rampage. Repercussions were widespread both on the local and "international" levels. The women moved the mighty British to alter their colonial administration of Eastern Nigeria (Nwabara, 1965; Gailey, 1970; Van Allen, 1972; Ifeka-Moller, 1975; O'Barr, 1984).

Innovation and Group Advancement

By improvising song texts, performers allude to people who are behaving in ways that retard innovation and group advancement, preventing others from acquiring power and material goods. The dance entitled "Omerigbo," meaning "Champion of Igbo," has the phrase, "You don't allow water to splash on us, we're in the boat," that is, don't spoil things. The "Zik Neme ka Odi Mma" ("Zik Tries to Make Things Good") dance has the sung phrase, "Don't sell the eating spoon."

Original creation and importation of dances gleaned from being "abroad" (visiting other areas) characterize creativity in the youth dances. These dances are a response to individual preferences and social and environmental pressures, and, in general, the dynamics of life's opportunities.

A popular teen dance draws its inspiration from the Ijaw people with whom the Ubakala have had numerous contacts. Dancers shimmy the upper torso and bounce their buttocks as they take small steps to the right, facing into a circle with their torsos at a right angle to the ground. The teenagers openly express themselves, displaying their sexual attractiveness and exhibiting their dancing skill, reflective of personal qualities. Their upper torso shimmy and pelvic rotations direct attention to pubescent body changes, the energy and strength for procreation and nurturance, along with the emergence of a new generation with its own innovations.

Teenagers of other villages, as well as marriage brokers, are attracted to the dance performance. In addition, the dance performance provides one of the few opportunities for young men and women to gain public recognition for their creativity.

The Nkwa Edere is a young girls' dance the Ubakala consider to be beautiful and a novelty. "Edere" refers to shaking the upper torso uniformly and symmetrically. In one of the dances, through parody, girls mime the "immoral" heterosexual physical contact of Europeans. Public physical contact between men and women is not traditionally approved, so that the embracing European ballroom dance positions, which seem too publicly intimate, is a subject of mimicry and parody.

At another level, the young girls are emotionally anticipating courtship in general, new ways of courtship in particular, married life in urban areas, and Western institutions. The fear of embracing and caressing in public, or of observing such activity, is partially overcome through the dance. Girls caressing each other is a less threatening event than boys and girls behaving similarly in public events in the *nkwa* medium. The Nkwa Edere is a channel for introducing change not only in the dance but in the larger society.

Respect for Seniority

The improvised themes of youth dances about chiefs, men's productivity in growing yams, and properly greeting one's elders and chiefs manifest respect. For example, in the dance "Unu Ahula Eze Anya Nabia" ("You Have Seen Our Chief Coming"), the song text includes these courteous and endearing phrases: "Come respect him," "Come recognize the chief," "Come open the door," and "Come pet his neck."

Reciprocity

The principle of reciprocity is a stimulus to creativity. Illustratively, if not received in a friendly manner when performing their dance to communicate important news, the performers express their displeasure by singing of the misdemeanor for all to hear.

Conclusion

Dancers perform known dance movement and song to socialize both young and old alike to the traditional norms of the culture. At the same time, each new generation is expected to introduce innovation. Ubakala allow a special kind of license in the dance that protects the individual and group from libel. Through dance movement, song text, and place of performance, women and young people can speak publicly, venting strong emotions without breaking those norms of etiquette related to interactions with males and seniors. Thus, there are digs at the conceited, protests against the overbearing, and movement and song text novelties for the community. But the *nkwa* has the potential for more than catharsis; it can guard against the misuse of power and produce social change without violence. Ubakala believe the youth reveal their personalities in the dance—their skill, creativity, and leadership in dance are indicators of how they will perform as marital partners and adult members of a democratic community. "No one knows the womb that bears the chief," say the Ubakala. And the dance, mostly play and pleasure, is not only an educational and display medium, but a key vehicle for protest and conflict resolution.

AFRICAN-AMERICAN CHILDREN'S SELF-CREATED DANCE

Children's spontaneous dance in a desegregated elementary school can be seen as a creative commentary on race relations, patterns of authority, and personal identity (Hanna, 1986, 1988a). Through dance, song, and mime, youngsters impulsively perform in school classrooms, in halls, and on the playground. Students create their own meaningful realm in play that is outside the formal educational relationship of adult teacher and child.

Several psychologists have provided relevant theoretical and empirical work on children's creative symbolization, which helps us understand how they are able to convey meaning through dance. In 1908 Sigmund Freud wrote, "Every child at play behaves like the creative writer, in that he creates a world of his own, or rather, rearranges the things of his world in a way that pleases him" (1958, p. 45). As a form of play, children's spontaneous dance is a vehicle for intuition and fantasy. Jean Piaget (1962; Levy 1978) believed that play acts are characterized by the primacy of assimilation over accommodation. Accommodation refers to a child modifying his teacher's instructions. Assimilation, seen in the children's dance, means the child incorporates elements of the outside world into his or her own view of reality and standards. Play, according to Jerome Bruner and his colleagues, is problem-solving (1976, p. 244 and passim). Rudolf Arnheim calls the creativity found in children's dance "a kind of reasoning...either intellectual or perceptual" (1972, p. 287). Howard Gardner (1973) with Dennie Wolf (Wolf & Gardner, 1980) translate two major views of human development, the cognitive approach of Jean Piaget and the affective view of Erik Erikson (who extended the work of Freud), into a model for the emergence of artistry. The phases they posit to characterize the child's development toward symbolic action support the theory of children's capability for creative symbolization in dance.

Other relevant research comes from studies of children who disrupt the classroom (Long, Morse, & Newman, 1976). Because children often learn that in our verbally oriented society the spoken word can be held against them as self-incriminating evidence, they use nonverbal forms of expression, including dance, to express themselves.

Dance on the Playground

At Pacesetter Elementary School in Dallas, Texas, during recess outdoors on a warm sunny day, groups of African-American girls spontaneously organized dances. Using the spatial form of children's dances probably of British origin and learned from white Americans, African-Americans meshed the African style of loose, flexible torso, extending and flexing knees with an easy breathing quality, shuffling steps, and pelvic swings and thrusts. Thus they created syncretistic dances of the sort that have been described as ring and line plays (Jones & Hawes, 1972, pp. 67–68). A leader either sang a phrase that the group answered or the leader led the performers. Movements accompanied and accented the song text or illustrated it. Hand clapping or other body percussion punctuated the performance to create a syncopated rhythm within the song and dance.

In one instance, when a white girl wished to join the African-American girls in one of the dances, an African-American girl stepped back, put her hands on her hips, and looked the white girl up and down about the hips and feet. Then, with a quizzical look and scowl, she said loudly for all to hear: "Show me you can dance!" Everyone watched as the white girl withdrew to the sidelines.

Later a different white girl joined the "Check Me" ring play in which the name of each participant in the circle was singled out in turn, going to the right. One girl's name was called by the girl standing to her immediate left; she identified herself, sang a refrain, and then called on the girl to her right.

Example one: "Check Me" ring play

Check, <clap>, check <clap>, check <clap>
My name is Tina,
I am a Pisces.
I want you to <clap>
check, check, check,
to check out Bridgette.
Check <clap>, check <clap>, check.

My name is Bridgette...

When it was the white girl's turn to be called, the African-American girl just passed her by and called the next African-American girl. Rejected, the white girl called out, "I can do it, too!" No one paid attention.

Dance in the Classroom

Let's look at another example. One day, during an unusual second-grade classroom period before the teacher had established control, several African-American children yelled out remarks and walked about the room. They played with furniture pretending it was gymnastic, musical, or military equipment, and pushed, pulled, or hit others. An African-American boy tried to cut a white girl's blond hair. An African-American girl kept talking loudly. In response to the white teacher's question, "Would you like to go out?" the youngster got up from her chair and walked into the aisle, where she stood, feet apart and knees bent. She brought her knees together and apart four times while crossing her hands together and apart in unison with her knees in a Charleston step. Then she scurried back to her assigned seat and sat down. Moments later she skipped to the door, opened it, picked up a book lying outside, and ran back to her place. Then she stood up on the chair seat and performed what in ballet is called an arabesque. Standing on the ball of one foot, she lifted the other leg backward as high as she could, one arm held diagonally up and forward, the other diagonally down. From this position she laughingly lost her balance and fell to the floor. The teacher picked her up and carried her out of the classroom. During the girl's performance, her peers gave her their undivided attention.

Dance in the Halls

Here's yet another illustration: At least once a week I saw one to six African-American children at a time spontaneously dance a few steps in short sequences in a variety of situations both inside and outside the classrooms in ways that did not disrupt formal teaching and learning. For example, as a second-grade class was being dismissed, one black boy exited performing a Charleston step three times (standing with feet apart, knees came together and apart as arms crossed in opposition to knees). This was the same step the African-American girl performed in the second illustration. After the first boy exited, a second African-American boy followed performing the same movement phrase. The sequences occurred repeatedly until six African-American boys had left the classroom. In a fourth-grade music class, several African-American boys "bebopped" (rhythmically walked) to the admiring looks of their peers. One African-American boy walked with exaggerated hip shifts, the upper and lower torso moving in opposition; another boy walked about while shimmying his shoulders. A third sat snapping his fingers and then got up and performed a step-kick walking dance sequence. A fourth boy shook his arms and rippled his torso. On another occasion, as a sixth-grade class was going through the halls to the cafeteria, several African-American boys and girls performed a variety of dance movement phrases.

What Is the Meaning of These Exchanges?

The historical context is illuminating. Pacesetter School is located in an African-American community that was created in the 1950s as a consequence of white terrorism and fire bombing of African-American homes that were purchased or being built in formerly all-white residential areas. Desegregation took away the African-Americans' control of the formerly segregated school. A five-year-long U.S. Justice Department civil rights effort culminated in a court case that led to the creation of a magnet school that required whites to be bused voluntarily to it.

Whites who volunteered to attend the school were interested in interracial mixing. Yet little interracial mixing was evident when African-American children would choose seats or partners for an activity. After all, black-white proximity in the past led to harassment of blacks, and, consequently, the black community was not unanimously in favor of having a desegregated magnet school. Because the territory occupied by African-Americans is historically small and precarious, it has been especially treasured. Thus the children's use of space, including their cutting shapes in space through dance, became especially endowed with meaning.

Many low-income youngsters neither value the pursuit of academic excellence nor do what is necessary to earn high marks. Indeed, at Pacesetter, some children devalued and belittled the ethics and activities of formal schooling. In spite of the low esteem some African-American children have for academic success, they are nonetheless sensitive to public revelation, such as in oral recitation, of their inadequate school work. This leads some of them to face-saving behavior, or what Bernard Siegel (1970) has described as defensive structuring that occurs among groups under stress and with limited resources. They seek arenas in which they can dominate and gain recognition; they attempt to establish a prideful group identity when they perceive external threats to that identity. This process involves the subordination of the individual to the group as it cooperatively masters challenges.

Expressive symbolic behavior, such as dance or athletics, are acceptable arenas for mastery that reinforces an individual's sense of being the kind of person that "significant others"—his or her peers—esteem. Through dance themes, participation criteria, and places of performance in a white-controlled school system, youngsters identified themselves as distinct from the "shuffling black" stereotypes of earlier historical periods and from the whites of today. They declared a wished-for privileged status and, in a sense, they attained it.

What are the fundamental bases of dance as a form for creativity, compensation, or defensive structuring? The primordial and most vital marker of identity consists of the ready-made set of endowments that each individual shares at birth with members of the group; the body itself "is at once the most intimate and inward and the most obvious and outward aspect of how we see ourselves, how we see others, and how others see us" (Isaacs, 1975, p. 47). The body in motion arrests even greater attention, for it implies a change in environmental conditions that may require reaction for one's safety. Easily perceptible, dancing readily attracts notice. If one has few material possessions and little power, as is the case with oppressed minorities and with children, the body and its use are likely to become particularly important. The significance of the African-American "body in motion" has roots in Africa, the American slave auction block, and antebellum labor markets. As is the case for the Ubakala Igbo described earlier, many African societies from which African-Americans originally came view the body in motion, especially in dancing, as predictive of an individual's personality, work capability, and creativity.

African-American girls at Pacesetter, for instance, asserted African-American power, in-group exclusivity and superiority, and the possibility of reversed black/white power relations. It seems reasonable to conclude that the African-American children's dance movements, contexts, and participation criteria creatively symbolized and mediated existing and possible social relations made visibly vital with prophetic yearnings. The children's social world embodied the image of possible adult life. Dancing at Pacesetter was concerned with respect and mutual recognition that positions of power and influence may be reversed or at least moderated. At Pacesetter this behavior did not mirror the concepts necessary to legitimize a social system of structured inequality in which they would be unequal to whites.

EXOTIC DANCE

Exotic dance (also referred to as erotic, striptease, and nude) is a stigmatized, controversial, and poorly understood form of adult entertainment in the United States. Although some dancers have danced with well-known ballet and modern dance companies, dance scholars have generally dismissed exotic dance without knowing about it. Some scholars consider it a "low" or "fringe" dance art.

The exotic dance establishments are a lightning rod for public conflicts in American society: Civil rights activists uphold dance as protected "speech" under the First Amendment of the U.S. Constitution, and certain feminists challenge religious groups and other feminists who view exotic dance as sinful and exploitative of women. Exotic dance offers the opportunity to transgress mainstream norms of sexuality and privacy; it is considered sinful or naughty to dance nude emphasizing sexuality, to look at such performers, and to engage in an economic dancer-customer transaction.

Diversity

Visiting clubs nationwide, from Seattle to Los Angeles, Las Vegas, Chicago, and New York, as well as talking with exotic dance stakeholders elsewhere, it became clear that exotic dance clubs are remarkably diverse. They vary, for example, in dancer training, physical appearance, motivation, and behavior; in hiring dancers who appear in upscale clubs on the nationwide circuit ("features") and regulars ("house girls"); in dancer-customer interaction and contact; in treatment of dancers; manager style; and in economic arrangements (clubs may be part of large corporations—one is on the stock exchange). Dancers may receive a salary from the club and tips from customers for their performances or be independent contractors paying "rent" for performance space and tipping staff, or paying a percentage of their dance sales and tips to management.

Facilities range from upscale to seedy. They may serve alcohol or be "juice bars." Some offer food. Entrance may be free or there may be a fee. Varying by gender, sex (there are transvestites and transsexuals), sexual orientation, and ethnicity, clubs primarily feature white women performing for heterosexual men (the focus of this discussion). Some clubs target gay men or lesbians, or offer men dancing for women. And there are different combinations (for example, some transvestites are part of the female dance corps and are accepted as females by the other dancers).

Performers vary educationally, including college students (Ivy League and other) and graduates (with degrees in such subjects as sociology and nursing), professionals (certified public accountant, law school intern, and stockbroker), and high school graduates and dropouts. Some performers have danced in prestigious ballet and modern dance companies or competed in gymnastics, while others have had no previous training.

Exotic dancers may or may not support boyfriends or husbands. Some dancers are battered by their male companions and forced to dance, although most are not. Some dancers are on drugs, but most are clean. Some dancers "hook" (prostitute), yet most do not (some clubs will fire a dancer who goes out with a club customer). Dancers may be single, married, or single mothers supporting their children.

The women dance for the money (like most jobs). Some also seek power, proudly assert their feminine sexuality, try to bolster self-esteem, or enjoy dancing. Dancers may like or dislike men.

Depending on local ordinances and club policy, dancers may retain some clothing or none and cover or flaunt their "private parts." In some clubs, dancers may not touch customers or be touched by them, while in other clubs some physical contact occurs. Dancers may be subjected to verbal and physical abuse or treated well.

Managers may be "dirty old men" or "kindly fathers." Some clubs require women to incur expenses, obey strict rules and suffer penalties for breaking them, and compete with each other through management overbooking or competitions, which may lead to their engaging in more sexual demeanor than had been customary.

The amount of government control over exotic dance clubs also varies in terms of the sale of alcohol and the opposition of local groups. Controls include the licensing of dancers, clubs, and managers; hours of operation; permissible body disclosure; kinds of exotic dance; self-touch; and distance between dancer and customer. Of course, there may be change over time in all of these variables.

Initiation

Exotic dance education comes from observation of strippers on film and in person, practice, and coaching from other dancers and club staff. Elaine said, "I was bartending. I learned just from watching for three years." A lawyer representing clubs told me he heard that there is a school for strippers somewhere in Wisconsin.

Eroticism

The semantics of exotic dance draw heavily on the metaphor and metonym of eroticism: sexuality transfigured, a representation that diverts or denies sex in action (Paz, 1995, pp. 8–9). The dancer tries to convey eroticism, desire, allure, a promise of ecstasy, the beauty of the body, and the fantasy of a romantic or noncommittal relationship: assignation, possession, foreplay, and consummation. Through a vocabulary of movements highlighting secondary and primary sex characteristics, dancers often simulate culturally specific rhythms of sexual behavior (Hanna, 1995). Costume, its color, and nudity also convey meaning; for example, white for purity, black for the night and associated lovemaking, red for passion, and nudity for intimacy and accessibility. Clothing affects the fantasy of intimacy; along with distance, it is armament that conveys unavailability and/or unapproachability. Dancers use costumes and props to create a particular image or scenario. A bikini with fluffy fringe; short dress with thigh-high leather boots, matching gloves, and spiked bracelet; and a full-length black evening gown are illustrative.

Stimuli to Creativity

Capitalism is the key stimulus to creativity. Its dimensions include the performer-audience connection, competition and other economic considerations, serendipity, personal motivation, change, and individual body shape.

Performer-Audience Relation

A dancer attempts to entice customers through the display of eroticism usually to elicit tips and sell personal dances. The aesthetic of exotic dance focuses on sensuality, beauty of the body, musicality, and the repertoire and quality of movement.

The performer-audience connection (Hanna, 1983b) of mutual fantasy depends on the dancer receiving feedback to validate the desirability, passion, and adoration she must project. Moreover, a patron who visibly or audibly manifests interest in a dancer may become part of the performance for other audience members in the club who may identify with the patron. Unpredictable spontaneous exchanges between the performer and patron create entertainment value for nearby guests.

Stage dances are dances performed on a main stage, and also ministages and runways, for the audience as a whole or large portions of it. These dances serve to showcase the performer for tips and/or advertise her for individual dances. Sometimes a dancer performs for a particular customer who is at the stage. During a stage dance, a performer removes some or all of her clothing in a striptease to one to three songs. The dancer moving in intentionally rhythmical patterns may appear clothed as some character/persona, become topless, and then finish in a thong or bottomless.

Table dances are dances performed by clothed (or initially clothed) performers close to an individual audience member at his or her table or in special places in a club. The performer focuses on the particular customer's responses to send a personal message not manifestly intended for the audience as a whole: interest in and understanding of the customer. The dancer is saying, "I am for you and you alone; you're special and important"—a king or queen for the cost of a table dance. Trying to create an illusion of concern and availability for the customer, the dancer seeks to transform the patron's fantasies and feelings in order to receive tips and sell more table dances. These customers may get the personal attention of an attractive female who would not otherwise relate to them, "give them the time of day"; they are reminded of what it is to be desired.

A couch dance is similar to a table dance except the customer sits on a couch, usually in a less public area of the club. In lap dancing a dancer usually places a towel on a customer's lap, and then sits there and gyrates for tips.

The use of space and the interaction between performer and an individual customer are the most distinguishing aspects of the table dance syntax or grammar. Moving within a circumscribed space commonly of one to twenty-four inches from the customer, facing toward or away while improvising movement toward and away from the customer or side to side, the dancer emphasizes different aspects of the body in response to the patron. There is a sense of intimacy through performer-customer multisensory and proximate interaction in response to indicators of attraction and satisfaction such as the mouth position, eye brightness, pupil dilation and expansion, facial color, breathing, and perspiration.

With the exception of the poorest performers, dancers create complex syntactic sequences of movement vocabulary for stage and individual dances. In an illustrative sequence, Deborah gracefully and fluidly moves from place to place on a mirrored stage: strutting, turning, and kneeling. During this time she ripples her torso and arches forward or backward, and rotates her hips. Her hands creatively sculpt lines and curves in space, scanning them over her own body out into space and then bringing them back toward herself, pointing to erotic zones and covering them in seductiveness and modesty. (See Appendix C for some movements in the exotic dance repertoire that dancers combine, depending on their creative inspiration, ability, club policy, and legal restrictions.)

Competition

Creativity often results from dancers competing for the attention of customers who show their appreciation by giving them tips or buying special dances. Club managers may encourage creativity and even hold contests. Media attention, too, is a stimulus for innovation.

American culture places a premium on novelty. Dancers may have a set choreography and improvise, or only make use of movement ideas in response to their own mood, the music, and, of most importance, customers' expectations and reactions.

If one dancer offers more in costume, movement, music, or interpersonal interaction, then there is pressure on other dancers to be creative in order to be competitive. The women who engage in illegal activity reinforce society's low esteem of exotic dance. Elaine was outraged to learn that for $30 a dancer would take a man's penis out of his pants: "I don't like having to fight a guy off because of what some other girl does....Some girls drop their morals."

Competitive pressures can be a detriment to creativity when dancers feel they can earn more money by repeating their standard moves.

Other economic considerations also spur creativity. Because pioneer stripteaser Carrie Finnel wished to prolong a theater engagement, she took off one item of her costume and promised the audience that she would take off one item a week for the limit of her engagement, which ran 52 weeks (Corio, 1968). Sally Rand introduced the fan to cover her nude body when she took a job and could not afford to buy a costume.

Serendipity

Creativity may be serendipitous. Dancers shimmying a costume off onstage came about when Hinda Wassau, one of the first stripteasers, went onstage with a costume that would not come off (Zeidman, 1967, p. 156; Corio, 1968, p. 71). A dancer explained her serendipitous creativity:

> Sometimes I don't take anything off. I can't look out at the audience. I just have to get into the music. Sometimes I just get into it. The back of my hand. I don't think about what I do. Creativity comes on. (Personal communication, 1995)

Personal Motivation

Creativity is the result of some dancers paying homage to the gods of love, Eros and Venus, and celebrating female beauty and fecundity in their performances. A dancer said, "Striptease is our one shrine to sexual feeling and the enjoyment and celebration of sexual feeling for its own sake" (Dragu & Harrison, 1988, p. 9). The nude body can bespeak nature, honesty, innocence, and intimacy. Some dancers honor the vagina, passageway of life for everyone.

The opportunity to perform, the physical workout, the narcissistic and exhibitionist thrill of being admired and desired, the fantasy about being the most beautiful woman in the world, and the attempt to feel empowered by controlling customers are other stimuli of creativity.

Social Change

Exotic dance has an evolving style with historical roots of deviance. Behavior disapproved of by mainstream society is an integral part of the art and entertainment and part of the lure for performers and patrons alike. As nudity became accepted in mainstream media, dancers created new "naughty" moves, such as bending the torso forward, almost touching the ground, to expose the clitoris. Touching one's own body became common in both the stage and table dance (cf. Longfield, 1994, p. 9).

Individual Physical Body Shape

Creativity often results from the dancer's physical capabilities and limitations. Body shape affects creativity; a short-legged dancer does not have the lengthy leg extension of a long-legged performers. Dancers who are "double-jointed" can create unique moves. In addition, dancers have their own individual nuance of performance.

Constraints on Creativity

Societal norms about the way the body, sexuality, and women are perceived and responded to, even in the context of a "deviant" setting, set parameters for dance creativity. Laws state what is permissible.

Moreover, clubs not only have local laws to abide by, but they have their own house rules. In some cases rigid performance standards are dictated by club owners, some of whom fire strippers for merely a slight deviation from the rules.

Of course, laws and rules are usually subject to many interpretations; they are at times broken and not enforced. Another constraint may be the dancers themselves, as noted above. They may exert strong peer pressure on dance performance style and structure.

CONCLUSION

People are socialized to ways of moving. In dance, whether a folk culture in Nigeria, children's performances in a school setting, or young adults in exotic dance clubs, creativity appears to have common catalysts. These appear to be cultural expectations and constraints, competition, serendipity, personality, audience reaction, current events, and external politics (see Appendix D).

Ubakala Igbo have a guiding principle of competition, black girls competed with white youngsters, and exotic dancers compete for income. Surprises are inevitable in improvised forms. Current events and external politics are seen in democratic contests in Nigeria, segregation and desegregation processes in Dallas, and cities and states imposing restrictions on exotic dance clubs.

Exotic dance differs from the other dance forms I have discussed in that it is professional, more directly interactive with and dependent upon audience members, and stigmatized. Mainstream society denigrates exotic dance establishments. Children, too, may be sanctioned for dancing in inappropriate places and ways. Children's own dance and exotic dance are sometimes considered as mere play and improper conduct, respectively, rather than dance.

Clearly dance is a form of communication, a barometer of life beyond dance itself. In dance discourse there is continuity and change. New elements or new works can be understood only in relation to what prevailed in the dance text (the style, semantics, and syntax) and its context (the ecology, history, and politics). Cultural conventions both evoke and constrain creativity.

APPENDIX A: DANCE MOVEMENT DATA CATEGORIES

Movement definition: The visual and/or kinesthetic result of energy release in time and space through muscular response to a stimulus is the essence of dance. Its structure (interrelation of parts) and style (characteristic mode and quality of all the contributing elements) can be analyzed in these terms:

Space (design):
  direction (path the moving body cuts through space)
  level (high—weight on ball of foot; low—body lowered through flexing knees; middle—normal stand; elevated; kneeling; sitting; lying)
  amplitude (size of movement, relative amount of distance covered or space enclosed by the body in action)
  focus (direction of eyes and body)
  grouping (overall spatial pattern of movement in relation to dancer, created dance space):
      free form or organized pattern (individual, couple, small group, team—linear or circular, symmetrical or asymmetrical)
      physical link (none, parts of body, length of contact)
  shape (physical contour of movement design—includes direction, level, amplitude)

Rhythm (time, flow):
  tempo (rate at which movements follow one another)
  duration (relative length of movements, patterns, performance)
  accent (rhythmically significant stress)
  meter (basic recurrent pattern of tempo, duration, and accent)

Dynamics (force, relative amount of energy, effort—tension and relaxation released by the body to accomplish movement):
  space (indulgence—minimum or maximum use; "direct" straight lines or "flexible" curves and deviations)
  flow (control, continuous transfer of energy which qualifies movement—free, unimpeded or bound, hampered)
  locomotion (means of moving from one place to another)
  projectional quality (texture produced by combination of elements—relative quickness or slowness of energy released in space)

Characteristic use of body (instrument of dance):
  posture (movement that activates or is largely supported through the whole body)
  locomotion (movement that involves a change of location of the whole body, e.g., walk, run, leap, hop, jump, skip, slide, gallop)
  gesture (movement of part of the body not supported through the whole body, e.g., rotation, flexion, extension, vibration)

APPENDIX B: SEMANTIC GRID

Semantic Grid

DEVICES		SPHERES							
		Event	Body	Whole Performance	Discursive Performance	Specific Movement	Intermesh with Other Medium	Vehicle for Other Medium	Presence
Concretization	c	★	★	★	★	★	★	—	—
	a	★	★	★	★	★	★	—	—
Icon	c	—	—	—	—	—	—	—	—
	a	—	—	—	—	—	—	—	—
Stylization	c	★	★	★	—	★	★	—	—
	a	★	★	★	—	★	★	—	—
Metonym	c	—	★	—	—	—	★	—	—
	a	★	★	★	—	—	★	—	—
Metaphor	c	—	★	—	—	★	★	—	—
	a	★	★	★	—	★	★	—	—
Actualization	c	—	—	—	—	—	—	—	—
	a	—	—	—	—	—	—	—	—

c = Conventional.
a = Autographical.
★ = Ubakala encoding.

165

APPENDIX C: SOME EXOTIC DANCE MOVEMENTS

Locomotion (movement from place to place):
strut
walk
turn
shimmy up a pole and lean back, often holding on with one hand
slide to floor
crawl
from kneeling position, move knees outward and inward
on right knee, place left foot on floor, then step with right
jump (restrained by the requisite four-inch high heels)
split
cartwheel
somersault into a split
Gesture:
self-touch:
  move hand(s) over body creating curvilinear designs
  brush stomach, breast, inner and outer thighs, genitals, buttocks
  press one's breasts together
  toss hair back with hand
  slap buttocks
  spread buttocks apart
  lick fingers
  flash (lower G-string to expose pubic area)
  open legs to reveal vagina ("spread show," "go pink")
pose, preen, pout
rotate head with loose hair
make eye contact to target and engage a customer with expectation of
  tip or sale of dance
gyrate hips and torso
thrust and rotate hips (bump and grind)
undulate body or body parts
shimmy breasts
bend torso perpendicular to ground
bend torso perpendicular to ground and
  shake buttocks
thrust buttocks toward spectator
snake arms upward
rotate knees toward and away from each other ("butterfly")
kneeling, hinge torso backwards
standing or prone, bend leg back from knee
on shoulders, extend legs up wall
hold foot and extend leg full length
swing leg over customer's head
standing, arch torso backward

bend backward (backbend) with hands and toes on floor
stand with torso bent over perpendicular to floor and extend one leg
and both arms out to side
seated with torso bent over parallel to floor, extend one leg out to
side, bend the other leg with foot toward center of body
breathe heavily
prone on floor, spread and close extended legs
prone on floor, raise buttocks up and down
pretend to be caged
supine on floor, arch torso
supine on floor, open and close extended legs
squat with knees turned outward
contract genital muscles ("wink vulva")
Level:
stand in pose
hang on a pole near ceiling
floor work (dancing off one's feet on floor or other horizontal plat-
form)

APPENDIX D: VARIABLES IN DANCE CREATIVITY

VARIABLE	NKWA	CHILDREN'S DANCE	EXOTIC DANCE
movements	X	X	X
emotional expression	excitement, pleasure, anger	excitement, pleasure, pride	eroticism
concept	traditional and current	identity, desegregation	fantasy, beauty of female
culture's response	treasured cultural expression	dismissed as frivolous play, black style	deviant, evokes legal constraint
culturally permissible movement	X	X	deviant
body part emphases	primary and secondary sex characteristics	hips, torso	primary and secondary sex characteristics
learning	observation, informal instruction	observation, informal instruction	observation, informal instruction
catalyst: current events	X	X	laws, club rules, peer pressure
cultural expectations	X	X	X
personality	X	X	X
song text	X	X	X
audience reaction	X	X	X

REFERENCES

Arnheim, R. (1972). *On inspiration: Toward a psychology of art.* Berkeley: University of California Press.

Bruner, J. S., Alison, J., & Sylva, K. (Eds.). (1976). *Play—its role in development and evolution.* New York: Basic Books.

Corio, A. (1968). *This was burlesque.* New York: Madison Square Press.

Dragu, M. and A.S.A. Harrison (1988). *Revelations: Essays on striptease and sexuality.* London, Ontario: Nightwood Editions.

Freud, S. (1958). *On creativity and the unconscious: Papers on psychology, art, literature, love, religion* (selected with introduction and annotation by Benjamin Nelson). New York: Harper & Row.

Gailey, H. A. (1970). *The road to Aba: A study of British administrative policy in eastern Nigeria.* New York: New York University Press.

Gardner, H. (1973). *The arts and human development.* New York: Wiley.

Gardner, H. (1993). *Creating minds: An anatomy of creativity seen through the lives of Freud, Einstein, Picasso, Stravinsky, Eliot, Graham, and Gandhi.* New York: Basic Books.

Hanna, J. L. (1983). *The performer-audience connection: Emotion to metaphor in dance and society.* Austin: University of Texas Press.

Hanna, J. L. (1986). Interethnic communication in children's own dance, play, and protest. In Y. Y. Kim (Ed.), *Interethnic Communication* (Vol. 10, *International and Intercultural Communication Annual*) (pp. 176–198). Newbury Park, CA: Sage.

Hanna, J. L. (1987). *To dance is human: A theory of nonverbal communication* (Rev. ed.). Chicago: University of Chicago Press.

Hanna, J. L. (1988a). *Disruptive school behavior: Class, race, and culture.* New York: Holmes & Meier Publishers.

Hanna, J. L. (1988b). *Dance, sex, and gender: Signs of identity, dominance, defiance, and desire.* Chicago: University of Chicago Press.

Hanna, J. L. (1988c). *Dance and stress: Resistance, reduction, and euphoria.* New York: AMS Press.

Hanna, J. L. (in press-a). *Undressing the First Amendment and corsetting the striptease dancer.*

Hanna, J. L. (in press-b). *Dance, Intelligence and Education for the 21st century.* Champaign, IL: Human Kinetics Press.

Hanna, J. L. (in press-c). *Nigeria's Ubakala Igbo dance: Life, death, and the women's war.* London: Harwood Academic Publishers.

Ifeka-Moller, C. (1975). Female militancy and colonial revolt: The Women's War of 1929, Eastern Nigeria. In S. Ardener (Ed.), *Perceiving women* (pp. 127–158). New York: Halsted Press.

Isaacs, H. R. (1975). *Idols of the Tribe.* New York: Harper & Row.

Jones, B., & Hawes, B. (1972). *Step it down: Games, plays and stories from the Afro-American heritage.* New York: Harper & Row.

Levy, J. (1978). *Play behavior.* New York: Wiley.

Long, N. J., Morse, W. C., & Newman, R. G. (1976). *Conflict in the classroom: The education of emotionally disturbed children* (3rd ed.). Belmont, CA: Wadsworth.

Longfield, C. (1994). Intimate interactions: The mitigation of objectification. Paper presented at the Southern Anthropological Meetings.

Meyer, L. B. (1967). *Music, the arts and ideas.* Chicago: University of Chicago Press.

Nwabara, S. N. (1965). *Ibo land: A study in British penetration and the problem of administration,* 1860-1930. Ph.D. dissertation, Northwestern University. Ann Arbor, MI: University Microfilms.

O'Barr, J. (1984). African women in politics. In M. J. Hay and S. Stichter (Eds.), *African women south of the Sahara* (pp. 140–155). London: Longman.

Paz, O. (1995). *The double flame: Love and eroticism.* New York: Harcourt Brace & Company.

Perkins, D. N. (1981). *The mind's best work.* Cambridge, MA: Harvard University Press.

Piaget, J. (1962). *Plays, dreams, and imitation in childhood.* New York: Norton.

Runco, M.A. & Albert, R. S. (Eds.) (1990). *Theories of creativity.* Newbury Park, CA: Sage.

Siegel, B. J. (1970). Defensive structuring and environmental stress. *American Journal of Sociology,* 76(1), 11–32.

Van Allen, J. (1972). "Sitting on a man": Colonialism and the political institutions of Igbo women. *Canadian Journal of African Studies, 6,* 165–181.

Wolf, D., & Gardner, H. (1980). Beyond playing or polishing: A developmental view of artistry. In J. J. Hausman (Ed.), *Arts and the schools* (pp. 47–78). New York: McGraw-Hill.

Zeidman, I. (1967). *The American burlesque show.* New York: Hawthorne Books.

chapter 8

Improvisational Theater: An Ethnotheory of Conversational Practice

R. Keith Sawyer
Washington University

Dr. Sawyer made use of the metaphor of improvisational performance in his study of pretend play in the nursery school, Pretend Play as Improvisation: Conversation in the Preschool Classroom. *This chapter is the first report on his current project, a multi-year ethnographic study of the improvisational theater community in Chicago. This chapter draws on Dr. Sawyer's observations of improv training classes, group rehearsals, and the performances of professional theater groups.*

To create dramatically effective improvised performances, the improv acting community has developed a fairly elaborate "ethnotheory" of everyday social interaction, a set of guiding principles that are taught to improvisational actors. This ethnotheory has intriguing implications for a range of contemporary theories of social action. Yet, these principles have not been presented to a social science audience. This chapter is a description of the interactional principles that are almost universally used by improvisational groups.

I am fascinated by everyday conversation. Because our conversations are not scripted in advance, I refer to them as *improvised*. Thinking about conversation as improvised allows me to apply my own performing experience to my study of conversation. I entered graduate study after 15 years of experience as a performing musician, primarily playing piano in bands that engaged in a large amount of group improvisation, or "jamming." My experience includes both jazz and improvisational rock. Both jazz and rock emphasize *group* improvisation, and it's this collective aspect of improvisation that I find particularly fascinating. Thus, in my scientific research, I focus on the collective, group dimensions of conversation. My first study explored how children acquire the improvisational skills needed to engage in everyday conversations, through peer play in preschool (Sawyer, 1997). While engaged in that study, I began to play piano with an improvisational theater group in Chicago, and I performed with this group for almost two years. I attended rehearsals and training classes, interviewed the actors and directors, and videotaped the performances. At the end of this two-year period, I expanded the study to include most of the major professional improvisational groups in Chicago, videotaping performances and interviewing actors and directors.

This chapter is the first report from this large body of data. I've chosen to begin my analysis at the point where the aspiring actor begins: with the training that actors receive in improvisation. Many of the professional theaters in Chicago offer training classes in improvisation as a way of supplementing their performance income. These classes are popular, and are attended by a broad range of people, including professional actors seeking to learn improvisational technique, as well as nonactors who hope that improvisational principles will help them be more comfortable in social settings.

The improvisational theater community is fond of saying that the best improv performances work because they are the most true to life. In one book of improv technique, Johnson wrote "Anyone can improvise. We all do it every day—none of us goes through our day-to-day life with a script to tell us what to do" (Halpern, Close, & Johnson, 1994, p. 9). In an improv training class, aspiring actors are taught a set of principles that, when followed, result in more interesting, more dramatically true performances. I am fascinated by these principles, because they form a theory of discursive action, developed not through armchair speculation, but through repeated experience with what works and doesn't work: a theory that has emerged from practice. Anthropologists use the term *ethnotheory* to refer to the theories that people have about their own behavior. Because improvisational actors spend so much time in training and rehearsal, they have developed a particularly elaborate ethnotheory about stage dialogues. Improvisational theater is a kind of "workbench" in which this ethnotheory of conversational interaction is tested in front of a live audience. What aspects of this ethnotheory confirm and echo social science theories of situated discourse? What aspects of the ethnotheory would not have been predicted by social science theory? Has the crucible of public performance led this community of practice to some insights about social life that have been underemphasized or neglected by the scholars in the Ivory Tower?

In this chapter I briefly summarize what I've learned about the principles that actors use to generate improvised dialogues on stage. Improvisational theater represents a special, highly marked sub-genre of conversational interaction. Like conversation, it is improvised; like some conversation, but unlike most, it is directed at a non-participant audience. I also discuss why I think that an analysis of this ethnotheory can shed light on the interactional processes underlying everyday conversations.

I've done many literature searches on improvisation. The references that I've found fall into two categories: (a) "how-to" books written for the theater community and (b) books of psychotherapeutic technique. Apparently, improvisational theater has not been studied by social scientists, nor by conversation researchers. Indirectly, research in disciplines that study conversation is relevant to an analysis of dialogue in improvisational theater, because improvised dialogues share many characteristics with everyday conversations. These disciplines include the ethnography of speaking, Goffman's *dramaturgical* theory of social interaction, semiotics, conversation analysis, and discourse analysis. Although I will point out some of these connections, the purpose of this chapter is not to use this ethnotheory to critique social science theories; that will have to wait for a later work. Rather, my purpose here is to begin the preliminary sense-making process, as I begin to work through the implications of the immense set of data I've gathered on improvisational dialogues.

METHODOLOGICAL BENEFITS TO THE STUDY OF IMPROVISATIONAL THEATER

I have several motivations for studying improvisational theater as an indirect method of studying ordinary talk, rather than studying ordinary talk directly. Because I am interested in understanding the mechanics, the structuring principles of interaction, rather than the motivations or intentionality of participants, I prefer to keep the focus of study on "how" rather than "why." Everyday talk involves intentionality and goals in a sense that is absent from an ephemeral performance. These are usually thought of as the "why" of an encounter: Why did you talk to him? Why for so long/so short? Are you happy with the conversation? Did you get what you wanted? These are all reasonable things to ask of a person after an encounter. The fact that these extra-interactional goals are absent from the improv performance allows a more direct focus on the principles of interaction themselves, the "how" of the encounter.

Improvisational theater not only allows us to focus more exclusively on "how," but also allows us to recast many "why" questions as "how" questions, since they are folded into the dramatic frame, as follows. Actors almost always introduce motivations and goals for their characters, because without having goals, there can be no dramatic performance, no development towards dramatic resolution. But in improvisation, these goals themselves become merged in with the "how" of interaction: How can I use this goal to make a better performance? How does this goal work to make a better performance, better or worse than another goal? How would my character work towards this goal?

There are several other methodological benefits to studying improvisational performance. First, the empirical study of everyday talk often requires an understanding of the personalities and past histories of participants, which can be difficult to capture without lengthy interviews or longitudinal analysis. Second, everyday conversation is usually not performed for an audience, so observation, which must be surreptitious to avoid influencing the talk, becomes problematic. In contrast, theater is a public performance, so that videotaping does not affect the phenomenon being studied. Third, since the participants are aware that they are performing, they concentrate more intently on their interaction, and thus may be able to provide more insights in post-performance interviews. It's hard to imagine a non-obtrusive study of everyday talk in which the participants could be interviewed about the conversation after it occurred. The distancing of "the self" from the stage role obviates many subjective personality issues which would make this latter study difficult.

A BRIEF HISTORY OF IMPROVISATIONAL THEATER

Improvisational theater has its roots in a series of games developed for children's peer play. These games were developed by Viola Spolin in the thirties and forties (Coleman, 1990; Spolin, 1963). Her son, Paul Sills, was a cofounder of the first improvisational comedy group, The Compass Players, at the University of Chicago in 1955. The Compass later evolved into the well-known improv group, The Second City, the model for the popular TV show *Saturday Night Live*.

Since its origins in the 1950s, improvisational theater has grown dramatically in Chicago and in other urban centers. With this growth has come a remarkable variety of styles and approaches to improvisation. These styles can be grouped loosely into two main approaches. The most well-known groups perform short *games*, 5 minutes or less, which start from one or two audience suggestions. There are dozens of different games widely used by improvisational ensembles; each game is distinguished by a unique set of constraints on how the performance will proceed. A common game is Freeze Tag. After asking for an audience suggestion, perhaps a location or a starting line of dialogue, two performers begin to improvise a scene. The actors accompany their dialog with exaggerated gestures and broad physical movements. The audience is instructed to shout "freeze" whenever they think the actors are in interesting physical positions. Immediately, the actors must "freeze" themselves in position; a third actor then walks up to these two and taps one of them on the shoulder. The tapped actor leaves the stage, and the new actor must take his place, in the same position, and then begin a completely different scene with her first line of dialogue, playing on the ambiguities inherent in the physical relationship of the frozen actors.

A second style of performance is referred to as *long-form improv*. The ensemble asks for an audience suggestion, and then begins to improvise a one-act play which typically lasts for 30 minutes without interruption. Although these performances often are so dramatically true that many audience members assume a script is being followed, this is never the case with authentic improv groups. The actors work very hard to avoid repeating even brief segments of a performance from a prior night. Long-form improv is less focused on comedy than are game performances, instead focusing on character and plot development.

All improvisational theater genres share two characteristics. First, there is no script, thus, they are created in the moment. Second, they are collective—no one person decides what will happen. Because the performance is collectively improvised, each performers' actions are influenced by the others. Although each actor's participation seems not to be scripted, a highly structured performance emerges. Studying improvisation thus requires being able to model the ways in which group processes constrain individual acts, and the mechanisms whereby actors may creatively influence the emerging performance. Because group improvisational genres are collective and unscripted, improvisational creativity is a collective social process.

THE COLLECTIVE CREATION OF IMPROVISED DIALOGUE

How do we collectively create coherent encounters that are not structured in advance? This is a question about intersubjectivity: How do participants in an encounter learn to arrive at shared understandings about social realities? One way to do this would be by talking about the ongoing interaction explicitly, taking on a director's off-stage voice. Bateson called such communication about the interaction itself *explicit metacommunication* (1955/1972, p. 180). Bateson introduced this concept to describe children's play. Children metacommunicate to collectively regulate the emergence of the play drama, and to integrate their distinct ideas about what is going on. Metacommunication provides a framework for interpreting each child's utterances.

In both improvisational theater and children's play, metacommunicative processes define and regulate an emerging performance. The following transcript of an improvised performance is an example of how *implicit* metacommunication is used to create new dramatic situations.

Example 1. Four actors stand at the back of the stage. Andrew begins the scene.

1. (Andrew steps to stage center, pulls up a chair and sits down, miming the action of driving by holding an imaginary steering wheel.)
2. (Ben steps to stage center, stands next to Andrew, fishes in pocket for something.)
3. Andrew: On or off?
4. Ben: I'm getting on, sir. (continues fishing in his pocket)
5. Andrew: In or out?
6. Ben: I'm getting in!
   I'm getting in!
7. Andrew: Did I see you tryin' to get in the back door
   a couple of stops back?
8. Ben: Uh...

At the end of this exchange, the actors have established a reasonably complex drama. They know that Andrew is a bus driver, and that Ben is a potential passenger. Andrew is getting a little impatient, and Ben may be a little shifty, perhaps trying to sneak on. But how do the audience and the actors know this? How was it decided? There are two points to emphasize about this example: One is the *contingency* of interaction at each utterance. For example, at turn 2, Ben had a range of creative options available. Ben could have pulled up a second chair and sat down next to the "driver," and he would have become a passenger in a car. At turn 3, Andrew had an equal range of options. He could have addressed Ben as his friend, searching for theater tickets. This doesn't begin to address the range of dramatic options that can occur on stage. For example, at turn 2, Ben could have addressed Andrew as Captain Kirk of Star Trek, creating a TV-show parody. A few minutes of examination of an improvisational transcript indicates many plausible, dramatically coherent utterances that the actors could have performed at each turn. A combinatorial explosion quickly results in hundreds of potential performances, branching out from each actor's utterance.

The other point to emphasize is the *implicitness* of metacommunication. None of the actors said what was going to happen explicitly. None of them stepped out of character to direct the scene. This is one of the basic principles of improv: "Show, don't tell." The actors are abiding by Goffman's (1974) observation that "breaking frame," stepping outside the interactional definition, is unnatural. Actors refer to this as "crossing the fourth wall," a wonderful metaphor. In improvisational theater, by design, metacommunication about how the drama will proceed is both *implicit* and *within frame*; Bateson referred to this as *implicit metacommunication*, and like Goffman, argued that most communication about the flow of interaction is implicit.

This is also true of everyday talk. In most everyday interactions adults metacommunicate implicitly, and they stay within frame. Adults are adept at using these interactional techniques. There is likely to be a great deal of similarity between the interactional techniques of improv and of everyday talk, not least because the actors are trying to create believable dialogue. To the extent that the metacommunicative techniques of improvisational theater are similar to those of everyday talk, its study could provide insights into our understanding of everyday talk.

PRINCIPLES OF EFFECTIVE IMPROVISATION

The improvisational theater community has developed a set of principles that are believed to result in more effective improvisations. "More effective" means that the scene works better as a performance, that it's more dramatically "true," and that it is funnier. Since these actors are all members of a community of practice, they all share an implicit definition of what makes a good improvisation. These principles are taught and shared by every group that I encountered in my study. In the following discussion, I draw on my own experiences with approximately 10 Chicago-area improv groups, and on the material in many of the available "how-to" improv books (Coleman, 1990; Goldberg, 1991; Halpern et al., 1994; Hodgson & Richards, 1966; Johnstone, 1981; Spolin, 1963; Sweet, 1978).

It's interesting how little disagreement there is about these rules. Because there are so many different professional groups and so many different teachers and schools of improvisation, it's easy to imagine different schools of thought emerging, groups that might have developed their own set of interactional principles that make for effective performances. But this hasn't been the case. There is a remarkable consensus about these principles among groups, regardless of the city, the age range, the professional level, or the style of improvisation. I think that makes the following rules even more important for the conversation researcher.

Yes, and...

This is the single most important rule of improv. In every conversational turn, an actor should do two things: Accept the material introduced in the prior turn, and add something new to the dramatic frame. The most important is to accept the proposal introduced in the prior turn. This is often phrased as "Don't deny." To deny a fellow actor is to reject whatever he has just introduced into the dramatic frame. Everything that is introduced by an actor must be fully embraced and accepted by the other actors on stage. Denial stops a scene dead. The director Del Close wrote about a scene in which a wife had proposed to her husband that they get divorced (Halpern et al., 1994, p. 48). The husband, distraught, introduced children into the dramatic frame, but was hit with denial:

Husband:	Honey, but what about the children?
Wife:	We don't have any children!

Close wrote, "Naturally, she got a huge laugh. Naturally, she had completely destroyed the scene" (1994, p. 48).

Actors keep the scene moving by introducing something new to the dramatic frame with every turn, for maximum efficiency. No turn is wasted. If an actor fails to add something, he is forcing the other actors to do more than their share of the creative building of the frame.

This principle has the effect of encouraging a democratic, balanced intersubjectivity. Performances are thought to be more effective if the frame is created collectively, better than if one person makes all the decisions about the frame and the other simply says "Yes" to each one.

No Questions

In a scene at the ImprovOlympic, a theater in Chicago, a man and a woman were taking a romantic stroll through the park. The woman had the idea that she would find a lottery ticket, a scenario rife with romantic possibility, and she initiated the scene change by pointing at the ground and saying, with surprise,

Woman:	What's that?
Man:	It's just a pile of shit.
Woman:	(Frustrated) No, it's a lottery ticket!

Asking the question was bad enough, but the actress also broke the first rule by following it up with a blatant denial. Instead of asking a question, actors are taught to make the assumption and go ahead and state it. The actress should have said "Look, a lottery ticket!" and bent down to pick it up. The scene would be three turns farther along, moving much more quickly.

What a question really does is to constrain the partner. A question limits the range of options, constraining the creativity. The question doesn't offer anything creative to the frame, and limits the other actors at the same time.

Don't Cross the Fourth Wall

The *fourth wall* is the imaginary barrier between the stage and the audience. The fourth wall is a metaphorical way of talking about Goffman's dramatic *frame*, and this rule is a restatement of Goffman's observation that interactants rarely "break frame" in social encounters. Although crossing the fourth wall is a common technique in twentieth-century theater, it generally doesn't work during improvisation. This may be because it's too easy to direct a scene using explicit metacommunication. Actors realize that implicit metacommunication is the essence of a good performance. Staying in frame is also an attempt to be true to life: In everyday life we rarely "break frame." As Goffman noted, when we do, something is usually very wrong.

Show, Don't Tell

This is another way of encouraging maximally implicit metacommunication. Even when the actors remain in frame, there are differing degrees of relative directness or indirectness, relative explicitness or implicitness (cf. Sawyer, 1997). If an actor decides to be holding an ax, he shouldn't say, "Look, I've got an ax!" Although this is in frame, and does not cross the fourth wall, it's a relatively explicit way of introducing material into the dramatic frame. It's almost like stepping out of frame into a director's voice. Instead, actors are taught to "show" the new information. One possibility for the ax would be for the actor to start to make chopping motions and to say, "Boy, I hope I get enough wood chopped before it starts raining!" The former version "tells" the audience, and doesn't get the scene anywhere. The latter version "shows" that he has the ax, and also introduces a lot of additional information into the frame. Because it is more implicit, it also has the effect of constraining the other actors even less, providing them with the maximum range of creative possibilities (Sawyer, 1996).

Be Specific, Not General

Specificity is always better. If an actor *were* to say "I've got an ax," it would be better to say "This new Runco AM-30 computerized ax was only $200 at the church auction!"

Specificity provides more detail for later connections. It builds a more elaborate, more complex dramatic frame. It provides inspiration for the other actors on stage; instead of just having "an ax" to respond to, they have "Runco," "computerized," "church auction," and "cheap."

Don't Make Jokes

Most people think of improv as a genre of comedy. Most audiences attend improv performances to laugh, to be entertained. The beginning improv actor is usually concerned with being funny, with getting a laugh out of the audience. The focus on making jokes almost always interferes with the development of an effective group improvisation. Even if a one-liner does get a laugh, it tends to break the continuity of the scene, because it's not the most natural action at that point. This is an issue of mental focus: If actors are thinking about being funny, looking for a good one-liner, then they won't be listening to the other actors and working on creating a believable scene together with their fellow actors. Being funny is often ego-driven, a way of competing with the other actors, rather than trusting the group to create the humor. Improv teachers tell students to focus on the other principles of good improv, and what will result is an improvisation that is true to life, and that is thus naturally funny.

Don't Write the Script in Your Head

Imagine the following two turns:

| Woman: | I've missed you, honey. |
| Man: | Yeah, sorry I haven't called more often, Mom. |

If the woman were writing the script in her head, she might have initiated this exchange thinking that the man was her husband, in the navy, and just back from a 6-month tour. Her mind would already be working on the romantic implications of the scene. But the man's response makes all of that mental work a waste. Because of the "no denial" rule, she has to proceed as the "Mother" now. But because she has written a different script in her head already, the scene won't flow as naturally.

Writing ahead is a common cause of denial; this is what happened in the "lottery ticket/shit" example above.

This rule encourages a balanced, group creation of a performance. It forces the actors to "stay in the moment," another way of phrasing the rule, rather than thinking ahead to the rest of the scene. Actors are taught to keep their minds from looking ahead. It's a hard thing to do, because it's so natural to think through the subsequent flow of an interaction. Try to imagine being the actress, saying "I've missed you, honey," and not having any specific idea of what your relationship is. Hard to do, isn't it? But that's exactly what a good improv actor will do. It involves a great deal of trust; the actress has to trust her partner to select the relationship. It involves relinquishing control to the group process. Actors often talk in terms of "trust," "losing one's ego," and refer to the "group mind."

Listen and Remember

Good actors remember everything that has been introduced into the dramatic frame. Not everything has to be resolved and connected right away, so there will always be small bits and pieces of plot and frame, waiting to be picked up and connected to the current scene. Making these connections is the sign of a skilled improviser, and knowledgeable audiences often applaud at such a connection. It's not a question of humor, it's not a joke; they applaud the making of the connection itself.

There Are No Rules

Having all of these rules is a contradiction of sorts. After all, it is "improvisation," right? Anything goes? Actually, this is true. The above rules are only guidelines, and there is always a right time to break one of the rules. A skillful breaking of a rule will often get applause from an audience, because they know the rules and they recognize when a rule is being broken in a "good" way.

Note that most of these rules are negatively phrased: They indicate what *not* to do. The rules say "Do anything you want *with these exceptions*." They don't prescribe, they proscribe.

The only rule that can never be broken is the rule of agreement, "No denial."

SOME CLASSIC GAMES

In short-form, or *game* improvisation, each skit lasts about 5 minutes. Usually, several skits are performed in a series. A game is defined by its advance setup, which usually involves asking the audience to suggest one or another parameter of the dramatic frame. The actors must start with the audience suggestion(s) as a given, and work with those suggestions, improvising the other properties of the dramatic frame.

Dubbing

The audience is asked to suggest a location, a theme, or a relationship. Two actors are onstage, and two other actors stand offstage, at opposite sides of the stage. The onstage actors do not speak at all during the scene. Instead, one offstage actor speaks for each onstage actor. In his turn, the onstage actor moves his mouth silently, as if talking, while his offstage actor talks for him. There is a competitive element to this game that often results in audience laughter, because the offstage "animator" can voice things that are embarrassing for the onstage actor. For example, if the offstage actor says "I think I'll roll around in this mud to cool off," the onstage actor will have to lie down on stage and start rolling. The onstage actor can be the initiator, as well; if he begins to mime an activity, the off-stage voice must be consistent with that physical activity or gesture.

This is an interesting game, reminiscent of Goffman's separation of the speaker into analytic roles in his classic "Footing" article (1981). It also demonstrates the importance of nonverbal action in human encounters, since the onstage actors contribute a great deal to the scene through purely physical actions.

Mutual Narrator Game

There are two actors on the stage. They take turns speaking. Each actor's turn consists of two utterances: (a) a line of dialogue in character, and (b) stepping to stage front, out of character, a line as the narrator. The narrator talk is usually a projection onto the other actor. The humor in this game comes from the "no denial" rule: Each actor has to enact their next turn in a manner that is consistent with the narration about them.

This game teases out two analytic levels of metacommunication—implicit and explicit, in-frame and out-of-frame, are both present in separate parts of the turn. What results is an interlacing of two different levels or "orders" of metapragmatic strategy (Sawyer, 1997; Silverstein, 1993).

Birthday Game

One actor is chosen as the guest of honor, the person having a birthday. He is escorted into the theater lobby by another actor. While this "target" is out of hearing range, the audience is asked to suggest a *profession* and then an *adjective* for each of three actors, who will be guests at a birthday party. The three roles that result are usually quite unlikely, novel characters such as the Paranoid Plumber. The target actor is then brought back into the theater, and sits down at stage center. Two other actors, standing, act as hosts of the party, welcoming each of the three mystery guests in turn. The goal is for the target to guess the adjective and the profession for each of the three guests, solely from the improvised dialogue.

The dialogue consists of typical party small talk and greeting rituals, as each of the three mystery guests arrives. As soon as the target guesses the identity of the mystery guest, that guest leaves the party (executing a socially appropriate closing ritual). All actors know the identity of each of the three guests except for the target. Thus these other actors structure their dialogue in such a way as to help the target identify the adjective and profession of the guest. The target speaks less often, usually to make tentative guesses or to ask clarifying (but indirect) questions. If the target mentions a portion of the adjective or profession, the audience is instructed to applaud.

The many techniques that the actors use to help the target are all interesting to the conversation researcher. First, the patterns of interaction between the two hosts and the mystery guests are themselves an *index* of the guest's identity. For example, if the guest is "paranoid," the host may show exaggerated concern for the safety of the guest, or possibly be dismissive of the fears of the guest. In this case, interaction patterns themselves are used to index denotational content. Second, the mystery guests must use the proper *voice* for the profession and adjective associated with them. This task is made more difficult by the unlikely combinations of adjective and profession; for example, we have probably never encountered a paranoid plumber before, yet we can imagine what the intersection of those two voices would be like. The speech of the mystery guest is often *dialogic* because they must merge two distinct types of voice. Some adjective/profession combinations are not so distinct, and the actor's skill then consists of identifying an appropriate single voice for that character. If the suggestion is "anal-retentive proctologist," typical of the sorts of suggestions that audiences come up with, it's consistent with our social stereotype of the "doctor" role that doctors are often uptight. In this case, a single "uptight professional" voice could be used.

The humor arises from the stereotypical behavior, the skillful inhabiting of these socially-recognized voices. Audiences clearly know these voices intimately. The audience also recognizes the host's stereotypically appropriate addressing of these roles. Although the hosts are not assigned a role, the job of the host is to *address* the guest in a manner appropriate to that guest's adjective and profession. This is a strange kind of "voicing" in Bakhtin's sense, since it's an "addressing" voicing. Audiences often laugh at a skillfully appropriate manner of addressing the guest.

Usually there is only one mystery guest on stage at a time, but occasionally a second guest will come on stage before the prior guest's identity is guessed. Usually they only do this if the target is having difficulty. These are often moments of peak laughter, when the two characters must address each other, combining as many as four distinct voices in their dialogue. The contrast with the dialogue with the host is instructive: The host's only constraint is to address appropriately; but the mystery guest must both (a) address appropriately, and (b) voice their own role appropriately. Possibly because of this difficulty, actors are instructed to try to keep only one guest at a time on stage.

SCENE CONSTRUCTION

The above are all short-form games. In addition to game, or skit improvisation, many groups perform *scene* improvisation. An improvised scene does not have the interactional constraints that the various games have. Instead, actors start with only one or two audience suggestions, and collectively develop a 5- to 30-minute scene. The audience can be asked to suggest any one of the dramatic parameters—a location, a title for the scene, a relationship, or even a more specific suggestion like "something that annoys you."

The improv guidelines itemized above all relate to micro-interaction, to the turn-by-turn flow of dialogue between actors. These rules are meant to be followed in both short-form and scene improvisation. In addition to these rules, in scene improvisation, actors are taught a set of general guidelines for how to construct an interesting, effective scene. These principles relate to scene properties like plot and character development, properties that are not so important in games.

Roles and Location

The first step in a scene is to answer the questions "who" and "where." In many improv games, these properties are fixed in advance of the performance, either by the structure of the game or by audience suggestion. In most scene improvisations, the location and the characters are not defined in advance.

A scene usually begins with two actors on stage; additional actors don't enter until these two actors have established identities, a location, and a relationship.

Relationships

Along with the roles of each actor, the actors must quickly establish a relationship between the characters. There are many different aspects of a relationship that can be collectively determined early in the scene. These include not only what we might think of as the stereotypic "relationship," such as mother-child, or brothers, but also the immediate situation of the pair (anger over a recent slight, unusually positive feelings due to being on vacation or winning the lottery), and the relationship history of the pair (actors can reference things that happened yesterday, last year, or even in long-ago childhood).

Goals

The goals of the characters are essential properties of all drama. In conventional theater, the goals are provided by the playwright, and the dramatic flow results from the motivations of the characters. The play has a trajectory that emerges from the character's motivations. In scene improvisation, the actors must provide motivations for their characters. As with all other aspects of the dramatic frame, goals for characters are provided collectively, and emerge from the dialogue of the actors. An actor doesn't necessarily choose his own motivation; sometimes the other actors propose the motivation for him.

Actors are taught to introduce these goals as soon as possible after identifying the roles and the location of the action.

Start Scenes in the Middle

In conventional, scripted theater, it's common for the play to begin with some sort of exposition, or a character-establishing scene, before the main action, that leads to the climax. Exposition doesn't work in scene improvisation. Actors are taught to start immediately with the climax, with the main action.

Rule of Threes

A *beat* is an identifiable subset of the scene. Three beats always seems to work better than two or four. Actors can generally agree on where the breaks are between the beats of a scene. In conventional theater, the beats are often exposition, climax, resolution. Since scene improv does not start with exposition, the three beats don't usually follow this conventional form. I didn't encounter any ethnotheory about what kinds of beats worked best, and in what order. The most common pattern that I observed was for the first beat to be one moment of action, the second beat to be a contrary or unexpected action, and the third beat to be a resolution or integration of the first two. The third beat resolves the discrepancies and disjunctions created by the first two.

Making It Interesting: Divergent and Convergent Processes

Performers are taught not to resolve contradictions and ambiguities immediately. This is a common mistake among intermediate-level performers; they have become adept at resolving a scene, and the natural tendency seems to be to resolve contradictions right away. Once actors reach this level, they must be explicitly taught to introduce contradiction and ambiguity, and to continue the improvisation in the presence of ambiguity. These ambiguities and inconsistencies then act as the source of tension that drives the performance. The connections will happen naturally, without being forced by the actors (Halpern et al., 1994, p. 74).

Especially in the first half of a scene, the first two beats, actors are encouraged to introduce new material, new characteristics of the dramatic frame, rather than to use their turn resolving or connecting items that have already been introduced. Actors are reminded not to be too clean and consistent with their projections during the early parts of a scene; some teachers will explicitly tell actors *not* to introduce something that they know will fit in with what is already established, but to introduce something radically different that they have no idea how to resolve.

By the second half of the scene, after a variety of dramatic material has been introduced, the actors still don't know how everything will be resolved and connected. Although individual actors may have some ideas, they can't "write the script ahead." The resolution is a collective process, and no one actor can know what is in the other actors' minds, or what will emerge from the subsequent dialogue. In many performances, the connections never quite happen, and the performance doesn't come to a good dramatic closure. This is an ever-present risk in improvisation; actors sometimes call it "performing without a net."

After the early work of introducing dramatic material, some of it inconsistent on purpose, the performance involves conversational work to construct a feasible dramatic frame within which all of this material makes sense. The actors must collectively solve a problem that they have created for themselves. This work is doubly difficult if multiple conflicting dramatic elements are in play.

These two stages are reminiscent of models of the creative process that distinguish between two stages of creativity. In the first, *divergent* stage, many ideas and concepts are proposed without concern for how they will work; this is what happens in a brainstorming session. In the second, *convergent* stage, the set of ideas is filtered, selected, and connected, to result in the final creative product. The two stages are also paralleled by the distinction between problem-finding and problem-solving (Csikszentmihalyi & Sawyer, 1995; Getzels, 1964); the first part of the scene is "problem-finding" in that the actors create a completely new dramatic problem for themselves; the second part of the scene is "problem-solving" as the actors work to solve this unique, one-time-only problem.

Note that both of these creativity theories were developed to describe the individual's creative process. However, in an improv scene, these stages and processes are collective. The divergent stage is accomplished by the group; the problem-solving is accomplished by the group. The interaction in the genre is defined in such a way that no one actor can accomplish these things alone. In fact, if an actor attempts to do this alone, it tends to cause problems; it's a form of "writing the script in your head." Actors are taught to trust in the "group mind" (Halpern et al., 1994), to allow these resolutions and connections to emerge from the performance of the group.

Endings and Edits

How is a scene ended? The scene ends when the lights are turned off and the stage goes black. This is such an important decision that the director of the group always sits at the lights, primarily to make this determination. The actors don't know when the lights will be cut. Although they know the approximate length assigned for this scene and they sometimes try to bring the scene to appropriate closure at about the right time, there's no guarantee that the director will agree with them. They can never assume that the scene is going to end, they always have to assume that it will continue.

In long-form improv, a one-act play that lasts 30 minutes, the play is often broken up into many shorter scenes, with "cuts" or edits between the scenes. In an edit, an offstage actor simply walks to the front of the stage while the actors are engaged in dialogue. Since actors face the audience, they notice the walk-on. The actors aren't expected to stop in mid-sentence, but continue their interaction one or two turns, however many are minimally necessary to achieve a natural-seeming closing to the scene. The walk-on actor begins the action of the next scene, and is usually quickly joined by one or two more actors who will develop the next scene together. These scene edits are only temporary closings, because the plot line will start again when those actors come back later for another scene.

It is sometimes obvious to the offstage actors that the onstage actors *want* them to edit the scene. They will be floundering, and even if the audience isn't aware a good actor will notice. It's better to edit too soon rather than too late, because the actors can always return to the idea later.

Conversational closings have been one of the focuses of conversation analysis (cf. Schegloff & Sachs, 1973). But there is a significant difference, since in improv, the actors don't accomplish their own closings; their scenes are "closed" by other actors or by the director, at the light board. The actors have a rough idea of when the scene is supposed to end, so they will modify their dialogue somewhat. Their dialogue might take on the properties of the early stages of the closing phase of an encounter. But it will still be quite different; just because the scene is ending doesn't mean the actors are actually leaving each other's company. A scene closing is not the same thing as a leave-taking. Actors are sometimes waiting for an opportunity to get in the perfect final punch line, or closing statement. However, I've seen performances in which an actor clearly thought they had made what would be the final utterance, and the lights were not turned off. The scene continued.

But there sometimes seem to be forms of closing discourse, when the actors sense that it's time to end the scene or act, and they work at achieving closure rather than introducing new dramatic elements. Although the actors can't actually "close" on their own, they are moving *toward* closure, toward convergence.

This is one topic that often is discussed post-performance: Was the blackout done at the right time? Were there earlier dialogue turns that would have been more appropriate endings? It's a difficult job for the director. How good is good enough? If the act is a little short, perhaps only 25 of the 30 minutes have gone by, he might wait for a better ending to emerge in the next five minutes. If the 30-minute mark is only seconds away, the director might settle for anything that remotely resembles an ending, whether it's a great line or not.

Although every performance is different, the ideal scene improvisation results in a trajectory that starts with divergence, with actors proposing new properties of the dramatic frame, followed by increasing convergence, as the actors work on bringing together the miscellaneous, diverse dramatic elements that have been introduced. The actors are solving a puzzle of which they have created the pieces. A talented improv ensemble is skilled in these two areas: effectively introducing material during this first portion, the kind of material that will work well as a "puzzle piece," and effectively resolving discrepancies, making connections, bringing the pieces of the puzzle together.

CONCLUSIONS: IMPLICATIONS FOR THE STUDY OF DISCURSIVE ACTION

This paper is exploratory, since it's my first attempt to analyze the large body of ethnographic data that I have gathered during my time in the improvisational theater community. It's also exploratory in that it's the first attempt that I'm aware of to connect improvisational theater with the social-scientific study of interaction. What can we learn from this ethnotheory? To what extent are our theories consistent with this ethnotheory? If not, why not? Are they bad theories, or are there differences between improvisational theater and everyday talk that could account for these differences?

The similarities, I believe, are primarily at the level of the metacommunicative regulatory principles that participants use to collectively construct an improvised encounter. The interactional techniques that improvisational actors use are the same ones that we all use in our everyday talk. And how could it be otherwise? The ensemble's goal is to create a dramatically true performance. It's hard to imagine a group of actors inventing a completely new set of principles to guide social interaction. Of course they are using the same implicit knowledge that we all have already, that we draw on in conducting everyday conversations. Since conversation researchers study exactly these interactional dynamics, improvisational theater performances provide empirical data that are as valuable as everyday conversations.

Of course, there are many differences between improvisational theater and everyday life. After I enumerate some of the differences, I'll discuss whether these differences are significant enough to affect the value of the phenomenon of improvisation to conversation researchers, and what qualifications we might need to place on interpretation and analysis.

1. *Stability of our lives from day to day.* Perhaps most obviously, improvisational theater is *more improvised* than everyday life. In our everyday lives, we don't get to select our social role and identity anew in every encounter. We have recent histories with most of the individuals that we encounter during the day, and these separate encounters together form a "relationship." The ways that we interact with each individual will not be invented anew each day, but will, to a large part, be determined by our relationship with them, our most recent

encounters with them, and at what point in our relationship we are (just getting to know them, good friends, old friends, family).

2. *Constancy of the self.* We usually remain the "same person," whereas in improvisation each actor chooses a new role at the beginning of each encounter. In each encounter, especially with strangers, we nonetheless have the task of performing our identity for others, which Goffman compared to a dramatic ritual. Goffman was fond of pointing out that most of the initial work of an encounter was taken up with presenting to our co-participants a definition of what role we inhabit; thus the need for ritual, since these roles are analogous to the roles that performers take on to conduct an effective ritual (1959). And symbolic interactionists were fond of, in fact criticized for, arguing that individuals do create themselves anew in each encounter (Stryker & Statham, 1985).

   Nonetheless, whereas improv actors are forced to create a role and character at the beginning of every scene, we don't do this in our everyday lives. We already have a role, or perhaps a limited set of distinct roles (the work role, the family role). And most of our daily interactions are with people who know us already.

3. *Differences in status.* In many of our everyday conversations, there is a status asymmetry between the participants. For example, workers talk differently to the boss than to someone working for them. During mealtime conversations, parents talk differently than children. In professional service encounters (as with lawyers or doctors) there are multiple asymmetries in role and status; you are paying them for a service, yet they are the expert with the knowledge that you need. In improvisational theater, there are no statuses determined in advance. Actors often improvise relationships with such status asymmetries (see Johnstone, 1981), but they get to create each relationship anew each time, it's not built into the status of the actors off stage. In our everyday lives, we don't have this flexibility. We can't change the fact that the boss has power over us. Also, in improvisation, the boss can't deny the subordinate, since the "no denial" rule applies regardless of the type of relationship between the characters. In everyday life, the higher-status individual often gets "denial rights" in interaction.

4. *Actions on stage don't have implications.* An actor can do any outrageous thing during a scene, and it doesn't really matter. An actor playing a lowly office gopher can rebel and tell off his boss. At the end of the scene, that's it. However, in our daily lives, our actions do have implications. If we curse at the boss, we may be out of a job the next day.

5. *Non-participant audience.* Improvisational theater is performed on stage, before a live, paying audience. The audience has paid to

attend because they anticipate being entertained. They have come to see a performance. The fourth wall prevents audience members from joining the performance. In everyday talk, there are often people nearby who can overhear the conversation. There may also be relatively peripheral participants, who are nominally included in the interaction, but who are not expected to talk (Goffman, 1981). Thus, it's not always accurate to say of everyday talk that there is no audience. Nonetheless, the participation status of this audience is different—peripheral participants can and do occasionally join in—and the goals of the speakers are not to entertain a paying audience.

It's important to keep these differences in mind while thinking of everyday life as improvised. Improvisational theater is more improvised than everyday life. Actors must be repeatedly creative, in ways that we never have to think about. Actors have the freedom to be creative in their stage role in areas where we are often constrained in our own lives.

I believe that all of these differences make improvisational theater an even more valuable phenomenon for study. It allows us to focus directly on the creative, interactional mechanisms that actors use to structure their interaction. In everyday social life, we don't need to rely on these improvising principles as heavily, since these other structuring factors are present. In everyday talk, we might not expect the metacommunicative level of interaction to be as important. But at those times when conversation is novel and improvised, these metacommunicative mechanisms become correspondingly more important.

Improvisational theater's highly marked status vis-à-vis ordinary talk provides the analyst with a wonderful tool with which to approach the study of conversation. My study of improvisational theater has provided me with a way to think about everyday social encounters, and has led me to read conversation theories from this perspective: I read them to evaluate how accurate they are in describing improvised talk. The study of improvisational theater can contribute to our understanding of two central aspects of everyday talk. The first aspect is the importance of discursive action in maintaining and constituting social life. Actors, through improvised dialogue, create an entire dramatic frame, an ephemeral social reality, in minutes or even seconds. Implicit, in-frame metacommunicative techniques are used to collectively create roles, characters, relationships, emotions, events, and a dramatic trajectory for the scene. To the extent that social actors are capable of creatively influencing their social reality, we might expect to identify some of these same interactional processes at work. Improvisation is characteristic of most small-group interaction in which the outcome is not predetermined, including classrooms, psychiatric encounters, and business meetings. Improvisation is also relevant to a second aspect of human action: how discursive interaction is influenced by, and in turn constitutes, the social and cultural context of that interaction. Although actors start a scene with only a few audience suggestions, a few minutes into the scene they are constrained by the dramatic frame that has been collectively created. At each moment, their creativity must be consistent with what has come before. The principles "no denial" and "make connections" attest to this. Because everyday social life is relatively more structured and stable than staged improvisations, the need to maintain coherence with the past is that much more critical. In improvisational encounters, participants must always balance the need to creatively contribute with the need to maintain coherence with the current state of the interactional frame. For these reasons, improvisation is more than a metaphor; by working out what improvisation is, one necessarily develops a theory of situated social action.

REFERENCES

Bateson, G. (1972). A theory of play and fantasy. In G. Bateson (Ed.), *Steps to an ecology of mind* (pp. 177–193.). New York: Chandler. (Reprinted from *American Psychiatric Association Research Reports*, 1955, *II*, 39–51).

Coleman, J. (1990). *The Compass: The improvisational theatre that revolutionized American comedy*. Chicago: University of Chicago Press.

Csikszentmihalyi, M., & Sawyer, R. K. (1995). Creative insight: The social dimension of a solitary moment. In R. J. Sternberg & J. E. Davidson (Eds.), *The nature of insight* (pp. 329–363). Cambridge: MIT Press.

Getzels, J. W. (1964). Creative thinking, problem-solving, and instruction. In E. R. Hilgard (Ed.), *Theories of learning and instruction* (pp. 240–267). Chicago: University of Chicago Press.

Goffman, E. (1959). *The presentation of self in everyday life*. New York: Anchor Books.

Goffman, E. (1974). *Frame Analysis: An essay on the organization of experience*. New York: Harper & Row.

Goffman, E. (1981). *Forms of talk*. Philadelphia: University of Pennsylvania Press.

Goldberg, A. (1991). *Improv comedy*. Hollywood, CA: Samuel French.

Halpern, C., Close, D., & Johnson, K. (1994). *Truth in comedy: The manual of improvisation*. Colorado Springs, CO: Meriwether Publishing.

Hodgson, J., & Richards, E. (1966). *Improvisation*. New York: Grove Weidenfeld.

Johnstone, K. (1981). *Impro: Improvisation and the theatre*. New York: Routledge.

Sawyer, R. K. (1996). The semiotics of improvisation: The pragmatics of musical and verbal performance. *Semiotica, 108*, (3/4), 269–306.

Sawyer, R. K. (1997). *Pretend play as improvisation: Conversation in the preschool classroom*. Norwood, NJ: Lawrence Erlbaum Associates.

Schegloff, E. A., & Sacks, H. (1973). Opening up closings. *Semiotica, 8*, 289–327.

Silverstein, M. (1993). Metapragmatic discourse and metapragmatic function. In J. A. Lucy (Ed.), *Reflexive language* (pp. 33–58). New York: Cambridge University Press.

Spolin, V. (1963). *Improvisation for the theater.* Evanston, IL: Northwestern University Press.

Stryker, S., & Statham, A. (1985). Symbolic interaction and role theory. In G. Lindzey & E. Aronson (Eds.), *The handbook of social psychology* (3rd ed., pp. 311–378). New York: Random House.

Sweet, J. (1978). *Something wonderful right away: An oral history of The Second City and The Compass Players.* New York: Avon Books.

part III
Performance in Everyday Life

chapter 9

School "Performance": Improvisational Processes in Development and Education*

Jacquelyn Baker-Sennett
University of British Columbia

Eugene Matusov
University of California, Santa Cruz

Dr. Baker-Sennett and Dr. Matusov study the development of planning skills. With Barbara Rogoff and others, they have studied the collective improvisational skills that children employ while developing puppet and other theatrical performances. In this chapter, they describe this "playcrafting" work, and extend their discussion to emphasize a variety of ways that improvisational performances unfold in classrooms.

Classroom interactions are often improvisational encounters, and the teacher often acts as a sort of performer. But the application of performance to educational settings goes beyond the notion of "teacher as performer." Rather, contemporary research in education focuses on the benefits of collaborative, participatory learning, in which the students take an active role, in rich unstructured interactions with both the teachers and with other students. In this view, the classroom is a "community of learners." In this type of learning environment, the researcher must consider the joint performances of all of the participants, not only the teacher. A collaborating group can be considered to be conducting an improvised performance, since such interactions are not structured in advance.

---

*This article is a revision and expansion of ideas presented in Baker-Sennett, J. (1995). Improvisacion, planificacion y el proceso creativo (Improvisation, planning, and the creative process), *Infancia y aprendizaje, 70*, 111–126. We would like to thank Barbara Rogoff for helpful suggestions on this paper and for her guidance and collaborative support.

The authors review a wide range of contemporary research on improvisational classrooms and on teaching as improvisation. For example, they argue that experienced teachers use a more improvisational style in their teaching, whereas the novice teachers plan ahead more and stick to the lesson plan more closely. Their discussion explores how both teaching and collaboration involve both structure and improvisation, how collaborative skills develop in childhood, and how improvisational teaching develops through a career.

The focus on the development of improvisational abilities is a theme linking this chapter to Berliner's and Henderson's chapters, since those authors analyze how a novice learns musical skills through participation in communities of practice. Their research on participation and collaboration in education is related to the chapters by Sawyer, Crease, and Silverstein on the improvisational qualities of everyday conversations.

I believe that our aesthetic sense, whether in works of art or in lives, has overfocused on the stubborn struggle toward a single goal rather than on the fluid, the protean, the improvisatory. We see achievement as purposeful and monolithic, like the sculpting of a massive tree trunk that has first to be brought from the forest and then shaped by long labor to assert the artist's vision, rather than something crafted from odds and ends, like a patchwork quilt.

—Mary Catherine Bateson, 1990

INTRODUCTION

T his chapter explores the relationships between improvisation, performance, and developmental process in schools and during everyday sociocultural activities and practices. We argue that an important aspect of development involves creating and employing cultural, social, psychological, and physical means on the spur of the moment, and in response to problem-solving situations. Examining development within the context of a discussion of improvisational performance is compatible with contemporary perspectives on human activity that are guided by the assumption that individual's minds are not passive receptacles for knowledge, but rather that cognitive processes are developed through ongoing engagement in everyday activities (Baker-Sennett, Matusov, & Rogoff, 1992; Rogoff, Baker-Sennett, & Matusov, 1994).

Much of our discussion focuses on improvisational performance and development in an educational context. We believe that developmental psychologists and educators can learn a great deal from performance

studies. While researchers and educators often emphasize the importance of memorizing, problem solving, and planning to guide actions,
some dramatists counter that humans are too skilled in suppressing
action. "All the improvisation teacher has to do is to reverse this skill
and he creates very gifted improvisers. Bad improvisers block action,
often with a high degree of skill. Good improvisers develop action"
(Johnstone, 1979, p. 95). Along these same lines, we argue that development and improvisational activities are integrally interwoven. When
educational opportunities for improvisation are blocked, children's
opportunities to learn and develop are often limited. To explore these
issues we draw on literature from psychology, anthropology, and education, as well as on a series of investigations of children's collaborative
creation of classroom plays that explores the ways that children participate in dramatic activities with both peer and adult directors (Baker-
Sennett, Matusov, & Rogoff, 1992, 1995).

Activity and Improvisation

Directors such as Charlie Chaplin (see Robinson, 1985), Konstantin
Stanislavsky (1946, 1949, 1961, 1962), and Jacques Copeau (Rudlin,
1986), as well as musicians throughout history (see Bailey, 1980; Ferand,
1961) have been recognized for their facility with improvisational techniques. In the performing arts, improvisation is typically viewed as the
"skill of using bodies, space, all human resources, to generate a coherent
physical expression of an idea, a situation, a character; to do this spontaneously, and to do it *á l'improviste*: as though taken by surprise, without
preconceptions" (Frost & Yarrow, 1990, p. 1). Improvisation in a theatrical or musical context provides important lessons for the social sciences and for an understanding of creativity (Randall, 1987; Schwartz &
Ogilvy, 1979). During these performances meaning is collectively created. By understanding improvisational performance we may learn
more about communication, risk taking, social relationships, and how
order derives from seeming chaos.

The study of dramaturgy in sociology and some studies of performance in anthropology and education have relied on the metaphor of
life as drama (Brissett & Edgley, 1990; Goffman, 1959; Schechner,
1985). Bruner has argued that, like drama, "so too a life can be
described as a script, constantly rewritten, guiding the unfolding internal drama" (Bruner, 1973, p. 216). Rather than viewing people as
objects that are shaped and influenced by outside forces, dramaturgical
analyses view humans as creators. Meaning is found in the manner in
which individuals express themselves in interaction with others (Burke,
1966; Engestrom & Kallinen, 1988; Heathcote & Herbert, 1985).

Improvisations are not simply by-products of goal-directed actions, but rather improvisation is the process of creating meaning.

The use of performance as a metaphor for development is compatible with contemporary perspectives on human activity (Leont'ev, 1978; Meacham, 1984; Wertsch, 1991). Sawyer (1995) distinguishes between *improvisational performance* and *product creativity*. He defines improvisational performance as a collective creative synchronous process that constitutes the creative product: an ephemeral public performance. Thus, in improvisational performance, the process is product (see also Rogoff, 1990; Wertsch & Stone, 1979). Product creativity involves the process of creating products over time "with potentially unlimited opportunities for revision by the creator before the product is displayed" (Sawyer, 1995, p. 172). It is characterized by a diachronic interaction between public and audience. However, in product creativity, improvisational processes are also involved. To be able to "use" the author's product, the audience must initiate an interactive process with the historically distant author mediated by the product. Because direct feedback from the audience is not typically available for the author's creative process, the collective and dynamic character of product creativity is often overlooked. Sawyer stresses that in Western white middle-class culture (and in current research), product creativity is overemphasized while improvisational performance is underemphasized. However, it is probably fair to say that improvisational performance and product creativity are aspects of any sociocultural activity. Sociocultural activities with strong improvisational performance aspects still create strong experiences and memories that can be referred to in future activities and hence, in this sense, they demonstrate diachronic product creativity (e.g., successful jazz improvisations can be used in future compositions or even recorded with musical scores). Similarly, sociocultural activities with strong product creativity (e.g. reading a classic novel or analyzing a museum masterpiece) involve synchronic improvisational elements during both the author's creation of the product and the audience's consumption or use of the product.

Improvisation, Performance, and Education

In his study of Portuguese immigrant students attending a Catholic school in Toronto, Peter McLaren (1986/1993) describes how students negotiate activity in home and school contexts. Before class each day students congregate on the playground and streetcorners. Activity in this "street corner state," according to McLaren, is filled with improvisations and spontaneous verbal and physical expression:

[It] embraces fantasy, experiment, hypothesis, and conjecture . . . meta-phors flourish and promote novel cultural forms. . . . There is apt to be more "flow" (after Csikszentmihalyi, 1990) in the matching of skills and abilities since students do things at their own pace. Students spend time experimenting with different roles—playing "as if" they were others. (p. 88)

When the school bell rings and students move in to the classroom, this spontaneous state is terminated. Students adjust by altering their behavior to a more formal "student state" where they participate in activities that are organized and preplanned.

Students move "offstage" from where they are more naturally themselves to the proscenium of the suite where they must write their student roles and scenarios in conformity to the teacher's master script; they move from the "raw" state of streetcorner life to the more "cooked" or socialized state of school existence. (McLaren, 1993, p. 90)

Any attempt by students to remain in the streetcorner state in the classroom, according to McLaren, is thwarted by educators through pointed stares or direct reprimands. Similarly, Zukerman (1993) remarks on the "double life" that children lead in Russian mainstream schools: They are involved in creative interaction and improvisational self-directed joint activities during recess time, whereas individual activities are controlled and monopolized by the teacher during classroom time.

Our own research (conducted in collaboration with Barbara Rogoff) also explores the contextualized nature of improvisational and pre-planned activities as they unfold in the classroom. Over the course of a year we observed and videotaped elementary school children as they planned and performed school plays (Baker-Sennett et al., 1992, 1995). In one series of analyses we compared plays that were produced in small groups in a public elementary school classroom under the direction of parent volunteers with plays that were produced under the direction of first- and second-grade student volunteers.

Baker-Sennett et al. (1995) found that when children directed plays without overt intervention on the part of a teacher or adult volunteers, the resulting *playcrafting* sessions—the play planning and production—were filled with instances of spontaneous planning and improvisation. During child-directed playcrafting, very few decisions were made prior to the sessions. Rather, children often began by trying on costumes and using props in ways that led to the development of germs of ideas and lines of dialogue that were developed through improvisational pro-cesses. Once themes were recognized by the children, groups often moved to more global and meta-planning activities necessary to reconcile individual children's understandings and thematic differences.

Conversely, during adult-directed playcrafting sessions, adults did most of the planning prior to entering the classroom. Parent volunteers typically presented their ready-made play plans and/or scripts to small groups of children who carried out these plans during the course of rehearsals and the final performance. During these adult-directed playcrafting sessions, children were encouraged to contribute to the play's minor details such as what type of costume to wear or the design of a particular puppet. However, themes, scripts, and other types of metacognitive decision making were typically controlled by the adult volunteers and decided upon before the adults entered the classroom.

Baker-Sennett, Matusov, and Rogoff (1995) argued that adults' efficiency was achieved at the expense of children's opportunities for learning and participation in planning and acting. Adults' planning processes were, for the most part, closed to the children. The adult volunteers in this classroom did not treat classroom time as an opportunity to plan together with the children and guide them through the process of planning, nor did they encourage child participants to engage in improvisations.

Adults never elected to perform or work as collaborative players in the productions. Instead, they took on the roles of directors and playwrights, by sharing their ready-made plans with the children. By monopolizing the planning process, adults were faced with the problem of revitalizing their plans for the children as prospective actors. According to the theater theoretician Konstantin Stanislavsky, in order to act the play, actors must understand the playwright's intentions and goals. The actors have to join the playwright's planning process.

> Need one point out that while the actor is on the stage all these desires, aspirations, and actions must belong to him as the creative artist, and not to the inert paper words printed in the text of his part; not to the playwright, who is absent from the performance; nor yet to the director of the play, who remains in the wings? ... An actor can subject himself to the wishes and indications of a playwright or a director and execute them mechanically, but to experience his role he must use his own living desires, engendered and worked over by himself, and he must exercise his own will, not that of another. The director and the playwright can suggest their wishes to the actor, but these wishes must then be reincarnated in the actor's own nature so that he becomes completely possessed by them. For these desires to become living, creative desires on the stage, embodied in the actions of the actor, they must have become a part of his very self. (Stanislavsky, 1961, p. 50)

In Stanislavsky's improvisational method, planning and acting are two aspects of one process. During classroom playcrafting, however, the adults' way of sharing the plan and guiding children through the playcrafting process did not facilitate social and cognitive opportunities for children's creative involvement. In the final production, the child participants were enacting the adults' plans rather than planning or improvising creatively. Based on the dramatic sensibilities of adult Western white middle-class mainstream culture, the adults may have created more coordinated and coherent performances than were created during child-directed playcrafting sessions. However, the adults did not usually contribute to children's development as planners or creative improvisers, participating in the planning process.

In contrast, playcrafting directed by child volunteers required the children to plan and improvise themselves. The planning process was open for participation and socially distributed among the children. In the child-directed playcrafting sessions the final performance was only a part of the playcrafting process. During the child-directed playcrafting sessions, the children's individual mastery of planning activity, as well as their collaborations with each other, seemed to be organic parts (and moments) of the unfolding sociocultural playcrafting activity.

Improvisational Classrooms

The British director Keith Johnstone writes of the "watcher at the gates of the mind" who examines and edits ideas. In the case of our playcrafting example, adult volunteers were the gatekeepers for children's creativity. Johnstone and other dramatists argue that in the case of improvisation, "the intellect has withdrawn its watcher from the gates, and the ideas rush in pell-mell, and only then does it review and inspect the multitude" (Johnstone, 1979, p. 79). Is there some merit to this metaphor?

Baker-Sennett and Ceci (1996) found developmental declines in ideational fluency, flexibility, and improvisational problem solving during the middle elementary school years. To date, there has been little research that examines why children show developmental declines in the uses of improvisational and creative processes during the elementary years. It has been suggested, however, that most North American children are discouraged from creating and improvising as they proceed through the educational system. The philosopher Robert Root-Bernstein argues that

> Students are evaluated on their ability to reach correct accepted conclusions. This sort of education is necessary, but it is also insufficient, serving only to verify what we know, to build up the edifice of codified science

without suggesting how to generate ideas of the sort that lead to new discoveries. (Root-Bernstein, 1988, p. 34)

In his work with Australia's Theatre in Education Programme, O'Toole (1992) points out that "teachers normally appropriate the functions of playwright and director, and they may also take role as a player and devolve some aspects of 'playwright' or 'director' to the other participants" (p. 38). By facilitating classroom activities that allow children to co-create roles and distribute responsibility across participants, we argue that opportunity arises for the development of active learning and creativity.

The educator Viola Spolin (1963) argues that a major difference among the many classrooms she encountered in her career can be attributed to their differential reliance on the use of improvisation as a context for instruction. Improvisational classrooms, according to Spolin, have three important features: Learning is a shared social activity, is self-regulated, and has a "point of concentration." Spolin and others argue that cooperation is a prerequisite for spontaneity and improvisation (Donmoyer, 1983). The social nature of improvisation sets the stage for cooperative activity. In theatrical improvisation this social emphasis promotes ensemble creations as opposed to a star system (Spolin, 1963). Extending this metaphor to a classroom setting translates to an emphasis on the successful completion of group projects as opposed to individual grades as a motivator for activity.

An improvisational classroom also de-emphasizes external authority over classroom activity. Echoing the ideas of Dewey (1963), Spolin argues that external authority inhibits spontaneity because students and teachers are constrained by predetermined possibilities. However, improvisational classrooms shift the burden of responsibility from the teacher, also relying on the class to keep the activity on track.

Finally, according to Spolin, improvisation provides a focus or a "point of concentration" that allows for learning efficiency as opposed to unbridled chaos. The point of concentration

> Gives the control, the artistic discipline in improvisation, where otherwise unchanneled creativity might become a destructive rather than a stabilizing force. . . . It provides the student with a focus on a changing, moving single point ("Keep your eye on the ball") within the . . . problem and this develops his capacity for involvement with the problem and relationship with his fellow players. (1963, p. 22)

This point of concentration functions as a boundary within which students operate and within which constant crises must be met. "Just as a jazz musician creates a personal discipline by staying within the best while playing with other musicians, so the control in the focus provides the theme and unblocks the student to act upon each crisis as it arrives" (p. 23). This point of concentration provides a focus and direction for experience without inhibiting spontaneity nor dictating the course of behavior. It also refers to the interplay of improvisational performance and product creativity discussed by Sawyer (1995).

Teaching as Improvisation

Dewey describes the impact of moving from an educational system that focuses on recitation to one that encourages improvisational communication:

> This change of the recitation, from an examination of knowledge already acquired to the free play of the children's communicative instinct, affects and modifies all the language work of the school. Under the old regime it was unquestionably a most serious problem to give the children a full and free use of language. The reason was obvious. The natural motive for language was seldom offered. In the pedagogical textbooks language is defined as the medium of expressing thought. It becomes that, more or less, to adults with trained minds, but it hardly needs to be said that language is primarily a social thing, a means by which we give our experiences to others and get theirs again in return. When it is taken away from its natural purpose, it is no wonder that it becomes a complex and difficult problem to teach language. (1990, p. 55)

Like improvisational actors, who arrive onstage with a set of guiding principles rather than a written script, interactive teachers are also improvising performers. Yinger (1980, 1987) argues that when improvising, a teacher begins with an outline of the classroom activity. Details are filled in during the class session as the teacher creates the lesson in the process of figuring out what students can do and what they know. Unlike traditional lesson plans that outline objectives and the steps necessary to meet these objectives, improvisational teaching involves creating general guidelines and then improvising on-site when unpredictability occurs.

Improvisational teaching seems to be based on a teacher's skill in planning and collaborating "on the fly" (Tharp & Gallimore, 1988). This skill is based on an educational philosophy of mutuality and collaboration in providing guidance that avoids traps of either an adult-run philosophy of teaching when classroom activity is monopolized by the teacher, or a children-run philosophy of teaching when the teacher only follows children's interests (Matusov & Rogoff, in press; Rogoff, 1994; Rogoff, Matusov, & White, in press). Improvisational teaching takes the form of "a transactional dialogue, in which the comments and contributions of the participants build organically on each other's views and in which alternative viewpoints, differing interpretations, and criticism are elements essential to the encounter" (Brookfield, 1986, p. 23). It involves bridging inquiries of students and the teacher and creating a "community of learners" that extends the walls of school, the time frame of the lesson, and children's participation in classroom activities. Tharp and Gallimore (1988); Moll and Whitemore (1993); Palincsar, Brown, and Campione (1993); Wells, Chang, and Maher (1990); and Rogoff, Matusov, and White (in press) provide many examples of transactional dialogue and improvisational teaching in classrooms functioning as a community of learners. Gallimore describes improvisational teaching as being the end and the means to that end in the following way:

> Historically, teachers have tended to control discourse in ways that greatly restricted students' participation. Efforts to diversify classroom discourse have often sought a more conversational, discursive style found in teaching/learning activities outside of school. Certain kinds of literacy functions cannot be taught through disjointed, question-answer sequences. In more conversational exchanges, children learn to critique multiple interactions of texts, to take multiple perspectives, and marshal and weigh evidence. As long as involvement in the activity is high, even silent participants get a "cognitive work-out." They are "participant-observers in the activity," a stage that precedes actual practice. (Gallimore 1984, quoted in Rogoff, Matusov, & White, in press)

To explore improvisational teaching, Borko and Livingston (1989) observed experienced and inexperienced teachers during mathematics classes throughout an entire week. They found that while experienced teachers created long-range planning blueprints of course content and sequencing, much of their teaching strategy was improvisational. That is, during interactive teaching they made final decisions about the specifics of instruction. Experienced teachers reported that much of their planning occurred outside of formal planning times and was never written down. One teacher described his planning in the following way, "A lot of times I just put the objective in my book, and I play off the kids." He viewed his improvisational teaching as comparable to a tennis match, "I sort of do a little and then they do a little. And then I do a little and then they do a little. But my reaction is just that, it's a re-action. And it depends upon their action what my reaction's going to be" (p. 485).

In contrast to experienced teachers, the inexperienced teachers in Borko and Livingston's study relied on short-term (as opposed to long-term) planning. Inexperienced teachers reported planning ahead a few pages or a section in the text. Plans were created for tomorrow. These teachers typically wrote down written scripts that included introductions and conclusions. They were aware of the impact that their inexperience had on their ability to plan and improvise. According to one inexperienced teacher,

> This is all so new to me that thinking up, I have to do a lot of thinking ahead of time. I really do. I have to think out what kind of questions to ask. I have to think out the answers to the questions . . . so that my answers are theoretically correct and yet simple enough to make sense. And I have to really think in math. I love it. But I have to really think carefully about it. I can't ad-lib it too well. (Borko and Livingston, 1989, p. 487)

When inexperienced teachers' lessons deviated from their *a priori* plans these teachers often ran into difficulty. For example, some teachers provided factually incorrect responses to student questions, others had difficulty relating their lesson to the curriculum, and still others had difficulty keeping the lesson on track when responding to students' questions. These experiences resulted in some of the inexperienced teachers deciding to minimize improvisation by eliminating the opportunity for students to ask questions. One teacher explained,

> It's better to cut off the questions, just go through the material, because it'll be much clearer to them if they just let me go through it. . . . I don't want to discourage questions, but there are times I'd rather get through my presentation and then get to the questions. (p. 488)

These examples suggest that improvisation may benefit from experience. For novice teachers with little experience, it was difficult to improvise. Experienced teachers were able to sketch a teaching plan and then improvise according to student needs and interests during the course of each lesson. It also appears that the difference between the teachers is not only characterized by length of time spent in teaching or quantitative adjustments of teaching skills but a "paradigm shift" in their teaching philosophy that involved relinquishing control of the educational process and re-viewing teaching and learning as a collaborative endeavor.

Does Improvisation Benefit From Structure and Experience?

While this question has never been thoroughly examined, we began to get a glimpse of how improvisation is used as a tool for creativity and communication in our studies of children's playcrafting (Baker-Sennett et al., 1992). While volunteering and conducting research for a different study of children's playcrafting at the same innovative public school described earlier, we also had the opportunity to observe and videotape a group of six second- and third- grade girls over the course of ten half-hour sessions as they collaborated on the planning and production of their version of the fairy tale "Snow White." With intermittent assistance from the classroom teacher the group spent 1 month planning and rehearsing their play. The sessions were transcribed and then examined for evidence of both advance and improvisational planning.

Five levels of planning were identified that ranged from considering such metacognitive issues as deciding how to plan the planning process, to more concrete and detailed decision making about specific words and actions. Over the course of the month the girls spent a good deal of time during the early sessions considering many of the meta-planning issues that would form the foundation for later concrete planning decisions. They discussed how to develop strategies and rules for handling disputes during the planning process and considered alternatives for deciding how to go about planning the play. During these early sessions they also spent time deciding on the main theme and events of the play and how to divide and distribute roles. Throughout these early sessions the group spent most of their time planning in advance "out of action," not enacting any roles. However, during the fourth session a shift in activities occurred. At this point the group began to create by improvising in character and planning opportunistically. They began to both improvise and modify preplanned actions, dialogue, and scenes. At the same time they created new plans while enacting portions of the play.

Baker-Sennett et al. (1992) argue that during the early sessions the group was building a social foundation that allowed them to both work effectively as a social group and to meet the cognitive challenges of their playcrafting task. For example, the solution to one interpersonal problem involved a student's suggestion to "mix ideas" and thus to welcome contributions of all participants. This resulted in a humorous modification of the traditional fairy tale "Snow White," based on reversing ideas, themes, and characters, which was reflected in the children's new play title, "Blue Night." The processes of solving interpersonal and task-oriented problems developed in parallel and resulted in a single playcrafting process that we describe as the creation of a *social foundation*. The social foundation was built through direct verbal communication and explicitly stated plans. Once this social foundation was developed, the group was able to communicate in a more indirect, implicit, and abbreviated fashion. Plans did not need to be explicitly stated; rather the group was able to communicate and plan improvisationally, often retaining the voice and mannerisms of the particular character they were assuming.

Children's playcrafting is a problem-solving situation that necessitates both creativity and flexibility. There are an infinite number of ways of negotiating the process and creating the final product. Besides open-ended goals related to the playcrafting activity itself, children also seem to pursue many specific goals in playcrafting, including building their friendships, managing interpersonal relations for their own gains, having fun, securing approval of the teacher and the classroom, and so on. The goal-development process was embedded in the activity and problem solving, and was bounded by the activities and relations outside the playcrafting.

Rogoff, Gauvain, and Gardner (1987) have suggested that for problems that have a number of potential solutions rather than a single "best" solution, it may be more efficient to plan improvisationally, in order to take advantage of circumstances and to avoid the mental effort and delays required to formulate an advance plan. This seemed to be the case with the creation of "Blue Night." In this example, the problem was open-ended, not all of the final outcomes of planning decisions could be foreseen, thus the group's decision to leave some aspects of the plan open to improvisation allowed for greater flexibility and creativity.

CONCLUSION

Learning how to improvise may be rather more than just getting used to botching things up, or doing something "on the spur of the moment." It may even be something like a skill for living. Not just doing anything in the moment, but learning how to make use of as much of ourselves and as much of the "context" as possible; learning how to fill the moment. (Frost & Yarrow, 1990)

As Frost and Yarrow argue, improvisation is more than acting in the moment and working with the imperfections that spontaneity brings. Improvisation is the intersubjective process of creating meaning. Schools do not typically teach students how to improvise, nor are the everyday failures that result from risky improvisations dealt with in the educational arena. In North America teachers are skilled at helping individual students become efficient at solving text-based, algorithmic problems. Although the problems of everyday life require opportunistic planning, school activities typically separate problem solving from problem defining and inquiry development (Lave, 1988).

In this chapter we have pointed to the importance of improvisational performance for development and educational practice. We have argued that it does not always make sense to follow a preplanned trajectory.

Rather, it is through improvisation that we weave familiar and unfamiliar activities and ideas in response to social, contextual, and individual needs. Traditional studies of learning in school settings have emphasized adult-directed, text-based learning. It has been interesting for us to explore what takes place when the text is gone and when students and teachers have the opportunity to improvise. By exploring the drama in everyday activities we are able to reevaluate existing perspectives on child development. We find that not only does improvisational performance provide children with opportunities to engage in sophisticated, collaborative problem-solving processes, it also serves as a tool that revitalizes the way we think about the relationships between teaching, learning, and development. As we have argued, the fields of education and developmental psychology have much to learn from drama. French director Jacques Copeau foreshadowed this article's conclusion more than 80 years ago when he argued; "Somewhere along the line of improvised play, playful improvisation, and improvised drama, real drama, new and fresh, will appear before us. And these children, whose teachers we think we are, will, without doubt, be ours one day" (Copeau, 1916, quoted in Rudlin, 1986, p. 44).

REFERENCES

Bailey, D. (1980). *Improvisation: Its nature and practice in music*. Ashbourne, Derbyshire, U.K.: Moorland Publishing.

Baker-Sennett, J., & Ceci, S. (1996). Cognitive insights: Examining clue-efficiency and strategies related to discovery. *Journal of Creative Behavior, 30,* 153–172.

Baker-Sennett, J., Matusov, E., & Rogoff, B. (1992). Social processes of creativity and planning: Illustrated by children's playcrafting. In P. Light & G. Butterworth (Eds.), *Context and cognition: Ways of learning and knowing.* Hertfordshire, U.K.: Harvester-Wheatsheaf.

Baker-Sennett, J., Matusov, E., & Rogoff, B. (March 1995). *Collaborative planning of classroom plays with child and adult direction.* Paper presented at the meetings for the Society for Research in Child Development, Indianapolis, Indiana.

Bateson, M. C. (1990). *Composing a life*. New York: Penguin Books.

Borko, H., & Livingston, C. (1989). Cognition and improvisation: Differences in mathematics instruction by expert and novice teachers. *American Educational Research Journal, 26,* 473–498.

Brissett, D., & Edgley, C. (1990). *Life as theater: A dramaturgical sourcebook.* New York: Aldine de Gruyter.

Brookfield, S. D. (1986). *Understanding and facilitating adult learning.* San Francisco: Jossey-Bass Publishers.

Bruner, J. (1973). *Beyond the information given: Studies in the psychology of knowing.* New York: Norton & Company.

Burke, K. (1966). *Language as symbolic action: Essays on life, literature, and method.* Berkeley: University of California Press.

Csikszentmihalyi, M. (1990). *Flow: The psychology of optimal experience.* New York: Harper and Collins

Dewey, J. (1963). *Experience and education.* New York: Collier Books.

Dewey, J. (1990). *The school and society.* Chicago: University of Chicago Press.

Donmoyer, R. (1983, January). Pedagogical improvisation. *Educational Leadership,* 39–43.

Engestrom, Y., & Kallinen, T. (1988). Theatre as a model system for learning to create. *The Quarterly Newsletter of the Laboratory of Comparative Human Cognition, 10,* 54–67.

Ferand, E. T. (1961). *Improvisation in nine centuries of Western music.* Koln, Germany: Arno Volk Verlag Hans Gerig KG.

Frost, A., & Yarrow, R. (1990). *Improvisation in drama.* London: Macmillan Education Ltd.

Goffman, E. (1959). *The presentation of self in everyday life.* New York: Doubleday & Co.

Heathcote, D., & Herbert, P. (1985). A drama of learning: Mantle of the expert. *Theory into Practice, XXIV* (3), 173–180.

Johnstone, K. (1979). *Impro: Improvisation and the theatre.* London: Faber and Faber.

Lave, J. (1988). *Cognition in practice: Mind, mathematics and culture in everyday life.* New York: Cambridge University Press.

Leont'ev, A. N. (1978). *Activity, consciousness, and personality.* Englewood Cliffs, NJ: Prentice-Hall.

Matusov, E., & Rogoff, B. (in preparation). *Educational philosophy differences related to parents' experience volunteering in a community of learners school.*

McLaren, P. (1986/1993). *Schooling as a ritual performance: Towards a political economy of educational symbols and gestures.* London: Routledge.

Meacham, J. A. (1984). The social basis of intentional action. *Human Development, 27,* 119–123.

Moll, I., & Whitmore, K. (1993). Vygotsky in classroom practice: Moving from individual transmission to social transaction. In E. Forman, N. Minick, & C. Stone (Eds.), *Contexts for learning: Sociocultural dynamics in children's development.* New York: Oxford University Press

O'Toole, J. (1992). *The process of drama.* London: Routledge.

Palincsar, A. S., Brown, A. L., & Campione, J. C. (1993). First-grade dialogues for knowledge acquisition and use. In E. Forman, N. Minick, & C. Stone (Eds.), *Contexts for learning: Sociocultural dynamics in children's development.* New York: Oxford University Press.

Randall, R. A. (1987). Planning in cross-cultural settings. In S. L. Friedman, E. K. Scholnick, & R. R. Cocking (Eds.), *Blueprints for thinking* (pp. 39–75). New York: Cambridge University Press.

Robinson, D. (1985). *Chaplin: His life and art.* New York: McGraw-Hill.

Rogoff, B. (1990). *Apprenticeship in thinking: Cognitive development in social context.* New York: Oxford University Press.

Rogoff, B. (1994). Developing understanding of the idea of communities of learners. *Mind, Culture, and Activity, 1*, 209–229.

Rogoff, B., Baker-Sennett, J., & Matusov, E. (1994). A sociocultural perspective on the concept of planning. In M. Haith, J. Benson, B. Pennington, & R. Roberts (Eds.), *Future-oriented processes* (pp. 353–373). Chicago: University of Chicago Press.

Rogoff, B., Gauvain, M., & Gardner, W. (1987). The development of children's skills in adjusting plans to circumstances. In S. L. Friedman, E. K. Scholnick, & R. R. Cocking (Eds.), *Blueprints for thinking* (pp. 303–320). New York: Cambridge University Press.

Rogoff, B., Matusov, E., & White, C. (in press). Models of teaching and learning: Participation in a community of learners. In D. Olson & N. Torrance (Eds.), *Handbook of education and human development: New models of learning, teaching, and schooling*. London: Basil Blackwell.

Root-Bernstein, R. (1988, May/June). Setting the stage for discovery. *The Sciences*.

Rudlin, J. (1986). *Jacques Copeau*. New York: Cambridge University Press.

Sawyer, R. K. (1995). Creativity as mediated action: A comparison of improvisational performance and product creativity. *Mind, Culture, and Activity, 2*, 172–191.

Schechner, R. (1985). *Between theater and anthropology*. Philadelphia: University of Pennsylvania Press.

Schwartz, P., & Ogilvy, J. (1979). *The emergent paradigm: Changing patterns of thought and belief*. Menlo Park, CA: Stanford Research Institute International.

Spolin, V. (1963). *Improvisation for the theatre*. Evanston, IL: Northwestern University Press.

Stanislavsky, K. (1946). *An actor prepares*. New York: Theatre Arts Books.

Stanislavsky, K. (1949). *Building a character*. New York: Theatre Arts Books.

Stanislavsky, K. (1961). *Creating a role*. New York: Theatre Arts Books.

Stanislavsky, K. (1962). *Stanislavsky on the art of the stage*. (trans. by D. Magarshack). New York: Hill & Wang.

Tharp, R. G., & Gallimore, R. (1988). *Rousing minds to life: Teaching, learning, and schooling in social context*. New York: Cambridge University Press.

Wells, G., Chang, G. L., & Maher, A. (1990). Creating classroom communities of literate thinkers. In S. Sharan (Ed.), *Cooperative learning: Theory and research*. New York: Praeger.

Wertsch, J. (1991). *Voices of the mind*. Cambridge: Harvard University Press.

Wertsch, J., & Stone, C. A. (February, 1979). *A social interactional analysis of learning disabilities remediation*. Paper presented at the International Conference of the Association for Children with Learning Disabilities, San Francisco.

Yinger, R. J. (1980). A study of teacher planning. *The Elementary School Journal, 80*, 107–127.

Yinger, R. J. (1987). *By the seat of your pants: An inquiry into improvisation and teaching*. Paper presented at the annual meeting of the American Educational Research Association, Washington, DC.

Zukerman, G. (1993). *Vidy obschenia v obuchenii* (Types of interaction in the classroom). Tomsk, Russia: Peleng.

chapter 10

Responsive Order:
The Phenomenology of Dramatic
and Scientific Performance

Robert P. Crease
State University of New York, Stony Brook

Dr. Crease is best known for his writings in the philosophy of science. His most recent book, The Play of Nature: Experimentation as Performance, *develops a performance analogy to analyze scientific practice. This book examined how practicing groups of scientists generate originality and novelty through collective performative processes. In this chapter, Crease draws on phenomenological philosophy to develop a broad concept of performance. Crease defines a "performance" to be a* presentation *of a phenomenon, that is related to a* representation, *but that is nonetheless able to be new; and the performance must be presented to a community that can* recognize *what is both old and new in it. Using this phenomenon-based definition, Crease argues that not only the performing arts are performances, but so too is experimental activity in science. The representation of the phenomenon is the theory, combined with the methodology of the experiment; the presentation is the execution of the experiment. What appears in performance—the results of the experiment—always has the potential to surprise not only the audience, but even the planners and executors of the experiment.*

To the extent that a performance represents a new phenomenon, creativity must be involved. But performance does not allow an "anything goes" creativity; it must evolve out of what exists—out of what we know and can already do. This is related to Csikszentmihalyi's concept of the domain *of creative activity. It is in this sense that performance is a* responsive order. *Performances are also responsive to the contingencies during performance, and in this sense are improvisational. This theme is related to the chapters by Sawyer and Berliner, since both emphasize the moment-to-moment responsiveness of improvising performers.*

The word "performance" is applied to a range of activities, including simple execution of purposive action ("job performance") social role-playing of any type (Goffman, 1959), the manner in which something takes place as opposed to content ("teacher performance"), as well as a wide variety of theatrical activity. The concept does not lend itself to definitive statements and final descriptions, and explorations of the word's applications continue. States recently observed that the word performance is still "ramifying," and concluded that, in his view, a definition of it "is a semantic impossibility" (States, 1996, p. 3). Allow me, in what Schechner calls the "broad spectrum" of performance (Schechner, 1988), to restrict my discussion to a narrow bandwidth. I shall treat performance as the conceiving, producing, and witnessing of an action in the service of an inquiry that cannot be furthered by consulting what we already have. More exactly,

> Performance is first of all an execution of an action in the world which is a *presentation* of a phenomenon; that action is related to a *representation* (for example, a text, script, scenario, or book), using a semiotic system (such as a language, a scheme of notation, a mathematical system); finally, a performance springs from and is presented to a suitably prepared local (historically and culturally bound) community which *recognizes* new phenomena in it. The field develops through an interaction of all three. (Crease, 1993, p. 100)

A performance in this sense is not merely a *praxis*—an application of a skill, technique, or practice that simply produces what it does—but a *poiesis*; a bringing forth of a phenomenon, of something with presence in the world; which is to say, something with the ability to appear in different ways in different circumstances, but exhibiting some lawlike behavior.

DRAMATIC AND EXPERIMENTAL PERFORMANCES

Works of the performing arts are clearly of this sort. Here, the lawlike behavior is represented or "programmed" in part by its texts, scripts, or notational systems, which are then correlated with techniques and practices so that a phenomenon appears: the work itself. The representation thus structures both performance process and product. A script, for instance, both structures the actions of the performers on the one hand, and describes what transpires onstage (the drama, the play) on the other. Expressed in phenomenological language, a representation read *noetically* is something to be performed; read *noematically*, it describes the object appearing in performance.

Experimental activity in science, too, is of this kind. In this case, law-like behavior is generally represented by theories (mathematical or otherwise), that are correlated with practices and procedures so that a phenomenon—some particle or behavior or structure—is revealed or produced. Here, too, the theory read noetically structures the actions necessary to produce the phenomenon (it is incorporated or programmed into the instruments), while read noematically it describes the phenomenon produced (the experimental object appearing in the lab). This is why a theory can be at once explanatory (an explication of when and how something appears which relates it to other phenomena), descriptive ("getting it right" with respect to how the phenomenon shows itself), and instructive (providing, recipe-like, the rules for how to produce a phenomenon) The theory of electromagnetism structures the instruments and techniques that produce electrons in the lab, provides a description of the observed "electrons" themselves, and tells us how they are "made."

There are, of course, important differences between the production of phenomena in the dramatic arts and in experimental science. One is the role of technology and instrumental mediation in the production of phenomena. Technology simultaneously extends and transforms perception and bodily praxes through what Ihde has called "embodiment relations"; it is absorbed and incorporated into bodily experience of the world like Heidegger's hammer or Merleau-Ponty's organ and blind man's cane (Ihde, 1979, 1991), and the phenomena that appear change as the forms of embodiment change. To a certain extent this also happens in the dramatic arts, as new techniques appear and become disseminated and standardized, but the nature and scope of technological embodiment is much more transformative in experimental science. Another difference between dramatic and experimental performances is that the latter are executed with an eye to *measurement*. Finally, in experimental science, *reports* of successful experimental performance for the most part suffice to those who do not immediately stage the performance, while this is not so in the dramatic arts. This is because the meaning of a dramatic work for each individual has to do with the experience of the work as it is occurring, whereas the meaning of a scientific entity for the scientific community has to do with the bare fact of its performability by someone.

Nevertheless, the first-person perspective of one who experiences (or fails to experience) the worldly presence of phenomena is essential to a complete understanding of not only the nature of performance, but also areas of inquiry, like drama and experimental science, that involve planning, executing, and witnessing performances. If these fields are viewed strictly from the third-person (social science) perspective, they are inevitably seen as purely *interest-driven*, or developed in response to changing human wants, needs, and utilities. Here the explanations given are at the level of social factors rather than those associated with individual, first-person experience. But performances are also and at the same time *event-driven*, or developed in response to physical performances (in the laboratory or theater, say), which involves reference to the first-person experience of the phenomenon appearing in performance.

The problematic nature of first-person experience cannot be jettisoned entirely without wholly misrepresenting the scientific process. Trevor Pinch has phrased the "most important thesis" guiding social constructivism as follows: "In providing an explanation of the development of scientific knowledge, the sociologist should attempt to explain adherence to all beliefs about the natural world, whether perceived to be true or false, in a similar way," but also says that the sociologist "endeavors to give explanations at the level of societal factors rather than those associated with individuals" (Pinch, 1986, pp. 3, 10). Yet a phenomenology that refers to first-person experience is ultimately essential in explaining human experience of the natural world, scientific and otherwise. If one views either the dramatic arts or experimental science solely from the third-person perspective, these fields look the way a soccer game might from an airplane, in which one sees an interesting and empirically describable spectacle involving ceaseless motion of the players, but without being able to apprehend a key ingredient to the play—the ball—whose immediate interaction with the players is essential to a full account of the game, and makes it compelling to watch and play.

For these reasons, as I argued in *The Play of Nature* (Crease, 1993), the structure of the performative act is essentially the same in the dramatic arts and experimental science. Performance is not a metaphor that is extended merely suggestively from the former into the latter. In both the dramatic arts and experimental science, the theory, language, or representation used in the performance does not completely determine the outcome, the product, the work, but only assists in the encounter with the new. What appears in performance can even startle and exceed the program used to represent it, and an experiment that has been planned, programmed, and executed on the basis of a certain theory, score, and so forth, can disclose things that lead us to adapt or change that theory. In the following discussion of performance and creativity, therefore, I shall discuss performance as something that happens alike in the arts and the sciences; to do otherwise would be to interpose a false disciplinary boundary. Yet that boundary has so much of a hold on thinking that what I say may sound abstract in trying to speak about performance in terms that straddle the false disciplinary fence. But to see experimental science and dramatic art as exhibiting one process sharing the same essential features, I claim, requires no more abstraction than is habitually practiced in either field.

CHARACTERISTICS OF PERFORMANCE

I have mentioned three related aspects involved in performance: presentation, representation, and recognition, which I now want to develop further.

Performances are first of all *presentative* in that they aim at being original rather than representative; revelatory and disclosive rather than imitative. They are not derivative with respect to the way they are represented or programmed. Performances are what they testify to; their appeal is direct. Were it otherwise, performance would be *superfluous* with respect to representation, and a performance of *Hamlet* no more than a means to transmit some pre-existing meaning or truth. To say that performances are "presentative" is also to say that they are actions done and witnessed for their own sake. Their purpose is internal to the process, and if some other motive is involved—money, prestige, problem solving, career advancement—it provides no indication as to how to perform well. What is presented, I suggested, is (a profile of) a phenomenon. By phenomenon, I do not mean anything to do with phenomenalism or illusionism; that is, not something that carries connotations of transience or ephemerality. Nor do I mean sense-data, nor something that is "pre-theory," as the term phenomenon often means in physics. Nor do I mean something with the ontological status of a mathematical object: abstract, unworldly, identical. By phenomenon, I simply mean something worldly that fulfills our expectations in a regular way. This formulation may sound vague, which is how I intend it. It merely expresses the fact that our ordinary living and thinking and acting reveal the world to possess a certain kind of order—what kind, I shall come to soon. This order includes things to which we can return, but differently. Works of dramatic art and experimental phenomena are examples; they are found and produced confidently again and again, though never exactly the same way each time.

While a performance is related to a *representation*, both the representation and the techniques and methods correlated with it *serve* the phenomenon. One may speak of a *primacy of performance* over the representations and techniques and methods used to get it, and these are often altered if the appearing of the phenomenon in performance demands it. One can speak of the *fragility* both of representations and of techniques; scores, scripts, and theories, as well as practices and methods, are not inviolate and sacred, but in actual use are often modified to fit what works in performance. One must be careful, however, to avoid a common confusion related to terminology that is addressed by Heelan's conception of the *dual semantics* of the language of science (Heelan, 1988). For a theorist, the terms are mathematical entities—"electron" is an abstract term in a theory—while for an experimenter the terms are descriptive of real worldly beings—an electron is a real phenomenon involved causally in laboratory events. We find the same contrast between a note in a score analyzed by a musicologist and a note heard in performance.

Recognition is the perceptual apprehension of a phenomenon *as* a phenomenon when what is at issue is its bodily presence. If I glance away momentarily from a group of people with whom I am speaking and then look back, the situation is too utterly familiar to say that I undergo a process of re-recognizing each and every one of them; I already *know* who they are. Rather, I recognize a phenomenon (a person) that I come across in an environment in which its presence is an issue to me—unanticipated perhaps, or alien. I say I recognize a person for I am looking in a sea of faces, or someone unexpected whom I encounter on the street. Recognition is a bodily experience and opens up new possibilities; I am surprised or relieved, and I can shun, linger over, or explore the recognized presence. The ability to recognize is relative to the historical, cultural, and technological embodiment of the observer. New forms of embodiment mean recognition of new phenomena, and I might recognize something as a horn, a saxophone, or a phrase by Ben Webster.

Presentation, representation, and recognition, then, are three essential characteristics of performance, and fields progress by the simultaneous development of all three. There is no need to secure any deeper grounding for either dramatic art or experimental science outside of the circle that these form. Now I shall address four features to help elucidate the connection between performance and creativity: multiple horizons, freshness, thrall, and atten tion.

Phenomena appear as able to show themselves in different ways; to use a classical phenomenological illustration, to apprehend the coffee mug is to apprehend it as able to be seen from the back, top, held in my hand, drunk from, and so forth—all of these anticipations of other ways I might also apprehend it. In phenomenological language, phenomena appear together with *horizons*, or sets of expectations, which may be determinate or indeterminate. Phenomena, that is, show themselves as able to be performed otherwise, as having potential answers to questions such as: What happens if I do *this*? How would it look if I do *that*?

Performances also aim at the bringing-forth of a *fresh* presence or phenomenon. By fresh, I mean that a performance offers a pure, vibrant, and original appearance that shines forth full of life, like fresh fruit or fresh hope. I also mean that a performance can stand out without being something entirely novel. Many things can be fresh—air, snow, flowers, appearance—while also being familiar. Nothing is as familiar to theater-goers as *Hamlet*—but can't a production of *Hamlet* be fresh? By fresh, I also mean forceful, as in a fresh stream or a wind that blows fresh. Such a fresh presence is something we linger over, and becomes the object of attention. By fresh, finally, I mean something we experience as invigorating and rejuvenating—something that refreshes. Freshness, therefore, refers to what we want out of a performance: what we come for, what we strive to get, what lies beyond the standard thing. One might distinguish here between the *technology* and the *artistry* of performance. The technology of performance refers to standardized practices whose successful operation we can take for granted. The artistry of performance, by contrast,

> coaxes into being something which has not previously appeared. It is beyond the standardized program; it is action at the limit of the already controlled and understood; it is risk. The artistry of experimentation involves bringing a phenomenon into material presence in a way which requires more than passive forms of preparation, yet in a way so that one nevertheless has confidence that one recognizes the phenomenon for what it is. (Crease, 1993, p. 110)

Performances are *enthralling*. "Enthralling" comes from the Old Norse for "slave;" to be enthralled means to be held captive by something more powerful than oneself. To say that performances are enthralling is to say that they can exert power over us. We are invested in them; something is at stake for us in their execution and outcome. The thrall of a performance is not derivative of whatever score, script, text, or other program or representation is used in its presentation, but rather from something that happens to us in its fleshy presence.

A performance also makes us *attentive*. "Attentive" is from the Latin for "to stretch towards"; we can stretch toward a performance, becoming watchful and alert and sometimes even edgy. Can't we be on the edge of our chairs even during a performance of *Hamlet*? We can not say that we are edgy because we don't know what happens next; in *Hamlet*, we know what happens next. It would also be wrong to say that our attention is due to curiosity at seeing how this particular production of *Hamlet* is going to pull things off. Instead, we are attentive, and we experience mounting tension because of something internal to the performance. For whatever reason, we are affected in our being by what transpires.

CREATIVITY AND PERFORMANCE

In our ordinary living and thinking and acting, I said above, we experience the world, not as a chaotic flux—as one complete novelty after another—but as containing a set of phenomena, or presences, to which we can return again and again, though differently each time. But neither does experience consist of always encountering what we expect; it often involves filling in, revising, and extending horizons in the exploration of phenomena. In fact, it is possible to add wholly new phenomena to the world. Let us call creativity the process by which new phenomena are sought and brought into the world. Performance is one means by which world enrichment can happen.

Let me now elaborate by discussing four features of new phenomena appearing in performance that are related to the features I just mentioned. First, a new phenomenon appears as *mysterious*, that is, as to-be-explored, as incompletely realized and thus requiring further investigation. To use the phenomenological terminology, a new phenomenon appears with unexplored horizons. Experience alone—additional performances—allows us to discover whether our expectations are fulfilled or not, and hence what kind of phenomenon it is.

Second, a new phenomenon, too, *imposes* itself. It has a life of its own; it seems to make its own choices in response to what I do; if I do this or that that it may grow stronger, disappear, or do something unexpected. A new phenomenon, moreover, *instructs* us how to reach it. Our familiar methods and techniques may not be suitable, and we may have to develop new ones. The development of a *technique*, in fact, involves just this kind of standardization. A classic and by now well known illustration of this process is found in Ludwik Fleck's *Genesis and Development of a Scientific Fact* (1979), about the development of the Wassermann reaction as a test for syphilis, in which the author describes how the necessary serological skills were at first possessed only by Wassermann himself, then slowly passed on to his coworkers and then to other laboratories, eventually resulting in a standardized, reliable technique. One may speak of a "trajectory of technique," in which a phenomenon moves, via a series of stages involving the standardization of performance ability, from effect to technique to technology (Crease, 1992). But while phenomena can instruct practice, they can also instruct theories. Here a classic example is provided by the history of the theory of electromagnetism. The theory as first formulated by James Clerk Maxwell was subsequently revised by the development of more appropriate notation, so that the early notation (used until the 1930s) came to seem hopelessly cumbersome in contrast.

A new phenomenon also *transforms* us. We are invested in a performance, and the reaction of a researcher to the appearance of something new is unlikely to be blasé. What appears in performance does so not magically, like a magician pulling a coin out of an ear, but from a coworking of elements that we observe. A performance is a *worldly* ("empirical") event and owes its thrall to the fact that the phenomenon present must be acknowledged in worldly ("objective") terms. If one is a scientist and is interested in the weak interaction, and a convincing performance has exhibited the phenomenon of parity violation in the weak interaction, one can hardly turn one's back or pretend the performance did not happen, but must acknowledge that worldly presence—*this* happens when the performance of *that* sort is staged—no matter how unexpected or shocking. (If one is convinced that the result is in error, one then has the burden of showing how it could be an epiphenomenon.) "Walked through door," cabled Robert Oppenheimer in 1957 to a friend upon hearing the news about parity violation.

Recognition of a new phenomenon is, finally, a *celebratory* event. Celebration, of course, is a phenomenon that takes place after successful performances of other kinds (consider the spiking of footballs after touchdowns) and occurs as well in the specific kinds of performances I am considering. Anyone who has rehearsed a complex ensemble performance is familiar with the reaction, not just of the performer but of members of the whole troupe, to the successful, first-time execution of a difficult performance segment. Such celebration is evidently part of the psychodynamics of creativity. It is true that one looks in vain for a description of the celebratory side of scientific performances in traditional philosophies of science, some of which have gone so far as to oppose aesthetic feelings to those that accompany genuine scientific inquiry. ("The question of truth," wrote Gottlob Frege in his most famous and influential article, "would cause us to abandon aesthetic delight for an attitude of scientific investigation," 1952, p. 63) Nothing could seem further from science than the celebratory moment. But as diaries, oral interviews, and reminiscences reveal, when scientists are not attempting to conform to an image of being detached observers, they also frequently express celebration and the enchantment of creation (Crease, 1993, p. 120).

CREATIVITY AND RESPONSIVE ORDER

I have treated creativity as the introduction of new phenomena into the world. Where were these new phenomena? Were they already there, merely unrecognized, all along? Or were they our own arbitrary constructions, the outcome of some process of negotiation that took place between human interests? What I have said shows that if new phenomena are viewed as either merely unrecognized beforehand or our arbitrary constructions, it would be a way of denying the authority of performance. (It would also be wrong to "split the difference" and say that performances are partly unrecognized and partly constructed.) Innovation in performance is neither an imposition of an arbitrary external order on the flux, on the one hand, nor a deductive or coerced process on the other. It is a *hermeneutical* process; it evolves out of an already existing involvement with and understanding of, a concrete situation, and the process I undergo in that situation that Gendlin calls *carrying-forward* (1996). In carrying-forward, I apply everything that has been culturally and historically transmitted to me, and inevitably wind up acting originally and with fresh involvements.

This is an illustration of a particular *kind* or order, that Gendlin has called *responsive order* (1995). With respect to the subject at hand, responsive order means that not everything works in performance. Neither scientists nor artists, that is, think up an idea in advance and then realize *that*, but are rather involved in an interactive process in which putting together a performance involves accommodating oneself to diversions, obstacles, and responses that are not *exactly* what we expected. Something new can appear in performance for which there are no concepts or words, even though the performance uses concepts and words. A new phenomenon shows itself as more than the program or theory, but not apart from it. It is tempting to believe in the fiction of a space that opens up in our heads, into which an insight drops from without, the gift of some mental angel. But there is not enough free space in our heads for that to happen. Such an insight can only enter through the carrying-forward of a situation we are already involved in.

Carrying-forward can happen in several ways. One is in the *workshop situation*, while one is in the course of working on an ongoing problem (by "workshop" I mean both the laboratory and rehearsal studio). In a recent talk, Martin Perl, the 1995 Nobel Prizewinner in physics, remarked that while experimenters often attempt to explain their reason for doing a particular experiment by saying that they want to find out something, the real reason is often simply that this is what they know how to do.

> We do these experiments because we do them—we know how to do them, we like to do them, we improve them a little bit, and we do them. In a way that's bad, but in a way that's the essence of science. Very few people, in the experimental world at least, can get an idea just sitting in their office or sitting in the library. It's working on a subject, working on an experi-

ment, that gives the idea—for improving the apparatus, or finding out it's not good, or how to do it some other way, or how to make a measurement. So the essence of science, in a difficult way, is working in the science already as individuals. And that's why "this is what we do" is deeper than it seems. (Perl, 1966)

What Perl describes—ideas befalling one in the course of working at the lab bench—feels familiar. In which situations are we more likely to be inventive: entirely open-ended situations when we are asked to "play something" at the piano, "paint something" on a blank canvas, or "say something about Heidegger"—or when we are in the course of being engaged in some concrete project of these kinds? The workshop situation can develop through the right way simply coming, or by some disturbance—something that turns us aside from the smooth path we expected. We could describe why this happens by saying that more of what one possesses in the way of cultural and historical resources is in play in a matrix when one is engaged in a concrete activity than when one attempts to stand back and take stock.

Another place where this happens is the dialogical situation, when one is clarifying for someone else what one is doing. If I have to reply to somebody's misunderstanding, all sorts of things may come that do not come by themselves. Here, too, what has been transmitted to me is in play, sometimes in fresh ways as I try to rephrase and rework an explanation. One is not speaking of an "it"—something already fixed—in different words, nor of replacing one "it" with a new and better one, rather one is carrying "it" forward. The need for such situations is revealed by the fact that they are often ritualized, as the cafeteria conversation at certain laboratories.

Another situation where carrying-forward can take place is the meditative situation, when one's thoughts freely drift over a problem, sometimes coming at it in unfamiliar and unexpected ways. These occasions, too, can be ritualized: the morning shower, the drive to the office, the leisurely morning spent in bed. This may look like an angel's gift but it is not; more can be in play in this kind of situation than when one is narrowly focused.

Another is the improvisational situation. In improvisation, something *must* be done. But without the guidance of a representation, the gestures of our performance come to us more like the way our moods and feelings come to us. Rather than come to us out of habitual pathways or thoughtfully considered patterns, they befall us out of our entire being-in-the-world. Again, one can (but not always) have in play more than what one can explicitly master (Crease, 1994).

The history of science, and of theater, can supply ample examples of each of these. The point is that we don't have to get mystical or agnostic about the process of creation, only understand it as the carrying-forward of a situation.

Let me make one final point related to what States has called the "pleasurable base" of performance (1996, p. 25). If, as I have argued, the phenomenon dominates the performance, then the distinction between the performer and audience is in some respects dissolved; the phenomenon that appears in performance does so equally to those who perform and those who watch only. One thing they share is the bodily feeling associated with the celebratory dimension of carrying-forward. Thus to understand how performance functions, either in dramatic arts or in experimental performances, one must begin prior to that differentiation in the urge to world enrichment. One must begin, as States put it, with the "abiding interest in the spectacular possibilities of the world" (1996, p. 25).

REFERENCES

Crease, R. P. (1992). The trajectory of techniques. *Science*, 257, 350–353.

Crease, R. P. (1993). *The play of nature: Experimentation as performance*. Bloomington: Indiana University Press.

Crease, R. P. (1994). The improvisational problem. *Man and World*, 27, 181–193.

Crease, R. P. (1995). The sculpture and the electron: The hermeneutics of the experimental object. *Science and Education*, 4, 109–114.

Fleck, L. (1979). *Genesis and development of a scientific fact* (trans. F. Bradley & T. J. Trenn). Chicago: University of Chicago Press.

Frege, G. (1952). On sense and reference. In P. Geach & M. Black (Eds.), *Translations from the philosophical writings of Gottlob Frege*. Oxford, U.K.: Blackwell.

Gendlin, E. T. (1996). *Experiencing and the creation of meaning*. Toronto: Collier-Macmillan. (Original work published in 1962.)

Gendlin, E. T. (1997). The responsive order: A new empiricism. In *Man and World, 30*, forthcoming.

Goffman, E. (1959). *The presentation of self in everyday life*. New York: Doubleday.

Heelan, P. A. (1983). *Space-perception and the philosophy of science*. Berkeley: University of California Press.

Heelan, P. A. (1988). Experiment and theory: Constitution and reality. *Journal of Philosophy, 85*, 515–524.

Ihde, D. (1979). *Technics and praxis*. Boston: D. Reidel Publishing Co.

Ihde, D. (1991). *Instrumental realism*. Bloomington: Indiana University Press.

Ihde, D. (1990). *Technology and the lifeworld*. Bloomington: Indiana University Press.

Merleau-Ponty, M. (1969). Cézanne's doubt. In A. L. Fisher (Ed.), *The essential writings of Merleau-Ponty*. New York: Harcourt, Brace.

Perl, M. (1996). Craft and art in experimental science. AUI Distinguished Lecture, Brookhaven National Laboratory, May 14, 1996.

Pinch, T. (1986). *Confronting nature*. Boston: Reidel.

Schechner, R. (1988). Performance studies: The broad spectrum approach. *The Drama Review, 32*, 4–6.

States, B. O. (1996). Performance as metaphor. *Theatre Journal, 28*.

chapter 11

Poetics and Performance as Critical Perspectives on Language and Social Life*

Richard Bauman
Indiana University

Charles Briggs
University of California, San Diego

This chapter is a reprint of an influential article in the Annual Review of
Anthropology. *It is a valuable resource for readers who want a concise, read-
able summary of a large body of exciting contemporary work in a range of disciplines, that focuses on the creativity of verbal performance in situations ranging
from ritual performance to everyday social encounters. Bauman and Briggs
begin their review with the late-1970s introduction of a performance focus in lin-*

*Reprinted from *Annual Review of Anthropology*, vol. 19, 1990, pp. 59–88. During the
writing of this chapter, both authors held fellowships from the National Endowment for
the Humanities, which are hereby gratefully acknowledged. We are also grateful to Indiana
University and Vassar College for travel funds in support of our collaboration. As noted,
the section on "Entextualization and Decontextualization" draws deeply on discussions of
the seminar on Texts and Power sponsored by the Center for Psychosocial Studies and
convened by Michael Silverstein and Greg Urban. We would like the thank the members of
the seminar for their intellectual contributions to this work: Donald Brenneis, James Collins, Vincent Crapanzano, William Hanks, John Haviland, Judith Irvine, Benjamin Lee,
John Lucy, Elizabeth Mertz, Richard Parmentier, Michael Silverstein, Greg Urban, Bernard Weissbourd. Michael Herzfeld and Hugh Mehan were discussants in an American
Anthropological Association session based on the work of the Texts and Power Group and
provided valuable comments. These colleagues are not, of course, accountable for logical
and expository flaws in our presentation. We also thank John Lucy for sharing with us, in
advance of publication, his work on reported speech.

guistic anthropology and folkloristics. This new focus on performance directed attention away from the study of formal patterns and symbolic contents in performance texts, toward the emergence of verbal art in the social interaction between performers and audiences. Their broad review covers discourse analysis, formalization and parallelism in ritual speech, conversation analysis, the influence of genre, and the relation of music and language in ritual. They note parallels with intellectual threads such as social constructionism, deconstruction, reader-response theories, hermeneutics, and cultural studies. Monson's chapter makes similar connections between the study of jazz improvisation, conversation, and current issues in poststructuralist theory.

In addition to their summary of current research, the authors introduce their own concepts of entextualization *and* contextualization *as ways of describing the dialectic relationship between the texts of performance and the creativity of the performer in using the text in a specific social setting. This framework allows the authors to explore how certain* poetic patternings *allow discourse to be extracted from particular speech events.*

INTRODUCTION

Scholars have vacillated for centuries between two opposing assessments of the role of poetics in social life. A long tradition of thinking about language and society argues that verbal art provides a central dynamic force in shaping linguistic structure and linguistic study. This position emerges clearly in the writings of Vico, Herder, and von Humboldt; attention from Sapir, the Russian "Formalists," and members of the Prague School to the role of poetics contributed to the development of performance studies and ethnopoetics in the last two decades. Nonetheless, poetics has often been marginalized by anthropologists and linguists who believe that aesthetic uses of language are merely parasitic upon such "core" areas of linguistics as phonology, syntax, and semantics, or upon such anthropological fields as economy and social organization.

The balance between these two views shifted in favor of poetics in the late 1970s and early 1980s as a new emphasis on performance directed attention away from study of the formal patterning and symbolic content of texts to the emergence of verbal art in the social interaction between performers and audiences. This reorientation fit nicely with growing concern among many linguists with indexical (as opposed to solely referential or symbolic) meaning, naturally occurring discourse, and the assumption that speech is heterogeneous and multifunctional. Anthropologists and folklorists similarly found performance-based studies responsive to their interest in play, the social construction of reality, and reflexivity. One dimension that particularly excited many practitioners was the way performances move the use of heterogeneous stylistic resources, context-sensitive meanings, and conflicting ideologies into a reflexive arena in which they can be examined critically.

A number of historical overviews and critical assessments of this literature are available (Bauman, 1982, 1987b, 1989a, 1989b; Bauman & Sherzer, 1975, 1989; Briggs, 1988a; Fine, 1984; Limon & Young, 1986; Stoeltje & Bauman, 1988). We accordingly turn our attention to several basic theoretical issues that have shaped both the way that scholars have studied performance and its rejection by other practitioners. These problems are evident in the way such key terms as performativity, text, and context have been defined, and in the presuppositions used in framing them. Our stress on these broader theoretical issues runs counter to a growing tendency to view this area as "the performance approach," thus downplaying the heterogeneous array of theoretical sources that have shaped it, and reducing performance to the status of a formula for the analysis of artful communication.

First, we examine several crucial presuppositions of both the partisans and critics of poetics research. These implicit metaphysical conceptions take culturally and historically specific ideas about the nature of language and its role in social life and elevate them to the level of purportedly objective and universally applicable theories. We argue that such assumptions are not only limited and ethnocentric but also often undermine the ability of scholars to grasp the heterogeneous and dynamic character of language use and the central place that it occupies in the social construction of reality. It is important to recognize the historical and cultural specificity and ethnocentricity of Western thinking about language and society and to explore a broader range of alternatives. In the context of these broader questions, performance-based research shares some of the central goals of deconstruction (Culler, 1981), reader-response and reception theories (Jauss, 1982; Tompkins, 1980), hermeneutics (Rabinow & Sullivan, 1987), the "poetics and politics" of ethnographic texts (Clifford & Marcus, 1986), and cultural studies (Carey, 1989).

Studies of performance can make a unique contribution to this larger project. As many authors have stressed, performances are not simply artful uses of language that stand apart from day-to-day life and larger questions of meaning, as a Kantian aesthetics would suggest. Performance rather provides a frame that invites critical reflection on communicative processes. A given performance is tied to a number of speech events that precede and succeed it (past performances, readings of texts, negotiations, rehearsals, gossip, reports, critiques, challenges, subsequent performances, and the like). An adequate analysis of a single performance thus requires sensitive ethnographic study of how its form and meaning index a broad range of discourse types, some of which are not framed as performance. Performance-based research can yield insights into diverse facets of language use and their interrelations. Because contrastive theories of speech and associated metaphysical assumptions embrace more than these discourse events alone, studying performance can open up a wider range of vantage points on how language can be structured and what roles it can play in social life.

Performance-based study challenges dominant Western conceptions by prompting researchers to stress the cultural organization of communicative processes. Linguists, of course, have long discounted native speakers' views of language structure and use; Boas (1911), for example, referred to such conceptions as "secondary explanations," and he regarded them as irrelevant, distracting, and patently false. Anthropologists, on the other hand, often follow Malinowski (1922/1961) in claiming to present "the native's point of view" (see Geertz, 1976). Presentations of "the native model" or "theory" generally overlook difficulties in deriving indigenous perspectives exclusively from the referential content of elicited data. They tend also to ignore the fact that such factors as gender and social class frequently generate competing perspectives on language and social life. To make more reliable use of native speakers' meta-level discourse on language we must regard performers and audience members not simply as sources of data but as intellectual partners who can make substantial theoretical contributions to this discourse. In addition, we must develop greater awareness of the way discourse is recorded and analyzed.

As ethnographers of performance, we regard the task of deconstructing dominant Western conceptions of language and social life as a vital, ongoing facet of a larger project. We accordingly turn to the complementary task of exploring alternative ways of viewing performance in a later section ("Entextualization and Decontextualization"). We attempt to provide a framework that will displace reified, object-centered notions of performativity, text, and context—notions that presuppose the encompassment of each performance by a single, bounded social interaction. Heeding calls for greater attention to the dialectical relationship between performance and its wider sociocultural and political-economic contexts, we introduce the concepts of *decentering* and *recontextualization* to stress the way poetic patterning extracts discourse from particular speech events and explores its relationship to a diversity of social settings.

Decentering and recontextualization have powerful implications for the conduct of social life. Investigating how this process takes place and how individuals gain rights to particular modes of transforming speech can therefore illuminate issues of central concern to anthropologists, linguists, folklorists, and literary scholars.

FROM PERFORMATIVITY TO THE SOCIAL CONSTRUCTION OF REALITY

J. L. Austin's *How to Do Things With Words* (1962) sparked both excitement and controversy. His rejection of an exclusive focus on truth-value semantics in favor of viewing language use as social action that emerges in the "total speech act" is echoed in Bauman's emphasis on the emergent properties of performance (Bauman, 1977b, 1987b). The impact of this characterization of language use as social action by such speech act theorists as Austin (1962), Grice (1975), and Searle (1969, 1976, 1979) was enhanced by its resonance with Sapir's emphasis on the dynamic character of language (Sapir, 1921, 1949), the Prague School's characterization of the multifunctionality of signs (Garvin, 1964; Matejka & Titunik, 1976; Mukarovsky, 1977a, 1977b), and Malinowski's view of language as a "mode of action" rather than primarily a "means of thinking" (Malinowski, 1923, 1935). The work of Bateson (1972) and Goffman (1974, 1981) has also been influential in this regard.

To say that language use is social action is, however, much easier than to develop frameworks that can identify and explain the nature of this dynamism. As Levinson (1983) notes, speech act theory has rested on a "literal force hypothesis" that posits a one-to-one correlation between performative utterances and illocutionary forces, even if most theorists admit that surface forms frequently do not directly signal illocutionary force. Silverstein (1979) suggests that speech act theory ultimately draws on the very referential reductionism it decries in asserting that the semantic content of "explicit performative verbs" can be used in correlating types of performative utterances with illocutionary forces. This equation becomes painfully apparent in Austin's conclusion that since "primitive languages" lack "precision" (that is, referential delicacy), explicit performatives will also be absent; it will accordingly be impossible to make clear distinctions between illocutionary forces. Far more than the reputation of speech act theory itself rests on sorting out these problems; they force practitioners to come to grips with basic recurrent issues regarding structure vs. event, context-free vs. pragmatic elements of language, and the role of language in social life. Performance-oriented research, particularly studies of political and ritual discourse, have played a special role in this undertaking.

Discourse analysis argues that a wide range of formal features can signal the illocutionary forces of utterances, often apart from or in spite of their referential content. One of the most controversial claims is Bloch's

(1975) characterization of political rhetoric in "traditional" societies. He argues that oratorical style places great constraints on linguistic form, suppresses creativity, and diminishes the importance of reference; this process of formalization nonetheless greatly enhances the ability of speakers to bring about a desired course of action. While many writers have attacked Bloch (Brenneis & Myers, 1984; Irvine, 1979; Paine, 1981; Parkin, 1984), his work has prompted researchers to examine the way that performativity can be tied to a vast range of formal features and patterns. Hanks (1984) argues, for example, that the formality of Yucatec Mayan ritual speech does not preclude creative responses to the shaman's personal history and the contextual parameters of the performance. McDowell (1983) suggests that formalization of ritual speech decreases its accessibility to both potential performers and audiences; this suppression of the referential function enhances its efficacy. He also argues in a study of riddles (McDowell, 1979, pp. 22–30) that framing speech as performance can signal a suspension or inversion of the felicity conditions outlined by Austin. Conversation analysts, such as C. Goodwin (1981), M. Goodwin (1982), Moerman (1988), Sacks (1974; Sacks, Schegloff, & Jefferson, 1974), and Schegloff (1968, 1982), have focused on the sequential organization of conversation, arguing that the communicative function of an utterance is relative to its location in the linear stream of discourse. In some speech communities, code-switching provides a central means of transforming the performative force of utterances (Amistae & Elias-Olivares, 1982). Hill (1985) has drawn on Bakhtin (1981) and Volosinov (1930/1973) in arguing that code-switching can heighten attention to competing languages and varieties to such an extent that identities, social relations, and the constitution of the community itself become open to negotiation (cf. Hill & Hill, 1986).

Similarly, drawing on Jakobson's work on parallelism, a number of researchers have demonstrated the way that parallelistic constructions at both micro and macro levels can signal illocutionary force (Caton, 1987; Jakobson, 1960, 1966, 1968; Silverstein, 1981, this volume). Haviland (1988) argues that the authority of elders in mediating conflict emerges from their ability to displace a cacophony of angry voices through use of the quintessential embodiment of Zinacanteco social and linguistic order: ritual couplets. A wealth of similar examples from eastern Indonesia is available in a recent volume edited by Fox (1988). Urban has argued that cultural stylization of the sonic embodiments of crying signal both affect and sociability in ritual wailing (Urban, 1988).

Studies have also suggested that performativity is not lodged in particular formal features alone but in larger formal-functional units. Abrahams (1980, 1986), and Bauman (1986) draw on Bakhtin (1968, 1981) Bateson (1972), Goffman (1974, 1981), Huizinga (1955), and Turner

(1969, 1974) in arguing that play frames not only alter the performative force of utterances but provide settings in which speech and society can be questioned and transformed. Participation structure, particularly the nature of turn-taking and performer-audience interaction, can have profound implications for shaping social relations (Bloch, 1975; Brenneis & Myers, 1984; Duranti, 1983; Goodwin, C., 1986; Goodwin, M. H., 1980; Myers, 1986; Shuman, 1986; Urban, 1986).

A number of authors have argued that genre plays a crucial role in shaping illocutionary force (Abrahams, 1976; Abu-Lughod, 1986; Bauman, 1990; Ben-Amos, 1976; Brenneis, 1978, 1988b; Briggs, 1988a; Gossen, 1972, 1974; Hanks, 1987; Hymes, 1972; Philips, 1987). These works suggest that genres are far more than isolated and self-contained bundles of formal features. A shift of genre evokes contrastive communicative functions, participation structures, and modes of interpretation. Moreover, the social capacity of particular genres and the relationship between genres are themselves patterned in ways that shape and are shaped by gender, social class, ethnicity, age, time, space, and other factors (Abrahams, 1976, 1983; Abrahams & Bauman, 1971; Abu-Lughod, 1986; Bauman, 1986, 1990; Bowen, 1989a; Briggs, 1988a; Glassie, 1982; Gossen, 1974; Levine, 1977; Sherzer, 1983, 1990). Similarly, pursuit of a particular interactive focus (teaching, exhorting, befriending, confronting, etc.) generally involves negotiated changes of genre in which features of one genre are embedded within a token of another. Bakhtin's (1981, 1986) pioneering work on this problem has been afforded greater depth and precision by several recent studies (Abrahams, 1985; Bauman, 1990; Dorst, 1983; Limon, 1983). The illocutionary force of an utterance often emerges not simply from its placement within a particular genre and social setting but also from the indexical relations between the performance and other speech events that precede and succeed it (of which more below). The illocutionary force and perlocutionary effects of courtroom testimony are highly dependent, for example, on evidentiary rules and broader semiotic frames that specify admissible types of relations to other bodies of written and oral discourse (Bennett & Feldman, 1981; Conley & O'Barr, 1990; Danet, 1980; Mertz, 1988; O'Barr, 1982; O'Barr & Conley, 1985; Philips, 1985, 1986).

This body of research has greatly enhanced our understanding of performativity by showing that illocutionary force is not simply a product of the referential content and/or syntactic structure of particular sentences. The formal properties of discourse, larger units of speech events, frames, keys, participation structures, and the like are not simply "felicity conditions" (Austin, 1962) or "preparatory conditions" (Searle, 1969) that activate self-contained performative utterances. Illocutionary force can be conveyed by a host of elements from micro to macro and, most importantly, by the interaction of such features. The ethnography of communication, discourse analysis, and research on performance have all contributed to shifting the locus of research from isolated sentences and features to, in Austin's terms, the total speech act.

This process has followed three loosely defined stages. A number of studies (published primarily in the late 1960s through mid-1970s) applied Austin's framework to a particular speech community and/or body of speech act types (Finnegan, 1969; Foster, 1974a, 1974b; Ravenhill, 1976). As a result, a lack of fit became apparent between speech act theory (as outlined by Austin, Searle, Grice, and others) and the way performativity was conceived of and used in a wide range of speech communities. Ethnographies of speaking both exposed the ethnocentricity and reductionism inherent in this theory, and helped researchers to find alternatives (Duranti, 1984; Hymes, 1974; Keenan, 1976; Ochs, 1984; Rosaldo, 1982; Silverstein, 1979). Eventually the use of speech act theory in framing research problems was to a great extent displaced in favor of, as Levinson has put it, "much more complex multi faceted pragmatic approaches to the functions that utterances perform" (Levinson, 1983, p. 283). Performance-oriented scholars no longer think of performativity primarily as the use of specific features in signaling particular illocutionary effects within a fixed set of conventions and a given social context. Instead, they view it as the interaction of complex and heterogeneous formal patterns in the social construction of reality. Works from this perspective (see particularly Abu-Lughod, 1986; Bauman, 1986; Bell, 1983; Brenneis & Myers, 1984; Caraveli-Chaves, 1980; Comaroff & Roberts, 1981; Herzfeld, 1985; Limon, 1982) resonate with the voices of such philosophers and literary critics as Burke (1941, 1950/ 1969), Gadamer (1960), Langer (1942/1951), and Williams (1977) in arguing that formal elaboration does not relegate discourse to a Kantian aesthetic sphere that is both purely subjective and carefully insulated from cognition, social relations, and politics. While Austin (1962, pp. 21-22) claimed that performance weakens the performative force of utterances, this literature suggests that poetic patterning, frames, genres, participatory structures, and other dimensions of performance draw attention to the status of speech as social action.

Researchers can go much further than they have in using the rich potential of performance-based research to question received notions about the nature of performativity and its role in social life. Three issues seem particularly in need of critical attention.

First, the relationship between formal features and communicative functions has generally been treated as one of means to ends, such that form becomes meaningful insofar as it is connected with some type of content or function. Saussure (1916/1959), for example, idealized form as a meaningless plane of undifferentiated sound that is constituted as a set of signifiers arbitrarily related to units of referential content. Just as telling is his capitalistic analogy, which equates the relationship between signifiers and signifieds with that between currency and goods. But some speech communities regard sound itself as a primary locus of meaning (see Monson, this volume). For example, Feld (1982, 1988) shows that the Kaluli view the patterning of linguistic and musical sound as emanating iconically from natural sounds, particularly bird calls and waterfalls; communicative functions and socially defined ends are derived from formal patterns, not vice versa. E. Basso (1985) and Seeger (1987) draw on South American data in arguing that musical dimensions of performances can shape linguistic patterning and social relations (see also Roseman, 1988; Stoller, 1984). Although more research is needed in clarifying these issues, these preliminary studies make it apparent that reifying form as a collection of empty containers waiting to receive small dollops of referential content or illocutionary force impoverishes our understanding of performance and of communication.

Second, Austin's suggestion that performance renders the performative force of utterances "hollow or void" cannot simply be inverted. Performance does not always connect discourse automatically and unimpeachably with particular illocutionary forces and perlocutionary effects. Keenan (1973) and Briggs (1988b) have noted that performances can by their very nature call into question the performative efficacy of speech forms, thus leading to negotiations of the relationship between utterances and illocutionary forces. Bauman (1983b), Silverstein (1985b), and, long before them, Sapir (1921) have shown how diachronic shifts between patterns for relating form and meaning are played out in conflicts between proponents of competing forms and ideologies. Briggs (1988a, pp. 328–331) argues that ritual speech can invoke a special form of signification in which the distinction between signifier and signified is itself collapsed. Bauman (1977b) and Hymes (1975a) have suggested that audience evaluation of the communicative competence of performers forms a crucial dimensions of performance. Particularly in ritual and political discourse, this concern with form and function is often extended to assessments of how (and even if) formal patterning becomes imbued with functional significance.

Finally, theories of performativity presuppose conceptions of the nature of language and social action. As Heidegger (1971) has argued, Western theories of language and poetics in turn presuppose Western metaphysics; Derrida (1974, 1978) has attempted to expose these connections by deconstructing Western discourse. The performances of non-Western societies and marginalized sectors of Western industrialized nations provide illuminating settings for furthering this pursuit.

Such performances do not simply reveal contrastive forms and functions; basic conceptions of language and social life differ as well (Friedrich, 1986). In the case of marginalized groups on the periphery of industrial capitalism, performances are often overtly concerned with deconstructing dominant ideologies and expressive forms (Briggs, 1988a; Farrer, 1975; Levine, 1977; Limon, 1982; Paredes, 1966a, 1968; Stewart, 1988; Weigle, 1978).

A striking illustration of the fruitfulness of this approach is an article by Rosaldo (1982). She uses Ilongot conceptions in showing how Searle "falls victim to folk views that locate social meaning first in private persons—and slight the sense of situational constraint" (p. 212). The Ilongot data prompt her to argue that Searle's analysis of performative verbs should be read less as universal laws of speech acts than as "an ethnography—however partial—of contemporary views of human personhood and action as these are linked to culturally particular modes of speaking" (p. 228). Such truly dialogical research does not view speakers as dupes who lack the ability to reflect meaningfully on their own communicative conduct. Rather, it accepts them as partners who have substantive contributions to make to the process of deconstructing Western views of language and social life and exploring a broader range of alternatives.

FROM CONTEXT TO CONTEXTUALIZATION

A crucial move in the establishment of performance approaches was a shift from the study of texts to the analysis of the emergence of texts in contexts. Malinowski (1923, 1935) emphasized early the cultural and interactional context of language use, paying attention especially to verbal art forms such as magical spells and narratives. Bateson's (1972) and Goffman's (1974) work on frames, Parry (1971) and Lord's (1960) emphasis on the role of the audience in oral composition, and the conceptualization of the communicative event proposed by Jakobson (1960) and expanded by Hymes (1962, 1964, 1974) provided important stimuli for students of performance (see Abrahams, 1968; Arewa & Dundes, 1964; Bauman, 1977b; Ben-Amos, 1972, 1977).

Nevertheless, a number of recent studies suggest that scholars are moving away from a focus on context, as conceived in normative, conventional, and institutional terms. Blackburn's work on Tamil bow songs provides a case in point. In an article published in 1981, Blackburn noted that "the influence of oral context on narrative content" provided a "central focus of this essay" (1981, p. 208). Five years later, while similarly declaring that "Performance . . . is whatever happens to a text in context" (1986, p. 168), he went on to argue that the analysis of text remained central to the study of performance. By the time that his monograph on bow songs appeared in 1988, Blackburn asserted that what is needed is a "text-centered approach to performance" that starts with the narrative outside its enactment" (1988, p. xviii).

Performance-centered scholarship has also been read of late in antithetical ways. Limon and Young (1986) argue, for instance, that studies of performance have not measured up to Bauman's (1977a, 1977b) call for analysis of the broader social, cultural, and historical context; they attribute this failure to the devotion of practitioners to microsociological or interactional analysis and to a focus on the poetics of verbal art. Bronner (1988, p. 89) argues in a somewhat similar vein that "in emphasizing display and performance, in the assumption of expressive actions as strategies used in specific situations, the nature of an actor was separated from the act, and the physical stage was isolated from its social surroundings." Thus in these and other recent accounts, performance-centered research emerges as the blind man's elephant. Blackburn seeks to recover "lost ground in the study of oral performance" by "reversing the direction that performance studies had charted" (Blackburn, 1988, pp. xxi, xvii); that is, to him performance studies seem too much concerned with context and too little concerned with textual detail. Limon and Young and Bronner, on the other hand, argue that performance approaches are too caught up in poetics to be able to discern broader social and political contexts.

These discrepancies are not simply the product of divergent trends in the field: These authors cite many of the same sources. Nor do such claims simply imply a circular movement from text to context to text. Rather, performance studies are in the midst of a radical reformulation wherein "text," "context," and the distinction between them are being redefined. This shift is signaled grammatically in the addition of affixes that effectively move the emphasis from product to process and from conventional structures to agency as the terms "entextualization" and "contextualization" gain currency. The remainder of this section is devoted to a consideration of the move from "context" to "contextualization"; we discuss the transition from "text" to "entextualization" in the following section.

Briggs (1988a, p. 13) identifies two problems inherent in the concept of context: inclusiveness and false objectivity. Some practitioners have proposed relatively circumscribed definitions. Dundes, for example, states that "The context of an item of folklore is the specific social situation in which that particular item is actually employed" (1964, p. 23). In his seminal formulation, Malinowski distinguishes "the context of cultural reality . . . the material equipment, the activities, interests, moral and aesthetic values with which the words are correlated" (1935, p. 22) from the "context of situation" or "social context," the "purpose, aim and direction of the accompanying activities" (1935, p. 214). Bauman (1983a) expands the list to six elements, including the "context of meaning," "institutional context," "context of communicative system," "social base," "individual context," and "context of situation." All such definitions of context are overly inclusive, there being no way to know when an adequate range of contextual factors has been encompassed. The seemingly simple task of describing "the context" of a performance can accordingly become an infinite regress.

The problem of false objectivity emerges from the positivistic character of most definitions of context. This equation of "the context" with an "objective" description of everything that surrounds a set of utterances has two important implications. First, since it is obviously impossible to point to all aspects of the context, the researcher becomes the judge of what merits inclusion. Second, positivistic definitions construe context as a set of discourse-external conditions that exist prior to and independently of the performance. This undermines the analyst's ability to discern how the participants themselves determine which aspects of the ongoing social interaction are relevant. It also obscures the manner in which speech shapes the setting, often transforming social relations. Reifying "the context" also implicitly preserves the premise that meaning essentially springs from context-free propositional content, which is then modified or clarified by "the context" (cf. Silverstein, 1992).

A number of writers have attempted to break out of this mold by focusing on the *metacommunicative* or *metapragmatic* (Silverstein, 1976) capacity of language. Cook-Gumperz and Gumperz (1976; see also Gumperz, 1982) incorporate insights of Bateson (1972), Goffman (1974, 1981), and others in proposing a shift from context to *contextualization*. They argue that communicative contexts are not dictated by the social and physical environment, but rather emerge in negotiations between participants in social interactions. The ongoing contextualization process can be discerned by attending to the *contextualization cues* that signal which features of the settings are used by interactants in producing interpretive frameworks. A rapidly growing body of literature points to the centrality of features of poetic patterning in contextualizing performances (Basso, E., 1985, 1992; Bauman, 1986; Bell, 1983; Blackburn, 1986; Briggs, 1988a; Goodwin, C., 1984; Haviland, 1988; Hymes, 1981, 1985; Kuipers, 1990; McDowell, 1985; Shuman, 1986; Urban, 1986, 1988). Performance-based analysis has a key role to play here in that poetically patterned contextualization cues are highlighted in performance; this heightened perceptibility can help researchers to determine how individual cues are linked in creating larger formal and functional patterns.

The shift in emphasis from context to contextualization suggests a reason why performance analysis has become simultaneously more textually and more contextually focused in recent years. In order to avoid reifying "the context" it is necessary to study the textual details that illuminate the manner in which participants are collectively constructing the world around them. On the other hand, attempts to identify the meaning of texts, performances, or entire genres in terms of purely symbolic, context-free content disregard the multiplicity of indexical connections that enable verbal art to transform, not simply reflect, social life. To claim that researchers must choose among analyses of poetic patterns, social interaction, or larger social and cultural contexts is to reify each of these elements and to forestall an adequate analysis of any.

The shift we identify here represents a major step toward achieving an agent-centered view of performance. Contextualization involves an active process of negotiation in which participants reflexively examine the discourse as it is emerging, embedding assessments of its structure and significance in the speech itself. Performers extend such assessments to include predictions about how the communicative competence, personal histories, and social identities of their interlocutors will shape the reception of what is said. Much research has focused on the way this meta-level process is incorporated into the textual form of performances, particularly in the case of narratives. Babcock (1977), Bauman (1986), Briggs (1990), McDowell (1973), and others have focused on *metanarration*, "those devices which comment upon the narrator, the narrating, and the narrative both as message and as code" (Babcock, 1977, p. 67). Metanarration includes a host of elements that have, as Georges (1981) argues, been marginalized, overlooked, and sometimes even deleted from transcripts, owing to their supposed irrelevance to the narrated events themselves. As Bauman has argued (1986), metanarrative devices index not only features of the ongoing social interaction but also the structure and significance of the narrative and the way it is linked to other events. For example, Texas storyteller Ed Bell embeds the following metanarrative comment in a story about a giant bee tree: "And I don't blame y'all if you don't believe me about this tree, because I wouldn't believe it either if I hadn'ta seen it with my own eyes. I don't know whether I can tell ya how you could believe it or not, but that was a big tree" (Bauman, 1986, p. 99). Bauman argues that such interventions bridge the gap between the narrated event and the storytelling event by reaching out *phatically* to the audience. Shuman (1986) details the way adolescent fight stories focus not only on the fights but also on situations that reveal the tenor of ongoing relationships between the involved parties. Such stories thus present both assessments of the causes and consequences of the fighting and assertions of the participants' rights to tell and hear the story.

A central device for connecting narrated and narrating events is *reported speech* (Jakobson, 1957); a growing body of research (Bauman, 1986, 1990; Briggs, 1988b; Hymes, 1981; Lucy, 1993; Silverstein, 1985a; Urban, 1984) has built upon the insights of Volosinov (1930/1973). Reported speech enables performers to increase stylistic and ideological heterogeneity by drawing on multiple speech events, voices, and points of view. As we show below, this *decentering* of the narrating event and of the narrator's voice opens up possibilities for renegotiating meanings and social relations beyond the parameters of the performance itself.

While much of the research on the metacommunicative functions of poetic patterning has focused on narrative, a number of studies have analyzed proverbs, riddles, rhymes, insults, greetings, and other genres, as well as poetic features of conversation (Abrahams, 1985; Basso, K., 1979; Bowen, 1989b; Briggs, 1988a; Cicourel, 1982; Goodwin, M. H., 1985; Gossen, 1974; Labov, 1972; McDowell, 1979, 1985; Silverstein, 1981, 1984). More research is needed in this area.

This shift in analytic perspective has fostered awareness of the active role that hearers also play in performances. In conversational narratives, audience members are often accorded turns at talk, thus rendering narration coperformance (Degh & Vazsonyi, 1976; Goodwin, C., 1986). The backchannel of audience members shapes the structure and content of the performance as speakers assess the involvement and comprehension of their interlocutors (Beeman, 1981; Briggs, 1988a; Duranti & Brenneis, 1986; Goodwin, C., 1981; Haviland, 1986, 1988). C. Goodwin (1986) argues that audiences are shaped by discourse in keeping with the differential involvement of members in what is said; the audience also plays a key role in assessing the significance of the talk. Performance-audience interaction is clearly not shaped by overt signals alone; K. Basso (1984) provides a striking analysis of the way that speakers can withhold overt contextualization cues, counting on culturally-defined patterns of response to enable listeners to work out the bearing of the narrative on the current setting. Even when audience members say or do practically nothing at the time of the performance, their role becomes active when they serve as speakers in subsequent entextualizations of the topic at hand (e.g., in reports, challenges, refutations, enactments of consequences, and the like).

The movement from context to contextualization and related concerns thus enables us to recognize the sophisticated way that performers and audiences use poetic patterning in interpreting the structure and significance of their own discourse. Researchers can accordingly ground their analysis in the participants' interpretive efforts. This change in orientation has profound implications for fieldwork. It facilitates greater awareness of the dynamics of performance in the ethnographic encounter itself.

The basic conceptual and methodological premise of the ethnography of performance is that the structure and dynamics of the performance event serve to orient the participants—including the performer. One might therefore expect assessments of the discourse emergent in ethnographic encounters to take into account both the ethnographic agenda and the role of the fieldworker. In fact, however, analysis of the effects of the ethnographer (his or her actions, research entourage, equipment, agenda, etc.) upon such discourse required the modification of a longstanding focus among folklorists and anthropologists on the *natural context*—that is, on the way in which the natives do (or did) things on their own, free of compromising outside influences. Ethnographers of performance needed a certain boldness to deconstruct this notion of natural context by confronting their own influence on what their local sources offered them. Nevertheless, after Haring's pioneering analysis (1972) of how his informants shaped what they told him to their conception of who he was, what he wanted, and what he should be told, numerous papers have examined contextualization in the ethnographic encounter. This work has illuminated variously the negotiation of the agenda of the interaction and the role of the participants within it as well as the choice, shaping, and framing of their discourse (Bauman, 1984; Briggs, 1985, 1986; Cicourel, 1974; Darnell, 1974; Hymes, 1975a, 1985; Mishler, 1986; Tedlock, 1983). Indeed, contextualization has been shown to extend beyond the boundaries of the fieldwork setting itself, insofar as the tape recorder introduces possible subsequent audiences into consideration (Bauman, 1986, pp. 78–111, Tedlock, 1983, pp. 285–301). Such reflexive attention to contextualization in the ethnographic encounter significantly affected the very formulation of performance theory: Hymes's foundational distinction between the reporting of an artistic text and the performance of it rests on an analysis of shifting and negotiated frames of contextualization in his ethnographic work with his Chinookan consultants (Hymes, 1975a).

By focusing on the dialogic foundations of ethnographic discovery, this reflexive line of performance-centered research anticipated the recent turn toward a more dialogic anthropology (Marcus & Fisher, 1986; Tedlock, 1983). In turn, the insights we have discussed here offer to "the poetics and politics of ethnography" a heightened awareness of the communicative work invested by our ethnographic interlocutors and a set of tools for analyzing the entextualization (Crapanzano, 1984) and contextualization of ethnographic dialogues.

The insights afforded by the studies we have cited stem from the special sensitivity of the ethnographers who produced them to the dynamics of contextualization and performance. Paredes (1977) goes on to offer a trenchant critique of ethnographic practices that fail to take performance within the ethnographic encounter into account. Paredes finds the literature on Greater Mexican (especially Texas-Mexican) society and culture to be riddled with interpretive inaccuracies that stem from the naively referential bias of positivist ethnographic practice: asking people for facts and assuming they will provide straight answers. Paredes shows that the ethnographic encounter invites the display of communicative competence, a touchstone of performance, just as the inequality that often characterizes the relationship between the native "informant" and ethnographer may invite joking, leg-pulling, or playing to stereotypes. There is thus a predisposition toward performance and other expressive framings of communication in the contextualization of discourse within the ethnographic encounter, regardless of whether the question at hand is verbal art or kinship. Paredes's work suggests that a sensitivity to performance must be a critical and reflexive part of any ethnographic investigation that involves the gathering of data by verbal means (see also Briggs, 1986; Grimshaw, 1981).

ENTEXTUALIZATION AND DECONTEXTUALIZATION

Much performance-oriented research on contextualization has focused on the grounding of performance in situational contexts. An alternative perspective has begun to emerge in performance studies and other areas that approaches some of the basic problems in linguistic anthropology from a contrary set of assumptions.

Consider for a moment why researchers have had to make such an issue of contextualization, to devote so much effort to establishing that the form, function, and meaning of verbal art cannot be understood apart from context. The reason is precisely that verbal art forms are so susceptible to treatment as self-contained, bounded objects separable from their social and cultural context of production. Taking the practice of decontextualization as the focus of investigation, we ask what makes it possible, how it is accomplished in formal and functional terms, for what ends, by whom, under what circumstances, and so on. We are currently far from having conclusive answers to these questions, but the inquiry can open up some productive new approaches.[1]

The past work of most investigators of contextualization has thus tended to take the opposite tack from the one on which we will now embark. It has established how performance is *anchored* in and inseparable from its context of use. Such work—on the ties of performance to the competence, expressive agenda, rhetorical strategy, and functional goals of the performer; on the phatic ties of the performer to the audience; on the indexical ties of the performed discourse to its situational surround, the participants, or other dimensions of the performance event; on the structure of the performed text as emergent in performance, and so on—served to establish how and why verbal art should be resistant to decentering, to extraction from context. We will contrastively ask what it is that makes verbal art decenterable despite all these anchoring counterforces. What makes it susceptible to decontextualization? What factors loosen the ties between performed discourse and its context?

One starting point for these inquiries is a distinction between discourse and text. At the heart of the process of decentering discourse is a more fundamental process—*entextualization*. In simple terms, though it is far from simple, it is the process of rendering discourse extractable, of making a stretch of linguistic production into a unit—a *text*—that can be lifted out of its interactional setting. A text, then, from this vantage point, is discourse rendered decontextualizable. Entextualization may well incorporate aspects of context, such that the resultant text carries elements of its history of use within it.

Basic to the process of entextualization is the reflexive capacity of discourse, the capacity it shares with all systems of signification "to turn or bend back upon itself, to become an object to itself, to refer to itself" (Babcock, 1980, 1984). In Jakobsonian terms (1960), with regard to language, this reflexive capacity is manifested most directly in the metalingual and poetic functions (Mannheim, 1986). The metalingual (or metadiscursive) function objectifies discourse by making discourse its own topic; the poetic function manipulates the formal features of the discourse to call attention to the formal structures by which the discourse is organized.

Performance, the enactment of the poetic function, is a highly reflexive mode of communication. As the concept of performance has been developed in linguistic anthropology, performance is seen as a specially marked, artful way of speaking that sets up or represents a special interpretive frame within which the act of speaking is to be understood. Performance puts the act of speaking on display—objectifies it, lifts it to a degree from its interactional setting and opens it to scrutiny by an audience. Performance heightens awareness of the act of speaking and licenses the audience to evaluate the skill and effectiveness of the performer's accomplishment. By its very nature, then, performance potentiates decontextualization.

We may approach the process of entextualization in performance in formal and functional terms by exploring the means and devices available to participants in performance situations to render stretches of discourse discontinuous with their interactional setting, thus making them into coherent, effective, and memorable texts. What discursive resources might serve this end? From a formal perspective, this line of inquiry takes us into familiar territory: the formal organization of texts, the devices of cohesion, and so forth. Here, the close formal analysis advanced in recent years under the stimulus of ethnopoetics (Hymes, 1981; Sherzer & Woodbury, 1987; Tedlock, 1983, 1989), the comparative analysis of parallelism (Caton, 1987; Fox, 1977, 1988; Kratz, 1990), and the analysis of folklore genres (Bauman, 1986; Ben-Amos, 1976; Briggs, 1988a; Gossen, 1974; McDowell, 1979, 1981) has expanded our understanding of the textuality of verbal art forms. The means and devices outlined as "keys to performance" by Bauman (1977b) may be seen as indices of entextualization. Conversational analysis (Goffman, 1981, pp. 5–77, Levinson, 1983; Schiffrin, 1988; Tannen, 1984) and language-oriented studies of disputing and conflict (Brenneis, 1988a; Briggs, 1988c; Goodwin, M. H., 1980; Grimshaw, 1990), offer vantage points on the formal analysis of discourse and entextualization and illuminate how the prepared-for detachability of texts may be interactively accomplished. They remind us that participants themselves may be directly and strongly concerned with the social management of entextualization, decontextualization, and recontextualization (Abrahams & Babcock, 1977).

Beyond formal features, frame analysis (Goffman, 1974), the phenomenological investigation of the "worlds" created in performance (Briggs, 1985; Young, 1987), studies of the interaction of verbal performance and accompanying media such as music, dance, and material objects (Feld, 1982; McDowell, 1981; Seeger, 1987; Stone, 1988), analysis of the composition process (Finnegan, 1977, 1988; Foley, 1988; Glassie, 1982), and a range of other lines of inquiry illuminate the process of entextualization in performance. The task is to discover empirically what means are available in a given social setting, to whom they may be available, under what circumstances, for making discourse into a text.

Performance is clearly not the only mechanism of entextualization. Our claim, rather, is that performance as a frame intensifies entextualization. It is also important to recall that performance is a variable quality; its salience among the multiple functions and framings of a communicative act may vary along a continuum from sustained, full performance to a fleeting breakthrough into performance (Bauman, 1984;

Hymes, 1975a). Likewise, entextualization is a matter of degree across the speech genres of a community (Basso, E., 1985, pp. 91–140, Brenneis, 1984; Briggs, 1988a; Glassie, 1982; Gossen, 1974; McDowell, 1983; Sherzer, 1983). Full performance seems to be associated with the most marked entextualization, but such correlation is far from perfect; a rigorously entextualized stretch of discourse may be reported, or translated, or rendered in a frame other than performance. This is an area that will reward further investigation.

The foregoing brief survey of entextualization must suffice here in establishing that discourse may be fashioned for ease of detachment from situational context. Processes that anchor discourse in contexts of use may be opposed by others that potentiate its detachability. If we now consider what becomes of text once decontextualized, we recognize that decontextualization from one social context involves recontextualization in another. For present purposes, we consider the decontextualization and recontextualization of texts to be two aspects of the same process, though time and possibly other factors may mediate between the two phases. Because the process is transformational, we must now determine what the recontextualized text brings with it from its earlier context(s), and what emergent form, function, and meaning is it given as it is recentered.

At this stage, we can only suggest schematically and programmatically what some of the dimensions of the transformation may be. It helps, of course, if one has good data on successive points in the process, but examination even of apparently isolated texts may be productive precisely because a text may carry some of its history with it (Abrahams & Babcock, 1977; Bauman, 1990; Briggs, 1988a). Moreover, a succession of recenterings may be encompassed within a single event (Proschan, 1981; Stoeltje, 1985, pp. 165–168).

For example, in performing a treasure tale popular among Spanish speakers in Northern New Mexico, Melaquias Romero provides a summary of the tale, a performance of his parents' version, and several retellings based on other versions of the narrative (Briggs, 1990). Such recenterings may also be simultaneous rather than serial. Mr. Romero thus presents a key scene in the treasure tale, a dialogue between a sheepherder and his boss, as it was retold by the boss to another sheepherder, who in turn recounted it to two friends; Mr. Romero then recounts the way these two individuals presented the narrative to him.

In mapping the dimensions of transformation one could employ any one of the following elements while keeping in mind the crucial task of examining their interrelations.

1. *Framing*—that is, the metacommunicative management of the recontextualized text. In Goffman's terms (1981, pp. 124–59), what is the

footing adopted toward the text in the process of recontextualizing it? Is it linked to prior renderings as a repetition or quotation? Here, the recent growth of interest in reported speech (Bauman, 1986, pp. 54–77, Lucy, 1993; Sherzer, 1983, pp. 201–207, Silverstein, 1985b) and metapragmatics (Silverstein, 1976) will be of special importance, as will developing research on blended genres, in which performed texts of one generic shape are embedded in texts of different generic shape (Bauman, 1990; Paredes, 1966b). The differential framing of texts as they are rendered in rehearsal as opposed to performance is also worthy of further research (Goffman, 1974, pp. 60–61, Tedlock, 1980).

2. *Form*—including formal means and structures from phonology, to grammar, to speech style, to larger structures of discourse such as generic packaging principles. Focus on this dimension of formal transformation from one context to another affords highly productive insights into the evolution of genres (Abrahams, 1987; Paredes, 1974). One especially interesting formal transformation is the recentering of text by metonymic substitution: mentioning the place where a narrated event happened (Basso, K., 1979, 1984) or a key portion of the plot (Kalcik, 1975), for example, to evoke the whole in the hearers' minds.

3. *Function*—manifest, latent, and performative (perlocutionary and illocutionary force; see above). A primarily ritual text, for example, may be used in entertainment, practice, or pedagogy (Sherzer, 1983, p. 118).

4. *Indexical grounding*, including deictic markers of person, spatial location, time, etc. The analysis of "metanarration" represents one productive vantage point on this problem (Babcock, 1977; Bauman, 1986, 1990; McDowell, 1973).

5. *Translation*, including both interlingual and intersemiotic translation (Jakobson, 1959). At issue here are the differential semiotic capacities of different languages and different media (Lucy, 1987). What happens if a text is transferred from Zuni to English or from oral narration to print? These issues have been central to the enterprise of ethnopoetics (Fine, 1984) and to the problematics of transcription (Ochs, 1979; Preston, 1982). They thus afford an important critical and reflexive vantage point on our own scholarly practice as linguistic anthropologists.

6. The *emergent structure* of the new context, as shaped by the process of recontextualization. Texts both shape and are shaped by the situational contexts in which they are produced.

To this point, we have sketched a framework for the investigation of decentering and recentering largely in formal terms. But just as the formal analysis of the processes and practices of contextualization is a means of investigating larger social and cultural problems, so, too, the analysis of decontextualization and recontextualization will stand or fall as an anthropological enterprise by the degree to which it illuminates problems of broader concern. Let us suggest, then, some problem areas in which such an investigation might be productive. In so doing, we begin to answer certain critics of performance-centered analysis (summarized in Limon & Young, 1986).

The decontextualization and recontextualization of performed discourse bear upon the political economy of texts (Gal, 1989; Irvine, 1989), texts and power. Performance is a mode of social production (Williams, 1977); specific products include texts—decentered discourse. To decontextualize and recontextualize a text is thus an act of control, and in regard to the differential exercise of such control the issue of social power arises. More specifically, we may recognize differential access to texts, differential legitimacy in claims to and use of texts, differential competence in the use of texts, and differential values attaching to various types of texts. All of these elements, let us emphasize, are culturally constructed, socially constituted, and sustained by ideologies, and they accordingly may vary cross-culturally. None of these factors is a social or cultural given, for each may be subject to negotiation as part of the process of entextualization, decentering, and recentering.

1. Access depends upon institutional structures, social definitions of eligibility, and other mechanisms and standards of inclusion and exclusion (even such practical matters as getting to where the texts are to be found).

2. The issue of legitimacy is one of being accorded the authority to appropriate a text such that your recentering of it counts as legitimate (Shuman, 1986). Cultural property rights, such as copyright, academic standards of plagiarism, and their counterparts in other cultures all regulate the exercise of legitimate power over performed discourse, as do such social mechanisms as ordination, initiation, or apprenticeship. Not only do institutional structures and mechanisms confer legitimate authority to control texts, but the reverse potential also exists: Contra Bourdieu (1977, p. 649), the appropriation and use of particular forms of discourse may be the basis of institutional power.

3. Competence, the knowledge and ability to carry out the decontextualization and recontextualization of performed discourse successfully and appropriately, may be locally conceived of as innate human capacity, learned skill, special gift, a correlate of one's position in

the life cycle and so on (e.g., Briggs, 1988a; Fox, 1988, pp. 13–16; Gossen, 1974, p. 239; Heath, 1983).
4. Finally, values organize the relative status of texts and their uses into a hierarchy of preference. Texts may be valued because of what you can use them for, what you can get for them, or for their indexical reference to desired qualities or states—Bourdieu's *cultural* capital (Bourdieu, 1984; Gal, 1989; Irvine, 1989).

All of these factors—access, legitimacy, competence, and values—bear centrally on the construction and assumption of authority. From Hymes's early formulation (1975a), in which performance consisted of the authoritative display of communicative competence, authority has held a central place in performance-oriented analysis. Hymes's definition highlights the assumption of an authoritative voice by the performer, which is grounded at least in part in the knowledge, ability, and right to control the recentering of valued texts. Control over decentering and recentering is part of the social framework and as such is one of the processes by which texts are endowed with authority (Bowen, 1989a), and this process in turn places formal and functional constraints on how texts may be further recentered: An authoritative text, by definition, is one that is maximally protected from compromising transformation (Bakhtin, 1981).

While the implications of the decentering and recentering of discourse for the construction and exercise of power may be approached from a variety of vantage points, including cultural conceptions of the nature and uses of performance, institutional structures, or ideology, the situated practice of decontextualization and recontextualization is an essential and foundational frame of reference. In this sense the investigation of decontextualization and recontextualization continues the program of the ethnography of speaking, adding a conceptual framework—centered on discursive practice itself—that links separate situational contexts in terms of the pragmatics of textuality. Moreover, the chain of linkages may be extended without temporal limit, for texts may be continuously decentered and recentered (Haring, 1988). At one level, this illuminates the process of traditionalization (Bauman, 1990; Hymes, 1975b)—the telling and retelling of a tale, the citing and reciting of a proverb—as these recenterings are part of the symbolic construction of discursive continuity with a meaningful past. Attention to such processes locates performance, texts, and contexts in systems of historical relationship. At another level, the tracing of chains of decentering and recentering offers a unified frame of reference for the analysis of control over discourse, a frame that extends from the small-scale and local to the global. A given folktale performance may be traced through connected processes of decentering and recentering in, for example, local oral tradition, the nationalization of culture as it is appropriated by learned elites in the service of nationalist ideology, or the internationalization of culture as it is held up to view as part of world literature (Appadurai & Breckenridge, 1988; Hymes, 1981, pp. 35–64; Moyne, 1963; Rothenberg & Rothenberg, 1983).

Our approach to the decontextualization and recontextualization of texts also contributes operational and substantive specificity to Bakhtin's more abstract notion of *dialogism* (Bakhtin, 1981), increasingly influential in linguistic anthropology and folklore. If indeed, as Bakhtin tells us, our mouths are filled with the words of others, the program we have outlined here is designed to elucidate how these dialogical relations are accomplished. This program takes full account of form-function interrelationships and the sociology and political economy of Bakhtinian dialogue.

A further significant payoff offered by the investigation of the decontextualization and recontextualization of texts is a critical and reflexive perspective from which to examine our own scholarly practice. Much of what we do as linguistic anthropologists amounts to the decontextualization and recontextualization of others' discourse (Haviland, 1987; Urban, 1987), which means as well that we exercise power along the lines outlined above. To be sure, the exercise of such power need not be entirely one-sided; our interlocutors may attempt to control how their discourse will be entextualized and recontextualized. These processes have significant implications for the methods, goals, and not least, ethics, of our profession.

CONCLUSION

Performance emerged as a key term in certain sectors of linguistic anthropology and folklore in the early to mid-1970s, drawing together under its rubric at least three critical reorientations then energizing those allied fields. The first of these involved a challenge to the conception of language that was promulgated under the banner of transformational generative linguistics. In that approach, performance—"natural speech," what the speaker actually does in using language—was excluded from the purview of linguistic theory, which centered instead on competence, an abstract, idealized, cognitive system of rules for the production and comprehension of grammatically appropriate sentences. It was conceptually and rhetorically effective, then, to advance performance as the center of an alternative, socially constituted linguistics (Hymes, 1974), in which social function gives shape to linguistic form, language has social as well as referential meaning, and the communicative functions of language in the constitution of social life are fundamental to its essence.

A second major shift of perspective captured by the notion of performance occurred in folklore, founded on a reorientation from a traditionalist view of folklore as reified, persistent cultural items—texts, artifacts, mentifacts—to a conception of folklore as a mode of communicative action (Paredes & Bauman, 1972). Here, performance was understood as the assumption of accountability to an audience for a display of communicative skill and effectiveness (Bauman, 1977b; Hymes, 1975a).

Third, the turn to performance marked an effort to establish a broader space within linguistics and anthropology for poetics—verbal artistry—against the conception, deeply rooted in Western epistemology and ontology, that poetics is an etiolation of language, functionally hollow or void, extraneous to what really makes language or society work (Friedrich, 1986; Sherzer, 1987). A focus on the artful use of language in the conduct of social life—in kinship, politics, economics, religion—opened the way to an understanding of performance as socially constitutive and efficacious, not secondary and derivative (Bauman & Sherzer, 1974, 1989).

All three of these critical reorientations relied centrally on the ethnographic and analytical investigation of form-function-meaning interrelationships within situational contexts of language use. As we have attempted to make clear in the early sections of this review, the further developments in performance studies have maintained the critical stance on which performance-centered analysis was founded, and have continued to exploit productively the basic situational frame of reference that characterized performance-centered lines of inquiry.

Recently, however, critics and practitioners alike have identified certain limitations engendered by a mode of analysis that hews too closely to speech or to the performance event as the primary frame of reference and unit of analysis (Limon & Young, 1986). The difficulties are several. First, there is the problem of history, the need to link series of speech events into historical systems of interrelationship in discourse-centered terms. Second, there is the perennial micro-macro problem of how to relate the situated use of language to larger social structures, particularly the structures of power and value that constitute the political economy of a society. Again, the problem is to identify discursive practices that mediate between the situated use of language within speech events and those larger structures. And finally, there is the problem of linking the artful speaking of performance to other modes of language use so that performance analysis does not fall into the trap of segregating poetics from other ways of speaking. The third major section of our review offers in preliminary outline a framework that we believe will help to overcome the limitations we have enumerated. Building upon the accumulated insights of past performance analysis, the investigation of the interrelated processes of entextualization, decontextualization (decentering), and recontextualization (recentering) opens a way toward constructing histories of performance; toward illuminating the larger systemic structures in which performances play a constitutive role; and toward linking performances with other modes of language use as performances are decentered and recentered both within and across speech events—referred to, cited, evaluated, reported, looked back upon, replayed, and otherwise transformed in the production and reproduction of social life. As we have suggested, the framework appears to us all the more productive in making our own scholarly practice continuous with the phenomena to which we devote our ethnographic attention. The poetics and politics of ethnography are illuminated by the poetics and politics of discourse within the communities about which and within which we write. Our dialogues with our ethnographic interlocutors are related dialectically to their dialogues among themselves and our own dialogues back home. Performance-oriented analysis is thus well positioned to continue the critical mission on which it was founded, testing our own conceptions of language and our own scholarly practices as it attempts to comprehend the role of language and poetics in the social life of the world's cultures.

NOTE

[1] The problem of decontextualization (and recontextualization, discussed further below) was the principal focus of a seminar at the Center for Psychosocial Studies, chiefly under the rubrics of the *decentering* and *recentering* of discourse. These terms draw on poststructuralist usage in the process of offering a critique of the perspectives in which that usage is rooted (Bauman, 1987a). Through the work of the group's members, these terms gained wider currency in linguistic anthropology (e.g., Hanks, 1989; Parmentier, 1989). We employ "centering," "decentering," and "recentering" here interchangeably with "contextualization," "decontextualization," and "recontextualization."

Because this section is a preliminary and programmatic formulation of a line of inquiry just beginning to take shape, we do not frame it as a review of the literature. Instead, by means of citations, we link our outline to past research on which the approach can be built. This section should be read in conjunction with William Hanks's article on "Texts and Textuality" in the 1989 *Annual Review of Anthropology* (Hanks, 1989).

REFERENCES

Abrahams, R. D. (1968). Introductory remarks to a rhetorical theory of folklore. *Journal of American Folklore, 81*, 143–148.

Abrahams, R. D. (1976). The complex relations of simple forms. In D. Ben-Amos (Ed.), *Folklore genres* (pp. 193–214). Austin: University of Texas Press.

Abrahams, R. D. (1980). Play. In V. Newall (Ed.), *Folklore studies in the twentieth century: Proceedings of the centennial of the Folk Lore Society* (pp. 19–22). Woodbridge, Suffolk: Brewer.

Abrahams, R. D. (1983). *The man of words in the West Indies*. Baltimore: Johns Hopkins.

Abrahams, R. D. (1985). A note on neck-riddles in the West Indies as they comment on emergent genre theory. *Journal of American Folklore, 98*, 85–94.

Abrahams, R. D. (1986). Complicity and imitation in storytelling: A pragmatic folklorist's perspective. *Cultural Anthropology, 1*, 223–237.

Abrahams, R. D. (1987). Child ballads in the West Indies: Familiar fabulations, creole performances. *Journal of Folklore Research, 24*, 107–134.

Abrahams, R. D., & Babcock, B. A. (1977). The literary use of proverbs. *Journal of American Folklore, 90*, 107–134.

Abrahams, R. D., & Bauman, R. (1971). Sense and nonsense in St. Vincent: Speech behavior and decorum in a Caribbean community. *American Anthropologist, 73*, 262–272.

Abu-Lughod, L. (1986). *Veiled sentiments: Honor and poetry in a Bedouin society*. Berkeley: University of California Press.

Amistae, J., & Elias-Olivares, L. (Eds.). (1982). *Spanish in the United States: Sociolinguistic aspects*. New York: Cambridge University Press.

Appadurai, A., & Breckenridge, C. (1988). Why public culture? *Public Culture, 1*, 5–10.

Arewa, E. O, & Dundes, A. (1964). Proverbs and the ethnography of speaking folklore. *American Anthropologist, 66*, 70–85.

Austin, J. L. (1962). *How to do things with words*. Oxford: Oxford University Press.

Babcock, B. A. (1977). The story in the story: metanarration in folk narrative. In R. Bauman (Ed.), *Verbal art as performance* (pp. 61–80). Prospect Heights, IL: Waveland.

Babcock, B. A. (1980). Reflexivity: Definitions and discriminations. *Semiotica, 30*, 1–14.

Babcock, B. A. (1984). Reflexivity. In M. Eliade (Ed.), *The encyclopedia of religion, Vol. 12* (pp. 234–238). New York: Macmillan.

Bakhtin, M. M. (1968). *Rabelais and his world* (H. Iswolsky, Trans.). Cambridge: MIT Press.

Bakhtin, M. M. (1981). *The dialogic imagination*. Austin: University of Texas Press.

Bakhtin, M. M. (1986). *Speech genres and other late essays* (V. W. McGee, Trans., C. Emerson, & M. Holquist, Eds.). Austin: University of Texas Press.

Basso, E. B. (1985). *A musical view of the universe: Kalapalo myth and ritual performance*. Philadelphia: University of Pennsylvania Press.

Basso, E. B. (1992). Contextualization In Kalapalo narratives. In C. Goodwin & A. Duranti (Eds.), *Rethinking context* (pp. 253–269). New York: Cambridge University Press.

Basso, K. H. (1979). *Portraits of "the whiteman": Linguistic play and cultural symbols among the Western Apache*. New York: Cambridge University Press.

Basso, K. H. 1984. "Stalking with stories": Names, places, and moral narratives among the Western Apache. In E. Bruner (Ed.), *Text, play, and story* (pp. 19–55). Washington, DC: American Ethnological Society.

Bateson, G. (1972). *Steps to an ecology of mind*. New York: Ballantine Books.

Bauman, R. (1977a). Settlement patterns on the frontiers of folklore. In W. Bascom (Ed.), *Frontiers of folklore* (pp. 121–132). Boulder, CO: Westview Press.

Bauman, R. (1977b). *Verbal art as performance*. Prospect Heights, IL: Waveland.

Bauman, R. (1982). Conceptions of folklore in the development of literary semiotics. *Semiotica, 39*, 1–20.

Bauman, R. (1983a). The field study of folklore in context. In R. M. Dorson (Ed.), *Handbook of American folklore* (pp. 362–367). Bloomington: Indiana University Press.

Bauman, R. (1983b). *Let your words be few: Symbolism of speaking and silence among seventeenth-century Quakers*. New York: Cambridge University Press.

Bauman, R. (1984). *Disclaimers of performance*. Paper presented at the 83rd annual meeting of the American Anthropological Association, Denver, CO.

Bauman, R. (1986). *Story, performance, and event: Contextual studies of oral narrative*. New York: Cambridge University Press.

Bauman, R. (1987a). *The decentering of discourse*. Paper presented at the 86th annual meeting of the American Anthropological Association, Chicago.

Bauman, R. (1987b). *The role of performance in the ethnography of speaking* (Working Papers and Proceedings of the Center for Psychosocial Studies, No. 11, pp. 3–12). Chicago: Center for Psychosocial Studies.

Bauman, R. (1989a). American folklore studies and social transformation. *Text and Performance Quarterly, 9*, 175–184.

Bauman, R. (1989b). Performance. In E. Barnouw (Ed.), *International encyclopedia of communications*, Vol. 3 (pp. 262–266). Oxford: Oxford University Press.

Bauman, R. (1990). Contextualization, tradition, and the dialogue of genres: Icelandic legends of the *kraftaskald*. In C. Goodwin & A. Duranti (Eds.), *Rethinking context* (pp. 125–145). New York: Cambridge University Press.

Bauman, R., & Sherzer, J. (Eds.). (1974). *Explorations in the ethnography of speaking*. New York: Cambridge University Press.

Bauman, R., & Sherzer, J. (1975). The ethnography of speaking. *Annual Review of Anthropology, 4*, 95–119.

Bauman, R., & Sherzer, J. (1989). Introduction to the second edition. In R. Bauman & J. Sherzer (Eds.), *Explorations in the ethnography of speaking* (pp. ix–xxvii). New York: Cambridge University Press.

Beeman, W. O. (1981). Why do they laugh? An interactional approach to humor in traditional Iranian improvisatory theater. *Journal of American Folklore, 94*, 506–526.

Bell, M. J. (1983). *The world from brown's lounge: An ethnography of black middle-class play*. Urbana: University of Illinois Press.

Ben-Amos, D. (1972). Toward a definition of folklore in context. In A. Paredes & R. Bauman (Eds.), *Toward new perspectives in folklore* (pp. 3–15). Austin: University of Texas Press.

Ben-Amos, D. (Ed.). (1976). *Folklore genres*. Austin: University of Texas Press.

Ben-Amos, D. (1977). The context of folklore: Implications and prospects. In W. Bascom (Ed.), *Frontiers of Folklore* (pp. 36–53). Boulder, CO: Westview Press.

Bennett, W. L., & Feldman, M. S. (1981). *Reconstructing reality in the courtroom: Justice and judgment in American culture*. New Brunswick, NJ: Rutgers University Press.

Blackburn, S. H. (1981). Oral performance: Narrative and ritual in a Tamil tradition. *Journal of American Folklore, 94*, 207–227.

Blackburn, S. H. (1986). Performance markers in an Indian story-type. In S. H. Blackburn & A. K. Ramanujan (Eds.), *Another harmony: New essays on the folklore of India* (pp. 167–193). Berkeley: University of California Press.

Blackburn, S. H. (1988). *Singing of birth and death: Texts in performance*. Philadelphia: University of Pennsylvania Press.

Bloch, M. (Ed.). (1975). *Political language and oratory in traditional society*. New York: Academic Press.

Boas, F. (1911). Introduction. In *Handbook of American Indian Languages* (Bulletin 40, Pt. 1, BAE, pp. 1–83). Washington, DC: U.S. Government Printing Office.

Bourdieu, P. (1977). The economics of linguistic exchanges. *Social Science Information, 16*, 645–668.

Bourdieu, P. (1984). *Distinction: A social critique of the judgement of taste*. Cambridge: Harvard University Press.

Bowen, J. R. (1989a). Narrative form and political incorporation: Changing uses of history in Aceh, Indonesia. *Comparative Studies in Society and History, 31*, 671–693.

Bowen, J. R. (1989b). Poetic duels and political change in the Gayo highlands of Sumatra. *American Anthropologist, 91*, 25–40.

Brenneis, D. L., (1978). The matter of talk: Political performance in Bhatgaon. *Language in Society, 7*, 159–170.

Brenneis, D. L. (1984). Grog and gossip in Bhatgaon: Style and substance in Fiji Indian conversation. *American Ethnologist, 11*, 487–506.

Brenneis, D. L. (1988a). Language and disputing. *Annual Review of Anthropology, 17*, 221–237.

Brenneis, D. L. (1988b). Telling troubles: Narrative, conflict, and experience. *Anthropological Linguistics, 30*, 279–291.

Brenneis, D. L. & Myers, F. R. (Eds.). (1984). *Dangerous words: Language and politics in the Pacific*. New York: New York University Press.

Briggs, C. L. (1985). Treasure tales and pedagogical discourse in Mexicano New Mexico. *Journal of American Folklore, 98*, 287–314.

Briggs, C. L. (1986). *Learning how to ask: A sociolinguistic appraisal of the role of the interview in social science research*. New York: Cambridge University Press.

Briggs, C. L. (1988a). *Competence in performance: The creativity of tradition in Mexicano verbal art*. Philadelphia: University of Pennsylvania Press.

Briggs, C. L. (1988b). Disorderly dialogues in ritual impositions of order: The role of metapragmatics in Warao dispute mediation. *Anthropological Linguistics, 30*, 448–491.

Briggs, C. L. (Ed.) (1988c). Narrative resources for the creation and mediation of conflict [Special issue]. *Anthropological Linguistics, 30*, (3 & 4).

Briggs, C. L. (1990). History, poetics, and interpretation in the tale. In C. L. Briggs & J. J. Vigil (Eds.), *The lost gold mine of Juan Mondragon: A legend from New Mexico performed by Melaquias Romero* (pp. 165–240). Tucson: University of Arizona Press.

Bronner, S. J. (1988). Art, performance, and praxis: The rhetoric of contemporary folklore studies. *Western Folklore, 47*, 75–102.

Burke, K. (1941). *The philosophy of literary form: Studies in symbolic action*. Baton Rouge: Louisiana State University Press.

Burke, K. (1950/1969). *A rhetoric of motives*. Berkeley: University of California Press.

Caraveli-Chaves, A. (1980). Bridge between worlds: The Greek woman's lament. *Journal of American Folklore, 95*, 129–158.

Carey, J. W. (1989). *Communication as culture: Essays on media and society*. Boston: Unwin Hyman.

Caton, S. (1987). Contributions of Roman Jakobson. *Annual Review of Anthropology, 16*, 223–260.

Cicourel, A. (1974). *Theory and method in a study of Argentine fertility*. New York: Wiley Interscience.

Cicourel, A. (1982). Language and belief in a medical setting. In H. Byrnes (Ed.), *Contemporary perceptions of language: Interdisciplinary dimensions* (pp. 48–78). Washington, DC: Georgetown University Press.

Clifford, J., & Marcus, G. E. (Eds.). (1986). *Writing culture: The poetics and politics of ethnography*. Berkeley: University of California Press.

Comaroff, J. L., & Roberts, S. (1981). *Rules and processes: The cultural logic of dispute in an African context*. Chicago: University of Chicago Press.

Conley, J. M., & O'Barr, W. M. (1990). Rules versus relationships in small claims disputes. In A. D. Grimshaw (Ed.), *Conflict talk: Sociolinguistic investigations of arguments in conversations* (pp. 178–196). New York: Cambridge University Press.

Cook-Gumperz, J., & Gumperz, J. J. (1976). *Papers on language and context*. Berkeley: Language Behavior Research Laboratory, University of California.

Crapanzano, V. (1984). Life histories. *American Anthropologist, 86*, 953–960.

Culler, J. (1981). *On deconstruction: Theory and criticism after structuralism*. Ithaca, NY: Cornell University Press.

Danet, B. (1980). Language in the legal process. *Law and Society, 14*, 445–564.

Darnell, R. (1974). Correlates of Cree narrative performance. In R. Bauman & J. Sherzer (Eds.), *Explorations in the ethnography of speaking* (pp. 315–336). New York: Cambridge University Press.

Degh, L., & Vazsonyi, A. (1976). Legend and belief. In D. Ben-Amos (Ed.), *Folklore genres* (pp. 93–123). Austin: University of Texas Press.

Derrida, J. (1974). *Of grammatology* (G. C. Spivak, Trans.). Baltimore: Johns Hopkins University Press.

Derrida, J. (1978). *Writing and difference* (A. Bass, Trans.). Chicago: University of Chicago Press.

Dorst, J. (1983). Neck-riddle as a dialogue of genres. *Journal of American Folklore, 96,* 413–433.

Dundes, A. (1964). Texture, text, and context. *Southern Folklore Quarterly, 28,* 251–265.

Duranti, A. (1983). Samoan speechmaking across social events: One genre in and out of a *fono. Language in Society, 12,* 1–22.

Duranti, A. (1984). *Intentions, self, and local theories of meaning: Words and social action in a Samoan context.* La Jolla: Center for Human Information Processing, University of California, San Diego.

Duranti, A., & Brenneis, D. L. (Eds.). (1986). The audience as co-author [Special issue]. *Text, 6,* (3).

Farrer, C. R. (Ed.). (1975). *Women in folklore.* Austin: University of Texas Press.

Feld, S. (1982). *Sound and sentiment: Birds, weeping, poetics, and song in Kaluli expression.* Philadelphia: University of Pennsylvania Press.

Feld, S. (1988). Aesthetics as iconicity of style, or "lift-up-over sounding": Getting into the Kaluli groove. *Yearbook for Traditional Music, 20,* 74–113.

Fine, E. C. (1984). *The folklore text: From performance to print.* Bloomington: Indiana University Press.

Finnegan, R. (1969). How to do things with words: Performative utterances among the Limba of Sierra Leone. *Man, 4,* 537–552.

Finnegan, R. (1977). *Oral poetry.* New York: Cambridge University Press.

Finnegan, R. (1988). *Literacy and orality: Studies in the technology of communication.* Oxford: Basil Blackwell.

Foley, J. M. (1988). *The theory of oral composition: History and methodology.* Bloomington: Indiana University Press.

Foster, M. (1974a). *From the earth to beyond the sky: An ethnographic approach to four longhouse Iroquois speech events.* Ottawa: National Museums of Canada.

Foster, M. (1974b). When words become deeds: An analysis of three Iroquois Longhouse speech events. In R. Bauman & J. Sherzer (Eds.), *Explorations in the ethnography of speaking* (pp. 345–367). New York: Cambridge University Press.

Fox, J. J. (1977). Roman Jakobson and the comparative study of parallelism. In J. D. Armstrong & C. H. van Schooneveld (Eds.), *Roman Jakobson: Echoes of his scholarship* (pp. 59–90). Lisse: Peter de Ridder.

Fox, J. J. (Ed.). (1988). *To speak in pairs: Essays on the ritual language of Eastern Indonesia.* New York: Cambridge University Press.

Friedrich, P. (1986). *The language parallax: Linguistic relativism and poetic indeterminacy.* Austin: University of Texas Press.

Gadamer, H. (1960). *Truth and method.* New York: Crossroads.

Gal, S. (1989). Language and political economy. *Annual Review of Anthropology, 18,* 345–367.

Garvin, P. L. (Ed.). (1964). *A Prague school reader in esthetics, literary structure, and style.* Washington, DC: Georgetown University Press.

Geertz, C. (1976). "From the native's point of view": On the nature of anthropological understanding. In K. H. Basso & H. A. Selby (Eds.), *Meaning in anthropology* (pp. 221–237). Albuquerque: University of New Mexico Press.

Georges, R. (1981). Do narrators really digress? A reconsideration of "audience asides" in narrating. *Western Folklore, 40,* 245–252.

Glassie, H. (1982). *Passing the time in Ballymenone: Culture and history of an Ulster community.* Philadelphia: University of Pennsylvania Press.

Goffman, E. (1974). *Frame analysis.* New York: Harper and Row.

Goffman, E. (1981). *Forms of talk.* Philadelphia: University of Pennsylvania Press.

Goodwin, C. (1981). *Conversational organization: Interaction between speakers and hearers.* New York: Academic Press.

Goodwin, C. (1984). Notes on story structure and the organization of participation. In J. M. Atkinson & J. Heritage (Eds.), *Structures of social action: Studies in conversation analysis* (pp. 225–246). New York: Cambridge University Press.

Goodwin, C. (1986). Audience diversity, participation and interpretation. *Text, 6,* 283–316.

Goodwin, M. H. (1980). "He-said-she said": Formal cultural procedures for the construction of a gossip dispute activity. *American Ethnologist, 9,* 76–96.

Goodwin, M. H. (1982). "Instigating": Storytelling as social process. *American Ethnologist, 9,* 799–819.

Goodwin, M. H. (1985). The serious side of jump rope: Conversational practices and social organization in the frame of play. *Journal American Folklore, 98,* 315–330.

Gossen, G. H. (1972). Chamula genres of verbal behavior. In A. Paredes & R. Bauman (Eds.), *Toward new perspectives in folklore* (pp. 145–168). Austin: University of Texas Press.

Gossen, G. H. (1974). *Chamulas in the world of the sun: Time and space in a Maya oral tradition.* Cambridge: Harvard University Press.

Grice, H. P. (1975). Logic and conversation. In P. Cole & J. L. Morgan (Eds.), *Syntax and Semantics, Vol. 3: Speech Acts* (pp. 41–48). New York: Academic Press.

Grimshaw, A. D. (1981). Some problematic aspects of communication in crossracial research in the United States. In A. D. Grimshaw, *Language as social resource* (pp. 57–96). Stanford: Stanford University Press.

Grimshaw, A. D. (Ed.). (1990). *Conflict talk: Sociolinguistic investigations of arguments in conversations.* New York: Cambridge University Press.

Gumperz, J. J. (1982). *Discourse strategies.* New York: Cambridge University Press.

Hanks, W. (1984). Sanctification, structure, and experience in a Yucatec ritual event. *Journal of American Folklore, 97,* 131–166.

Hanks, W. (1987). Discourse genres in a theory of practice. *American Ethnologist, 14,* 668–692.

Hanks, W. F. (1989). Texts and textuality. *Annual Review of Anthropology, 18,* 95–127.

Haring, L. (1972). Performing for the interviewer: A study of the structure of context. *Southern Folklore Quarterly, 36,* 383–398.

Haring, L. (1988). Interperformance. *Fabula, 29,* 365–372.

Haviland, J. (1986). "Con buenos chiles": Talk, targets, and teasing in Zinacantan. *Text, 6,* 249–282.

Haviland, J. (1987). *Text from talk in Tzotzil.* Paper presented at the 86th annual meeting of the American Anthropological Association, Chicago.

Haviland, J. (1988). "We want to borrow your mouth": Tzotzil marital squabbles. *Anthropological Linguistics, 30,* 395–447.

Heath, S. B. (1983). *Ways with words: Language, life, and work in communities and classrooms.* New York: Cambridge University Press.

Heidegger, M. (1971). *Poetry, language, thought* (A. Hofstadter, Trans.). New York: Harper Colophon.

Herzfeld, M. (1985). *The poetics of manhood: Contest and identity in a Cretan mountain village.* Princeton: Princeton University Press.

Hill, J. (1985). The grammar of consciousness and the consciousness of grammar. *American Ethnologist, 12,* 725–737.

Hill, J., & Hill, K. (1986). *Speaking Mexicano: Dynamics of syncretic language in Central Mexico.* Tucson: University of Arizona Press.

Huizinga, J. (1955). *Homo ludens.* Boston: Beacon.

Hymes, D. H. (1962). The ethnography of speaking. In T. Gladwin & W. Sturtevant (Eds.), *Anthropology and human behavior* (pp. 15–53). Washington, DC: Anthropological Society of Washington.

Hymes, D. H. (1964). Toward ethnographies of communication. *American Anthropologist, 66,* 1–34.

Hymes, D. H. (1972). The contribution of folklore to sociolinguistic research. In A. Paredes & R. Bauman (Eds.), *Toward new perspectives in folklore* (pp. 42–50). Austin: University of Texas Press.

Hymes, D. H. (1974). *Foundations in sociolinguistics: An ethnographic perspective.* Philadelphia: University of Pennsylvania Press.

Hymes, D. H. (1975a). Breakthrough into performance. In D. Ben-Amos & K. S. Goldstein (Eds.), *Folklore: Performance and communication* (pp. 11–74). The Hague, Holland: Mouton.

Hymes, D. H. (1975b). Folklore's nature and the sun's myth. *Journal of American Folklore, 88,* 346–369.

Hymes, D. H. (1981). *"In vain I tried to tell you": Essays in Native American ethnopoetics.* Philadelphia: University of Pennsylvania Press.

Hymes, D. H. (1985). Language, memory, and selective performance: Cultee's "Salmon's Myth" as twice told to Boas. *Journal of American Folklore, 98,* 391–434.

Irvine, J. T. (1979). Formality and informality in communicative events. *American Anthropologist, 81,* 773–790.

Irvine, J. T. (1989). When talk isn't cheap: Language and political economy. *American Ethnologist, 16,* 248–267.

Jakobson, R. (1957). *Shifters, verbal categories, and the Russian verb.* Cambridge: Harvard University Russian Language Project.

Jakobson, R. (1959). Linguistic aspects of translation. In R. A. Brower (Ed.), *On translation* (pp. 232–239). Cambridge: Harvard University Press.

Jakobson, R. (1960). Closing statement: Linguistics and poetics. In T. A. Sebeok (Ed.), *Style in language* (pp. 350–377). Cambridge: MIT Press.

Jakobson, R. (1966). Grammatical parallelism and its Russian facet. *Language, 42*, 399–429.

Jakobson, R. (1968). Poetry of grammar and grammar of poetry. *Lingua, 21*, 597–609.

Jauss, H. R. (1982). *Toward an aesthetic of reception: Theory and history of literature, Vol. 2* (T. Bahti, Trans.). Minneapolis: University of Minnesota Press.

Kalcik, S. (1975). "...like Ann's gynecologist or the time I was almost raped": Personal narratives in women's rap groups. In C. R. Farrer (Ed.), *Women in folklore* (pp. 3–11). Austin: University of Texas Press.

Keenan, E. O. (1973). A sliding sense of obligatoriness: The polystructure of Malagasy oratory. *Language in Society, 2*, 225–243.

Keenan, E. O. (1976). On the universality of conversational implicatures. *Language in Society, 5*, 67–80.

Kratz, C. A. (1990). Persuasive suggestions and reassuring promises: Emergent parallelism and dialogic encouragement in song. *Journal of American Folklore, 103*, 42–67.

Kuipers, J. (1990). *Power in performance: The creation of textual authority in Weyewa ritual speech.* Philadelphia: University of Pennsylvania Press.

Labov, W. (1972). Rules for ritual insults. In T. Kochman (Ed.), *Rappin' and stylin' out: Communication in urban Black America* (pp. 265–314). Urbana: University of Illinois Press.

Langer, S. K. (1942/1951). *Philosophy in a new key.* New York: New American Library.

Levine, L. W. (1977). *Black culture and Black consciousness: Afro-American folk thought from slavery to freedom.* Oxford: Oxford University Press.

Levinson, S. (1983). *Pragmatics.* New York: Cambridge University Press.

Limon, J. E. (1982). History, Chicano joking, and the varieties of higher education: Tradition and performance as critical symbolic action. *Journal of the Folklore Institute, 19*, 141–166.

Limon, J. E. (1983). Legendry, metafolklore, and performance: A Mexican-American example. *Western Folklore, 42*, 191–208.

Limon, J. E., Young, E. J. (1986). Frontiers, settlements, and development in folklore studies, 1972–1985. *Annual Review of Anthropology, 15*, 437–460.

Lord, A. B. (1960). *The singer of tales.* Cambridge: Harvard University Press.

Lucy, J. (1987). *From performance pragmatics to "Practical Pig."* Paper presented at the 86th annual meeting of the American Anthropological Association, Chicago.

Lucy, J. (Ed.) (1993). *Reflexive language: Reported speech and metapragmatics.* New York: Cambridge University Press.

Malinowski, B. (1923). The problem of meaning in primitive languages. In C. K. Ogden & I. A. Richards (Eds.), *The meaning of meaning* (pp. 296–336). London: Routledge and Kegan Paul.

Malinowski, B. (1935). *Coral gardens and their magic* (2 Vols.). London: Allen and Unwin.

Malinowski, B. (1961). *Argonauts of the western pacific.* New York: E. P. Dutton. (Original work published 1922)

Mannheim, B. (1986). Popular song and popular grammar, poetry and metalanguage. *Word, 37,* 45–75.

Marcus, G., & Fischer, M. M. J. (1986). *Anthropology as cultural critique: An experimental moment in the human sciences.* Chicago: University of Chicago Press.

Matejka, L., & Titunik, I. R. (Eds.). (1976). *Semiotics of art: Prague school contributions.* Cambridge: MIT Press.

McDowell, J. H. (1973). Performance and the folkloric text: A rhetorical approach to "The Christ of the Bible." *Folklore Forum, 6,* 139–148.

McDowell, J. H. (1979). *Children's riddling.* Bloomington: Indiana University Press.

McDowell, J. H. (1981). The *corrido* of Greater Mexico as discourse, music, and event. In R. Bauman & R. D. Abrahams (Eds.), *"And other neighborly names": Social process and cultural image in Texas folklore* (pp. 44–75). Austin: University of Texas Press.

McDowell, J. H. (1983). The semiotic constitution of Kamsa ritual language. *Language in Society, 12,* 23–46.

McDowell, J. H. (1985). The poetic rites of conversation. *Journal of Folklore Research, 22,* 113–132.

Mertz, E. (1988). Consensus and dissent in U.S. legal opinions: Order-creating narratives. *Anthropological Linguistics, 30,* 369–394.

Mishler, E. G. (1986). *Research interviewing: Context and narrative.* Cambridge: Harvard University Press.

Moerman, M. (1988). *Talking culture: Ethnography and conversation analysis.* Philadelphia: University of Pennsylvania Press.

Moyne, E. J. (1963). *Hiawatha and Kalevala: A study of the relationship between Longfellow's "Indian Edda" and the Finnish epic* (Folklore Fellows Communication No. 192). Helsinki, Finland: Suomalainen Tiedeakatemia.

Mukarovsky, J. (1977a). *Structure, sign, and function: Selected essays by Jan Mukarovsky* (J. Burbank & P. Steiner, Trans. and Eds.). New Haven, CT: Yale University Press.

Mukarovsky, J. (1977b). *The word and verbal art: Selected essays by Jan Mukarovsky* (J. Burbank & P. Steiner, Trans. and Eds.). New Haven, CT: Yale University Press.

Myers, F. R. (1986). Reflections on a meeting: Structure, language, and the polity in a small-scale society. *American Ethnologist, 13,* 430–447.

O'Barr, W. M. (1982). *Linguistic evidence: Language, power, and strategy in the courtroom.* New York: Academic Press.

O'Barr, W. M., & Conley, J. M. (1985). Litigant satisfaction versus legal adequacy in small claims court narratives. *Law and Society Review, 19,* 661–702.

Ochs, E. (1979). Transcription as theory. In E. Ochs & B. Schieffelin (Eds.), *Developmental pragmatics* (pp. 43–72). New York: Academic Press.

Ochs, E. (1984). Clarification and culture. In D. Schiffrin (Ed.), *Meaning, form, and use in context: Linguistic applications* (pp. 325–341). Washington, DC: Georgetown University Press.

Paine, R. (Ed.). (1981). *Politically speaking: Cross-cultural studies of rhetoric.* Philadelphia: ISHI.

Paredes, A. (1966a). The Anglo-American in Mexican folklore. In R. Browne (Ed.), *New voices in American studies* (pp. 113–128). Lafayette, IN: Purdue University Press.

Paredes, A. (1966b). The *décima* on the Texas-Mexican border: Folksong as an adjunct to legend. *Journal of the Folklore Institute, 3*, 154–167.

Paredes, A. (1968). Folk medicine and the intercultural jest. In J. Helm (Ed.), *Spanish speaking people in the United States* (pp. 104–119). Proceedings of the 1968 Annual Spring Meeting of the American Ethnological Society. Seattle: University of Washington Press.

Paredes, A. (1974). Jose Mosqueda and the folklorization of actual events. *Aztlan, 4*, 1–29.

Paredes, A. (1977). On ethnographic work among minority groups: A folklorist's perspective. *New Scholar, 7*, 1–32.

Paredes, A., & Bauman, R. (Eds.). (1972). *Toward new perspectives in folklore*. Austin: University of Texas Press.

Parkin, D. (1984). Political language. *Annual Review of Anthropology, 13*, 345–365.

Parmentier, R. (1989). *The semiotics of ritual performativity*. Paper presented at the 88th annual meeting of the American Anthropological Association, Washington, DC.

Parry, M. (1971). *The making of Homeric verse: The collected papers of Milman Parry* (A. Parry, Ed.). Oxford: Clarendon Press.

Philips, S. U. (1985). Strategies of clarification in judges' use of language: From the written to the spoken. *Discourse Processes, 8*, 421–436.

Philips, S. U. (1986). Reported speech as evidence in an American trial. In D. Tannen & J. E. Alatis (Eds.), *Languages and linguistics: The interdependency of theory, data, and application* (pp. 154–170). Washington, DC: Georgetown University Press.

Philips, S. U. (1987). *The concept of speech genre in the study of language and culture* (Working Papers and Proceedings of the Center for Psychosocial Studies No. 11, pp. 25–34). Chicago.

Preston, D. (1982). 'Ritin' folklower daun 'rong: Folklorists' failures in phonology. *Journal of American Folklore, 95*, 304–326.

Proschan, F. (1981). Puppet voices and interlocutors: Language in folk puppetry. *Journal of American Folklore, 94*, 527–555.

Rabinow, P., & Sullivan, W. M. (Eds.). (1987). *Interpretive social science: A second look*. Berkeley: University of California Press.

Ravenhill, P. L. (1976). Religious utterances and the theory of speech acts. In W. J. Samarin (Ed.), *Language in religious practice* (pp. 26–39). Rowley, MA: Newbury House.

Rosaldo, M. Z. (1982). The things we do with words: Ilongot speech acts and speech act theory in philosophy. *Language in Society, 11*, 203–235.

Roseman, M. (1988). The pragmatics of aesthetics: The performance of healing among the Senoi Temiar. *Social Science & Medicine, 27*, 811–18.

Rothenberg, J., & Rothenberg D. (Eds.). (1983). *Symposium of the whole: A range of discourse toward an ethnopoetics*. Berkeley: University of California Press.

Sacks, H. (1974). An analysis of the course of a joke's telling in conversation. In R. Bauman & J. Sherzer (Eds.), *Explorations in the ethnography of speaking* (pp. 337–353). New York: Cambridge University Press.

Sacks, H., Schegloff, E. A., & Jefferson, G. (1974). A simplest systematics for the organization of turn-taking for conversation. *Language, 50,* 696–735.

Sapir, E. (1921). *Language: An introduction to the study of speech.* New York: Harcourt, Brace and World.

Sapir, E. (1949). *Selected writings of Edward Sapir in language, culture, and personality* (D. G. Mandelbaum, Ed.). Berkeley: University of California Press.

Saussure, F. de. (1916/1959). *A course in general linguistics* (W. Baskin, Trans.). New York: McGraw-Hill.

Schegloff, E. A. (1968). Sequencing in conversational openings. *American Anthropologist, 70,* 1075–1095.

Schegloff, E. A. (1982). Discourse as an interactional achievement: Some uses of "uh huh" and other things that come between sentences. In D. Tannen (Ed.), *Analyzing discourse: Text and talk* (pp. 71–93). Washington, DC: Georgetown University Press.

Schiffrin, D. (1988). Conversation analysis. In F. J. Newmeyer (Ed.), *Linguistics: The Cambridge survey, Vol. 4. Language: The socio-cultural context* (pp. 251–276). New York: Cambridge University Press.

Searle, J. (1969). *Speech acts.* New York: Cambridge University Press.

Searle, J. (1976). The classification of illocutionary acts. *Language in Society, 5,* 1–23.

Searle, J. (1979). *Expression and meaning.* New York: Cambridge University Press.

Seeger, A. (1987). *Why Suya sing: A musical anthropology of an Amazonian people.* New York: Cambridge University Press.

Sherzer, J. (1983). *Kuna ways of speaking.* Austin: University of Texas Press.

Sherzer, J. (1987). A discourse-centered approach to language and culture. *American Anthropologist, 89,* 295–309.

Sherzer, J. (1990). *Verbal art in San Blas: Kuna culture through its discourse.* New York: Cambridge University Press.

Sherzer, J., & Woodbury, A. C. (Eds.). (1987). *Native American discourse: Poetics and rhetoric.* New York: Cambridge University Press.

Shuman, A. (1986). *Storytelling rights: The uses of oral and written texts by urban adolescents.* New York: Cambridge University Press.

Silverstein, M. (1976). Shifters, linguistic categories, and cultural description. In K. H. Basso & H. A. Selby (Eds.), *Meaning in Anthropology* (pp. 11–55). Albuquerque: University of New Mexico Press.

Silverstein, M. (1979). Language structure and linguistic ideology. In P. R. Clyne, W. Hanks, & C. L. Hofbauer (Eds.), *The elements: A parasession on linguistic units and levels* (pp. 193–247). Chicago: Chicago Linguistic Society.

Silverstein, M. (1981). *Metaforces of power in traditional oratory.* Paper presented to Department of Anthropology, Yale University. Unpublished manuscript, University of Chicago.

Silverstein, M. (1984). On the pragmatic "poetry" of prose: Parallelism, repetition, and cohesive structure in the time course of dyadic conversation. In

D. Schiffrin (Ed.), *Meaning, form, and use in context: Linguistic applications* (pp. 181–199). Washington, DC: Georgetown University Press.

Silverstein, M. (1985a). The culture of language in Chinookan narrative texts; or, on saying that...in Chinook. In J. Nichols & A. C. Woodbury (Eds.), *Grammar inside and outside the clause* (pp. 132–171). New York: Cambridge University Press.

Silverstein, M. (1985b). Language and the culture of gender: At the intersection of structure, usage, and ideology. In E. Mertz & R. Parmentier (Eds.), *Semiotic mediation* (pp. 219–259). Orlando, FL: Academic Press.

Silverstein, M. (1992). The indeterminacy of contextualization: When is enough enough? In P. Auer & A. Di Luzio (Eds.), *The contextualization of language* (pp. 55–76). Amsterdam: John Benjamins.

Stewart, K. (1988). Nostalgia—a polemic. *Cultural Anthropology, 3,* 227–241.

Stoeltje, B. J. (1985). The rodeo clown and the semiotics of metaphor. *Journal of Folklore Research, 22,* 155–177.

Stoeltje, B. J., & Bauman, R. (1988). The semiotics of folkloric performance. In T. A. Sebeok & J. Umiker-Sebeok (Eds.), *The semiotic web 1987* (pp. 585–599). Berlin: Mouton deGruyter.

Stoller, P. (1984). Sound in Songhay cultural experience. *American Ethnologist, 11,* 559–570.

Stone, R. M. (1988). *Dried millet breaking: Time, words, and song in the Woi epic of the Kpelle.* Bloomington: Indiana University Press.

Tannen, D. (1984). *Conversational style: Analyzing talk among friends.* Norwood, NJ: Ablex.

Tedlock, B. (1980). Songs of the Zuni Kachina society: Composition, rehearsal, performance. In C. Frisbie (Ed.), *Southwestern Indian ritual drama* (pp. 7–35). Albuquerque: University of New Mexico Press.

Tedlock, D. (1983). *The spoken word and the work of interpretation.* Philadelphia: University of Pennsylvania Press.

Tedlock, D. (1989). Ethnopoetics. In E. Barnouw (Ed.), *International encyclopedia of communications,* Vol. 2 (pp. 116–117). Oxford: Oxford University Press.

Tompkins, J. P. (Ed.). (1980). *Reader-response criticism: From formalism to post-structuralism.* Baltimore: Johns Hopkins University Press.

Turner, V. W. (1969). *The ritual process: Structure and anti-structure.* London: Routledge and Kegan Paul.

Turner, V. W. (1974). *Dramas, fields, and metaphors.* Ithaca, NY: Cornell University Press.

Urban, G. (1984). Speech about speech in speech about action. *Journal of American Folklore, 97,* 310–328.

Urban, G. (1986). Ceremonial dialogues in South America. *American Anthropologist, 88,* 371–386.

Urban, G. (1987). *On the "Psychological Reality of the Text."* Paper presented at the 86th annual meeting of the American Anthropological Association, Chicago.

Urban, G. (1988). Discourse, affect, and social order: Ritual wailing in Amerindian Brazil. *American Anthropologist, 90,* 385–400.

Volosinov, V. N. (1930/1973). *Marxism and the philosophy of language* (L. Matejka & I. R. Titunik, Trans.). New York: Seminar Press.

Weigle, M. (1978). Women as verbal artists: Reclaiming the sisters of Enheduanna. *Frontiers, 3*, 1–9.

Williams, R. (1977). *Marxism and literature*. Oxford: Oxford University Press.

Young, K. G. (1987). *Taleworlds and storyrealms: The phenomenology of narrative.* Dordrecht, Holland: Martinus Nijhoff.

chapter 12

The Improvisational Performance of Culture in Realtime Discursive Practice*

Michael Silverstein
The University of Chicago

Since the mid-1970s, Dr. Silverstein has developed an influential theory of situated linguistic action. He originated the concept of metapragmatics, *and has published seminal articles on* linguistic ideology *and its relationship to language structure. Silverstein begins this chapter with a theoretical discussion of the interactional mechanics of improvised conversations, and the powerful relationship between them and "culture." The relationship is so powerful, in fact, that Silverstein claims that culture is created and reproduced through these encounters, which are fundamentally improvisational and creative. In doing so, he makes the methodological point that discourse analysis is meaningless without incorporating a notion of "culture" into the analysis.*

Silverstein then demonstrates this approach by analyzing a transcript of a conversation between two native English speakers. This analysis demonstrates that

*This chapter completely revises major portions of a draft, "A Minimax Approach to Verbal Interaction: Invoking 'Culture' in Realtime Discursive Practice," written at the invitation of Professor Joan A. Argente of the Autonomous University of Barcelona for a November 1993 Workshop on Language, Cognition, and Computation (sponsored and generously supported by the Fundació Catalana per a la Recerca and the Institut d'Estudis Catalans). I am most grateful to Professor Argente and to my coparticipants in that conference. This revision has benefited greatly from copious marginalia on that draft by Keith Sawyer, as well as from a critical discussion with Robert E. Moore. I have presented various accounts of the transcript material and of this analysis over the last few years in lectures in such places as Tel Aviv, Minneapolis, Bloomington, Buffalo, etc., to the audiences of which occasions—as to my attentive "Language in Culture" course students over the last decade— I am indebted for insightful questions and responses. I continue to be in the debt of my colleague Starkey Duncan for access to and use of these data.

*creativity, performance, and improvisation are found even in informal encoun-
ters, and that the poetic patternings summarized by Bauman and Briggs are used
in everyday encounters. This analysis is a powerful demonstration that everyday
encounters are improvisational. In its close focus on the turn-by-turn, micro-level
mechanics of interaction, it is reminiscent of Berliner's and Monson's musicological demonstrations of jazz "conversation."*

I n this chapter, I give a close analytic reading of how "what is said"
by two interacting conversationalists maps onto "what is done
(accomplished)" by them in the course of their spontaneous language use. I argue that this is improvisationally achievable precisely
because it is effectively a mapping of textual objects, mediated or
enabled by context. Particularly important is the perduring context of
culture, group-relative truths and schemata of value that in effect underlie—because they are necessarily semiotically invoked by—interactants'
mutual positionings and repositionings vis-à-vis communicable signs.

By this account, "culture" exists only by virtue of its being invoked—
indexically called into being—primarily in discursive interaction, the
kind of social action[1] that occurs through the use of language and its
dependent sign systems. This means that anyone can know about culture
only by studying language-in-use *as* a form of social action, that is, as a
by-degrees improvisational performance of a meaningful cultural *text* in
context (terms to be discussed below). Conversely, anyone can understand
the nature of language use as social action only by understanding the
necessary and enabling role of culture as the framework that gives interactional potency to participants' behaviors *as* symbolic interaction. Further, "culture" has continuity beyond the microsociological moment of
its invocation only as it perdures, with gradual consequential change, in
a macrosociological order of virtual communication over multiple
improvisational, invocational performances of it.

Language performances, like all the rest of social action, can thus be
seen to have "event" characteristics. That is, language-in-use constitutes
sociohistorically-located happenings of the functioning social order.
(This is termed by social anthropologists the social organization of society.) In this order such happenings are causally contingent and causally
consequential events. But, insofar as different instances of such happenings can be said to recur, like multiple playings of "the same" game (ref-
erencing at once a Saussurean and a Wittgensteinian image), this fact of
recurrence manifests an order of types of events of social action realized
by genres of performed texts-in-context, even if these are, in each
instance, characteristically "improvisational" in nature.[2]

We want to get some preliminary sense of how people's realtime communicative behavior of just "saying something to someone" by using

particular sign-forms in particular arrangements can count as doing (accomplishing) at least one socially (in)appropriate/(in)effective act—note the 2 x 2 table implied!—in whatever durational expanse we are considering.[3] With such a sense it should be possible to see why we can never find any genred order in improvisations without reference to culture as an essential part of the context of their accomplishment.

What then are the characteristics of such texts-in-context? Of what are they composed such that biographical individuals can participate with one another in achieving them? The problem as stated has two primary components, text and "in-context," which we can attempt to clarify in turn. Further, to differentiate the "saying something" from the "doing something" aspects of our problem, then, let us recognize not one but two types of textuality(-in-context) for the social action of language-in-use.

One is at the plane of *denotational* coherence—coherence of referential and modalized predicational meaningfulness over a stretch of linguistic usage. Under such a model of textuality, a text is evaluated for the ways in which, and degree to which, it is an organized structure-in-realtime representing states-of-affairs of distinguishable entities in universes-of-reference, along with indications of propositional attitudes or orientations communicative participants take with respect to such representations. The latter forms a matrix of relational positionings towards represented states-of-affairs—such as epistemic, ontic, and phenomenal—of communicating self and other in the frame of interactants' role-inhabitances. This is a basic and frequently highly grammatically coded set of deictic parameters for calibrating represented states-of-affairs with respect to the presumed and consequent ones affecting the participants in the communicative-act.

Here as prototypical denotational text, we include especially logical discourse in its natural-expository presentation, that is, such stretches of language as can be at least reconstructed as syllogistic or inferentially coherent propositional organization of conceptual information. Such evaluations of linguistic form for denotational textuality-in-context have more or less been the limits of consideration of textuality by students of linguistic structure or cognitive process in the West; this view of language-in-use certainly underlies our Western post-Enlightenment notions of grammar as a perduring order of language-as-structure invoked by each use of language particularly in the denotational-textual function.

Concerned with denotational textuality, we are interested in how specific pieces of information or conceptual content are brought out into the intersubjective field of communication. Are there "orderly" and "disorderly" ways of doing so that are dependent on, that is, in more or less conformity with, formal mechanisms of grammatical structure as well as with formalizable understandings of propositionality such as are modeled by logical syntax? Are such mechanisms universal tendencies towards transparent mappings—"picture theories" of propositional coding in natural language—or at least universal in some structural sense? More specifically, to exemplify this kind of interrogation of discourse, what are the *topicalization* devices, the ways that a denotatum is intersubjectively singled out to be the referential fulcrum of propositional information here-and-now unfolding in the formal scope of a clause or sentence? What are the *topic-continuity* devices, the ways that an established referent is marked as still the fulcrum of propositional information of the clause or sentence where its formal mark functions? Analysis of language use as denotational text yields up a model of how, over smaller-scope and larger-scope signal-stretches of behavioral duration, modalized propositional information can be seen as an orderly process of increasingly dense coherence, mutual interrelationships of logically (inferentially) consequential kinds.[4] Such coherence allows us to say that the sign-vehicles involved in achieving its intersubjective marking show a formal relationship of "(denotational-textual) cohesion" with one another.

By contrast to denotational coherence and its associated formal cohesion, another type of textuality-in-context is characterizable by its types and degrees of *interactional* coherence. An interactional text, in such a view, is a structure-in-realtime of organized, segmentable, and recognizable event-units of the order of social organizational regularity, the ways that individuals of various social characteristics are "recruited" to role-relations in various institutionalized ways, and consequentially, through semiotic behavior, reinforce, contend with, and transform their actual and potential inhabitance of such roles. People act one with respect to another according to default, or plausible, or by-degrees possible, or even newly emergent identities of a macrosociological order; that is to say, social action in event-realtime has the capacity to be causally effective in the universe of identities as a basis for relationships and further social action. The macrosociological order is invoked as the microsociological context of role-inhabitances relevant to an interaction, and in these terms using language in its interactional text-forming capacity is, semiotically, the mapping of the "presupposed" social situation, the one thus far established by defaults and by any prior social action, into the "entailed" one, the one that might be said to result from the semiotic behavior of language-use. Observe that insofar as this takes place with a certain balletic multiparticipant consistency (or at least relative non-inconsistency) over a span of interactional realtime, we have a coherent, intersubjectively accomplished interactional text, the interpersonal achievement of a "doing" of something—an instance of some generically understood social act—to which more than one individual has contributed. We can, then, in parallel fashion to denotational text coherence, evaluate stretches of discourse forms as having *interactional-textual cohesion* one with respect to another to the extent there is a specially recognizable interactional coherence to their co-occurrence in the course of discursive interaction.

But let us note again that, by hypothesis, this interpersonal achievement of interactional textuality occurs through the medium of what participants *say* to each other, that is, through their co-production of a particular denotational text. To the extent that this is the case, we have the problem of specifying the precise role in this interactional-textual achievement of the specific arrangement of signs for "what is said" by the use of certain sign-forms. We have the problem of showing that the specific pattern of denotational-textual cohesion generated across interactional realtime is effective in constituting—in "counting as"—a particular interactional text in its dynamically intersubjective context of occurrence. The problem of showing *that* this is the case becomes, scientifically, the problem of showing *how* this is and can be the case, in particular and in general. Hence the worked example below, as illustrative.

Keep in mind that we are dealing with structures of cohesion of sign-vehicles as the mnemonic models for corresponding types of coherence. Let us call the problem of the relationship of denotational text to at least one associated interactional text the *textual mapping problem*. We see immediately that so-called "speech-act" theory (see notes 3 and 4) foundered in multiple ways on shoals of ambiguity, indeterminacy, arbitrariness, etc., when it attempted to solve the textual mapping problem as an empirical (as opposed to ideal-speculative) approach to the analysis of real interactional events. Below I will propose instead a particular assumption about realtime achievement of formal cohesion of realtime discursive signs used in an interaction, the assumption of *maximization of global and local transparency* relating denotational and interactional textual cohesions. This is an assumption about mapping purely at the level of textuality, as stated. However, because of the nature of what constitutes discursive interaction as a semiotic enterprise, viz., the intersubjective generation or achievement of text-in-context, such a stipulative resolution of the textual mapping problem implicates at the very same time a (i.e., at least one) *minimally-rich contextualization* of this now composite text-structure, a contextualization within the micro- and macrosociological orders that critically invokes "culture," the framework for giving valuated meaningfulness to intersubjectively deployable signs.

But why should a stipulation about the textual mapping problem yield an interpretation of the culturally specific interpretability of an interaction? I think this rests ultimately on the fact that text as a set of relationships constituting a developmental structure in (real)time is a function of establishing complex *indexical relationships*, or *indexicalities*, just as are relationships of text to context. All interaction rests on indexicality "all the way down"; and thus, indexically invoked, culture turns out to be the decisive component for achieving the text/context divide in a discursive interaction, however improvisational such interaction may be. By understanding the logically autonomous nature of events of indexicality, we will understand the necessity for a *principle of biplanar textuality* in particular, and hence we will understand the necessity for relating those two planes of textuality by a stipulative maximization assumption about the mapping across them.

We might then pause to observe that the text/context divide in a discursive interaction is an achieved one; indeed, we might emphasize this by speaking instead of processes of *entextualization* and of *contextualization* (see Bauman & Briggs, this volume; also Silverstein & Urban, 1996, for many case studies). The first labels the achievement in discursive realtime of a relatively stable textual cohesiveness (with its understood or at least experienced intuition of coherence); and the second labels a correspondingly understood functional effect of appropriateness-of-text to context or effectiveness-of-text in context. For as structures of cohesion, texts are nothing more than by-degrees complex and multiply overlaid patterns of *co-occurrence* of (token) sign-forms one with respect to another. In this sense, knowing the location of some particular sign in its cohesive modality of sign-configuration permits us to predict at least something of where another particular sign will be located with respect to it; that is, both particular signs have an orderly and stipulable textual occurrence by virtue of a structure of co-occurrence in a semiotic medium that can be modeled as such. One particular sign "points to" (indexes) the other under the principle of textual co-occurrence that covers their mutual appearance. Each is an index of the other, of course, and the co-occurrence pattern indexes the general regularity that underlies their appearance. *Cotextuality*, as we call this relationship, is thus a special, text-internal form of indexicality, the semiotic property that we more usually associate with something *in* a text that points *out* to its context of occurrence. As a developmental structure in realtime, note, patterns of cotextuality are indexical patterns in which the rest of a text, under whatever complex patterns of co-occurrence are being implemented, is the text-internal context (no oxymoron here!) of any particular sign-form bound up in such relationships.

Further, such indexical relationships, both text-internal cotextuality and indexes pointing to aspects of context, can be seen to comprise two functional kinds in their definitional order of cause and effect: either the indexical sign-token is *presupposing*, where a sign-token points to a co(n)text that is already an intersubjective reality at the interactional moment of its occurrence, or the indexical sign-token is "performative" or *creative* or (as I rather call them) *entailing*, where a sign-token points to a co(n)text that may become an intersubjective reality—and thus subject to further or other indexical presupposition—precisely as a causal consequence of the occurrence of that particular sign. Presupposing indexes rely on having intersubjective validity at the point of their occurrence of co(n)text as already processually gelled, by initial-state defaults or givens plus any en/contextualization processes up to that point; entailing indexes effectuate that intersubjective validity, causing expectations of co(n)textualizations-abuilding into the interactional future. Empirically, any indexical sign-form is always balanced at a borderland between presupposition and entailment; as a rule their underlying indexical sign-types—at the level of conventions or regularities of indexicality associable with particular forms like words, expressions, and grammatical categories—have a characteristic degree of relative presupposing/entailing value in different generic or at least asymptotically autonomous co(n)textual usages.[5]

Defined in this way, as events whereby the occurrence of a sign-vehicle indexically presupposes or indexically entails the occurrence of its object of semiosis, the realm of indexicality is merely a complete congeries of "pointings-to." There is no orderliness that transcends the individual indexical happening. Principles of cotextuality, however, are, in effect, criteria for carving out of this mass of indexicalities pointing every-which-way in every-which-manner a kind of orderliness of *co*-occurrence that we call simply, text. Textuality is an achievement of at least one distinctive *co*textualization, serving the discursive-interactional end of giving even improvised semiotic behavior a genre-based form and interpretability, insofar as principles of co-occurrence are invoked by indexical presupposition.[6] We have already appealed to two great realms of such cotextualization principles for language-centered discursive interaction, the denotational and the interactional. These planes of cotextualization are, thus, principles that give essentially indexical behavior—hence essentially individuated realtime pointings—a more encompassing or overarching effect, which we call their cumulative coherence in the intersubjective universe of sociocultural fact. So to study cotextuality is to study modes of such coherence. To relate one kind of cotextuality and its coherence to another is to understand how coherence of, for example, "what is said" can count as coherence of "what is done."

Now for any particular interactional happening, we may be able to discern its textuality, hence its cotextualization principles, on an increasingly improvisational series of bases. There is clearly a range of possibilities, starting from the at least theoretical instance that an interactional happening is a mere replica of another textual occasion or of more than one such textual occasion, up a scale of uniqueness-of-text to the again theoretically imaginable situation of complete and utter uniqueness of an interactional event (Sawyer, 1996). Interactional texts of the first extreme have some of the experiential and observational excitement of games the outcome of which everyone knows in advance; "performance" is merely the regular, mechanical execution of "competence," we might say, and there is no real potential for contingent novelty in a sociohistorical sense, such as seems to be the case with all human facts even including actual use of language.[7]

Human discursive interaction in general seems to be very far from this possibility of completely predictive ritualization, of course, at least partly because the possible textualities manifested by any chunk of human interactional behavior are always—forever—at least asymptotically subject to retrospective revision, both as the text is being achieved by participants in its creation and ever afterward as it is subject to reinterpretation by them and by others acting as interpreters. The work of textuality is never finished, as this theorization of the problem indicates; any achievement of textuality-in-context is "perspectivally-dependent" therefore in the sense that we humans always approach what-is-said/what-happens in discursive interaction as inhabitants of some role with respect to understanding what is said/what happens. And this is no less true of would-be objective "observers" and "analysts" after-the-fact as it is of admittedly subjective direct and intentional "participants in" discursive interaction. Hence, note, it can never be our aim to say, definitively and once and for all, what a discursive interaction means or effectuates, either in its realtime earlier-to-later unfolding (where surprises of textually-retrospective reinterpretation happen all the time). Nor can we be exhaustively definitive after a given interaction unfolds, when for example as analysts we study the *in vitro* trace, a good transcript, of the *in vivo* reality we seek to give an account of. We must therefore be content as analysts to find a plausible, minimally rich account of the meaning and effectiveness of discursive interaction that has some predictive power in a number of collateral ways. It is this level of *plausible minimality of interpretation* that we achieve by applying our principles of *maximality of locally/globally transparent mapping* across denotational and interactional textualities.

This must be our stance as analysts. But it must be emphasized that while individuals intentionally participate in creating both denotational and interactional textualities,[8] they are only indirectly parties to them. Such texts inhabit a sociocultural and sociohistorical realm that is interpersonal and intersubjective. As already discussed, for better or worse for our attempts at empirical study, in this dialectically constituted realm there is only relatively local stability of textuality, irreducibly indexical in its epistemological characteristics even as we analysts seek to model and understand it and certainly also as any individual bound up in the primary creation of textuality can seek to do so. While individuals of course have cognitive and affective involvement in creating such orders of textuality each time they use language, we should not lose sight of the fact that the structure of contingent and consequential events in the real social world is, of course, only partly, if at all, "consciously" understood (hence, modeled) by actors caught up in them through their individual mental functioning, including conscious, purposive thought about the real social world. And when participants do try to model or understand what is going on, they do so in perhaps spontaneous and untutored terms; in their individual and culture-specific "folk-theoretic" modalities such folk understandings are very different from any systematic attempt social scientists make to treat the matter of textuality in the micro- and macrosociological orders. We claim as social scientists of textuality the perhaps privileged stance of systematized, generalizing predictiveness, despite our recognition that in some sense our perspective is perforce continuous with that of others, both in its limits and its prejudices.

Improvisational texts-in-context are thus complex objects; they demand characterization in ways that capture their contingent, processual, and dialectic nature, and make us realize that we can, at best, study them *in vitro*, though never *in vivo*. Recalling the terms entextualization/contextualization, we see that the achievement of relative fixity or stability at some point of interactional time (including points beyond a particular participation framework, as for example analytic scrutiny by someone who was not there originally) depends on intuitively—or explicitly—understanding this ratio accomplished through the very unitary medium of indexicality. We claim that our method of maximization of projected cotextualities gives a sufficient—minimal—account of such relative fixity in a sociocultural order of significance.

The method grows out of a semiotic reconstruction of the so-called "Formalist" literary-critical tradition of analyzing "poetic function," as Jakobson (1960, pp. 356–358) termed pervasive and principle-based cotextuality in a denotational text. Strongly marked indications of supervening cotextuality, as in the construction of denotational text by use of metered, or recurrently positioned formal units, frequently serve to put a discursive interaction over the minimal threshold of determinate interactional entextualization. As Jakobson noted, any actual denotational-textual "poetry" uses multiple compositional principles of metrical equivalence of underlying unitizations of a text, like verses, lines, hemistichs, feet, syllables, etc., of phonological form, though one can use words, grammatical categories, sentences, etc., of grammatical form just as well. With respect to such overlaid unitizations of text, consider denotational linguistic forms that occur in metrically multiply-characterized positions—think of hemistich-final stressed units in alternate even-numbered lines of respective verses of a whole text as a kind of complexly definable metrical position. Such units are generally interpretable as contributing to overall entextualization only by understanding them as tropes one of another, in a meta-level reading that appears figuratively to transform their normal denotational senses associable with lexicon and grammar in the asymptotically literal mode. All of the classical types of poetic and rhetorical figures are classifications of the types of transformations seemingly undergone by literal senses of words and expressions in various poetically situated occurrences in denotational text.

Thus note two important principles to extract and generalize beyond self-styled literary composition and beyond denotational textuality in its narrowest sense. First, *poetry* in the sense of using textually bound figurative language indexically presupposes—and hence invokes—the existence of grammar and lexicon in some asymptotically literal denotational modality, which literalness is thus experienced (and experienceable) only to the degree to which and in the manner in which we can experience entextualizing figuration. Literalness in any empirically experienceable denotational entextualization is just poetic figuration degree zero, that is, meaningfulness (or that aspect of meaningfulness) of words and expressions completely independent of emerging (en)text(ualization)-in-context—an obviously merely theoretical extreme invoked by actual usage.[9] Second, insofar as units of poetic figuration do not merely *occur* in particular local meta-semiosis, but *recur* in certain determinate positions across the durational realtime of a metricalized (en)text(ualization), we might read earlier-to-later in emerging text-structural metricalization as an icon or diagram of process: This potentially becomes a *dynamic figuration* that implicitly transforms one literal/figurative occurrence into another, at an even higher, global meta-level of semiosis that can be read as a significance of the whole textual segment in which recurrences are located. The local figurations thus become organized, under this *iconic* reading of entextualization, into a global figuration or movement that might be seen as the message of the whole text-segment over which its sign-vehicles take place.

We shall see how, precisely, these two principles operate across the planes of denotational and interactional textuality in the extended example below. To do so, we need to define some particular kinds of textual structures achievable as maxima of cohesive organization in the course of discursive interaction. Though the terms we use for character-izing them are consistent with the framework introduced here, their properties ought to be familiar to readers from one or another approach already in the literature of studying realtime interaction.[10]

First, for any discursive interaction we can conceptualize at least one *maximally coherent interactional text*. This is characterized cohesively by maximally unified indexical structure, the closest realization for the hap-pening at issue of a "once-and-for-all" organized structure-in-durational-realtime. It is laid down by the greatest number of mutually consistent indexical relationships, densely co-occurring so as to reinforce one another cotextually as well in the dialectic of indexical presupposition and indexical entailment. Note that there need not be a unique such text-in-context, only at least one.

For any discursive interaction engaged in by participants, the theoreti-cal maximum of coherence would be recognizable as balletic fluency of coherently cumulating interactional contributions both by each partici-pant and across their interactional turns: fluency that builds consistently over actual earlier-to-later realtime to a structurally perfect execution of some genred social-actional event, never faltering or going back to redo a stretch so as to make clear its contribution to some structure abuilding, never requiring meta-interactional work of repair or explicitly stipula-tive metapragmatic discourse of any sort (like checking to see what genre of segment one is at that point intersubjectively understood to be engaged in).

Observe that at issue are degrees and modalities of fluent vs. dysfluent ways of sedimenting *interactional texts* of particular sorts; the denotational content of verbal interaction, contributing to denotational textuality as such, is not at all at issue. Thus, note that Schiffrin (1984) discovered among middle-aged Jewish ethnic couples fluently executed patterns of maintaining pairwise exclusivistic solidarity through arguing over deno-tational factuality or accuracy, while they were participating in larger conversational groupings. The denotational text was at issue and vigor-ously contested by them, while the precision of the mutually stroking intimacy of "argument" itself maintained boundaries of what we might call rights and responsibilities of caring for each other, troping as it were upon one's care for the partner's accuracy of recollection, of narra-tion, and of informed opinion.

It should also be clear that such a theoretical maximum is an ideal compared to which most discursive interactions fall short. Nevertheless, the idea is that from any *in vitro* transcript of a discursive interaction, one can construct a proposal for structured cohesion of indexicals in what appears to be a most densely cotextual and most (non-in)coher-ently cumulative earlier-to-later performance of social acts. For any empirical interaction, to be sure, we may have to recognize this as the implicit social action, in terms of which then certain transcripted happenings are non-contributory side- or by-sequences, places where participants seem to try to set right what must at a certain point have seemed to be going terribly wrong for one or another participant, etc. But, in keeping with the analogical concept of a poetics of interactional textuality (see Silverstein, 1985b), *the analytic rule of thumb is to find, that is, to discern, in a transcript a cohesive model of indexical signs as though at each phase of a discursive interaction the sign is determined by the densest possible lamination of multiple metrical principles of placement-within-an-emerging-textual-whole*, as a syllable in many traditions of actual poetry is simultaneously determinate as to its status within a foot, a hemistich, a line, a verse, a section, and the whole poem.[11]

Next, we add to the concept of the maximally coherent interactional text the stipulation that at each moment of discursive interaction, each social actor's role-incumbency be a strategically discernible one, that is, one that has integrity as a *move* of that social actor constituting at least one coherent and genred interactional text-segment, a locally-maximally-coherent interactional "textlet." In a discursive interaction characterized by turns that are distributed over individual role-incumbents, for example, each such turn here is stipulably a coherent interactional text, that is, each turn sediments an internally cohesive and maximally-locally-dense cotextual structure, considered, insofar possible, all by itself.

Under such conditions applied to each and every putative segment of discursive interaction, we can define a *maximally-coherent, maximally-strategic interactional text* as a maximal interactional text in which the functional integrity is maximized of each role-incumbent's contribution, e.g., each turn at communication, as a co(n)textual indexical structure: Each role-incumbent turn contributes its contextualizing effect as autonomously as possible, though it is of course subordinate to the emergent cotextual structure of the whole, with which it must be compatible, i.e., non-incoherent.

In such a maximization, we are obligated to seek to read each interactant's behavior by the criterion that it constitutes a complete performance of some known genre of social action. Note that the so-called "pair-part" structure of alternating $(A_1;B_1);(A_2;B_2);(A_3;B_3)$ ... form—with A_i and B_i representing the respectively paired contributions of two individuable participants, A and B, alternately having the communicational floor—constitutes an analytic hypothesis about the perhaps cumulatively-coherent as well as certainly *strategic* interactional text to be found in the discursive interaction of A and B. That A's and B's respective behaviors can be so modeled does not, of course, imply that each participant interacts consciously knowing at that instant the particular position of the current contribution to the overall poetics of pair-part interaction. But were one designing a strategic engine of maximally coherent interaction (in which case, let us recall, each interactional phase is made unerringly as a contribution to an emerging coherent whole), one would have to model the equivalent of at least the local pair-part position toward counting as which the particular contribution would be made.

In such a strategic model, each interactant's contribution could also explicitly indicate which other interactional pair-part contribution it relates to (as first or second pair-part), by virtue of including what have been called in the speech-act approach (Searle, 1969, pp. 30–33, 68–69) "illocutionary force indicating devices." Thus, one could use an explicit interrogative syntactic construction to lay down a contribution that counted as a "question" first pair-part, at least so intending with a certain degree of compulsive entailment for what a segment of interactional text that followed it should be *qua* second pair-part. One could seek to answer such a question in a second pair-part contribution that indexically presupposed its having occurred as a question, for example by using an emphatic assertorial syntactic construction. The point is, of course, that these are only statistical relationships of "counting as" one or another pair-part position in a genred type of interactional move when viewed against norms or expectations of interactional appropriateness-to-co(n)text   and   interactional   effectiveness-in-co(n)text.   As Levinson (1983, pp. 332–336) points out in introducing a typological chart of folk-terminologized interactional-textual *adjacency pairs*, for example (Request; Acceptance/Refusal) or (Blame; Denial/Admission), various degrees of indexically presupposing/entailing compulsiveness relate the parts of such interactional-textual structures, which interactants *as agentive actors* can certainly strategically exploit in yielding to the genred adjacency-pair expectations (norms), or in creatively avoiding (violating) them.

An important consequence of such a maximally strategic interactional text is that it is possible to build up an overall or global coherence of interactional text by repeatedly constructing very local coherence across interactionally integral adjacency pairs, requiring interactants to keep track only of reasonably local developments in sedimenting a much longer interactional text. It might be reasonable to think of human improvisational actors as doing so, engaged in a banal interactional poetics of dyadic parallelism that yields a structure of the form $(A_i;B_i)^n$, that is, n repetitions of adjacency-pairhood. Of course, the overall interaction has its own culminative integrity only to the extent that over the course of this structure there is another, dynamic figuration developing as well, one that is a function of positionality of an interactional segment S_j in a larger sequence of such ranging over $1 < j < n$. We might think of all the ways that this might be otherwise introduced as well, from a very abrupt change in either A's or B's interactional contributions, or a sudden metapragmatic stipulation by one or another that some interactional-textual state has been/will-have-been reached, etc. American telephone conversations, frequently to be experienced as chatty pair-part meanderings between well-acquainted parties, suddenly are ready to be brought to a conclusion when one party comes back to the first (denotational) topic of discursive interaction; then can follow a quick coda (though it is possible, of course, to avoid the coda and get back into meandering pair-partism once more).

Now nothing so far in our theoretical account of kinds of interactional-textual maximizations is inherently and specifically language-centered, despite the linguistic examples. Stated simply in terms of interactional textuality, we might be dealing with any improvisational medium in which such things are definable as maximally coherent and thus cohesively "integral" participant turn structures (Sawyer, 1996). We come now to the specific link to natural language. We want to be able to stipulate that making denotational text is a necessary condition of how a specifically linguistic-discursive interactional text is generated, even if—as is clearly the case—in some intersubjectively literal sense of A's "saying something" and B's (as well as A's) "understanding what A says," generating such denotational text is not a *sufficient* condition for discursive interaction between A and B. Sometimes, as the worked example will demonstrate, rather dysfluent denotational text is the basis for what seems to be the interactional text it determines, precisely revealed by our reading of the culturally specific local tropology of "what is being said" and of the dynamic figuration of such cultural tropes at a more global scope of interactional textuality.

Denotational text is, of course, a cohesive structure-in-time that unfolds in text-sentence-long scopes or segments; we can project such segments onto signal-form under our normal assumptions about their being a maximal domain of grammatical analysis. To be sure, there is a great deal in interactional signal-form that escapes grammatical analysis in the normal sense of that enterprise. However, when we center our understanding of the entire envelope of signal-form on grammatically stipulated unitizations like text-sentences, we have in effect maximized the *transparency to denotational-textual unitization* of whatever interactional-textual cohesion emerges in a discursive interaction. *By stipulating a maximum of "relevance" (see note 4) of grammatically projected signal-form to modeling any interactional text, we give ourselves a heuristic for analysis. We have made it possible for words and expressions of denotational text viewed through the lens of grammatically given construction in effect to constitute as well the medium of* interactional *textuality. What one "does" with language now depends in some way on what one "says" in it*: This means that since words and expressions viewed through their implicit grammatical-analytic structures make up the essential core of denotational-textual structure, these very partials of grammatical structure at all levels and planes of analysis can contribute as well to the cohesive structure of interactional text (though of course not in the same way they do to denotational text).

We are now providing a theorized underpinning for the asymptote of what is really a familiar object of intuitive folk-contemplation of language use, though our constructed term for it, viz., a *maximal, maximally (denotationally) transparent, maximally strategic interactional text* (MAX^3TSIT), may be daunting. It is the familiar kind of object—certainly the basis for much philosophical and other speculation about discursive interaction—in which people as participants are thought to have the distinct sense that what they "mean" and "say" (thereby generating denotational text) is consequential in some determinate (i.e., regular or genred) way for what goes on interpersonally, that is, what they agentively feel they do in-and-by meaning and saying it in a turn-length communicative contribution to discursive interaction. And, by construction, we have modeled a structure that makes explicit at least one possible explanation for that intuition even in the real-world case of non-maximal discursive-interactional situations. Of course, being based in the problem of microsociological and interpersonal/intersubjective events, the account it gives of the relationship of the "said" to the "done" is generally quite at variance with folk reconstructions of how we improvise coherent interaction that begin in imputed intentionalities-to-say-that-*p* (*p* is a proposition) of autonomous communicating actor-agents.

But the account we offer through this approach to improvisation is quite at variance with such other accounts for perhaps a more subtle reason having to do with the way that we view "what is said," that is, the way we view denotational text as it (maximally to any case at hand) projects its interactional-textual relevance. For in general, we read as denotational text a poetic arrangement of words and expressions that (a) merely uses the machinery of grammar to arrange them as semiotic (indexical) operators in (b) structures of segmented figuration one with respect to another that (c) over durational realtime constitute dynamic tropes of their interactional effect or purport. Let me briefly review these three factors.

The orderliness of arrangement of words and expressions into text-sentences that depends on (presupposes) the existence of grammar (factor (a)) is a constraint on the way that, in ordinary discursive interaction at least, the various interactionally significant signs are introduced into emerging denotational text. Words and expressions comprised among the grammatical forms of a language get a particular aspect of their denotational meaningfulness—which I call their *Saussurean sense*—as a correlate of their privileges of distribution within that grammar (see note 9). We might say that insofar as their text-sentence usage indexes (presupposes) the grammar in which they are construable as indeed well-formed words and expressions, their Saussurean senses are always available as a basis for making denotational text. Under our assumption of maximal denotational transparency, we can asymptotically rely on the grammar of each text-sentence in a discursive interaction for the literal reading of it.[12]

But there are other components of the denotational meaningfulness of words and expressions in any language, components that actually differentiate most of what the dictionaries call the senses of specific linguistic forms, or that thesauruses group words by according to related shadings of sense. These components of meaning are a function of the way particular sociohistorical groups of people or even particular individuals use them in making-text-in-context. These cultural(:) beliefs about the world in the form of by-degrees presumptively true/false attributions about phenomena—thus, attributes of the very phenomena of denotation—are indexed when speakers of a language use words and expressions to which they have been indexically attached by complex sociohistorical processes of text-making. After Putnam (1975), we can call these schemata of attribution *stereotypes* about denotata, or stereotypic beliefs about the n, that are much more important and certainly much more salient in most cases for the denotationally differential use of words and expressions than are their Saussurean senses under normal grammatical analysis. Such stereotypes and such (Saussurean) senses as are indexed by words and expressions in text-sentences are the stuff at the basis of how one makes interactionally relevant denotational text.

But factor (a) does more than provide senses and stereotypes (and further components of meaning). The principal mode of communicative "orderliness"—denotational coherence—projected by the fact of grammar is the way that words and expressions co-occur with, and are grammatically framed by, various explicit *deictic* categories at the level of grammatically-construable form. Such indexical-denotational categories come in paradigms (viz., English *here* : *there*, 'past' Tense : 'nonpast' Tense, etc.) and their Saussurean sense essentially incorporates information about the conditions of indexical (co)occurrence *as* their denotational contribution. At once deictics and related indexicals do two things: (1) They anchor any denotational text being generated to the actual context of communication in which it is emerging, an effect which, when viewed in the opposite direction, I have termed their *calibration* of the interaction itself by creating a shared, intersubjective representational-universe-to-hand that provides a medium for adjusting mutual role inhabitance (Silverstein, 1993, pp. 40, 48–53). And (2), at the same time deictics arrayed in discourse constitute a secondary, virtual framework of poetically arrangeable positions of (co)occurrence for other, nondeictic words and expressions that independently carry sense and stereotypy invocations. We might think of this as the deictic skeleton on which is arranged the interactionally significant flesh of discursive interaction (or, alternatively, we can think of the deictically constituted clothespins on which the word-and-expression linens are hung out to dry in the (now multidimensional) intersubjective space of denotational text). Both of these effects of deixis (and indexicality more broadly) are centrally important as the most literal mechanism grammar provides to make the "how" of what is said count as what is done.

Let us turn to factor (b). By their arrangement with respect to grammar and to textually-present deictic paradigms, senses and stereotypes associated with words and expressions are brought into determinately structured relationships. We generally find that words and expressions that invoke the same cultural realms of belief and value are organized by grammatical arrangement and deixis into discernibly local segments of text. Such text-segments present the denotata of words and expressions as terms of comparison and contrast, as terms of taxonomic, partonomic, and serial differentiation, as terms of identity or various forms of "oppositeness," and so forth. In short, the denotata, knowable by invoking sense-schemata of language, by invoking such other cultural schemata as go into stereotypes, and by invoking the emergent co(n)text of interaction itself, are the foci of relatively local denotational-textual segments.

We can measure the orderliness of local denotational-textual information or content precisely by the segmentability and clarity of the semantic figures constructed in-and-by a signal-form. A number of factors, as we now can see, contribute to such an impression of orderliness and clarity of interactionally-pregnant information. Words and expressions used to make senses and stereotypes intersubjectively "in play" must invoke particular cultural *domains of knowledge* relative to *group memberships* that are plausible for interactants at the particular point in interaction.[13] Deictic systems, including, for example, reference-tracking (topicality, anaphora) mechanisms, tense/aspect/modality sequencing mechanisms, and theme/rheme mechanisms,[14] must be deployed in grammatically conforming signal-structures that comprise slots of *parallelism, repetition*, and other types of explicit *metricality of form* to constitute the space of *virtual form* (or virtual arrangement of denotational content) we described under (a). Certainly rhetoricians or instructors in composition and communication skills address aspects of some of these maximizing principles as guidelines to good composition or communication, even though they do not necessarily understand the phenomena with more than aesthetic or strategic connoisseurship.

Finally, to address the last factor, (c), we maintain that such local figurations are more globally organized in relation to *role-inhabitances of the participants* in discursive interaction. These role-inhabitances range from mere epistemic/ontic/phenomenal stance with respect to the informational content of "what has been said," which constitutes a basis for a primordial and contextually specific groupness of like-mindedness among participants,[15] to those macrosociologically-derived social identities of participants invoked in the context of discursive interaction and in relation to which a particular interaction may constitute a fulcrum of (re)creation or transformation of participants' identities, as happens in rites of passage (focused ritual discursive interactions of the human life cycle). Certainly in the latter, somewhat densely scripted discursive interactions, social scientists have long discerned the characteristic of *iconicity* or, more particularly, *diagrammaticity of figuration*: that between the already frequently figurative denotational text of what is said and otherwise signaled and the ritual's transformative purport in a culturally understood universe of social identities and statuses, there is a dynamic isomorphism that, for enculturated participants, the performance of the (communicated denotational) text instantiates instrumentally on "this one"—"here"—"now." Our point is that such a (c) dynamic or processual figuration of participants' contextually created and transformed "groupness" characteristics—in short a real social act—happens *improvisationally* each time there is discursive interaction. We seek to be able to use our maximizing analytic technique to show that for any swatch of discursive interaction, it is possible to discern such transformations' having been at work when we study the in vitro fixing of a sufficiently detailed transcript.

IMPROV: "GETTING TO KNOW YOU"

My vehicle of exemplification of the techniques involved is a snippet of conversational transcript that I have discussed before (Silverstein, 1985b). In that earlier discussion, I constructed in some detail one obvious MAX^3TSIT structure, at least by analyzing the denotational textuality that appears to be interactionally relevant. Having thus earlier established the basis for the form of the transcript here given in Figure 12.1, I want here to consider this extract once again, explicating in particular how the denotational text can, in fact, be read by us analysts as a

FIGURE 12.1. Metrically Arranged Transcript.
(continued on next two pages)

(continued on next two pages)

A

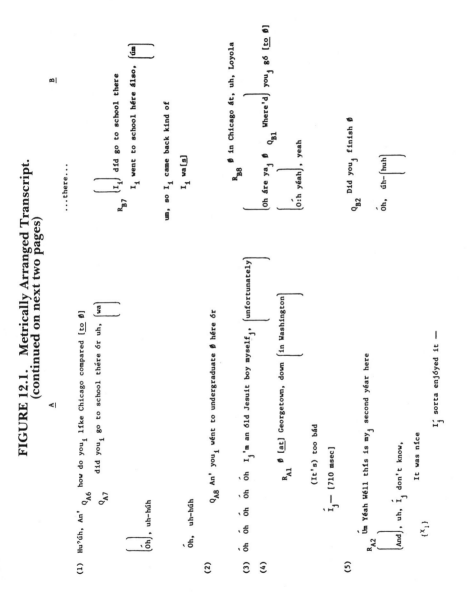

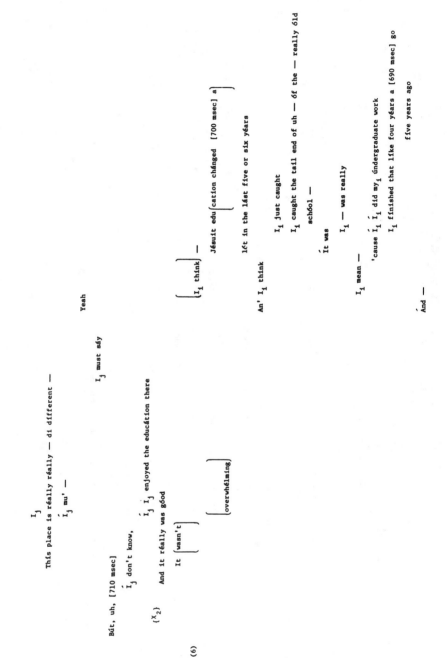

(6)

Bút, uh, [710 msec]
İⱼ don't know,

(X₂) İⱼ İⱼ enjoyed the educátion there

And it réally was góod

It [wasn't]
   [overwhélming]

Iⱼ
This place is réally réally — di different —
İⱼ mu' —

Iⱼ must sáy

Yeah

[İ₁ think] —

Jésuit edu[cation chánged [700 msec] a]

lót in the lást five or six yéars

An' İ₁ think

I₁ just caught

I₁ caught the tail end of uh — óf the — really óld
   schóol —

It was

I₁ — was really

İ₁ mean —

'cause İ₁ İ₁ did my₁ úndergraduate work

I₁ finished that líke four yéars a [690 msec] go
   five years ago

Ánd —

I_i think

Nów — próbably Loyola is a lót different

an' a lot bétter [690 msec]

y'$_j$ knów

a lót more — variety of courses

being offered et cetera

ánd —

yóu$_j$ know

I_i — I_i...

tropic figurement of the interactional text thus revealed to have occurred in this discursive interaction.

Referring interested readers to that earlier discussion, I therefore presuppose familiarity with the tools and results of the grammatical analysis of the denotational text. Let me point out some of the conventions by which the spatial arrangement of the transcriptional text-artifact in Figure 12.1 is intended as a perspicuous presentation of the denotational text. First, it keeps the temporal dimension of turn-segments strictly vertical in its visual display, preserving and uniting the contributions of each participant in its own column of a split-page columnar presentation.[16] The parallelisms of grammatical form and lexicon within each participant's utterance-part are indicated by degrees of indented paragraphing within the column arrangement. When they occur across utterance-parts (hence in different columns), many such parallelisms are generally adjacent in the vertical dimension, and they have, moreover, been paragraphed in their respective columns in identical fashion; but to capture long-distance parallelisms across columns, a full transcript would need something like poetic notation of grammatical "line"-types, as in formal analysis of poetry, using either a hierarchical alphanumeric notation as in a lecturer's outline, or appropriately differentiated connecting lines and brackets.

Let me call attention also to the braces inclusive of portions of two lines of printing, one line in each column of utterance. These are intended visually to synchronize adjacent-turn material that is simultaneously verbalized—thus "overlapping" in the resulting denotational-textual realtime—while visually preserving the convention that at most one participant's column contains a segment of transcript at any point in the top-to-bottom vertical array.

Let me now recapitulate and expand upon the sociocultural scene of this discursive interaction. During the late 1960s, my colleague, Starkey Duncan, interested in the systematicity of turn-taking in dyadic conversation and other matters involving the study of "nonverbal communication," paid graduate students at the University of Chicago to take a battery of tests and then to participate in a systematic videotaping of dyadic conversation (see Duncan & Fiske, 1977). While on camera, participants interacted with two interlocutors (one male, one female) previously unknown to them.[17] Duncan's assistants transcribed each conversation, the transcripts generated being then electronically stored in a data bank having millisecond-calibrated transcriber's codings of verbalizations, including denotational language, as well as codings of postures, body movements, gestures and other hand-arm motions, gazes, and so forth. I have extracted from one of these records the central, denotational text of a randomly selected short chunk of one such transcribed conversation, a chunk, however, that proved upon analysis to be a kind of crux of the likely interactional text of the interaction.

One of the cultural regularities of the unmarked American bourgeoisie is exemplified in the overall interactional text, a kind of "Getting to Know You" genre. One experiences this genre when two (or a small group of) people find themselves anonymously put into interactional proximity by constraining institutional circumstances, some joint outcome of which is the aggregate concern. What characterizes the subgenre evidenced in this interaction is mutual introductions by name, which is generally reserved for an interactional context of at least stipulative egalitarian group-membership: here, two educated white males in their mid-twenties, previously unacquainted, but each known by the other to be a graduate student at the University of Chicago; both are participating in a reasonably strange form of psychological experiment (see instructions in note 17) involving the then-new technology of videotaping (being in front of a television camera, perhaps for the first time in their lives).

Both students have professional aspirations of the kind that depend upon use of language in such social situations as much as upon specific other techniques of accomplished professionalization. Student A, the interlocutor whose utterances appear in the *left* column, is in the Law School, where for the most part graduates could expect in those days to be snapped up as associates by the leading private law firms in the major cities of the United States, in this way trained in corporate specializations. He obviously would have looked forward to a high level of financial reward and, if coming from modest family origins, would have contemplated dramatic upward mobility. Student B, the interlocutor whose utterances appear in the *right* column, is in the School of Social Service Administration, where for the most part graduates could expect to become entry-level caseworkers or supervisors in social work specialties, such as psychiatric social work, work with delinquent young people, etc.; in short, entering some kind of essentially governmental or para-governmental ("NGO") bureaucracy, through which any further professional mobility would occur. It is not overwhelmingly known to be a route to great financial rewards, and one's daily associates are, at least for the caseworker, to a large extent the "problem" people of mainstream bourgeois society, whether by psychiatric dysfunction, victimization, age, bodily condition, illegal activities, what bourgeois society considers demographic excesses (like motherhood early in puberty), or some combination of these.

There is thus a tension. On the one hand, we have the signs of easy and seemingly spontaneous egalitarianism of the within-group encounter (where "Getting to Know You" includes exchanging names) with a safe, mirror-image stranger from within the University of Chicago community. On the other hand, we can observe the clear asymmetries that emerge almost from the beginning of the flow of self-characterizing denotational information, to the effect that student A is in the Law School, student B in Social Service Administration,[18] and we can, with them, understand the probable implications of this for their aspirations to status and even wealth within the larger stratified social order, etc. In inhabiting the "Getting to Know You" interactional text, Messrs. A and B follow the general expectations of participants in the genre and move from the initial "here-now" denotational frame of mutual introductions to the "there-then[=before]" frame of "who they are." That is to say that in this way, Messrs. A and B develop an interactionally relevant biography for each'participant, exhibiting for intersubjective registration an orderly set of identities and associations by which each can be known to the further-interacting dyad.

It is these biographies, constructed from the denotational text Messrs. A and B narrate about themselves and their experiences, that continue to present certain potential problems for resolution in respect of Mr. A's and Mr. B's initial "default" expression of symmetric in-groupness. In the transcribed segment presented here, we can follow the intersubjective emergence of status-asymmetry in Mr. A's favor, and we can follow its further elaboration on the basis of Mr. A's pressing for specific biographical information about Mr. B, to whom he then offers his own counterpart autobiography. Once Mr. A offers a potentially negative autobiographical evaluation, however, Mr. B follows with an interesting, interactionally consequential contribution that seems to resolve the status-asymmetry in his own favor, or at least no longer in Mr. A's. The mode of improvising these interactional-textual dynamics is for Messrs. A and B to employ, or (were they strategically intensional) to deploy expressions—especially names—laden with cultural symbolism as part of the stereotype knowledge associable with their use. The poetics of how this projects into interactional figurement can be seen in the transcriptional fragment before us.

To enter into the flow of the transcripted segment, let us first consider the immediately-prior interactional sequence from which Messrs. A and B are proceeding at this point. At the point our transcript begins, among the asymmetries of identity in play is the interval-of-time "here" for each participant—note the vagueness of exactly what this word denotes, absent some specification—given in (academic) years as a matriculated graduate student at the University of Chicago.[19] Mr. B has revealed that he is a first-year graduate student "here." Mr. A has then asked his fifth question, Q_{A5}, of Mr. B, "Where did you come from before?" Note that the temporal frame in play at this point was established in terms of academic years at academic institutions, and hence the grammatical form *before* in its cotextual (poetic) position (end of text-sentence preposition!) ought to be denotationally equivalent to the fuller phrase PP[*before* NP[*this* (*,your first academic*) *year*]], while the *where* of Q_{A5} would thus seem to interrogate some contrasting institution of affiliation before the University of Chicago. Mr. B has, however, replied to the query, "Mm, Iowa. I lived in Iowa."

In its interactionally relevant frame, this reply presents perhaps incongruous denotational information in a number of ways.

1. The idiom *come from* used by Mr. A in his question Q_{A5} is generally used in the nomic or "tenseless" present all by itself in the default mode to inquire about place of personal or familial origin/birth/ethnic-national derivation ("Where do you come from?"). But here the past tense[20] plus the truncated phrasal preposition *before* seems specifically to ask about origin relative to the framework at denotational issue, at this point intervals of association with colleges and universities.

2. Observe that the first part of Mr. B's response would be fine as a coherent second pair-part, since there does, in fact, exist a University of Iowa, in Iowa City, which is termed *Iowa* in short reference form (in contrast to Iowa State University, in Ames, termed *Iowa State* in short reference form). However, the second sentence in Mr. B's reply, "I lived in Iowa," with its locational phrase *in Iowa* can only be formulating a place of residence or domicile in contrast to where Mr. B is now living—as distinguished from where he is going to school for post-baccalaureate training (to indicate which he would be obligated to use, depending on the school, one of the phrases *at Iowa* or *at Iowa State*).[21]

3. The geopolitical framework indexically invoked by the expressions "Iowa...in Iowa" contrasts states of the union in a simple partitioning taxonomy. As mapped political entities, however, states are clustered within the informal region-level cultural concept as well; here, that of "the Midwest," in which, among others, Iowa contrasts with Illinois (the state in which Messrs. A and B know themselves to be at the moment of interaction). More particularly, this culturally *regional* perspective implies an urban-rural distinction, with its radial geometry of central cities and rural hinterlands. The degree of urban-rural contrast of the region's states—for example corresponding to the number of and population rank of a state's major metropolises vs. the extent and sparseness of its rural areas—is reflected in stereotypes about the relative "urbanity" vs. rurality of the several states of a region. These stereotypes are part of the inhabitable identities of someone who "comes from" them.

Here, Iowa as a whole contrasts not only with Illinois, but, culturally, with Illinois-encompassing-Chicago, the region's definitively major metropolis (where Messrs. A and B also find themselves at the moment of interaction), as the quintessential, frequently negatively invoked stereotype of attitudinal and experientially wholesome rurality. Hence, we might understand that Mr. B's multiply ambiguous response, "Iowa"—is it denoting where he "comes from" or where he was "at" undergraduate university "before" the University of Chicago?—seems to be "repaired" by stipulating that he "*lived* in" Iowa, at once negating both possible indexical inhabitances that seem to have been interactionally in play up to this point (also see note 23 below).

Mr. B having introduced this technically frame-breaking irrelevance to the conversation, Mr. A then launches himself into a recitation of facts about the state of Iowa, using a variant of mentioning a common acquaintance that is so frequently a part of "Getting to Know You"; it is a kind of "I-already-know-you" contribution, in fact, by virtue of presumed commonality of knowledge between interactants. Mr. A hangs his recitation of knowledge on the line that he has "a good friend from Iowa . . . from the Amana . . . area," who has told him lots about Iowa, hence offering himself to Mr. B as a person consocial with a like person to him and, even though by hearsay, similarly knowledgeable: The interactional-textual figurement is that Messrs. A and B can be to this extent familiar equals.

In response to this, interestingly, Mr. B himself begins a recitation of information about the Amana area in Iowa with a disclaimer of any *personal* knowledge ("I really don't know . . . much about it. . . . I've never been there. . .")—a somewhat curious claim for someone who has "lived in Iowa," but one which does the interactional work of declining the offer of likeness to Mr. A's friend, and hence linkage to Mr. A as an equivalently consocial in-group member. Mr. B having thus declined to inhabit the identity of a knowledgeable native Iowan, the interactants are left with the unresolved scheme earlier established about institutional affiliation. As we will be able retrospectively to see, this whole "Iowa" segment will have been constituted, notwithstanding its slightly informative yield, as an interactional side-sequence of attempted, but declined, egalitarian familiarity. And it is at this point that our transcript starts, with Mr. A pressing forward on the main business of discovering Mr. B's undergraduate school affiliation.

In the genre of "Getting to Know You," observe, for each participant, Mr. A and Mr. B, certain aspects of inhabitable identities are being serially and cumulatively indexed in interactional realtime. The mechanism of this indexing is the explicit denotational text, which builds up information about each participant by introducing denotational descriptors of entities (such as places) that bear culturally emblematic value and states-of-affairs involving these entities and the participants. It is important to see that the various parts of the total denotational information are cohesive one with another, constituting an orderly, interactionally relevant social-structural biography for each participant—but one that gets its orderliness only in terms of how each piece of the information has been subtly calibrated (Silverstein, 1993, pp. 48–53) with the presupposed "here-and-now" of the framework of basic communicational roles that Messrs. A and B know themselves to be inhabiting. Observe that the information is structured by English two-term deictic oppositions, *here* (: *there*), *this* (: *that*), *now* (: *then*), the first term of each of which denotes the ongoing interactional "here-and-now" from which a distinct "there-and-then" universe of denotation is constructed as though beyond a circumferential perimeter. The "there-and-then" denotational universe is in this instance keyed by past tense usage as well as by *there*-deixis, each descriptor giving thus the biographical structure of a personal past-to-present retrospected in the discursive interaction to hand. And, being each calibrated to the here-and-now through the use of a consistent deictic framework, the pieces of information are computably calibrated one with another.

At the point we enter the transcript, we already have a partial cumulative and thenceforth indexically presupposable structure of such a biography for each participant. Mr. A's questions have seemingly been directed to the end of filling in Mr. B's biography, along with elaborate relational self/other-positioning with respect to in-group (or similar) vs. out-group (or differentiated) interactional figurations that this suggests. Mr. A and Mr. B each knows a different amount of the other's biography at this point, though what has been made intersubjective shows the two men to be partly alike and partly different in the various frameworks they have implicitly (by presupposition) or explicitly (by denotation) established.

The array of Figure 12.2, below, lays out this biographical information in play at this point, that about Mr. A in a left column, and that about Mr. B in a right column for the "here-and-now" vs. the "there-and-then" of each, along all the relevant dimensions of information, or cultural frameworks indexed, that are critical to the course of the interaction under this analysis. I enclose the indexically presupposable, but up to this point denotationally implicit entities in brackets.

Note in Figure 12.2 that each of the frameworks of emblems of identity has its own particular dimensionalization of interactionally relevant threshold intervals between "here : there" and "now : then." Recall that

		Mr A	Mr B
[Conv. Role]:	'here-now'	[Initiator]	[Respondent]
	:	:	:
	'there-then'	["]	["]
Experiment:	'here-now'	this-exper. conversation	
	:	:	
	'there-then'	previous-exper. conversation	
Curriculum:	'here-now'	Law School	SocServAdmin
	:	:	:
	'there-then'	[ ]	[ ]
[University]:	'here-now'	[(University of) Chicago]	
	:	:	:
	'there-then'	[ ]	[(U of)Iowa?]
City/Town:	'here-now'		[Chicago]
	:	:	:
	'there-then'		not Amana
State:	'here-now'		[Illinois]
	:	:	:
	'there-then'		Iowa

$\downarrow \Delta t$

		Mr A	Mr B
[Conv. Role]:	'there-then'	[Initiator]	[Respondent]
	:	:	:
	'here-now'	[Respondent]	[Initiator]
Curriculum:	'here$_A$-then$_A$'	Law School-1	[?]
	:	:	:
	'here-now'	Law School-2	SocServAdmin1
University:	'there$_B$-then$_B$'		Loyola-Chicago
	:		:
	'there$_A$-then$_A$'	Georgetown	[(U of)Iowa?]
	:	:	:
	'here$_{A-B}$-now$_{A-B}$'	The University of Chicago	

FIGURE 12.2.   Initial-to-final deictically-spaced personal emblems of Mr. A and Mr. B

all such intervals are projectable only from the constantly moving "here-and-now" of the interactional process, and that to conceptualize them as in the figure is an act of abstraction that lays out the intervals of mensuration of the poetics of improvisational performance so as to align them one with another. Thus consider the temporal opposition, for example. It is clear that the scale of the interval size defining "now" vs. "then" for the interactional pair-part role incumbency within the conversation—who is "now" first pair-part "initiator" and who second pair-part "respondent," and who so functioned "then" (earlier)—can alternate on a rather more local scale, differing from the temporal scale on which the participants have been earlier—"then"—in the first conversation (probably as both initiator and respondent in many, many pair-parts) and are "now" in the second conversation of the "now-then" interval of participation in the experiment as a whole.[22] Both of these differ from the quanta of difference measuring the participants' respective years of academic study in their curricular framework, from the framework of time until/time since a degree in a particular school of affiliation, and so forth. Yet at every "here-this-now" moment of discursive interaction, all of these intervals that have been introduced can be calibrated one with respect to another so as to underlie their figuration in an interactional text.

For the "here-there" dimensions of contrast of locus in Figure 2, we might recall that there is a culturally salient urban-rural interval framework that applies to every region in the country and determines intervals, one of the poles of which is a metropolis of a sufficient rank. It seems already to have been operative for both Messrs. A and B in the way Mr. B introduced specifically where he *lived* before "now," i.e., "there-then," not actually "coming from" there (i.e., Iowa), and as well in the way that a "region" even within rural Iowa ("the Amana area") has been described by its townish center.[23]

Mr. A has probably all along been pursuing the piece of Mr. B's biography involving his previous university affiliation. Note that by the point we enter our transcript, Iowa has been only ambiguously revealed to have been Mr. B's "there" with respect to the university-affiliation interval of differentiation[24]—or so, in the rapid-fire course of interactional flow, it might at first have seemed to be. Hence we can understand that Mr. A persists in taking up again, more explicitly this time, the biographical detail about Mr. B that he seems, by cotextual structure, to have been seeking earlier at Q_{A4}. His pair of questions, Q_{A6} and Q_{A7}, start to ask if Mr. B "*likes*" (rhematic emphasis) the presupposed and now explicitly denoted "here$_B$," "Chicago," by comparison. But in which framework of the two available is he doing so, the institutional or the geopolitical (for each of which a term of a contrast set is available of identical linguistic form, *Iowa*)? Hence, in Q_{A7}, by which point Mr. A must himself have come to an interactionally strategic cognition of the distinction now in play between ^{U}Iowa:Chicago$_B$ and $^{C/S}$Iowa:Chicago$_B$—Mr. B having said specifically that he "lived in" (not *at*) Iowa, but not for example that he had "lived in" Ames or Iowa City (cf. note 21)—he formulates his probe about Mr. B's "then$_B$" using the slightly more disambiguating predicate *go to school* (*in/at*) to elicit information about what he must have long been after about Mr. B's relationship to the "there$_B$."

Now from our perspective of bottom-up maximization of the poetic cotextuality of denotational text, we can see that the most textually recent denotational frame in play, that of States and Cities, is the default one for the rhematically emphasized "thére" of Q_{A7}.[25] Yet even at this point, in the abstract the form *there* can substitute for either *in Iowa* or *at Iowa*, that is, it can theoretically be designating $^{C/S}$there$_B$ or ^{U}there$_B$ were we to consider nothing more than a text-sentence by text-sentence concept of interaction. Mr. B does nothing to disambiguate this in his R_{B7}, where he repeats the precise formulation of Mr. A's Q_{A7}, using the predicating phrase *go to school* (modulo inflectional morphology varying over assertorial past [*díd go to school*] vs. non-assertorial past [*went to school*]). And he creates the denotationally explicit paradigm in that predicated past of "there$_B$" vs. (contrastive-emphatic) "hére$_B$" "álso"— that is, he creates a triple deictic space, in effect "here-now$_B$" : "there-then$_B$" : "here-then$_B$," with "here$_B$" and "there$_B$" still ambiguous as to framework of deictic differentiation.

Punctuated by intercalated back-channels of recognition and registration by Mr. A ("óh, uh-húh"), Mr. B continues by clarifying the temporal order of the paradigm he has now established: He has gone to school "here$_B$" as well as "there$_B$" in relation to the presupposed reality at the very moment of interaction of his going to school "here$_{A,B}$" as well. "I came back kind of," he informs Mr. A. Thus note the deictically organized progression for Mr. B's biography that the conversation has now established:

$$^{U/C}\text{here-then}_B = \text{Chicago} > {}^{U/S}\text{there-then}_B = \text{Iowa} > {}^{U/C}\text{here-now}_B =$$
Chicago.

Is Mr. B speaking of "the University of" or "the city of" Chicago? Mr. A pursues this matter once again, pointedly asking for confirmation of what he must by now have been led to infer, that Mr. B was an undergraduate at the University of Chicago. In Q_{A8} Mr. A uses a noninverted, confirmatory question that, continuing an established framework, preserves the exact surface form of Mr. B's most recent use (in R_{B7}) of the predicate *go to school* that has been in play for some turns at this point.

Yet, he seems to blend two simultaneous informational quests in his utterance, which makes for a rather strange discontinuous colloquial phrase with focal stress, "wént . . . hére,"[26] superimposed upon the modified, hence more specific (via the complex nominal *undergraduate* [*school*]) repetition of the earlier construction, "wént *to undergraduate* [*school*] hére," de-stressing the modifier.

The different focalization of these two blended constructions leaves no doubt to us analysts which is the more important piece of information being asked for; it is the undergraduate institution with which Mr. B's identity can be affiliated. But we should note that even this formulation of Mr. A's is not without its own denotational-textual wiggle room. Using the context of cotextual parallelism only, and discounting Mr. A's locally blended-in construction *go to* "attend," it would be possible for Mr. B to respond to Mr. A's Q_{A8} in round (2) as though it were asking if he "went to undergraduate [school] ^{C}hére$_{A,B}$," that is, in the city of Chicago as opposed to the state of Iowa. So Mr. B could simply reply minimally in the affirmative and Mr. A's quest of some long interactional standing would still be on.

But for whatever reason—perhaps Mr. B has now caught the interactional point of the denotational text Mr. A has apparently been dialogically seeking to build in this improv performance of "Getting to Know You"—Mr. B does now reveal that most important of emblems of identity in professional- and upper-class America, the "old school tie."[27] At this point, therefore, he delivers the apparently long-desired information in R_{B8}, carefully—though apparently with some hesitation—differentiating city and university for Mr. A, so that he establishes the following clarified deictic structure ($>_t$ indicating temporal order):

^{C}here$_B$-^{U}there$_B$-then$_B$ = in Chicago - at Loyola $>_t$
^{S}there$_B$-^{U}there$_B$-then$_B$ = in Iowa [?- at (Iowa?)] $>_t$
^{C}here$_B$-^{U}here$_B$-now$_B$ = in Chicago - at Chicago.

Based on widely shared understanding of the system of stratification of educational institutions, Mr. B's apparent hesitation in making this sought-after clarifying revelation is itself probably an index of his having at least by this point really understood the nature of the game of "Getting to Know You" as it has developed for Mr. A: Whatever asymmetries of identity-status are already intersubjectively known to the two participants, this self-revelation of Mr. B's having gotten a then radically unprestigious bachelor's credential, certainly by comparison with his current position in-and-at Chicago, reinforces his marginality and inferiority with respect to Mr. A by most likely giving temporal depth to it.

Mr. B has thus apparently filled out the interactionally relevant paradigm of self-identification sought after by Mr. A. In exchange (3), Mr. A now immediately jumps in with a metadiscursively proffered framework of mutual identities, at once a commentary registering the significance of Mr. B's self-revelation and a (meta-level) stipulation of a universe in which Mr. B's credential and what will later be his credential can be compared. Starting with his five-times repeated exclamation of "Oh!" he reveals that the framework now to be denotationally (hence interactionally) in play is Jesuit institutions of higher learning in particular. Such a framework, all the while making Messrs. A and B seem to be comparable in biography, both being "óld Jesuit boy"s, further serves interactionally to drive home their diachronic differences.

For, following upon his rhetorical (exclamatory) question ("Oh, áre ya!"),[28] Mr. B now seems to oblige Mr. A by at last reversing roles and asking Mr. A for comparable biographical detail. Observe that this is Mr. B's first actual question of the entire interaction up to this point, Q_{B1} (exactly parallel to and following upon Mr. A's Q_{A7}), "Where'd you gó [to (undergraduate) school]?" and Mr. A responds to it with a full, deictically calibrated set of descriptors, yielding up the information that

$$^C\text{there}_A\text{-}^U\text{there}_A\text{-then}_A \; = \; \text{down in Washington - [at] Georgetown} >_t$$
$$^C\text{here}_A\text{-}^U\text{here}_A\text{-now}_A \; = \; \text{in Chicago - at Chicago.}$$

Interestingly, though this is not shown on our purely verbal transcript, just as Mr. A is saying "unfortunately,"[29] he begins to smile, as does Mr. B, mirroring, as he begins to respond with "Oh áre ya [an old Jesuit boy, too, yourself]?" Mr. A holds his smile nearly to the end of (4), adding a bit of laughter during his long pause; Mr. B keeps his smile until his concurrent "Oh, úh-huh" back-channel during Mr. A's R_{A2} of (5).

This has clearly constituted an interactional moment of exceeding importance, acknowledged in this way by both participants. What Messrs. A and B have been able to invoke here is not merely the larger cultural paradigm of middle- and upper-class "old school tie," but more particularly the framework of a savvy Catholic male's knowledge about Jesuit institutions of higher learning in the U.S. In this framework, Mr. B's then large, urban commuter school, with lots of evening-class students of modest and even impoverished means, Loyola University of Chicago, is compared with Mr. A's oldest, richest, toniest, politically connected, "almost Ivy [League]" college, Georgetown University, "down in Washington," as Mr. A says, actually being "up" indeed!

There is a sense in which, perhaps even unbeknownst to the participants as conscious, agentive actors, this game of "Getting to Know You" has moved decidedly into realms of biographical knowledge the gradual revelation of which constitute another kind of improvisational genre, termed "One-Upsmanship," a dyadic interaction often understood to be critically under the agentive control of the interrogator who elicits information that can be valuationally "trumped," as it were, in response. As Mr. B complies, in round (4), with the symmetric mirror-image demands of the emerging denotational text, becoming the Initiator and asking his first question of Mr. A, he elicits in R_{A1} information that completes a temporalized paradigm of perduring asymmetry of status between the two participants; during this phase of interaction they are mirrored to each other in mutual smiles. Notice that the role-incumbencies of Messrs. A and B seem also to have shifted at this point, Mr. B asking his first question in (4) and Mr. A responding with his valuable cultural symbolism, elicited by the question. This shift is maintained for the rest of the transcribed interaction, but probably with shifting significance as turns (5) and (6) play themselves out.

For the "One-Upsmanship," however intended or unintended to the agentive consciousness of Mr. A, is foiled—and by his own doing. After a pause filled with a burst of nervous laughter, in (5) Mr. A replies to Mr. B's second question (Q_{B2}, "Did you finish [(at) Georgetown]?") with the revelation that he is a second-year student in the Law School at Chicago, hence outranking Mr. B in this curricular respect as well. And then he goes on in (5) to offer a remarkable, self-revelatory observation bespeaking his reaction to the transition from undergraduate experience at Georgetown to graduate experience at Chicago. In a somewhat disjointed syntax that, however, constitutes an exquisitely well-crafted utterance poetics of two parallelistic rhetorical periods, he tells Mr. B that things for him have gone from enjoyable to "overwhelming." He smiles at Mr. B. while he is delivering this, starting at the first "I don't know," and abruptly terminating his smile just before delivering the word "overwhélming." His move out of the Jesuitical undergraduate world, however well-placed the school, and "up" into the graduate university milieu of one of the then three or four most prestigious law schools in the country has obviously not been without difficulty, to Mr. A's own denotational participant perspective. And we should note the barrage of explicitly evaluative terms, in which Mr. A contrasts a "nice" and "good" state-of-affairs in his retrospected undergraduate experience, the one located at $^{U/C}$there$_A$, to the one located $^{U/C}$here$_A$ that has proved in his estimation to be "réally réally different" (in its negative colloquial vernacular use) and "overwhelming."[30] In short, as we diagram Mr. A's turn, we get the cumulative, deictically calibrated paradigm as follows:

^{U}there$_A$-[^{C}there$_A$-]then$_A$ = Georgetown[-Washington] = nice/good/
enjoy[able] $>_t$

^{U}here$_A$-[^{C}here$_A$-]now$_A$ = Chicago[-Chicago] = réally réally different/over=
whélming

And this transformation of Mr. A's experience takes places in the curricular and university framework-interval of merely two years from "then$_A$"
to "now$_A$."

With some overlaps in the speaker-transition of turns (5) and (6), note,
Mr. B then begins his mirroring response, formulated in poetic units
that are, structurally, strikingly reminiscent of Mr. A's (see Silverstein,
1985b, pp. 192–196 for detailed analysis). By the measure of strict logical coherence, Mr. B's contribution in (6) is something of a propositional
non sequitur; it has only generally similar informational content, the
principal sentence-subject referents being "Jésuit education" and later—
in parallel position in the second rhetorical period—"Loyola." Mr. B's
contribution also includes a nice sub-routine in which he establishes that
he is in fact Mr. A's chronological and curricular senior, having completed his baccalaureate degree at Loyola some four or five years prior to
"now$_{A,B}$." This should not surprise us, of course; our intuitive experience
of so much of the denotational content of the improvised conversation of
daily encounters has exactly this quality of vaguely related associativity as
it meanders along doing its interactional work—work, we argue here,
that becomes understandable and plausible only when subjected to the
kind of analysis we are doing here, involving moving beyond sentence-
by-sentence or turn-by-turn unilevel consideration of denotational text.

In this light, what is of central importance to the dynamics of this
interaction is Mr. B's pointed, mirror-image focalizing and rhematizing
of the evaluative terms like "good" and its implied and explicit oppo-
sites in Mr. A's prior turn, (5). Note particularly in Mr. B's denotational
text in (6) how "a lót different" (cf. Mr. A's "réally réally—di different")
is now parallelistically equated with "a lot bétter . . . a lót more—
variety. . ." and how this equation reverses their experiential and perspectival mapping into the deictically calibrated framework of the two
men's biographies already in play: Loyola University of Chicago, and
the less status-conferring Jesuit education it has thus far represented in
the interaction, has, according to Mr. B's perspective, gotten a lot
better[31] since he has completed his undergraduate work there. In schematic terms, we can diagram the transformation Mr. B describes with its
deictic calibration from his participatory perspective, as follows:

^{U}there$_B$-[^{C}here$_B$-]then$_B$ = really óld schóol - [Chicago -] [more than] 4-5
years ago $>_t$

^{U}there$_B$-[^{C}here$_B$-]now$_B$ = a lót different an' a lot bétter [Loyola] - [Chicago -] nów

Let us consider this further in terms of its relevance for interactional textuality. By logical presupposition of what he explicitly says, Mr. B in effect denotationally concedes the point that there is emblematic status asymmetry between a graduate of Georgetown and a graduate of Loyola-Chicago as these have been introduced thus far—for the latter was, indeed, a college run in the "óld [Jesuitical] schóol" at the time ("then$_B$") that he was an undergraduate there. But observe: Mr. B was an undergraduate at Loyola-Chicago *before* Mr. A had even begun his undergraduate work at Georgetown; Mr. B is implicatively asserting, in effect, that he is Mr. A's elder, symmetrically filling in the time interval information about the scale of interactant's respective "then : now" that mirrors and completes Mr. A's self-disclosure in R_{A2} at the beginning of turn (5). In making the time intervals of their educational careers more precise, Mr. B has just used the heretofore vague "then : now" interval of opposition at the denotational-textual plane as a means of projecting (tropically inhabiting) an interactional-textual identity of "older/senior$_B$" with respect to Mr. A's now entailed interactional identity of "younger/junior$_A$."

And further: According to Mr. B, Loyola-Chicago at a time coeval with Mr. A's Georgetown experience was already "a lot bétter" than when Mr. B had been there—perhaps becoming even at least as good as Georgetown? Recall from our schematization above that in Mr. A's first pair-part contribution in (5), beginning with "And, uh, I don't know," he has made manifest his participatory perspective that for him things have gone from "good$_A$" to "bad$_A$" in making the institutional transition from "then$_A$" to "now$_A$." Mr. B's second pair-part response of (6), in perspectivally describing a temporal transformation from implicit [bad$_{A,B}$] to not only good but "a lot bétter$_B$" makes manifest precisely the contrary evaluated movement, predicated, to be sure, of the school and its circumstances that Mr. B is emblematically wearing. Figuratively projected, on this dimension, also, Messrs. A and B have reversed their indexed interactional stances on what they are respectively talking about even though in terms of "logical" coherence, they are not strictly talking about the same thing.

In a real sense, then, Mr. B's contribution in (6) is doubly positioned. On the one hand, it is precisely cotextually related to Mr. A's turn (5), particularly when we consider syntax, word choice, phraseology of denotational-poetic units, and its ultimate conversational point, however long it takes to get to it. But on the other hand, it is also recapitulating his understanding of what has been—with only the interruption of Q_{B1} and

Q_{B2} and other perfunctory back-channels—a monologic flow in Mr. A's transcripted column all the way from turn (3) through turn (5). In an interactional preamble, Mr. B first makes denotationally explicit the frame already in play, "Jésuit education" (cf. Mr. A's (3)), and then announces (6) as a segment with an interactional-textual positioning relative to (4-5) by using a kind of *interactional topic sentence*[32] that indeed restates the theme Mr. A has put in play in (5), of how things have (temporally) "chánged ... a lót." He then clarifies his own personal biographical time-interval (cf. Mr. A's opening of (5)), in the first rhetorical period of a two-period discourse, and then, in the second and matched rhetorical period delivers the interactional punch line, as it were, the statement of adjudged temporally bound transformation that is completely opposite in sense to the one earlier offered in (5) by Mr. A.

Observe, then, that after the framework-restating preamble, the first rhetorical period of Mr. B's contribution in (6) completes the establishment of biographies for both participants to *Mr. B's* advantage, he being the "senior," and the second period, declaring the movement of the circumstances of Loyola-Chicago to be from bad_B to $good_B$—or at least to "a lot bétter$_B$"—pointedly responds to Mr. A's sorry, seemingly regretful nostalgia with an upbeat ameliorationist image. How does this project into an interactional text, and how can this be seen in terms of the MAX^3TSIT model?

First, whatever specifically "One-Upsmanship" improv variant of "Getting to Know You" had been in play, consciously or otherwise, especially on Mr. A's part, has been, as it were, foiled. Viewed as a specimen of this genre, the game turns decisively in Mr. B's favor precisely at this point. Mr. B has made the temporally based dimension of "seniority" relevant, on which he has the advantage. Mr. B has inverted the trope of perspectival worsening to perspectival betterment, thus indexing an inhabitance of a superior—desired—position of retrospection. And, as one can confirm from looking at the entire transcript—beyond what we have been intensively studying—from this point on, one can see that Mr. A and Mr. B have in fact decisively exchanged interactional role-incumbencies as initiator and respondent by turn (6), a trend not yet obvious when Mr. B asks his first question Q_{B1} in (3b) as a mirroring compelled by Mr. A's coy partial revelation in (3a). From here on in, Mr. B asks all the questions, and Mr. A asks no further questions. This reversal in the potential to control the conversation by compulsive pair-part initiation is also something that is metaphorically understandable, i.e., can be projectively "read as" the interactional-textual import of Mr. B's self-assertion and rhematic "contradiction," abstractly speaking, of Mr. A in the exchange of (5-6). As an abstract mapping between denotational text and interactional text, this realtime, figured contrariety of propositions asserted in the flow of the denotational text precipitated—first things going from $good_A$ to bad_A for Mr. A, yielding to things going, second, from bad_B to $good_B$ for Mr. B—is perforce *a diagrammatic icon of* how things are going in the interactional text, according to our MAX^3TSIT-based construal of it.

Second, though it seems to constitute a denotational-(co)textual non-sequitur at first, the particular way that Mr. B's contribution in (6) mirrors and responds to Mr. A's contribution in (5) at the same time serves as a pointed and effective *commentary upon* Mr. A's revelation of his obvious unhappiness or distress in the $here_A$-and-now_A. Mr. B responds to the very personal, highly temporally specific, first-person predications of Mr. A's in (5) by offering impersonal, nomic or generic, third-person— in fact corporately institutional-referent—predications in return.[33] Such giving of generic predications in response to highly specific ones makes Mr. B's contribution something of a *meta-level discourse* with respect to Mr. A's, in addition to a mirroring response to it in pair-part structure, offering generalities that respond to and suggestively frame personal experiences.[34]

In fact, this role of creating a denotationally meta-discursive frame around the discursive contributions of Mr. A, can be seen as additive to the role-incumbency of Initiator (e.g., interrogator posing questions in pair-part sequence) that Mr. B has just assumed (it later turns out). So Mr. B will no longer be constrained to ask just those questions suggested by the denotational-textual poetics required in proper response to Mr. A's own earlier Initiator role-incumbency (as did Mr. B in exchange (3), for example, in contributing Q_{B1}). As an Initiator who also makes responsive commentary about Respondent's contributions, Mr. B has, lo and behold, taken on something of the professional role for which he is in fact training at the School of Social Service Administration, the case worker in a social intervention agency with a troubled client! Mr. B maintains the twin role-incumbencies of Initiator and Commentator-Putting-Things-in-Perspective-for-Other for the entire rest of the interaction, from this point.

Third, there is the point most important for understanding the MAX^3TSIT here. Mr. B's denotational contribution has never explicitly contradicted anything in Mr. A's denotational-textual contribution (cf. the "no denial" rule of improvisational theater, Sawyer, this volume). *The effectiveness of the interactional work is seen only at the abstract level of a dynamic, though improvised figuration: cultural-emblematic (stereotypic) information indexing intersubjective context, and arrayed by deictic anchoring into a systematic structure, parts of which the denotational content of conversation serves to create, fill-in, and transform over interactional realtime.* There is no explicit "illocution" in the standard Oxonian (and now Berkeleian) modalities that does the culturally conventional interactional work we claim is done here. There is no explicit, denotational appeal to the institutionally located identities and positional interests ultimately indexed as the stuff of interactional context—the contingent point, as it were, of such improvised, but "real" discursive interaction in the first place.

Such is the nature of the cultural work done in conversation as we can experience it, and this dynamic work is the object of explicit modeling and hypothesis-formation ("interpretative reading") that a MAX^3TSIT perspective makes at once formal and predictive. Here, by "reading" up to this point of transcripted material, we predict that the conversation takes a particular turn, based on an elaborate maximizing model that tells us *where* the cultural symbolism is being applied, *how* it is being applied, and thus *what* perspectival array of likely *outcomes* in intersubjective, interpersonal social reality its effective application indexically entails. So we might say that consciously or not, Mr. B has used his contribution in (6) to recoup and even reverse much of the status-asymmetry disadvantage that was emerging in the interactional text up to this point. It has been transformative as a contribution to Goffmanian "interactional ritual."

And what culturally characteristic interaction rituals are these improvised genres of "Getting To Know You" and "One-Upsmanship"! That is the point that vividly emerges from our methodology of constructing a maximally locally-contingent, but cumulatively coherent structuring of denotational text along the dimensions of denotational content suggested by poetic structuring in morphosyntactic and lexical form. And by criteria of predictive value, there is good reason to believe that Messrs. A and B are indeed participating at or near the level of interactional-textual coherence that this model stipulates, with highly dependably shared intersubjective cultural understandings and values, and impressively fluent and even efficient ways of articulating them to get to and through a dense, improvised, series of interactional segments. And all this, even though—based on our merely in vitro studies of transcript—we see Messrs. A and B only sometimes clearly acting as conscious and agentive parties to their own interactional-textual creation of an inhabitable and genred cultural form.

NOTES

[1]We use the term here in the traditional Weberian sociological sense, to mean consequential personal orientations-to-context, for example in behavioral terms (including verbalization), that involve a person's understanding of the "meaning" or significance of such orientation-to-context within some frame-

work(s) of interpretation that are themselves a function of the existence of social structure.

[2] Bakhtin (1986), of course, saw clearly the problematic relationship of a theory of "genres" with the basically constantly "improvisational" nature of textuality. His work informs this one in both general and specific ways.

[3] This is, of course, the problem attacked by so-called "speech act" theory from Austin (1962/1975) to Searle (1969) and beyond, though I purposefully do not limit the problem to the agentive, intentional behavior of a single interactional participant uttering a single, grammatically conforming sentence (or equivalent) in the durational expanse of a single turn-at-talk. Hancher (1979), for example, demonstrates that the two-party pair-part exchange is frequently the minimal interactional expanse for even defining the nature of certain "speech-acts," addressing just one of the many problems with this approach. See Levinson (1983, pp. 226–283) for a summary critique, with references, and Silverstein (1987, pp. 23–36) for a placement of "speech-act" theory within a framework of broadly "functional" analyses of language form, here attempted by folk-theorists with no technical linguistic competence or social scientific background, whatever their good intentions.

[4] This kind of modeling of language-in-use was clearly the project of H. P. Grice (see his papers collected in Grice, 1989). Note that in instances Grice recognized the apparent breakdown of logically conforming informational flow from his folk-theoretic perspective of what was explicitly denotationally signaled by words and expressions of language, he proposed to generate further, only implicit, propositions communicated in the guise of *implicatures* that he claims follow from certain folk-theoretic *maxims* a hearer relies on about the relation of kinds, amounts, and orderliness of information for which an intentional speaker is conventionally and perhaps morally responsible in events of discursive interaction. To a certain extent, it becomes clear, Grice happened upon the existence of culture, notwithstanding the hokey pseudopsychologism of so-called "conventional intentions," and the reduction of everything interactional to participants' internal states of propositional coherence; but his scheme is completely unworkable from an empirical point of view, no matter what one's social scientific sophistication. Sperber & Wilson (1986) seem to code this Gricean view of culture-as-cognitive-belief-state under the rubric of the (conventional? commonsensical?) "relevance" of beliefs to a communicative interaction.

[5] See Silverstein (1976, pp. 33–36) for an early but example-rich discussion of this. The idea is that, all other things in discursive-interactional co(n)text being equal, members of indexical paradigms, like deictics *here* : *there* :: *this* : *that* :: *now* : *then*, show asymmetries of presupposition/entailment, in each of these parallel cases the first member of the opposition being more entailing or creative than the second, and thus, for example, at the plane of denotational usage being associated more with "presentational topicalization," that is, introducing new entities as potential topics, rather than, by contrast, making resumptive reference to an already established referent (see also Silverstein, 1992, pp. 61–65). The linguistic anthropological literature now generally invokes the distinction for a number of important consequences, such as differences in availability to

ideological consciousness of indexical types of these two polar opposite functional characteristics in token-context.

[6]In the more technical development of this matter, I have written about the *metapragmatic* function of cotextuality with respect to the *pragmatic* functions of the realm of indexicality (see Silverstein, 1976, pp. 48–51; 1981; 1985a pp. 217–230; and esp. 1993). In the last in particular I have outlined the analytic dimensionalities by which we can classify semiotic forms ranging from explicit *metapragmatic discourse*—denotational "talk about talk"—to the most implicit of metapragmatically-functioning regimentations of indexicality through multi-order poetics.

[7]Without wishing here to reprise the entire history of the debate between "analogists" and "regularists," I do want to call attention to how central has been this issue to theorists' understanding of the relationship of grammar to denotational textuality, and in particular to those fractional segments of denotational text popularly and philosophically called "words and expressions," technically seen by linguists as various occurring tokens of grammatical collocations of lexical forms. To what extent, when we hear such a form-token, a word or expression, do we know its (denotational) meaning by analogy to a prior occasion of textuality, a prior occasion of use we have managed to commit to memory or equivalent, and to what extent do we know the form-meaning relationship by rule of grammar that applies, indifferently, as the generative principle of "competence" underlying any and all of the infinite "performances" of the form-meaning mapping in this as well as in any other use of it? And what is the nature of the rules, if any, by which this might be accomplished? Are such rules based on properties of denotational textuality-in-context directly, or on partially or even completely autonomous kinds of properties, for example of different kinds of mental objects? Of course, the recent tradition of professional linguistics as a field has resoundingly rejected all but autonomous principles of a kind that factors out anything involving textuality-in-context as underlying the way that words and expressions get their denotational values in context. Observe further how, with a misplaced enthusiasm for a then-convincing formalized "generative-grammatical" model based in infinitely recursive rules for characterizing syntactic (phrasal) structure of expressions in natural languages, many linguists and psychologists tried creating, by analogy (or theoretical calque) *text grammars*, or *story grammars* with somewhat dubious results. As one can see, text is a dynamic, realtime accomplishment of intersubjective significance, different from but viewable through the lens of formal cohesion; grammatical structure in the now classic generative modality is a complex of dependencies of aspects of signal form completely abstracted from spatiotemporal and other such realms, and intendedly autonomous of any principles of meaningfulness. So even at the denotational plane—let alone at the interactional!—neither is a text like a sentence only larger, nor is one like a logical-conceptual sense, only more complex.

[8]Aren't we—you and I—doing so now through the medium of visual artifactuality?

[9]Such "literal" denotational meaning is to be identified with the Saussurean *signifié*, or Saussurean sense, as I term it, projectable as just those denotational consequences that follow from the fact of systematic grammatical organization of

language. Of course such a conceptualization still lives in the various attempts of Chomskian linguists and cognitive scientists to discern principles of "semantic interpretation" or "conceptual representation" that correspond to, and follow from, grammatical analysis of sentences in the usual way, abstracted as these are from any textuality as such. Observe that empirical words (even word-stems in obligatorily inflecting languages) and expressions containing them have much more to their denotational meanings than Saussurean senses; and that conversely, textual usage in context is no guide at all to the Saussurean senses associable with lexical items and grammatical collocations built from them by productive rules of syntax. Saussurean sense is just one of several components of the meaningfulness of empirical words and expressions.

[10]See also Silverstein (1992, pp. 73–74), where these are first introduced in the context of trying to solve the otherwise hopeless problem raised by Gumperz's *contextualization cues* approach (Gumperz, 1992, and references therein), that without further specification indexicality—signs-in-co(n)text—is multiply indeterminate, multiply ambiguous, and multiply defeasible.

[11]As a formal structure in which simultaneously exist all of these hierarchically inclusive levels of metricality, a poem would seem indeed to preclude simple, straightforward, earlier-to-later utterance in discursive realtime. For one would have to be monitoring or paying attention to all of these levels simultaneously if each were in fact independently operative as an autonomous principle of exhaustive structuration into constituents of one's emerging textual whole, while as well monitoring the apparent structured relations of constituency among each of these independently stipulated unitizations, such as that a "foot consists of a sequence of such-and-such syllable-types." One would have the problem of directly generating the formal equivalent of an augmented transition network, a serially ordered, hence temporally producible, constituency structure of hierarchical constituencies. This is difficult if not impossible to model for syntax at the level of grammar. However, here is the difference between metrical textuality and the constituencies of syntax: The textual constituencies are merely virtual; they rely on finite equivalence possibilities across the units stipulated by each of the laminated metricalizations of text, without such things as recursive constituency relations ("The cat that the dog that the boy that the...struck bit ate the mouse.") and other known phenomena of grammar. As we shall see, moreover, by constructing richer maximizations of interactional text, the functional effect of poetic structure is to be able to build up large, global (or, durationally, long) poetic forms by constant repetition-with-variation of a very local metrical device.

[12]Indeed, sometimes in (metapragmatic) argumentation about what one has interactionally done in-and-by "saying something," participants turn to interpreting denotational text under default assumptions about grammatically driven meaningfulness, that is, about their folk concepts of Saussurean sense, looking for the logic of denotational text-sentences in grammar, and thence the interactional-textual import of what has been said. In actual folk usage, however, Saussurean sense is generally undifferentiated from stereotypy (discussed below) and from various other indexical components of meaningfulness of words and expressions.

[13] And note that discursive interaction up to that point can establish such knowledge and such memberships ad hoc through emergent cotextuality—as for example, to the degree it is successful, this discursive interaction in which you are the reader.

[14] There are immense, sometimes confusing literatures on these matters. Sometimes one must even be alert to the fact that writers use the same term, e.g., *topic*, to denote both a stretch of linguistic form and an element of conceptual representation with particular properties in either intersubjective or individual-conceptual realms! However, good places to begin exploration, following out references, are Brown & Yule (1983), van Dijk (1985, vol.2), and Halliday & Hasan (1976). A number of self-styled "functional" approaches to grammar are centrally concerned with matters of "information packaging" in structures of linguistic form, that is, how linguistic forms correspond to, or "code," information-as-communicable, e.g., Foley & Van Valin (1984) and further developments of their "Role and Reference Grammar" in Van Valin (1993), or Givón (1984) and developments of it. Similarly, special topics within this "coding" view of grammar have been treated as typological-comparative domains of relatively comparable functional (denotational-textual) effect in various languages, e.g. Haiman & Munro (1983) on a particular formal device common to many reference-tracking systems (Foley & Van Valin 1984, pp. 321–367) now called "switch-reference" (Jacobsen, 1967). Observe that in these "functional" approaches to grammar in particular, assumptions about the unity of a phenomenon in denotational (or even interactional!) text as well as in the text-sentential domain of traditional, self-styled "formal" syntax, generally underlie analyses of linguistic form.

[15] Though, to be sure, a groupness that may have lasting causal effects: for example any groupness based on scientific understanding (beliefs-and-practices) that a scholarly communication may bring into being—such as the one we are engaged in as you encounter this text-artifact. Such groupness of scientific understanding is its only ideologically legitimated interactional function.

[16] Even though such an array is rotated 90 degrees in its use of a page's visual space, note the parallelism to a conductor's musical score, in which compositional (metricalized durational) time is represented along the horizontal stafflines for each type of instrumental participant, while each of these participation structures is placed along the vertical in a metrically synchronized array from top to bottom of the page. Note that at any left-to-right point, representing a performance-moment in the composition/realization of the piece, a conductor can read across all of the parallel and metrically aligned staves to get an instantaneous picture of the harmonies, chords, and so forth. in play at that moment. And by reading across the left-to-right duration of a particular staff or two, one can see the text of a single such participant's music. Within the parameters of left-to-right and top-to-bottom alphanumeric printing conventions, we retain these representationalities along, respectively, the vertical-column individual participant's contributions, and the horizontal-line glimpse of simultaneous verbalizations.

[17] Duncan and Fiske (1977, pp. 36–37) report as follows about the research design:

The two participants were seated in adjacent chairs turned slightly toward each other, facing a videocamera. Each had a small lavaliere microphone suspended around his neck. A female experimenter gave the following instruction: "I would like the two of you to have a conversation for the next seven minutes or so. You can use the time to get acquanted with each other or to talk about anything else that interests you." She then left the room. When the first conversation was terminated, one member from each dyad [participating at the same time] exchanged places, the instructions were repeated, and a second conversation was recorded for each of the new pairings. . . . There was wall-to-wall carpeting in both rooms, and both carpets and walls were of a light gray color. The rooms were comfortably furnished with couches, arm chairs, and tables, and coffee tables. The lighting in the rooms consisted of an assortment of floor and table lamps.

In characterizing the contents of the transcripts generated this way, Duncan & Fiske report

[T]he subjects were requested merely to get acquainted with each other and to talk about anything that was of interest. The topics proved to be of the sort that might be expected in such an acquaintance process between professional-school students: home towns, colleges attended, present course of study, work experiences, career goals, and the study in which the subjects were participating. (1977, p. 150)

Indeed, Messrs. A and B in this particular transcript cover the range of these topics in one or another way in both the transcribed and the videotaped but not transcribed portions of their interaction. This was the second interaction of the experiment for both of them.

[18] It must be understood that even as units of the same university, these professional schools operate in a microcosm of the larger world of social and economic asymmetry between their professions. Everything, the very architecture of their university homes, the administrative lavishing of attention, funds, and so forth upon faculty and students, the prominence of their members in councils of the university, and so forth, reinforces the distinctions of identity one would see outside the university context as well.

[19] Mr. B has revealed that he is in his first year of his degree program at the School of Social Service Administration. Observe that it will not be until R_{A2} in the course of the transcript turn (5) of Figure 12.1 that Mr. A reveals to Mr. B that he is in the second year of the three-year Law School curriculum leading to the degree of J.D. Up to this point, then, only Mr. A knows that he is more advanced as a student in his respective graduate course than is Mr. B. However, it also develops in turn (6) that Mr. B is probably chronologically older than Mr. A, since his undergraduate work seems to have ended four to five years earlier, while Mr. A seems to have gone from undergraduate to graduate university directly.

[20] Observe that in interrogative syntax, verbs such as (past tense) *came from* require so-called "*do*-support" where the auxiliary *do* carries the past tense

marker, thus: did ... come from. The question is thus the colloquial register equivalent of the present perfect—*Where have you come from?*—that would be demanded in good literary-register standard.

[21]Two remarks are important here. First, in the sphere of American public higher education, there is generally a systematic distinction in naming between institutions termed *University of* [+State Name] and those termed [State Name+] *State University*: The former set stereotypically connote academically more prestigious and research-oriented schools, having some status as the "flagship" institution in the state's system of campuses, and so forth, as opposed to the latter set, whose names frequently invoke stereotypes of an institution that is the historical outgrowth of colleges with heavily agricultural and other "applied" fields of practical subject matter, dominated by undergraduate-level teaching to unsophisticated audiences, and so forth. (There are a few exceptions in the Midwest, e.g., *Ohio State University* (short form, *Ohio State*), but here note there is no opposed term *University of Ohio* for a public institution, and the lesser-prestige public institutions in that particular state do, indeed, have the naming formula [Name+] *State University*, where the name—for example, of a city—is in a partonomic relation to the state name.)

Seconed, there is an alternative formulation possible of particular relevance to this interaction. Particularly in "in-group talk," one can use the characterizing expression *at* [+ city or town name] to indicate an entity's association with the particular educational or other kind of institution in the culturally relevant set that happens to be located in that place. Hence one can designate an entity's being "at" the University of Iowa by *at Iowa City*, and one can designate an entity's being "at" Iowa State University by *at Ames*. (Note how this indexically presupposes and invokes knowledge of the relevant locators as part of one's conversational competence.) This is, in fact, key to an ambiguity of the simplex term *Chicago* for both the city and the educational institution, which seems to constitute a kind of fulcrum of this interaction. Mr. B, furthermore, uses this very formulation much later in the interaction, after the segment analyzed here, when he talks about the experiences one would have "if you were doing graduate work *at*, say, *Madison* or *Champaign* or someplace like that," i.e., at the University of Wisconsin in Madison, Wisconsin or at the University of Illinois in Urbana-Champaign, Illinois (then still termed Champaign-Urbana and abbreviated with its first component), both the premier campuses of their respective state systems by common knowledge among Midwesterners and many people more widely. By the way, precisely because the University of Chicago has a name that fits these canonical patterns, it is frequently—and erroneously—assumed to be a city version of a public state university system by native speakers of English who just do not happen to know the historical particulars.

[22]Recall from note 17 that each participant was participating in two conversational interactions as the terms of his experimental role, and that the transcript at issue records interaction with the second conversational partner for each.

[23]Mr. A, it turns out, speaks much later in the interaction of his own intentions of "returning" to New York [City] at a later time, emphasizing in the verbal perspective that New York is the conceptual point-of-origin, Chicago the place "here-now" but later to be "there-then" once more. Further, if more gen-

eral, inter-regional cultural stereotypes operate here, they conceptualize the entire United States, or even North America, as region-like in this same way as we have described the Midwest. Given Chicago's "second city" status with respect to New York in this framework of cities' ranks, note that Iowa and its inhabitants become doubly marked in an overall framework: un-urbane with respect to a city that is itself un-urbane with respect to Mr. A's place for return.

[24] I symbolize the deictically calibrated points in the various frameworks thus: ^{U}there$_B$, i.e., a value in the U[niversity] schema of denotational differentiation brought into "there" calibration with respect to the interactional here-this-now role-incumbency of the individual [Mr.] B. This means that some piece of information identifiable as culturally within this U-framework was introduced into the conversation with distal, that is "there," deixis or equivalent, for instance an explicit university involvement evaluable for truth/falsity as predicated about Mr. B, its propositional argument. Where two or more frameworks are invoked, I use "/" to separate "either-or" relations, e.g. U/C = "university or city" framework, and "," to separate "both-and" relations, e.g., A,B = both Mr. A and Mr. B. Such deictically hung-out pieces of *information about* Mr. B depend on the presupposed (indexed) configuration in-play of relational role-incumbencies of the discursive interaction, with respect to a schematization of which deixis projects a conceptual location in a universe of reference-and-predication. That is to say, it depends on an indexed (presupposed) *participatory perspective on* the information by virtue of presupposed role-incumbency. Participatory perspective—underlying the achievement of deixis in the first place—is here represented by the subscript following the deictic. Furthermore, when I introduce denotational descriptors with following subscripts (e.g., "good(Georgetown)$_A$"), these, too, indicate participatory perspective, as for example "for whom" someone or something is predicable as "good," no matter the subject. (It is of course the grammatical category of "person" in which are indicated the identity or non-identity of denotatum and participatory perspective.) Importantly, it is through participatory perspective as subscripted, not merely or at least only denotation as noted in argument-position schematic, that the figuration of "what is said" by "what is done" takes place.

It is important to call attention to one related matter. Languages frequently have as part of their denotational machinery a scheme for coding *denotational participant perspective* with a range of devices from left-dislocated topic-like noun phrases, e.g., the well-known Japanese *wa* phrases, to pseudo-case-marked adjuncts like the well-known Latin *datives of interest, ethical datives,* etc. and similar indirect-object/locative-like noun phrases in benefactive/malefactive constructions, all the way to subtle, complex interactions of modality and predicate case-marking, as in the *participant role perspective* category of Tibetan (Agha, 1993, pp. 155–202). This *grammaticization* in denotational code of denotable (hence indexically presupposed) participants of the universe of denotation interacts with—and hence presupposes—the role inhabitances that underlie the category of "person." As variously grammaticized, this is a complex area of empirical investigation I do not deal with in this chapter.

[25] Notwithstanding the default value of anaphoric (resumptive) referentiality for the word *there*, in the usage of Q$_{A7}$ the heightened stress on it as the intona-

tional peak definitively puts it into the text-sentential "focus." Moreover, in parallelistic denotational text—consisting of a string of Wh- and predicate-inversion questions on a grammatical subject *you*—it clearly is the functional rheme of the rhetorical period, i.e., it is the maximally indexically entailing information-coding unit of the text-sentence.

[26]The lexeme *go to* + [institution name], particularly in the simple present or other constructions of non-specific habitual state, as in *She goes to Yale*, indicates regular attendance at an institution for some culturally conventional purpose like matriculation, absent further specification. Of course, the default deictic substitutes for *to* + [name] are *here* or *there*.

[27]Within these social strata and sectors, it is being an alumnus/-a of at least some undergraduate (baccalaureate degree) institution, and in addition perhaps of some private preparatory academy as well. It is not my purpose here to enter into a lengthy discussion of social stratification and the role in it of educational institutions, which in this respect function as institutions of credentialing and inculcation of identity-value. To the degree that there is a commodity culture of emblematized affiliations with such institutions, from students and their families to alumni to faculty and other employees, such things as the institutional degree become permanent indexes within an economy of prestige, access-to-valued people, things, and places, and so forth, as in any aspect of a system of social stratification. There is a gendered aspect of all this as well, with a much more pronounced or explicit emphasis in either traditionally or restrictively male spheres of social action, though the reflected positionality of females affiliated with such males has long been noted by society (some traditionally all-female institutions once constituting themselves as places that produced fit wives and mothers of male counterparts), and there have emerged the stimuli to create a parallel institutional realm for and among women of these classes as an important social force, sometimes even perceived as being "feminist" pressure in some sense. Certainly in the world in which Mr. A hopes to circulate, such emblems are an important part of one's professional identity and perquisites.

[28]In one, completely unilevel, turn-by-turn way of looking at discursive interaction, this would just be an elaborate "back-channel" signal, co-occurring temporally with the latter part of Mr. A's turn in exchange (3), and not necessarily leading to a change of turns. However, the turn does, indeed, change, with Mr. B continuing so as to ask his substantive question Q_{B1}. More significantly, the cotextual elaborateness of the reply, with its conventional indexical expression of surprise by emphasis in grammar, stress, and intonation, would seem within the more plurileveled and structured poetics of textuality here espoused to be an index of registering the major shift of interactional segment that is now underway. Mr. A has stipulated a framework for revelation of *his* biographical information, in a turn, (3), that is not so much a question from Mr. A to Mr. B— as has been the rule thus far—as a response/commentary/statement that fits into a poetics of pair-part exchanges as a denotationally superordinate (meta-level) "third" segment. Thus Mr. B both preserves the pair-part structure by his exclamatory rhetorical back-channel, and goes on to take the role of Initiator in the Q:R pair-part structure all in the same turn. Note how Mr. B's contribution has refashioned Mr. A's next turn, in (4), into in effect constituting a response

R_{A1} to his first pair-part contribution Q_{B1}—even if from Mr. A's intentional point of view (to sink into folk metapragmatics for a moment) he had intended his contribution in (4) to follow on with nothing more than a back channel from Mr. B. The remarkable *inter*personal structure of $((Q_{A8};R_{B8});(Q_{B1};R_{A1}))$ is but one simple demonstration of the force of cotextuality-in-process at work here.

[29]Recall that such an evaluative adverb or equivalent outer indexical frame enclosing a predication or modifying use of a stereotypically "good" descriptor, filters the expected interactional participant perspective of the utterer of the descriptor in a determinate direction in a universe of what folk metapragmatics sees as "emotions" or "attitudes." Here, the effect seems to be "(mock) regret" with respect to circumstances beyond the utterer's control that have brought about the truth of the description we might diagram, "Jesuit-boy(Mr. A)$_A$". Mr. B is invited to share in the mock regret with respect to himself, "too"—inviting interactional solidarity of participant perspective at this point.

[30]Observe how the distal referent, "Georgetown-down-in-Washington," is initially introduced as "it" in poetic contrast to "thís place" in the first half of Mr. A's rhetorical period. Purely on the basis of rules of sentence syntax, the first occurrence of *it* in "It was níce" might be taken as a dummy Subject. The continuities over cotextual realtime all become clearer by the second rhetorical unit of (5), where Georgetown-down-in-Washington is referred to—in contrast to the quite precise deictic $^{U/C}this_{A,B}$ *place*—with the relatively thematic "there"—i.e., $^{U/C}there_A$—in the more particular explanatory phrase "the educátion there" (where *educátion* marks the focus/rheme). In this second period, the form *it* of "And it réally was góod. It wasn't overwhélming." might at first be taken to be an anaphoric resumption of the prior full noun phrase, *the education there*, independent of its cotextual relations. Within the overall structure, however, *it* seems to be coreferential with *there*, that is, also to refer to Georgetown-down-in-Washington rather than being just a dummy Subject of no determinate referential value.

[31]Observe in (6) how Mr. B first introduces the rheme "chánged...a lót" for the theme (and sentence Subject) "Jésuit education," resuming in the first segment of his first rhetorical period the focalized phrase "the educátion $^{U/C}there_A$ [i.e., "(at) Georgetown in Washington"]" of the first segment of the second rhetorical period of Mr. A's turn (5). In his second major rhetorical period, then, Mr. B elaborates the resultative state-of-affairs consequent upon change, namely that "Loyola is a lót different an' a lot bétter," using the stress-focalized comparative degree of *good*, and going on then to specify the matters of the *education* $^U there_B$ that lead to this judgment.

[32]This is a segment of denotational text in which the interactionally-projectable stereotypes in the rheme (generally coded in grammatically focalized form in text-sentences) are, in effect, entitling the interactional segment as to the genre that is abuilding. Here, it is denotationally *described* change mappable into interactionally *experienced* change. It is important to understand that, were we limited to examining denotational text and trying to derive interaction from it on a sentence-by-sentence basis, as in all the standard approaches rejected here, we would have to say that Mr. B's text-sentence at the outset, "I think Jésuit education...six yéars." was the denotational-textual "topic sentence," that he

goes on to "logically" develop as an "argument" [he is after all chatting with a future lawyer!], supporting it with experiential and conjectural points one by one. To this MAX³TSIT approach, this is at best an inadequate, at worst a useless, way of modeling how "what is said" improvisationally effectuates "what is done."

²³We except here the framing discourse markers "I think" and "I mean," of course, as well as the first substantive rhetorical period of (6) in which Mr. B establishes his "seniority" with respect to Mr. A. That this latter, first-person and temporally specific predication *asserts* an entailed mutual asymmetry between the two men in Mr. B's favor actually is totally consistent with our seeing the rest as responsive commentary to Mr. A, in fact constituting just one culturally accepted ground from which Mr. B can so speak, age-and-experience speaking to youth-and-inexperience.

²⁴See (Wortham, 1994) for a fascinating, MAX³TSIT-based study of how "participant examples" used in improvised classroom discourse to illustrate general propositions and nomic truths become a site of interactional struggle.

REFERENCES

Agha, A. (1993). *Structural form and utterance context in Lhasa Tibetan: Grammar and indexicality in a non-configurational language.* New York: Peter Lang.

Austin, J. L. (1962/1975). *How to do things with words: The William James lectures delivered at Harvard University in 1955* (J. O. Urmson & M. Sbisà, Eds.). Cambridge: Harvard University Press.

Bakhtin, M. M. (1986). The problem of speech genres. In *Speech genres and other late essays* (pp. 60–102). (C. Emerson & M. Holquist, Eds.; V. McGee, Trans.). Austin: University of Texas Press.

Brown, G., & Yule, G. (1983). *Discourse analysis.* New York: Cambridge University Press.

Duncan, S., Jr. & Fiske, D. W. (1977). *Face-to-face interaction: Research, methods, and theory.* Hillsdale, NJ: Lawrence Erlbaum Associates.

Foley, W. A., & Van Valin, R. D., Jr. (1984). *Functional syntax and universal grammar.* New York: Cambridge University Press.

Givón, T. (1984). *Syntax: A functional-typological introduction.* Amsterdam: John Benjamins.

Grice, H. P. (1989). *Studies in the way of words.* Cambridge: Harvard University Press.

Gumperz, J. J. (1992). Contextualization revisited. In P. Auer & A. Di Luzio (Eds.), *The contextualization of language* (pp. 39–53). Amsterdam: John Benjamins.

Haiman, J., & Munro, P. (Eds.). (1983). *Switch-reference and universal grammar.* Amsterdam: John Benjamins.

Halliday, M. A. K., & Hasan, R. (1976). *Cohesion in English.* London: Longman Group, Ltd.

Hancher, M. (1979). The classification of cooperative illocutionary acts. *Language in Society, 8*, 1–14.

Jacobsen, W. H., Jr. (1967). Switch-reference in Hokan-Coahuiltecan. In D. Hymes & W. E. Bittle (Eds.), *Studies in Southwestern ethnolinguistics: Meaning and history in the languages of the American Southwest* (pp. 238–263). The Hague, the Netherlands: Mouton & Co.

Jakobson, R. (1960). Closing statement: Linguistics and poetics. In T. A. Sebeok (Ed.), *Style in language* (pp. 350–377). Cambridge: MIT Press.

Levinson, S. C. (1983). *Pragmatics*. New York: Cambridge University Press.

Putnam, H. (1975). The meaning of "meaning." In H. Putnam, *Philosophical papers, Vol. 2, Mind, language, and reality* (pp. 215–271). New York: Cambridge University Press.

Sawyer, R. K. (1996). The semiotics of improvisation: The pragmatics of musical and verbal performance. *Semiotica, 108*, 269–306.

Schiffrin, D. (1984). Jewish argument as sociability. *Language in society, 13*, 311–335.

Searle, J. R. (1969). *Speech acts: An essay in the philosophy of language*. New York: Cambridge University Press.

Silverstein, M. (1976). Shifters, linguistic categories, and cultural description. In K. H. Basso & H. A. Selby, Jr. (Eds.), *Meaning in anthropology* (pp. 11–55). Albuquerque: University of New Mexico Press.

Silverstein, M. (1981). *Metaforces of power in traditional oratory*. Paper presented to Department of Anthropology, Yale University. Unpublished manuscript, University of Chicago.

Silverstein, M. (1985a). The functional stratification of language and ontogenesis. In J. V. Wertsch (Ed.), *Culture, communication, and cognition: Vygotskian perspectives* (pp. 205–235). New York: Cambridge University Press.

Silverstein, M. (1985b). On the pragmatic "poetry" of prose: Parallelism, repetition, and cohesive structure in the time course of dyadic conversation. In D. Schiffrin (Ed.), *Meaning, form, and use in context: Linguistic applications* (pp. 181–199). Washington, DC: Georgetown University Press.

Silverstein, M. (1987). The three faces of "function": Preliminaries to a psychology of language. In M. Hickmann (Ed.), *Social and functional approaches to language and thought* (pp. 17–38). Orlando, FL: Academic Press.

Silverstein, M. (1992). The indeterminacy of contextualization: When is enough enough? In P. Auer & A. Di Luzio (Eds.), *The contextualization of language* (pp. 55–76). Amsterdam: John Benjamins.

Silverstein, M. (1993). Metapragmatic discourse and metapragmatic function. In J. A. Lucy (Ed.), *Reflexive language: Reported speech and metapragmatics* (pp. 33–58). New York: Cambridge University Press.

Silverstein, M., & Urban, G. (Eds.). (1996). *Natural histories of discourse*. Chicago: University of Chicago Press.

Sperber, D., & Wilson, D. (1986). *Relevance: Communication and cognition*. Cambridge: Harvard University Press.

van Dijk, T. A. (Ed.). (1985). *Handbook of discourse analysis, vol. 2. Dimensions of discourse*. London: Academic Press, Ltd.

Van Valin, R. D., Jr. (Ed.). (1993). *Advances in role and reference grammar.* Amsterdam: John Benjamins.
Wortham, S. E. F. (1994). *Acting out participant examples in the classroom.* Amsterdam: John Benjamins.

Author Index

Subject Index